Territorial Patterns of Innovation

T0295609

This edited volume presents a new interpretative framework of innovation in space. A wide variety of theoretical and empirical analyses exist in the literature dealing with knowledge creation and diffusion processes, and their effects on regional performance. However, much of our understanding of the relationship among knowledge, innovation and regional growth is strongly influenced by popular beliefs which hold in a general framework, but which may exhibit important peculiarities when analyzed through a particular lens, that of a regional approach. This book shows that different *territorial patterns of innovation* can occur at regional level, defined as spatial breakdowns of variants of the knowledge → invention → innovation → development logical path, depending on the presence/absence of local preconditions for knowledge creation, knowledge attraction and innovation.

Territorial Patterns of Innovation provides evidence that local knowledge intensity does not necessarily guarantee higher innovation performance. Moreover, the book shows that the growth benefits deriving from innovation do not necessarily match the strength of the formal local knowledge base, and that regions innovating in the absence of a strong local knowledge base can be as successful as more knowledge-intensive regions in turning innovation into a higher growth rate.

Together, the contributions in this book offer a new understanding of the relationship between knowledge, innovation and regional performance by delving beyond generally held beliefs. The empirical results support a new design for innovation policies at the regional level, which could help the European Union to achieve the targets set up in its 2020 Agenda. The book will be of value to regional scientists, industrial economists and policy-makers.

Roberta Capello is professor of regional and urban economics at Politecnico di Milano.

Camilla Lenzi is assistant professor of regional and urban economics at Politecnico di Milano.

Routledge Advances in Regional Economics, Science and Policy

1. **Territorial patterns of innovation**
    An inquiry on the knowledge economy in European regions
    Edited by Roberta Capello and Camilla Lenzi

Territorial Patterns of Innovation

An inquiry on the knowledge economy in European regions

Edited by
Roberta Capello and
Camilla Lenzi

Routledge
Taylor & Francis Group

LONDON AND NEW YORK

First published 2013
by Routledge
2 Park Square, Milton Park, Abingdon, Oxfordshire OX14 4RN

Simultaneously published in the USA and Canada
by Routledge
711 Third Avenue, New York, NY 10017

First issued in paperback 2015

Routledge is an imprint of the Taylor & Francis Group, an informa business

British Library Cataloguing in Publication Data
A catalogue record for this book is available from the British Library

Library of Congress Cataloging in Publication Data
  Territorial patterns of innovation : an inquiry on the
  knowledge economy in European regions /
  edited by Roberta Capello and Camilla Lenzi.
  pages cm
  Includes bibliographical references and index.
  1. Knowledge economy–Europe. 2. Economic development–Europe.
  3. Technological innovations–Economic aspects–Europe.
  I. Capello, Roberta. II. Lenzi, Camilla.
  HD30.2.T477 2013
  303.48'33094–dc23
  2012049035

ISBN 13: 978-1-138-92364-5 (pbk)
ISBN 13: 978-0-415-63606-3 (hbk)

Typeset in Times New Roman
by Swales & Willis, Exeter, Devon

Contents

Notes on contributors

Roberto Camagni is professor of urban economics and economic assessment of urban transformation at Politecnico di Milano. Past-President of the European Regional Science Association (ERSA). Head of the Department for Urban Affairs at the Presidency of the Council of Ministers, Rome, under the first Prodi Government, 1997–98. Author of many scientific papers and a textbook in urban economics published in Italian, French and Spanish.

Roberta Capello is professor of regional and urban economics at Politecnico di Milano. Past-President of the Regional Science Association International (RSAI). Editor in chief of *Papers in Regional Science* (Wiley Blackwell) and of the *Italian Journal of Regional Science* (FrancoAngeli). Past co-editor of *Letters in Spatial and Resource Science* (Springer Verlag). Author of many scientific papers and a textbook in regional economics, published in Italian and English.

Andrea Caragliu is a postdoctoral fellow at Politecnico di Milano. He holds a PhD in management, economics and industrial engineering, from the same University, and a master's degree and a degree in economics at Università Commerciale Luigi Bocconi, Milan. He has been frequently a visiting scholar at the Spatial Economics Department of the Free University of Amsterdam, Netherlands. His research interests focus on non-material regional growth determinants, non-geographical forms of proximity, and urban development.

Alessandra Colombelli is assistant professor at Politecnico of Torino and research associate at the CRENoS (Center for North–South Economic Research) and the CNRS-GREDEG, University of Nice Sophia Antipolis. Author of several scientific papers in the fields of economics of innovation and regional economics.

Riccardo Crescenzi is lecturer in economic geography and programme director of the MSc in local economic development at the London School of Economics. He has a long track record of research in regional economic development and growth, innovation and EU regional development policies. He has also recently published a book (with A. Rodríguez-Pose) on *Innovation and Regional Growth in the European Union* (Springer, 2011). He was principal investigator for the LSE Unit in the EU/applied project/ESPON 2013 KIT and he is currently co-investigator in two EU-funded FP7 research projects.

Marta Foddi has a MA in economics at the University of Louvain-la-Neuve and she is currently a research assistant at CRENoS (Center for North–South Economic Research). Her main research interests are regional economics, innovation and evaluation of public policies.

Camilla Lenzi is assistant professor of regional and urban economics at Politecnico di Milano. She holds a PhD in economics from University of Pavia and master's degree in industry and innovation analysis from SPRU – University of Sussex (UK). She has published several papers in international peer-reviewed journals in the fields of innovation and urban and regional growth, entrepreneurship, human capital mobility and technology transfer.

Emanuela Marrocu is associate professor of econometrics at the University of Cagliari, Italy, and research fellow of CRENoS (Center for North-South Economic Research). Her main research interests are: spatial econometrics and productivity analysis at regional and firm level; tourism industry and economic performance; time series econometrics; and forecasting evaluation.

Ernest Miguelez is research fellow of the Regional Quantitative Analysis Group, where he did his PhD. He currently holds a research economist position at the Economics and Statistics Division of the World Intellectual Property Organization.

Rosina Moreno is professor of applied economics at the University of Barcelona. She was a visiting scholar at the Regional Research Institute of the West Virginia University, at the Bruton Center for Development Studies of the University of Texas at Dallas and at the CRENoS Center at Cagliari (Italy). Her teaching areas are mainly econometrics. Her current research interests are focused on regional growth, public and human capital impact, sectoral and regional externalities, spatial econometrics, innovation capabilities in SMEs and innovation diffusion.

Raffaele Paci is professor of applied economics at the University of Cagliari (Italy) and Jean Monnet Chair on 'Regional Economic Integration in the European Union'. He is author of many papers on innovative activity and externalities, intangible assets, spatial spillovers and regional economic performance which have been published in leading international journals.

Andrés Rodríguez-Pose is professor of economic geography at the London School of Economics and a current holder of a European Research Council Advanced Grant. He has published more than 80 papers in peer-reviewed journals on regional growth and disparities, fiscal and political decentralization, regional innovation, and development policies. He is the joint managing editor of *Environment and Planning C*, and editor of *Economic Geography*, and sits on the editorial board of 18 scholarly journals.

Jordi Suriñach is professor of applied economics at the University of Barcelona, director of the Institute of Applied Economic Research (IREA-UB) and president of the Spanish Regional Science Association. He has led several projects funded by the European Commission and has participated in Spanish and European competitive public projects. His teaching areas are mainly econometrics. His current research interests are focused on regional growth, public and human capital impact, sectoral and regional externalities, labour markets, innovation capabilities in SMEs, and innovation diffusion.

Stefano Usai is associate professor of economics at the University of Cagliari, Italy, and the director of CRENoS (Center for North–South Economic Research). He is currently on the editorial board of *Regional Studies*. Author of several scientific papers on regional economics and the economics of technological change.

Abbreviations

BRIC	Brazil, Russia, India and China
CIS	Community Innovation Survey
DEA	Data Envelopment Analysis
EFTA	European Free Trade Association
EIS	European Innovation Scoreboard
EPO	European Patent Office
ERA	European Research Area
ESPON	European Spatial Observatory Network
EU	European Union
EU15	Austria, Belgium, Denmark, Germany, Finland, France, Greece, Spain, Ireland, Italy, Luxembourg, Netherlands, Portugal, Sweden, United Kingdom
EU12	Bulgaria, Cyprus, Czech Republic, Hungary, Estonia, Latvia, Lithuania, Malta, Poland, Romania, Slovakia, Slovenia
FDI	Foreign Direct Investment
FP	Framework Programme
GDP	Gross Domestic Product
GMR	Gross Migration Rate
GPT	General Purpose Technology
HE	Higher Education
ICT	Information and Communication Technologies
IMR	Inward Migration Rate
IPC	International Patent Classification
KIS	Knowledge-Intensive Services
KIT	Knowledge, Innovation and Territory
KPF	Knowledge Production Function
MHHT	Medium High-Tech Manufacturing
MNC	Multinational Corporation
MNE	Multinational Enterprises
MS	Member States
MSA	Metropolitan Statistical Areas
NEG	New Economic Geography
NMR	Net Migration Rate

NMS	New Member States
NUTS	Nomenclature d'Unités Territoriales Statistiques
OECD	Organisation for Economic Cooperation and Development
OMR	Outward Migration Rate
OST	Observatoire des Sciences et des Techniques
PCA	Principal Component Analysis
PF	Production Function
R&D	Research and Development
RIS	Regional Innovation Scoreboard
S&T	Science and Technology
SAR	Spatial Autoregressive Model
SEM	Spatial Error Model
SME	Small-Medium Enterprises
SNA	Social Network Analysis
TAR	Technologically Advanced Region
TFP	Total Factor Productivity
UK	United Kingdom
US	United States

1 An inquiry on the regional dimension of the knowledge economy

Aims and novelties of the book

Roberta Capello and Camilla Lenzi

1.1. Knowledge, innovation and regional growth: what novelties in this book?

The decisive globalization process of the past decade and the economic downturn in recent times have brought severe pressure to bear on economic actors and policymakers in search of ad hoc strategies and policies to support competitiveness. Innovation is interpreted as a fundamental resource for economic efficiency and growth; knowledge accumulation is essential for economic systems to be able to face world competition; new and appealing products become vital for stimulating scarce demand; and new organizational and managerial solutions are crucial for increasing firms' efficiency.

Attempts in these directions are not new. In 2000 the European Union (EU) set itself the goal of becoming the most competitive and dynamic knowledge-based economy in the world. It subsequently confirmed that goal in 2005, allocating its Structural Fund resources to achieving it, and, in 2010, with the launch of the Europe 2020 Agenda, stressing once again the need for the achievement of 3% of GDP invested in research and development (R&D) (EC, 2010a). Since the Lisbon (March 2000) and Europe 2020 Agendas (EC, 2000 and 2010a), all policy levels have contributed to the creation of the knowledge economy and to the reinforcement of innovation, since access to knowledge is generally considered a key condition for innovative activities in a modern economy. The idea of knowledge as the main discriminating element in economic and social performance was put forward even before the Lisbon Agenda by some national governments, like that of the United Kingdom, where in 1998 a white paper on 'Our Competitive Future, Building the Knowledge-Driven Economy' was produced by the Department of Trade and Industry.

A complex indicator for regional achievement of the Lisbon performance was circulated during the Luxembourg meeting, which concentrated on private R&D investment and expenditure, educational level of the labour force and productivity level. An increasing flow of public resources into the scientific research system was requested until the economic crisis (i.e. mid-2008) and it was likely to be accepted by public authorities, giving rise to huge scientific engagement in the measurement of the internal efficiency, productivity and impact of the research system itself (Okubo, 1997; Joly, 1997).

Most of the original initiatives and policy suggestions were initially located in the context of European or national economies, but it soon became evident that the same reasoning should be applied at a more territorially disaggregated level of analysis, namely *the regional level*. A bottom-up approach to the development of the knowledge economy was thought to be of interest, given the high spatial concentration of knowledge creation and innovation activities. Clusters of technologically advanced firms, like Silicon Valley in California, Route 128 in the Boston area, Baden-Württenberg in Southern Germany, Jutland in Denmark, Småland in Sweden, and Sophia-Antipolis close to Nice, to cite only some examples, testified to the presence of some form of increasing returns on the concentration of innovative activity.

Different reasons were given for the importance of space in the creation of a knowledge economy: externalities stemming from urban environments, knowledge spillovers subject to strong and visible distance decay effects, and collective learning based on a relational space where economic and social interactions take place and are embedded in geographical space. This new approach links with the idea that knowledge develops and accumulates through slow individual and collective learning processes, and grows through information, interaction and local knowledge. Knowledge creation is therefore a local process rooted in the historical development of the area. It is accumulated over time through experience, local culture, the local labour market and the local context, and it is therefore difficult to transfer elsewhere.

Accordingly, broad consensus arose in the scientific domain on the fact that regional competitiveness – and consequently regional growth – was no longer dependent on the traditional production resources: i.e. capital and labour. The hypermobility that today characterizes these factors reduces their geographical concentration, and shifts the elements on which competitiveness rests from the availability of material resources to the presence of immobile local resources like local culture and competences; in general: knowledge and innovation.

In this spirit, even in recent times, the European Commission's Green Papers on Territorial Cohesion and the European Research Area have called for particular attention to be paid to the territorial dimension of knowledge creation and innovation (EC, 2008). The diversity of innovation activities, of the spatial diffusion of innovation throughout the European territory, and of the capacity of regions to create knowledge and to exploit knowledge coming from outside requires in-depth analysis of the territorial dimension of the knowledge economy on which the so-called 'third generation of innovation policy at Community level' can rely. In fact,

> innovation policy at community level is now moving into its third generation. It is moving away from the approach of the first generation of innovation policy which focused on R&D through a linear process for the development of innovations, beginning with laboratory science moving through successive stages up to the inclusion of knowledge in commercial applications. Equally, it is building on the approach of the second generation which recognized the

complexity of innovation systems (national, regional, local, sectoral), with many feedback loops between the different stages. In the approach of this third generation, innovation is not considered as a linear process that starts with research, eventually leading to development, translated later into growth in the territories that have more capabilities. Instead, it is the product of a policy mix, including several bodies and stakeholders in which the territories, their specificities and conditions are paramount.

(Hübner, 2009; p. 2)

This book takes up the challenge of elaborating on a 'third generation of innovation policy' and presents a comprehensive study on both the spatial trends of knowledge and innovation and their impacts on regional performance for all NUTS2 regions in the 27 European countries, the aim being to derive policy suggestions useful to increase regional innovation standards and competitiveness in Europe. It represents a second, and more advanced, development of ideas first discussed in a research programme undertaken as part of an EU ESPON (European Spatial Observatory Network) project developed in the 2010–2012 period.[1]

The general subject of the book is not a new one. A wide variety of theoretical and empirical analyses exist in the literature dealing with knowledge creation and diffusion processes, and their effects on regional performance.[2] Overall, it is probably fair to say that our current understanding of knowledge and innovation and their relationships with economic growth is quite advanced. However, what becomes clear when considering the issue more closely is that much of our understanding of the relationships among knowledge, innovation and regional growth is strongly influenced by common beliefs which hold in a general framework but which may exhibit important peculiarities when analysed through a particular lens, that of a regional approach.

In fact, it is generally quite difficult to ignore the role of knowledge and innovation in a modern economy. Financial capital, general information, consolidated technologies and codified knowledge are today readily available virtually everywhere. However, the ability to organize these 'pervasive' factors into continuously innovative production processes and products is by no means pervasive and generalized; rather, it exists selectively only in some places where tacit knowledge is continuously created, exchanged and utilized, and business ideas find their way to real markets (Camagni and Capello, 2009). This also means that the presence of knowledge does not necessarily guarantee innovation, contrary to what is usually thought. Innovation can take place in different forms, even with a lack of local knowledge. It can be the result of knowledge acquired from other places or it can result from the diffusion of an already existing innovation; these modes of innovation exist in reality, and different patterns of innovation can occur at regional level as spatial breakdowns of variants of the knowledge → invention → innovation → development logical path, depending on the presence/absence of territorial preconditions for knowledge creation, knowledge attraction and innovation.

The aim of the book is to understand the relationship between knowledge, innovation and regional performance by going beyond, when necessary, some general beliefs on this relationship. For the first time, to our knowledge, this understanding is based on a systematic analysis of all NUTS2 regions of the 27 European countries. In particular, the book introduces:

- a multidimensional definition of a knowledge economy, which is successfully applied at empirical level for the European regions (Chapters 2 to 4);
- a new and unique database with which to measure innovation at regional level (Chapter 5);
- a new analytical framework for the interpretation of alternative spatial innovation modes and the measurement of the efficiency of each alternative spatial innovation mode (Chapters 6 to 11);
- a reorientation of the normative strategies behind present European innovation policies, based on the conceptual approach and empirical results obtained (Chapter 12).

The book first elaborates on a *multidimensional definition of a knowledge economy*. Although use of the term dates back to the work of Fritz Machlup (Machlup, 1962), only in recent years has the concept of the knowledge-based economy begun to spread in the scientific and political literature. This is mainly due to work sponsored by the OECD (David and Foray, 1995; Foray and Lundvall, 1996). The well-known European strategy defined at the Lisbon and Luxembourg ministerial meetings (2000 and 2005) commits the Union to becoming the most competitive and dynamic knowledge-based economy in the world.

But what does this concept really mean? Vaguely, we know that research, human capital, creative utilization of scientific concepts and information should merge to give rise to continuing innovation and advanced production. The OECD has suggested using about 60 indicators – among which R&D and high technology activities play the dominant role – to measure the knowledge-based economy (OECD, 2004; Van Oort and Raspe, 2006). In the history of the concept, alternative and non-mutually-exclusive definitions have been provided, all with pros and cons. This book espouses a multidimensional definition of knowledge economy in which the presence of high-tech sectors, of scientific functions, and of scientific cooperation can be the source of a knowledge economy.

How can a knowledge-based economy be measured? How can its degree of penetration into a local economy be calculated? This book elaborates on these questions, and provides an operational answer which makes it possible, for the first time to our knowledge, to produce a map of the diffusion of the knowledge-based economy in European regions. This is already an interesting achievement from the *empirical point of view*.

The key novelty of the book, however, is its development of a conceptual approach that envisages a logical sequence among knowledge, innovation and economic performance which follows an abstract but consistent 'linear model of innovation', and calls for spatial separation between *knowledge and innovation*, between the invention (i.e. knowledge creation) and commercialization of new ideas (i.e. innovation) (Schumpeter, 1934 and 1942). If one accepts the idea that the two phases do not necessarily occur in the same place, a number of different possible spatial breakdowns of variants of the knowledge → invention → innovation → development logical path, built on presence/absence of territorial preconditions for knowledge creation, knowledge attraction and innovation, are available for interpreting regional modes of innovation. This means that we conceptually allow innovation to be generated from an internal knowledge base, or from local creativity even in the absence of local knowledge, or from innovative applications of knowledge developed elsewhere and acquired via scientific linkages, or finally from imitative processes. The implementation of one of these modes of innovation depends on the local preconditions that accompany knowledge and innovation creation and diffusion.

From this perspective, the book proposes a new theoretical framework in which all the empirical analyses are developed: that of regional (territorial) patterns of innovation. A *territorial pattern of innovation* is defined as a combination of *context conditions* and *specific modes of performing the different phases* of the innovation process. For several reasons, widely explained in the book (see Chapter 6), we strongly support the concept of a 'spatially diversified, phase-linear, multiple-solution model of innovation' in which the single patterns represent linearizations, or partial block linearizations, of an innovation process in which feedbacks, spatial interconnections and non-linearities play a prominent role. As regards the context conditions, the existing literature largely suggests that local elements perform a major role in the various phases, from knowledge creation to the exploitation of internal and external knowledge for innovative purposes.

Once the alternative modes of innovation have been empirically identified, the book measures *the degree of efficiency, in terms of knowledge and GDP growth, of each pattern of innovation*. Knowledge output elasticity to internal and external knowledge inputs, and GDP elasticity to innovation and to knowledge are estimated for the different kinds of regional innovation patterns, with an interesting result: none of the innovative modes is by definition superior to any other, and each of them shows distinctive forms of knowledge creation and exploitation that should be understood and utilized in order to obtain the greatest advantages from innovation.

The new theoretical paradigm requires good and reliable measures of both knowledge and innovation. In this regard, the book presents the implementation of a unique database at NUTS2 level of all kinds of innovations, from product to organizational and managerial innovation, obtained from the Community Innovation Survey (CIS) data available at NUTS0. The book suggests a sound methodology for estimating data at NUTS2 for those countries where the regional disaggregation is not available. The results testify that the invention–innovation co-location does not exist in many European regions and that there is consequently an urgent need to conceptualize possible alternative situations.

Last, but not least, the book decisively joins the debate on the most *efficient regional policy innovation with which to boost smart growth*. The present innovation policy debate stresses the need to conceptually integrate the tasks put forward by the Europe 2020 Report and the new cohesion policy reform into a common framework. On the one hand, Europe 2020 is seen as lacking a more explicit territorial dimension, a way in which to stimulate all potential and dispersed actors to contribute to the Agenda with their decision processes, doing so in a bottom-up manner (Camagni, 2011). On the other hand, the EU policy reform should be conceptualized so that it can contribute to the achievement of the three pillars (smart, sustainable and inclusive growth) of the Europe 2020 Agenda. In particular, the first pillar might become the occasion to relaunch a knowledge-intensive growth model for Europe on a regional base, supplying operational answers to the requirement of one of its 'flagship initiatives', namely 'Innovation Union'.

1.2. A multidimensional definition of the knowledge economy

Much research has been produced since the 1980s on the idea of a knowledge-based economy, and on the preconditions for knowledge creation. However, careful inspection of the existing literature reveals two striking aspects. On the one hand, it is evident that the knowledge-based economy does not have a unique interpretative paradigm. Rather, it has been (and still can be) defined on the basis of different approaches ranging from the earliest sectoral approach, through a more recent functional one, to the latest relation-based one. As a consequence, the term is still vague and imprecisely defined, which leads to rather different policy suggestions. On the other hand, it appears evident that the different approaches to the concept have a feature in common: that of the central role played by spatial elements in the creation and diffusion of knowledge, as either evidenced by empirical analyses or deductively derived from theoretical elements.

Should one want to adopt a historical approach to the interpretation of the concept, sector-based definitions and function-based definitions have long been proposed and maintained. While human capital has always been considered a basic condition for any knowledge-based development, different factors have been indicated as the driving forces of change. At an early stage, which can be located in the late 1970s and 1980s, most attention was directed to 'science-based' (Pavitt, 1984) or high-technology sectors. Regions hosting these sectors were considered to be 'advanced' regions leading the transformation of the economy. New jobs were expected to be mainly created by these new sectors, while more traditional sectors were expected to restructure or even to flow offshore, giving rise to serious tensions in local labour markets.

It soon became evident that the dichotomy was too simplistic, and that many knowledge-based advances were possible and were actually being introduced by 'traditional' sectors – such as textiles and car production – in their paths to rejuvenation. Furthermore, complexification of technological filières within the value chain increasingly highlighted the importance of advanced tertiary sectors taking mainly the form of consultancy for process innovation (proper acquisition and use of advanced technologies, tailor-made software, systems integration in production, administration and logistic processes, organizational support) and for product innovation (marketing, design, testing, advertising, finance, distribution).

In the second stage, which developed mainly during the 1980s and 1990s, a function-based approach was preferred (even though it conceptually overlapped with the previous one). This approach stressed the importance of pervasive and horizontal functions like R&D and high education. 'Scientific' regions, hosting large and well-known scientific institutions, were studied in detail, and relationships between these institutions and the industrial fabric were analysed, with some disappointments in regard to an expected but not often visible direct linkage (MacDonald, 1987; Massey et al., 1992; Monk et al., 1988; Storey and Tether, 1998). Indicators of R&D inputs (like public and private research investment and personnel) and, increasingly, indicators of R&D outputs (like patenting activities) were used to measure the commitment of firms and territories to knowledge, regarded as a necessary long-term precondition for continuing innovation (Dasgupta and Stiglitz, 1980; Antonelli, 1989; Griliches, 1990). This approach, which equated knowledge to scientific research, was the one relaunched by the European strategy defined in the Lisbon Agenda.

It is difficult to escape the impression that both the sector-based and the function-based approaches to the knowledge-based economy – both driven by the need to measure and quantify it – produced a simplified picture of the complex nature of knowledge creation and its relation to inventive and innovative capability. The presence of advanced sectors and advanced functions like R&D and higher education are special features of only some of the possible innovation paths and, though relevant, they cannot be considered as necessary or sufficient preconditions for innovation. Furthermore, emphasizing the stock of human capital, advanced functions and sectors may overlook the interaction among the different actors of knowledge development, which is increasingly seen as the crucial element in knowledge creation and evolution. This element is typical of production contexts characterized by the presence of small and medium enterprises (SMEs), but also of contexts where large firms develop their own internal knowledge, culture and know-how by enhancing internal interaction and boosting selective external interaction with industrial partners, schools, professionals and research centres. Therefore, a rather different approach should be taken, namely a cognitive one which stresses the relational and cultural elements that define the preconditions for knowledge creation, development, transmission, and diffusion.

The third stage of reflection, typical of the present preference for a relation-based approach, concentrates on identification of a 'cognitive capability' (Foray, 2000): the ability to manage information in order to identify and solve problems, or, more precisely in the economic domain, the ability to transform information and inventions into innovation and productivity increases through cooperative or market interactions. The 'learning' region is identified as the place where such cognitive processes play a crucial role by combining existing but dispersed know-how, interpretations of market needs, information flows with intellectual artifacts such as theories and models and enabling exchange of experiences and cooperation (Lundvall and Johnson, 1994). Especially in contexts characterized by a plurality of agents – like cities or industrial districts – knowledge evolution 'is not the result of individual efforts in R&D within individual firms, but rather the combination of complementary capacities and of widespread interactive learning processes, which involve many 'customers' and 'suppliers' along a well-defined filière or supply chain' (Cappellin, 2003a, p. 307).

What is striking about all the above-mentioned approaches is the central role played by spatial elements in creating new knowledge and in supporting inter-regional flows of knowledge, either evidenced by empirical analyses or deductively derived from theoretical elements. Each approach defines a type of innovative region: with a sector-based approach, t*echnologically advanced regions* are highlighted; with a functional approach, *scientific regions* are evidenced; and with the relational approach, *knowledge networking regions* are analysed.

All these kinds of region belong to a knowledge economy; they differ in terms of territorial elements that explain their innovative performance, as well as the spatial elements that support knowledge creation. A modern definition of a knowledge economy should embrace all these 'innovation modes'.

The tendency of high-technology activities to cluster along valleys, corridors, glens and high-tech districts was early empirical evidence: externalities arising from the presence of advanced education facilities were invoked to explain these facts, but international accessibility, advanced urban atmosphere, traditional industrial competencies under reorientation (Malecki, 1980; Saxenian, 1994) were also suggested.

The role of space in function-based approaches is important in two respects. Firstly, space acts as a strong concentration mechanism of advanced facilities, which are mainly located within large agglomerations or city-regions in order to benefit from scale effects in both input markets (human capital, private financial capital) and output markets (higher education services, research services) (Scott, 2001). Secondly, space acts as a driver of knowledge spillovers from R&D clusters, which are subject to strong and visible distance decay effects.

The relational approach assumes spatial elements more directly. Knowledge flows and information channels are made interdependent by the presence of a relational space, a space where functional and hierarchical economic and social interactions take place and are embedded in geographical space. The local milieu – a 'territory' identified by both geographical proximity (agglomeration economies, district economies) and cognitive proximity (shared behavioural codes, common culture, mutual trust and sense of belonging) – supplies the socioeconomic and geographical substrate on which collective learning processes can be incorporated.

The different approaches to the knowledge economy are complementary views on the role of space in knowledge creation and diffusion and they highlight different spatial elements that can be the territorial pre-conditions for knowledge creation to occur. In this sense, a *multidimensional definition of the knowledge economy* enriches interpretation of the phenomenon as well, and it highlights the diversity and variations between a regional knowledge economy and a regional innovation economy.

The book presents an empirical analysis for each approach to the knowledge economy, suggesting indicators able to capture each definition and measure its penetration into each regional economy. Only by having a clear picture of these regional variations can specific innovation policies relevant to each territorial innovation mode be distinguished.

1.3. The need for a new interpretative framework of innovation in space: territorial patterns of innovation

The paradigmatic leap in interpreting regional innovation processes today consists in the capacity to build – on the single approaches developed for the interpretation of knowledge and innovation – a conceptual framework interpreting, not a single phase of the innovation process (either knowledge or innovation creation or knowledge and innovation diffusion), as has been the case to date in the literature, but the different modes of performing the different phases of the innovation process in each region, highlighting the context conditions that accompany each innovation pattern.

Consequently considered is a *multiple-solution model of innovation* where innovation builds on internal knowledge, or where local creativity produces, even when local knowledge is lacking, an innovative application thanks to knowledge developed elsewhere and acquired via scientific linkages, or where innovation is made possible by imitation of innovations developed outside the region.

The concept of territorial innovation patterns stresses complex interplays between phases of the innovation process and the territory. By doing so, it adds three new elements to the previous theoretical paradigms. Firstly, it separates knowledge from innovation as different (and subsequent) logical phases of an innovation process, each phase requiring specific local elements for its development. This approach rejects the generalization of an invention–innovation short circuit taking place within individual firms (or territories), like the one visible in some advanced sectors, as well as the assumption of an immediate interaction between R&D/higher education facilities, on the one hand, and innovating firms on the other, thanks to pure spatial proximity. Secondly, the concept of 'patterns of innovation' identifies the different necessary context conditions, that may support the single innovation phases and that generate *different modes of performing and linking the different phases of the innovation process.* These context conditions become integral parts of each territorial pattern of innovation. The third new element concerns the superseding of a purely geographic concept of proximity to interpret inter-regional knowledge spillovers, moving towards a concept of 'cross-regional cognitive proximity'. This concept links knowledge spillovers to the presence of a common technological domain within which cumulative search processes and inventions can be performed through inter-regional cooperation (Capello and Caragliu, 2012).

Among all possible combinations between innovation modes and territorial elements, the 'archetypal' ones may be indicated as follows, where each reflects a specific piece of literature on knowledge and innovation in space:

a) *an endogenous innovation pattern in a scientific network*, where local conditions fully support the creation of knowledge, its local diffusion and transformation into innovation and its widespread local adoption. Given the complex nature of knowledge creation today, this pattern is expected to show a tight interplay among regions in the form of international scientific networks. From the conceptual point of view this advanced pattern is the one considered by most of the existing literature dealing with knowledge and innovation creation and diffusion (Camagni, 1991; Audretsch and Feldman, 1996; Boschma 2005; Capello, 2009a);

b) *a creative application pattern*, characterized by the presence of economic actors interested and curious enough to look for knowledge outside the region – given the scarcity of local knowledge – and creative enough to apply external knowledge to local innovation needs. This approach is conceptually built on the literature on regional innovation adoption/adaptation, as also proposed by the smart specialization approach (Foray, 2009; EC, 2010b);

c) *an imitative innovation pattern*, where the actors base their innovation capacity on imitative processes, which can take place with different degrees of adaptation of an already existing innovation. This pattern is based on the literature dealing with innovation diffusion (Hägerstrand, 1952; Capello, 1988).

Conceptually speaking, these three patterns by and large represent the different ways in which knowledge and innovation can take place in a regional economy. Each of them represents a different way of innovating, and calls for different policy styles to support it.

Regional 'innovation patterns' are identified empirically in the book in the way that knowledge and innovation are developed within regions according to the nature of their traditional knowledge base and productive specificities and/or how they are captured from other regions via cooperation, the mobility of scientists and professionals, market procurement, and trans-regional investments. The empirical results show that the pathways to innovation and modernization are differentiated among regions according to local specificities, and that there is a larger variety of possible innovation patterns than are conceptually envisaged, still consistent with the archetypal theoretical patterns identified.

Therefore, from the scientific point of view, the interesting research question to test is whether any innovation pattern is superior to another, or, rather, whether high efficiency levels can be achieved in each pattern.

Importantly, the variety of innovation patterns that emerge from this analysis explains the failure of a 'one-size-fits-all' policy for innovation like thematically/regionally neutral R&D incentives. Innovation patterns specific to each area must be identified: for it is on these patterns that targeted innovation policies can be devised.

1.4. A new and unique innovation database for European regions

The conceptual distinction between invention and innovation is important for interpreting the different modes of innovation. However, empirical analysis of the distinction requires a clear separation between indicators of knowledge and those of innovation: a distinction able to capture the invention phase separately from the phase of commercialization of new ideas. In fact, factors that enhance the implementation of new knowledge are different from the factors which stimulate innovation. The firms and individuals leading an invention are not necessarily also leaders in innovation or in the widespread diffusion of new technologies. The real world is full of examples of this kind: the fax machine, first developed in Germany, was turned into a product that was successful worldwide by Japanese companies. Similarly, the anti-lock brake system (ABS) was invented by US car makers but became prominent primarily due to German automotive suppliers (Licht, 2009).

In this book this empirical distinction has been made possible by the development of a unique database on innovation at regional level. Based on the Community Innovation Survey (CIS) available from Eurostat at national level (and for a few countries at regional level), the effort in this book has been to propose and test a methodology able to estimate regional data for those countries on which regional data were missing. In particular, innovation indicators have been built based on national CIS4 wave figures (covering the 2002–2004 period) for all NUTS2 of the 27 European member countries. Table 1.1 reports the number of NUTS2 regions by country that are at the basis of the innovation data and of the empirical analysis

Table 1.1 Number of NUTS2 regions by country

Code	Country	NUTS level	Number of NUTS2 regions
AT	Austria	2	9
BE	Belgium	2	11
BG	Bulgaria	2	6
CH	Switzerland	2	7
CY	Cyprus	0	1
CZ	Czech Republic	2	9
DE	Germany	2	39
DK	Denmark	2	5
EE	Estonia	0	1
ES	Spain	2	19
FI	Finland	2	5
FR	France	2	26
GR	Greece	2	13
HU	Hungary	2	7
IE	Ireland	2	2
IS	Iceland	0	1
IT	Italy	2	21
LI	Liechtenstein	0	1
LT	Lithuania	0	1
LU	Luxembourg	0	1
LV	Latvia	0	1
NL	The Netherlands	2	12
NO	Norway	2	7
PL	Poland	2	16
PT	Portugal	2	7
RO	Romania	2	8
SE	Sweden	2	8
SI	Slovenia	2	2
SK	Slovakia	2	4
UK	United Kingdom	2	37

throughout the whole book. Tests for robustness of the estimates have been run with striking positive results that encourage their use.

Different questions of CIS were used to measure different types of innovation: only product innovations, only process innovations, product and process innovations (both types of innovation simultaneously as well as all the first three main types together), and marketing and/or organizational innovations.

The traditional R&D and patenting indicators capture in great detail the invention phase, which, as the empirical evidence shows, does not necessarily go hand in hand with the innovation phase, especially at the regional level. This empirical result supports the theoretical idea that different patterns of innovation exist. Probably none of them is superior to the others; rather, they are all efficient, given the local characteristics in which they are embedded.

1.5. The need for a reorientation of regional innovation policies

The variety of territorial innovation patterns calls for analysis of the efficiency of each territorial pattern in terms of innovative performance and regional growth. The book conducts an impact analysis of knowledge and innovation on regional dynamics, and it stresses the difference in GDP elasticity to knowledge and innovation for each pattern of innovation.

Increasing European competitiveness through knowledge and innovation is a strategic and correctly formulated goal. However, the far-reaching empirical analysis developed in this book highlights in many respects the inappropriateness of the 'one-size-fits-all' policy which might be derived from a rapid and superficial reading of the Lisbon and Europe 2020 agendas.

When a regional perspective is adopted, in fact, an aggregate policy goal of 3% of the EU's GDP (public and private) to be invested in R&D/innovation shows its fragility in supporting the increase of the innovation capacity of each region in Europe. In fact, the analysis of knowledge/innovation impact on the regional performance developed for the different patterns of innovation yields interesting and unexpected results, namely:

- required for R&D to have a substantial impact on GDP is a critical mass of R&D investments. In Europe, there are only a few regions that have achieved this critical mass. Moreover, R&D investments suffer from decreasing returns, which oblige areas highly endowed with R&D activities to target new R&D funds on new technological domains;
- similarly, formal knowledge, in the form of R&D and patents, generates innovation only in those areas that register a critical mass of formal knowledge;
- human capital, in the form of a highly educated population, requires a critical mass if it is to create new knowledge (patents). However, notwithstanding the decreasing returns associated with this knowledge input, the elasticity of new knowledge to human capital is higher than to R&D investments. This reminds us that R&D investments *tout court* is too narrow a policy tool to enhance knowledge creation;

- R&D investment on its own does not guarantee high efficiency in the production of new knowledge; it is instead the efficient combination of different knowledge inputs that guarantees high efficiency levels in knowledge production;
- external knowledge (in the form of inventor attraction and scientific research collaborations) contributes to the creation of local knowledge in regions in which there is already a high level of knowledge. The idea that R&D investments and knowledge production in general spill over to neighbouring regions is not so obvious when a certain receptiveness to external knowledge is lacking; receptivity is defined as the local tacit knowledge embedded in local culture rather than formal knowledge, usually labeled absorptive capacity à la Cohen and Levinthal (1990);
- regional growth potentials arising from innovation activities do not always match the intensity of the local formal knowledge basis.

All these findings highlight unconventional policy warnings with regard to:

- the high expectations that R&D investments are the right policy tools with which to develop new knowledge, innovation and growth;
- the general belief that, if a knowledge economy is developed, this will give rise to the same growth opportunities everywhere;
- the idea that knowledge produced outside the region can be easily and automatically used efficiently by other regions;
- the general belief that an innovation-driven economy is necessarily linked to a knowledge economy;
- the idea that formal knowledge is the main and most strategic knowledge asset on which a knowledge economy rests.

These unconventional policy warnings suggest that European innovation policies should move away from a thematically/regionally neutral and generic innovation strategy; instead, they should be based on a *thematically/regionally focused innovation policy* approach.

The empirical results help suggest a reorientation of innovation strategies at the regional level thanks to the superseding of some general beliefs that might be misleading in regard to coherent and efficient policy implications.

The book enters the debate on the smart specialization strategies suggested by the 'Knowledge for Growth' expert group advising the former European Commissioner for Research, Janez Potocnik (Foray, 2009; Foray et al., 2009), and it advocates a consistent match between investments in knowledge and human capital and the present industrial and technological 'vocations' and competences of territories. Supported by the empirical results, the book stresses the need to go beyond the simplistic dichotomy between core and periphery in the Union, between an advanced 'research area' (the core) and a 'co-application area' of general purpose technologies (the periphery), present in the original but also in subsequent contributions of the smart specialization group. The results of our empirical analyses indicate that the geography of innovation is much more complex than a core–periphery model. The capacity to pass from knowledge to innovation and from innovation to regional growth differs among regions, and identification of specific 'innovation patterns' is essential for building targeted normative strategies well beyond those envisaged in a first phase of the smart specialization. Also the identification of specific innovation policies based on specificities of single regions – suggested more recently by the same experts (EC, 2012a) – is certainly fundamental for the implementation of projects, but not for strategies, which call for the identification of *common approaches for similar types of regions* in order to prevent misallocation of public resources and unlikely local strategies. For this purpose, a *territorial taxonomy* is necessary for the development of a regional innovation strategy.

1.6. Structure of the book

The book has been structured with the aim of producing a systematic work which encompasses theoretical underpinnings, methodological analyses, and policy implications. It is a monograph that starts with analysis of the spatial trends of knowledge and innovation, moves to identification of the territorial patterns of innovation and the impact of knowledge and innovation on local performance in each pattern of innovation, and concludes with the policy implications that the empirical evidence suggests for the current debate at European level.

The chapters have a clear logical interconnection if read in sequence. However, efforts have been made to give each of them methodological autonomy and self-containment, together with evidence of its position in the full logical chain.

The book is organized into three main parts (Figure 1.1). Part I sets out the empirical measurement of the knowledge economy and of innovation potential at the regional level. The knowledge economy measurement is based on the conceptual definition provided above. Technologically advanced regions are identified when a sector-based approach is used (Chapter 2). Scientific regions recall the function-based approach (Chapter 3). The relational approach identifies the knowledge networking regions on the basis of spatial proximity, on the one hand, and scientific cooperation, mobility of scientists and exchange of knowledge through citations (irrespective of geographical proximity) on the other (Chapter 4). A picture of the knowledge economy in Europe at the regional level is provided as the sum of all possible definitions, and it is compared with the spatial innovation trends, showing a discrepancy in the spatial distribution of the two variables (Chapter 5).

Part II discusses the new interpretative paradigm of innovation in space, and the empirical analysis of the impact of knowledge and innovation on regional performance. The first chapter in Part II describes the logic of the conceptual framework and its steps forward with respect to the literature (Chapter 6). The application of the new conceptual framework to the European reality is presented in Chapter 7, and the territorial patterns of innovation are identified.

The impact analysis of knowledge and innovation is developed by reading the European territory through the lens of the alternative patterns of innovation. In particular, the analysis measures:

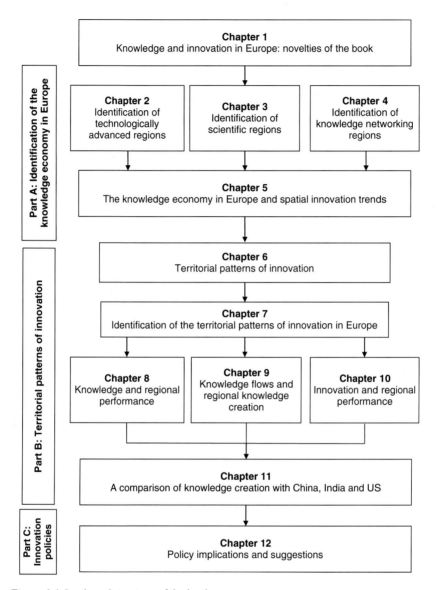

Figure 1.1 Logic and structure of the book

- the elasticity of knowledge output to knowledge input (Chapter 8);
- the elasticity of GDP to knowledge (Chapter 8);
- the elasticity of knowledge output to internal and external knowledge spillovers (Chapter 9);
- the elasticity of GDP growth to knowledge and innovation (Chapter 10).

Comparison of knowledge-creation factors at regional level between Europe and other countries is an important exercise with which to highlight similarities and differences in the European context. For this reason, in Chapter 11, a unique database of regional patents and innovation-enabling factors in the US, India and China yields lessons for European regions.

Part C is devoted to the policy suggestions built from the empirical results obtained. It enters the debate on smart specialization strategies by stressing the need to move beyond the simplistic dichotomy between core and periphery in the Union, between an advanced 'research area' (the core) and a 'co-application area' of general purpose technologies (the periphery), present in the original but also in subsequent contributions. In fact, the geography of innovation is much more complex than a simple core–periphery model, and the capacity to pass from knowledge to innovation and from innovation to regional growth differs among regions. Therefore, identification of specific 'innovation patterns' is essential for building targeted normative strategies well beyond what is proposed by the smart specialization model (Chapter 12).

This structure provides the reader with a comprehensive roadmap that goes from the definition and measurement of the knowledge economy, through the clear empirical evidence that knowledge and innovation do not always overlap at the spatial level, the new conceptual framework that might allocate the distinction between knowledge and innovation, to identification of the different regional patterns of innovation in Europe, and, lastly, to empirical analyses on efficiency in exploiting knowledge and innovation for growth across innovation patterns. Innovation policies that start from local specificities and the established innovation patterns in each region are suggested and elaborated within the framework of the smart specialization strategy.

Notes

1 The first ideas were developed within the EU ESPON 2013 applied project KIT – Knowledge, Innovation, Territory – led by Politecnico di Milano, in cooperation with CRENoS – Università di Cagliari, IREA-AQR, University of Barcelona, LSE – London School of Economics and Political Science, University of Economics in Bratislava and Cardiff University. In the work presented here, additional quantitative analyses, both descriptive and econometric, are developed. The authors wish to thank all researchers involved in the project for their invaluable contribution to, and their joint effort on, the project. The authors would like to thank, also, Ann-Gritt Neuse from ESPON CU, and the two sounding board members, for comments and suggestions on earlier drafts of the KIT report, partially reflected in this book.

2 For a review of innovation and regional growth theories, see Johansson and Karlsson (2009). For different aspects of innovation and regional growth see Cooke et al. (2011).

Part I

Measuring the territorial dimension of knowledge and innovation in Europe

2   Technologically advanced regions

Roberta Capello and Andrea Caragliu

2.1. Introduction

In the second half of the 1990s, a surge in knowledge-related activities and industries prompted the emergence of a new paradigm, namely that of the *knowledge-based economy*. Apparently, the term 'knowledge-based economy', which enjoyed much success in the 1990s, dates as far back as the late 1960s. Already in 1969, in his book *The Age of Discontinuity*, Peter Drucker titled one of his chapters 'The knowledge economy'. The success of the term, however, only came when it entered the policy arena, often being adopted by such institutions as the World Bank and the OECD.

In the early stage of reflection on the knowledge economy, attention therefore concentrated on 'science-based' (Pavitt, 1984) or high-technology sectors. Regions hosting these sectors were considered to be 'advanced' regions leading the transformation of the economy. New jobs were expected mainly from these new sectors, while more traditional ones were expected to restructure or even to flow offshore, giving rise to severe tensions in local labour markets.

In 1996, the OECD stated that the increasing importance of knowledge in Western economies warranted a specific definition, as follows:

> Knowledge-based economies [are defined as] economies which are directly based on the production, distribution and use of knowledge and information. This is reflected in the trend in OECD economies towards growth in high-technology investments, high-technology industries, more highly-skilled labour and associated productivity gains.
>
> (OECD, 1996, p. 229)

In the same period as the OECD definition, many studies were developed at the regional level, demonstrating both deductively and inductively a natural tendency for high-tech firms to cluster in space. Using both input (e.g. expenditure on research and development) and output indicators (e.g. number of patents) of innovative activity, these studies showed that innovation was concentrated in central and metropolitan areas. Moreover, in all the industrialized countries, analyses of the location of high-tech firms revealed marked polarization effects due to the pronounced preference of these firms for central locations with strong sectoral specialization. European examples of this pattern included Baden-Württenberg in Southern Germany, Jutland in Denmark, Småland in Sweden, and Sophia-Antipolis close to Nice in France. These cases seemed to replicate in Europe the experience of the celebrated Silicon Valley in California, or Route 128 in the Boston area (Saxenian, 1994).

Explanations for high-tech clustering appeared to be straightforward. Concentrated locations facilitate the exploitation of technological and scientific knowledge developed by research centres and universities; they grant easier access to the tacit, non-codified knowledge required for imitation and reverse engineering; and they ensure the ready availability of skilled labour and advanced services. In theoretical terms, this means that a concentrated location of industries benefits from the existence of agglomeration economies.

The role of agglomeration economies (at both urban and sectoral levels) in explaining the concentration of innovative activity was demonstrated long ago by Marshall (Marshall, 1920). However, interest in dynamic agglomeration economies (the agglomerative advantages fostering the innovative behavior of firms) has grown considerably in recent years, as agreement has emerged on the importance of innovation for the competitiveness of local systems.

Starting from this literature and assuming the industry-based approach[1] in the definition of the knowledge economy, this chapter proposes a classification of the EU territory according to the regional specialization in high-technology sectors; regions hosting these sectors are labelled as technologically advanced regions (henceforth, TARs). Because of the deep technological content of both manufacturing as well as service activities, neither are ex ante excluded from the definition. For this reason, regions are classified as 'technologically advanced' if both technologically advanced manufacturing and services characterize the region.

The structure of the chapter is as follows. Section 2.2 briefly presents the theoretical explanation for the agglomeration of high-tech sectors, and then summarizes the main empirical verifications of such paradigms. Section 2.3 links the summary of the existing literature with identification of a taxonomy for TARs. Section 2.4 presents a regional analysis on high-tech specialization patterns between 2002 and 2007. Section 2.5 sets out the empirical results, with statistical and graphical evidence concerning the location of TARs. Finally, Section 2.6 concludes the chapter.

As widely explained in Chapter 1, the industry-based definition of the knowledge economy is only one of the definitions to be found in the literature. Two more recent definitions proposed in the literature are based respectively on a functional and relational approach to knowledge. These modern interpretations of the knowledge economy identify other types of regions, namely the scientific regions characterized by the presence of knowledge creation functions like R&D and higher education (Chapter 3), and knowledge networking regions, an expression which refers to the presence of relational, cultural and psychological elements that define the preconditions for knowledge creation, development, transmission and diffusion (Chapter 4).

2.2. Why do high-tech firms agglomerate in space? A brief survey of the literature

Understanding the clustering of high-tech firms became of particular interest in the 1980s. In that period, under the impetus of profound technological changes, innovation came to be considered the driving force of economic development, and knowledge the key factor in local economic success. For this reason, high-tech industries were considered to be at the basis of the knowledge economy in what can be defined as the 'industry paradigm' (Figure 2.1).

In the 1980s, the industrial organization literature found evidence on the existence, and importance, of intra-industry (Bernstein and Nadiri, 1989) and inter-industry (Bernstein and Nadiri, 1988) knowledge spillovers in high-tech industries which caused lower unit production costs and hence higher productivity for firms active in industries with high average levels of R&D capital. Intra-industry and inter-industry spillovers were found to be stronger because firms in high-tech sectors share both technological as well as geographical proximity. Nevertheless, technological proximity fosters the exchange of knowledge across industrially compatible economic activities even at large distances (Coe and Helpman, 1995).

In the same period, the uneven spatial distribution of innovative activity was taken to be the primary cause of regional imbalances, and given evident signs of the hypermobility of labour and capital, the most immobile factors were considered to be knowledge and the intangible elements connected with culture, skills and creativity: it was on these elements that the competitiveness of local systems depended. Therefore, in a spatial approach, the main theoretical rationale behind identification of the knowledge-based economy consists in the notions of localization and agglomeration economies (Figure 2.1). Firms obtain agglomeration

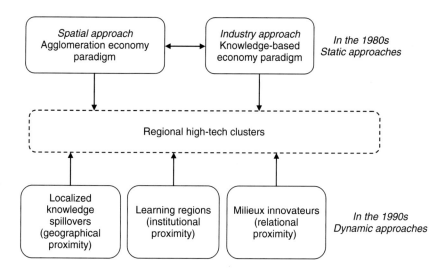

Figure 2.1 Theoretical approaches behind regional high-tech clusters

economies when they co-locate near to each other ('agglomerating'). This concept relates to two main rationales, i.e. the idea of economies of scale and the related network effects. Simply put, as more firms in related industries cluster together, average production and transportation costs significantly decrease. Such effects can be classified into three typologies (Hoover, 1936): economies internal to the firm (namely, scale economies); economies external to the firm but internal to the industry (localization economies); and finally economies achieved from localization in cities (urbanization economies). These last are formed outside both the firm and the industry.

Economies of scale typically concern indivisibilities proper to certain production lines, technologies, or products (Edwards and Starr, 1987). Therefore, it could be argued that the optimal distribution of firms across space, in the presence of indivisibilities (i.e. economies of scale), and transport costs (i.e. distance-caused spatial impedance) implies an equilibrium finite set of very large, vertically integrated firms incorporating the core of worldwide production. Stylized facts demonstrate, however, the existence of a very large number of small and medium-sized enterprises located in relatively small clusters and specializing in activities up and down the value chain. The rationale for these firms not to integrate vertically such activities is the agglomeration advantages that they obtain from clustering (Feldman, 1999).

Neoclassical economics explained the existence of clusters mainly on the basis of extra-firm, intra-industry indivisibilities. This approach, summarized in Duranton and Puga (2004), posits that sharing costly production factors and enjoying a diversified labour market are the biggest advantages for firms and workers deciding to co-locate. No reference is made to any concept of proximity beyond pure geographical nearness, and savings in transport costs are the ultimate reason why firms co-locate (Glaeser, 2010).

However, even classical economists such as Alfred Marshall (Marshall, 1920) noted that there should have been something more in the agglomeration economies' 'black box' than pure proximity advantages:

> The mysteries of the trade become no mysteries; but are as it were in the air, and children learn many of them unconsciously. Good work is rightly appreciated, inventions and improvements in machinery, in processes and the general organization of the business have their merits promptly discussed: if one man starts a new idea, it is taken up by others and combined with suggestions of their own; and thus it becomes the source of further new ideas.
>
> (Marshall, 1920, rep. 2009, p. 225)

The challenge of adding something more to pure geographical proximity was taken up in the 1970s, when the industrial district literature (Becattini, 1979 and 2004) paved the way for a new generation of theories convincingly advancing explanations for the existence of clusters of specialized SMEs beyond the achievement of lower transport costs (Capello, 2009a). The industrial districts literature for the first time identified the genetic elements responsible for the existence of agglomeration economies: in particular, the paramount importance of sociocultural proximity among firms, average small/medium size, and industrial specialization, which add to spatial proximity advantages. This contribution, however, proved helpful for explanation of pure co-localization processes, and consequently for a higher-than-average economic performance, but it did not consider innovation activities.

Empirical evidence collected in the 1980s on several EU regions demonstrated the increasing importance of specialization in high-tech manufacturing. Empirical studies providing such evidence included, among many, Stöhr and Tödling (1977), Ciciotti and Wettmann (1981), Johannisson and Spilling (1983), Garofoli (1981), and Courlet and Pecqueur (1992). This new stylized fact implied the need to focus on specific advantages linked to the Marshallian district, namely dynamic/learning advantages.[2]

Knowledge was interpreted as a long-term process crucial for the competitiveness of high-tech firms, and the explanation for the clustering of high-tech firms centred on dynamic agglomeration economies (Figure 2.1). In this vein, a large body of research explained the agglomerated spatial location of high-tech firms through the existence of dynamic advantages on regional innovativeness.

Pure geographical nearness, and a higher probability of knowledge accumulation via easier face-to-face contacts, was at the basis of the literature on localized knowledge spillovers (Audretsch and Feldman, 1996, 2004). The aim of this approach was to stress the importance of geographical proximity as a vehicle for the diffusion of local knowledge: firms located in areas characterized by a high number of high-tech firms registered increasing returns in innovation processes thanks to the knowledge that they acquired from the external environment.

One criticism brought against a pure geographical approach like the knowledge spillover one was that synergy and cooperative elements were left to pure probability contacts that increased as distance decreased (Capello, 2009a). This simplified approach also impoverished interpretations of the mechanism by which knowledge flows are spread, which was reduced to a simple epidemic process. Thus one of the most crucial aspects of the innovation process was ignored: how people (or the context) actually learn, and how agglomeration can support learning processes through interaction, networks, and exchange of labour and knowledge (Capello and Faggian, 2005).

Even on very traditional, cost-savings-oriented lines, the empirical literature on the positive effects of agglomerated spatial structures on productivity argued that agglomerated areas were also more innovative (Puga, 2010). There was insufficient work which extended the rationale beyond pure geographical nearness and higher innovativeness in agglomerated areas. Shearmur (2012) was a rare example of this kind: by using establishment-level data on knowledge-intensive business services in the Canadian city of Montreal, he provided evidence that localization and urbanization economies play a prominent role in firms' innovative performance. Such evidence was clearly geography-driven, and the pure probability of contact among individual knowledge-keepers increased the chances of knowledge accumulating locally.

Theoretical approaches took a step forward in explaining dynamic agglomeration economies (Figure 2.1). The milieu innovateur (Aydalot, 1986; Camagni, 1991) and the learning region literature (Lundvall and Johnson, 1994) are examples in this regard. Both approaches departed from simple geographical proximity as the element behind the higher innovativeness of some areas, and they conceptualized different forms of proximities as the bases of interactive and collective learning.

Relational proximity is at the basis of dynamic agglomeration economies in the milieu innovateur theory. In fact, this theory gives a conceptual role to social interactions, interpersonal synergies, and collective action among actors – in short, what it calls 'relational proximity' – as factors which account for the greater innovative capacity of spatially concentrated small firms, and of the areas in which they are located. Cooperation and relational attitude are at the basis of collective learning. In a milieu, such learning takes place in a spontaneous and socialized manner within the local labour market through forms of stable and enduring collaboration between customers and suppliers based on loyalty and trust (Camagni, 1991). Moreover, the socialization of the risks associated with innovation explains the greater innovativeness of these areas – as has also been empirically demonstrated (Capello and Faggian, 2005).

Dynamic agglomeration economies in the learning region theory are dependent on institutional proximity. The latter emphasizes the importance for increasing innovation activities of cooperation and interaction between firms and the local scientific system, between different functions within the firm, between producers and customers, and between firms and the social and institutional structure. Innovation, in fact, is more and more dependent on informal learning processes based on direct experience, or on that of others, which comes about through activities focused on finding solutions to specific technological, productive or market problems (Capello, 2007). Innovation, therefore, cannot be understood properly unless it is examined within the sociocultural and institutional context in which it takes place. In areas where there is 'institutional proximity' – meaning the set of norms, codes and rules of behaviour which help economic actors (people, individual firms, public and private institutions) to adopt forms of organization that facilitate interactive learning – the innovative process comes about more rapidly and gives competitiveness to the economic system. Areas with a rich endowment of cooperative actors for innovation (including not only R&D centres but also public institutions and universities) are found to be more innovative (Asheim and Isaksen, 1996).

The dynamic agglomeration advantages show their effects in most industries, but they are particularly active in areas characterized by high-tech industries in which the complexity and systemic nature of innovation, and the brevity of the product life cycle imposed by a high rate of technological change, increasingly call for interactive processes, collective learning, and risk socialization.

Ever since the 1990s, the OECD definition of a knowledge-based economy as an economy where knowledge-intensive industries agglomerate has found solid grounding in the extensive and articulated theories just presented, and it still receives large attention in the policy arena. This, therefore, calls for identification of TARs in Europe.

2.3. Technologically advanced regions: a taxonomy

The identification of TARs in Europe is based on a sector-oriented approach. Because of the above-summarized theoretical grounding, knowledge-intensive industries represent a standard referent for the definition of a knowledge-based economy. Through technological, relational, institutional, and geographical proximity, high-tech firms co-located in agglomerated areas enjoy innovativeness enhancements.

In order to identify knowledge-based regions, now presented is a definition of what exactly is meant by 'high-tech', followed by a proposed taxonomy of high-tech industries in high-tech manufacturing and high-tech services.

The definition of high-tech industries may be rather arbitrary. Consequently, a broad definition has been chosen, one which encompasses industries with medium-high and high-tech content (henceforth, MHHT) in order to capture a wide range of industries characterized by remarkable high-tech creation and deployment.

High-tech industries are classified according to the OECD methodology (OECD, 2005). Such industries include manufacturing of aircraft and spacecraft, pharmaceuticals, office, accounting and computing machinery, radio, TV and communications equipment, and medical, precision and optical instruments.[3] Also high-tech services follow the OECD classification, being labelled 'Knowledge-Intensive Service Activities' (henceforth, KIS).

The level of specialization is captured here with a location quotient calculated with respect to the EU27 average value; regional data include industry-specific employment in MHHT manufacturing and KIS industries.[4] Specialization is calculated for two years (2002 and 2007) in order to identify time trends, along with its spatial distribution.

The definition of TARs is summarized in Figure 2.2. Regions specialized only in high-tech manufacturing or KIS are labelled *high-tech manufacturing regions* and *KIS regions*, respectively. TARs are instead those regions which simultaneously specialize in both MHHT and KIS industries. *Low-tech regions*, instead, have no specialization in either manufacturing or service activities.

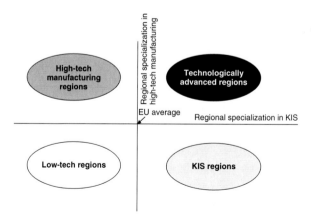

Figure 2.2 Typology of regions according to industrial and high-tech service specialization

Before highlighting the TARs in Europe, examination should be made of the high-tech specialization patterns of European regions in order to understand the trajectories followed by the regions. An especially interesting aspect to understand is the extent to which high-tech manufacturing is substituted by knowledge-intensive services, and whether the substitution effect is common to all countries in Europe and takes place at all geographical levels, i.e. across regions in Europe, across European countries, or across regions of the same country.

2.4. High-tech specialization in European regions

Maps 2.1 and 2.2 show the location quotients (LQ) for both MHHT manufacturing and KIS in 2002 calculated on employment shares in MHHT manufacturing and KIS industries. In order to provide time comparisons, Maps 2.3 and 2.4 represent the same indicators for the year 2007.

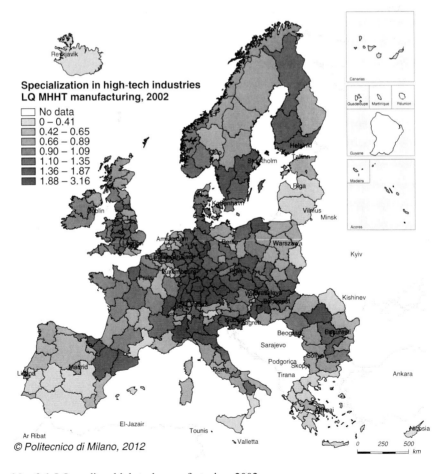

Map 2.1 LQ medium high-tech manufacturing, 2002

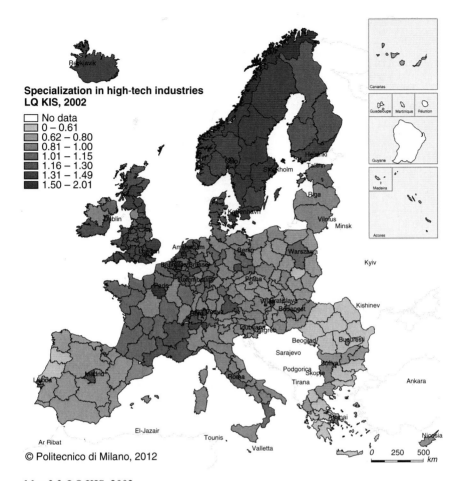

Map 2.2 LQ KIS, 2002

While specialization in manufacturing high-tech seems to be much more diffused across the European space (Map 2.3), specialization in KIS (Map 2.4) displays impressive concentration rates. At the national level, the result is already striking: as many as twelve countries present no specialization at all, neither in MHHT nor in KIS industries.[5]

The urban–rural distribution of specialization levels present interesting patterns. Using the Agglomerated-Urban–Rural ESPON classification (Bengs and Schmidt-Thomé, 2005) of EU regions[6] yields strong statistical evidence in favour of a higher MHHT specialization in urban regions (Figure 2.3) i.e. regions characterized by the presence of medium-sized cities. By contrast, KIS specialization (Figure 2.4) is found to be much stronger in more densely inhabited areas, i.e. agglomerated regions (dense regions hosting at least one large city).

Classical pairwise t-tests demonstrate, at all the usual levels of statistical confidence, that such differences are striking in both the MHHT and the KIS cases.

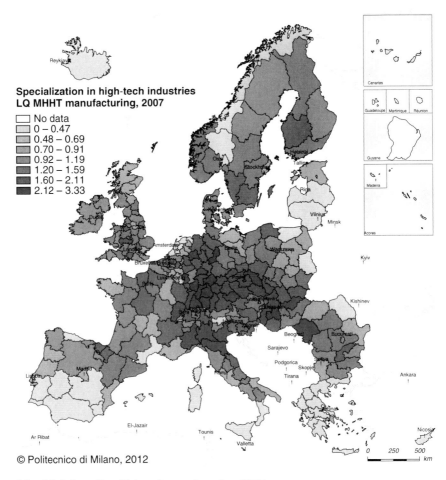

Map 2.3 LQ medium high-tech manufacturing, 2007

Urban regions are roughly 20 per cent more specialized in high-tech manufacturing than agglomerated regions, and 40 per cent more than rural ones, while agglomerated regions display 40 per cent more specialization in KIS industries than rural regions and 20 per cent higher than do urban ones.

Maps 2.5 and 2.6 show the region-specific absolute change in MHHT and KIS location quotients. These maps allow inspection of the geographical distribution of evolution in European regions for the levels of specialization in both high-tech manufacturing and service industries. A first-hand visual examination suggests the existence of markedly different evolution patterns in different areas – namely Western vs. Eastern countries, densely inhabited vs rural areas – along with non-negligible country effects.

The graphical evidence calls for more detailed analysis. Graphically, it seems that a very weak negative correlation may exist between specialization levels in

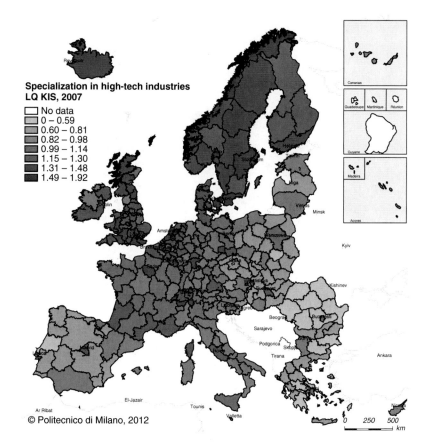

**Specialization in high-tech industries
LQ KIS, 2007**

- ☐ No data
- 0 – 0.59
- 0.60 – 0.81
- 0.82 – 0.98
- 0.99 – 1.14
- 1.15 – 1.30
- 1.31 – 1.48
- 1.49 – 1.92

© Politecnico di Milano, 2012

Map 2.4 LQ KIS, 2007

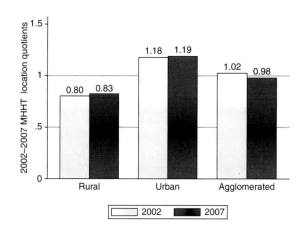

Figure 2.3 LQ in MHHT in 2002 and 2007 by settlement structure

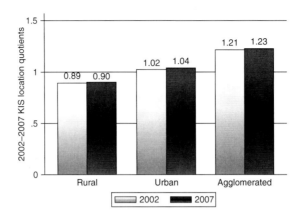

Figure 2.4 LQ in KIS in 2002 and 2007 by settlement structure

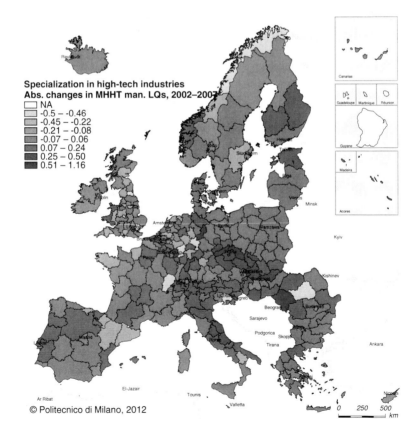

Map 2.5 Absolute changes in medium high-tech manufacturing LQs, 2002–2007

Source: Capello et al. (2012)

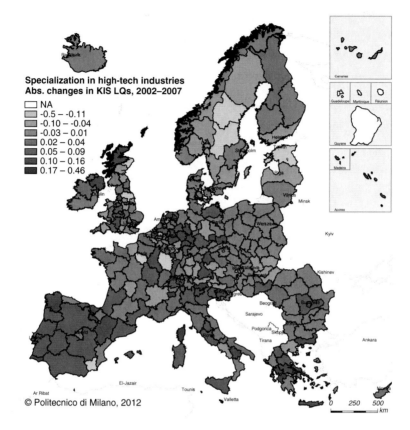

Specialization in high-tech industries
Abs. changes in KIS LQs, 2002–2007

- NA
- -0.5 – -0.11
- -0.10 – -0.04
- -0.03 – 0.01
- 0.02 – 0.04
- 0.05 – 0.09
- 0.10 – 0.16
- 0.17 – 0.46

© Politecnico di Milano, 2012

Map 2.6 Absolute changes in KIS LQs, 2002–2007

Source: Capello et al. (2012)

the MHHT and KIS industries; this statement is verified in Figure 2.5. Such correlation is also slightly non-significant: the Pearson correlation index equals 0.24, with p-value equal to 0.19.

Within-country evidence confirms that a slight decrease in MHHT manufacturing activities has taken place in major industrial countries in the past decade. Regional specialization in the MHHT industry markedly declined between 2002 and 2007 in most French, Polish, British, Bulgarian and Greek regions (Map 2.5).[7] At the same time, a relative positive shift in MHHT occurred in most regions belonging to two belts, one running north–southwards and the other stretching west–eastwards across the continent.

This evidence allows one to draw conclusions similar to those emerging from inspection at country level: the analysis of the regional correlations between MHHT and KIS specialization (Figure 2.6) allows the inference that the change in MHHT and KIS specialization between 2002 and 2007 (measured with the

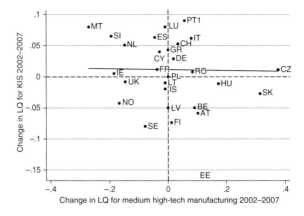

Figure 2.5 Country average changes in LQs for medium high-tech and KIS industries, 2002–2007

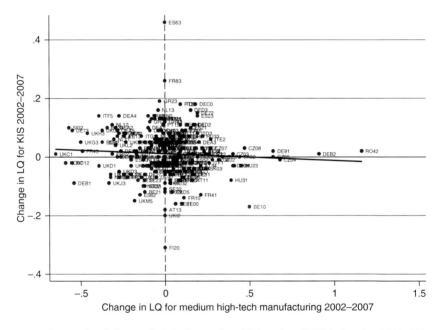

Figure 2.6 Regional changes in LQs for medium high-tech and KIS industries, 2002–2007

Pearson index) was equal to –0.06, again not significant at any conventional level.[8] Both at the national and regional level, therefore, the data suggest that a counter-mechanism – i.e. increasing specialization in KIS – was not necessarily at work in countries and regions where specialization in MHHT decreased in the last decade. These findings imply that the type of knowledge required to succeed in high-tech manufacturing activities may not be interchangeable with the set of skills necessary to thrive in KIS industries. This result has important policy implications: when policymakers respond to a crisis affecting regional employment in high-tech manufacturing, they should consider measures to facilitate the shift towards a rather different set of skills by taking long-term industrial evolution into account.

In order to clarify the structural differences emerging from inspection of Maps 2.5 and 2.6, and Figures 2.5 and 2.6, Table 2.1 tabulates the absolute rates of change for MHHT and KIS location quotients across different areas.

Table 2.1 Average absolute changes in MHHT and KIS LQs, 2002–2007

Area	Average abs. change in MHHT LQs	Average abs. change in KIS LQs
EU27	−0.01	0.01
EU15	−0.02	0.01
NMS	0.10	0.00
Country averages:		
AT	0.10	0.06
BE	0.09	−0.05
BG	0.00	0.00
CH	0.03	0.05
CY	−0.03	0.04
CZ	0.38	0.01
DE	0.02	0.03
DK	0.00	0.00
EE	0.10	−0.16
ES	0.05	0.06
FI	0.01	−0.07
FR	0.04	0.01
GR	0.00	0.04
HU	0.17	0.01
IE	−0.19	0.01
IS	−0.01	−0.02
IT	0.08	0.06
LT	−0.01	−0.01
LU	−0.01	0.08
LV	0.00	−0.05
MT	−0.27	0.08
NL	0.15	0.05
NO	0.17	0.04
PL	0.00	0.00
PT	0.06	0.09
RO	0.08	0.01
SE	−0.08	−0.08
SI	−0.20	0.07
SK	0.32	−0.03
UK	0.15	0.01
Average values by settlement structure		
Rural regions	0.02	0.01
Urban regions	0.01	0.01
Agglomerated regions	−0.04	0.01

Note: NMS = new member states

Table 2.1 shows that, over the period 2002–2007, the average absolute change in MHHT location quotients over the whole European sample was equal to –0.01, while an opposite average change (equal to +0.01) occurred in terms of KIS specialization. From a general perspective, the stylized fact about the loss over time of high-tech manufacturing in the EU27, and the consequent shift of productive plants towards areas in the eastern part of the continent with lower labour costs, is confirmed by our data. In fact, while in the EU15 countries an average decrease in high-tech manufacturing took place, with location quotients decreasing by –0.02, a significant increase in MHHT specialization (location quotients increasing by +0.10) occurred in new member states (Table 2.1).

At the country level, massive decreases in MHHT specialization affected Ireland, Malta, and Slovenia. Simultaneously, some Eastern countries (namely Czech Republic, Estonia, Hungary, and Slovakia) increased their levels of specialization in high-tech manufacturing. Interestingly, a few Western and European Free Trade Agreement (henceforth, EFTA) countries, viz. Austria, the Netherlands, Norway, and the UK, gained more than 0.1 in absolute terms in their MHHT specialization levels (Table 2.1).

The picture is much clearer for KIS specialization. Most European countries increased their specialization levels, with only a few notable exceptions (Belgium, Estonia, Finland, Iceland, Lithuania, Latvia, Sweden, and Slovakia) (Table 2.1).

In terms of the geographical distribution/urban patterns of such changes (Table 2.1, third block, column 2), rural regions show an increasing specialization in MHHT industry which is mirrored by a simultaneous weak increase in regions hosting medium-sized cities, and a pronounced decrease in more urbanized (agglomerated) areas. A more widespread increase in KIS specialization instead took place in the three above-mentioned areas, with a similar absolute increase in the KIS location quotient equal to 0.01 (Table 2.1).

The evidence presented in Maps 2.5 and 2.6 and Table 2.1 suggests that, within each country, a region's loss of high-tech manufacturing specialization is not necessarily matched by a simultaneous process of increasing specialization in advanced services. In fact, only three countries register significant within-country correlations between the change in MHHT and the change in KIS specializations (Table 2.2), namely Greece, Italy, and Sweden (in italics in Table 2.2), where regions apparently switched regime by swapping a focus on advanced manufacturing with a specialization in advanced services. Elsewhere, insignificant relations suggest that manufacturing jobs flowing to regions characterized by lower labour costs are not necessarily replaced with similarly advanced services.

This last result is of particular interest, since these data suggest that a loss of high-tech manufacturing is not necessarily matched by an increase in high-tech services. The type of knowledge needed successfully to perform high-tech manufacturing activities, therefore, seems to be different from the set of skills required to be competitive in high-tech service industries. This point opens further research avenues, in particular ones focusing on theoretical explanation and empirical verification of the type of knowledge needed for such a switch, which

Table 2.2 Within-country correlations between changes in medium-high tech and KIS specialization levels, 2002–2007

Country	Correlation	p-value
Austria	0.44	0.24
Belgium	−0.33	0.32
Czech Republic	−0.62	0.11
Finland	0.04	0.95
France	−0.16	0.46
Germany	−0.02	0.92
Greece	*−0.61*	*0.03*
Hungary	−0.21	0.65
Italy	*−0.41*	*0.06*
Netherlands	−0.08	0.82
Norway	0.01	0.99
Portugal	0.15	0.75
Romania	0.06	0.90
Slovakia	0.80	0.20
Spain	0.17	0.48
Sweden	*−0.70*	*0.06*
Switzerland	0.22	0.63
United Kingdom	−0.16	0.35

Notes:
Significant (at least at the 90% confidence level) correlations in Italics.
Correlations are not calculated for single-region countries, since no significance level can be identified.

in turn poses policy challenges for governments wanting to support this evolutionary process.

2.5. Technologically advanced regions in Europe

Figure 2.2 is translated into its empirical version in Figure 2.7 for the most recent observed period, i.e. 2007. The figure suggests that TARs are located in the core regions of Europe; most of them are in fact to be found in Germany, Switzerland, Belgium, France, and the UK. Relevant geographically peripheral areas boasting at least one TAR, moreover, include Denmark, Finland, Italy, Norway, Sweden, Slovenia, and Slovakia. Given the small changes in the location quotients between 2002 and 2007, the results would not change if the TARs were identified on the basis of the 2002 data.

In order to facilitate visual inspection of the geographical distribution of TARs, Map 2.7 shows TARs classified according to classes with the colors used to draw Figure 2.2.

In more detail, twenty-one regions identified as TARs with our methodology are German, thirteen are British, eight French, five Belgian, four Swiss, three Swedish, two Finnish and Danish, and one each for Italy, Norway, Slovenia, and Slovakia (Map 2.7, Figure 2.3). The geography of technology in Europe is indeed highly concentrated, although peripheral regions and regions with capital cities

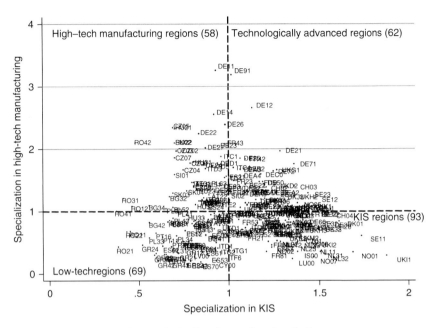

Figure 2.7 Scatter plot of technologically-advanced regions in Europe

in new member states play a major role. The productive fabric of Europe therefore displays a remarkable concentration of technology related either to advanced
manufacturing or services activities. This visual impression is confirmed by the
Moran's I index measuring the degree of spatial autocorrelation among regions
and calculated on the basis of a rook contiguity matrix of second order. In this
case, the Moran's I index is equal to 0.18, and significant at all conventional
levels.

Table 2.3 shows the distribution of the EU27 regions according to the four
categories described in Section 2.3 and depicted in Figure 2.3, as well as to their
location, breaking down EU countries among EU15, new member states, and the
EFTA countries, and their settlement structure.

The results show that TARs are mostly located in the EU15 (55 of the 62 regions
thus identified belong to Western Europe), while only 3% are located in the new
member countries. The rest of the TAR sample is instead located in the EFTA
countries, in particular in Norway and Switzerland.

In terms of the levels of specialization only in either high-tech manufacturing or
services, the evidence shows that high-tech manufacturing is much more strongly
concentrated in new member states. In fact, more than half the sample of high-tech
manufacturing regions is located in the countries which entered the EU between
2004 and 2007. This result is as expected, and in line with the findings of many
recent policy reports (see for instance Calleja Crespo and Groebner, 2012).

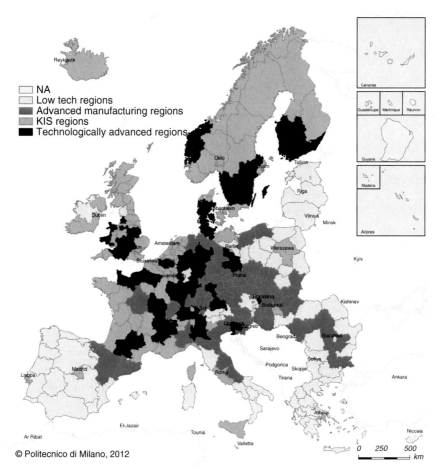

Map 2.7 Technologically advanced regions in Europe (2007)

Source: Capello et al. (2012)

Table 2.3 Count of TARs by typology of region and settlement structure

Classes	All regions	Subsamples			Settlement structure		
		EU 15	NMS	EFTA	Rural	Urban	Agglomerated
Technologically advanced regions	62	55	2	5	11	24	27
High-tech manufacturing regions	58	31	27	0	21	28	9
High-tech services regions	93	79	4	10	23	29	41
Low-tech regions	69	46	23	0	50	10	9

Note: NMS = new member states

What really makes a difference in terms of the remarkable concentration of TARs in the EU15 is the importance of high-tech services: 85% of the sample of regions specialized in KIS is actually located in the Western Europe.

2.6. Technologically advanced regions in Europe: a dynamic perspective

Although the 2002–2007 time span considered may be too short to draw safe conclusions, it is interesting to note that no region acquired or lost the status of TAR; all regions that were TARs in 2002 maintained their status, while no region became a TAR in 2007.

In fact, examination of the top ten performers over the time span analysed (Table 2.4) shows rather stable overall behavior by the entire regional sample, with very few dynamics characterizing the regions identified as technologically advanced. In fact, only one change takes place between 2002 and 2007 for MHHT (Franche-Comté being substituted by Severovýchod), while more changes occur in the KIS case (five out of ten regions in the 2007 top ten table were not listed in 2002). The hierarchy of high-tech manufacturing therefore seems to be rather hysteretic, with more change taking place in the KIS industries, where in particular a strong specialization of capital city-regions seems to take place.

Table 2.5 classifies TAR regions only according to whether their levels of specialization in MHHT and KIS increased or decreased (over columns), and also according to their settlement structure (over rows), again using the ESPON classification mentioned in Section 2.3. This exercise is useful in order to assess what happens 'below the surface': in fact, although no region left or entered the TAR subsample over the 2002–2007 span analysed, changes in the intensity of the levels of specialization in the two axes of the TAR definition are to be expected.

Table 2.5 clearly shows that, while relatively few dynamics affected the levels of specialization in high-tech manufacturing, with TARs either slightly increasing or decreasing their levels of specialization (first two columns), the opposite

Table 2.4 Top ten regions in terms of LQs, 2002–2007

Location quotient	Medium- and high-tech manufacturing 2002	Medium- and high-tech manufacturing 2007	Knowledge-intensive services 2002	Knowledge-intensive services 2007
Region #1	Stuttgart	Stuttgart	Inner London	Inner London
Region #2	Tübingen	Braunschweig	Stockholm	Stockholm
Region #3	Braunschweig	Karlsruhe	Oslo og Akershus	Oslo og Akershus
Region #4	Franche-Comté	Tübingen	Outer London	Hovedstaden
Region #5	Közép-Dunántúl	Rheinhessen-Pfalz	Brussels	Åland
Region #6	Karlsruhe	Unterfranken	Hovedstaden	Zürich
Region #7	Niederbayern	Freiburg	Övre Norrland	Berlin
Region #8	Unterfranken	Severovýchod	Mellersta Norrland	Noord-Holland
Region #9	Rheinhessen-Pfalz	Közép-Dunántúl	Île de France	Utrecht
Region #10	Freiburg	Niederbayern	Surrey and Sussex	Övre Norrland

Source: Capello et al. (2012)

Table 2.5 Change in the number of TARs by high-tech industry specialization and settlement structure, 2002–2007

	Increase in MHHT LQ	Decrease in MHHT LQ	Increase in KIS LQ	Decrease in KIS LQ
Rural TAR	2	4	3	6
Urban TAR	14	8	14	8
Agglomerated TAR	10	16	18	7
Total TAR	26	28	35	21

Note: A few regions in the sample registered no change in the LQ of high-tech industries; hence, they do not appear in this table. Therefore, the total number of TAR regions classified by changes in the LQs and settlement structure does not sum to 62.

holds for the levels of specialization in KIS. In this latter case, the evidence demonstrates that regions labelled as technologically advanced in 2002 (i.e. showing levels of specialization in both MHHT and KIS above the EU average) maintained their status mostly because their levels of specialization in KIS increased. This, together with the evidence presented above, suggests that even in the absence of a substitution of specialization in high-tech manufacturing with KIS, regions labelled as TARs at the inception of the last decade tended to remain technologically advanced, and in large part underwent a process of increasing specialization in knowledge-intensive services.

The urban pattern depicted in Table 2.5 shows that, while for MHHT industries, an increase in the levels of specialization affects urban TARs and, to a lesser extent, agglomerated TARs, a much clearer picture pertains to urban and agglomerated TARs in terms of increases in KIS specialization levels. By the same token, while a non-negligible number of agglomerated TAR regions are affected by a decrease in MHHT specialization levels, many fewer urban and agglomerated TARs face de-specialization in KIS industries. Table 2.5 therefore provides further evidence on the shift of high-tech regions towards a relatively higher role of KIS vis-à-vis high-tech manufacturing. Even if, as said, this does mean that a substitution effect takes place with regions previously specialized in MHHT shifting towards a KIS specialization, within the TAR subsample the negative correlation between the change in specialization in MHHT and KIS is found to be relatively stronger (Figure 2.8). This is further evidence that KIS industries have been of crucial importance for TAR regions in the past decade.[9]

2.7. Concluding remarks

This chapter has proposed a classification of the EU territory according to regional specialization in high-tech industries. The reason for a definition of knowledge economy based on high-tech intensity is contained in a conceptual intersection between the industry and spatial approaches to the knowledge-based economy: the former has always emphasized the knowledge-intensive character of high-tech industries, and their higher learning processes; the latter emphasizes the static and, more recently, dynamic advantages of firms' clustering in space.

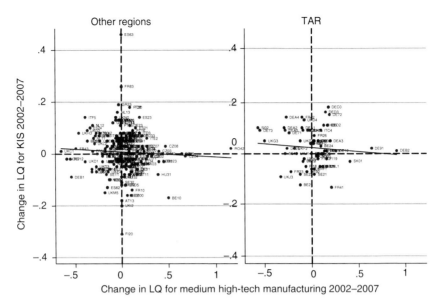

Figure 2.8 Regional changes in LQs for medium high-tech and KIS industries and by TAR vs. non-TAR regions, 2002–2007

The chapter has presented a taxonomy of TARs based on the simultaneous specialization of regions in high-tech manufacturing and advanced service activities. The results show that TARs are mostly located in the EU15, with a few notable exceptions in new member states and EFTA countries. The spatial pattern of such regions implies a remarkable concentration in more densely inhabited areas (mostly urban and agglomerated regions), and presents no major dynamics over time: in particular, no region that was a TAR at the beginning of the last decade exits or enters the subsample over the observed time span. Dynamic behavior nevertheless affects both the axes in our definition of TAR: a remarkable increase in KIS specialization between 2002 and 2007 affects several TAR regions, thereby enhancing their qualification as TARs. Since there is little evidence on the possible substitution between specialization in MHHT and in KIS, empirical verification supports the conjecture that the type of knowledge needed to succeed in high-tech manufacturing is different from that needed to thrive in knowledge-intensive services.

The evidence presented in this chapter is certainly solid, but a few caveats are in order. In particular, it is quite clear that only some of the features needed to identify a knowledge economy have been properly captured. During the late 1980s, the limits of an 'industry approach' to the knowledge economy were clearly identified. It became evident that many knowledge-based advances were possible, and were actually introduced by 'traditional' sectors – such as textiles and car production – in their path towards rejuvenation. Several examples of innovative low-tech industries were evident in the Western world (Von Tunzelmann and Acha, 2005).

As mentioned in Chapter 1, at a later stage of reflection a function-based approach was preferred (even though it conceptually overlapped with the previous one). This stressed the importance of pervasive and horizontal functions such as R&D and higher education. Scientific regions hosting large and well-known scientific institutions were closely studied, and the relationships between these institutions and the industrial fabric were analysed, with some disappointment due to the fact that the expected direct linkage among them was often not clearly visible. The functional approach, which equates knowledge with scientific research, has been recently relaunched by the well-known European strategy defined at the Lisbon and Luxembourg Ministerial meetings (2000 and 2005) and which committed the Union to becoming the most competitive and dynamic knowledge-based economy in the world.

Finally, a third stage of theoretical reflection has preferred a relation-based approach to definition of the knowledge economy centred on identification of a 'cognitive capability' (Foray, 2000): the ability to manage information in order to identify and solve problems, or, more precisely in the economic sphere, the ability to transform information and inventions into innovation and productivity increases through cooperative or market interaction. This approach amplifies the importance of cooperation and interaction for innovation activity. In doing so, it explicitly directs attention to cooperation in spatially concentrated areas, opening the black box of 'dynamic agglomeration economies' presented in this chapter by directly measuring both intra-regional and inter-regional linkages – the former mostly driven by spatial proximity, the latter by an a-spatial approach.

In our opinion, a realistic and broad picture of what the knowledge economy looks like in the European territory requires extension of the empirical analysis to encompass the other two more recent conceptual definitions: those based on the functional and relational approaches. To this end, the next chapters provide evidence on scientific and knowledge networking regions respectively.

Notes

1 The industry-based approach and sector-based approach are considered as synonymous and will be used interchangeably in this chapter.
2 Wide-ranging empirical studies on innovative activity were carried out in the UK by CURDS (Centre for Urban and Regional Development Studies) of the University of Newcastle (see Goddard and Thwaites, 1986 and Oakey et al., 1980) and by SPRU (Science Policy Research Unit) of the University of Sussex (see Clark, 1971); in the USA by Malecki (see Malecki and Varaiya, 1986); and more recently also in Italy (see Breschi, 2000; Paci and Usai, 2000). Studies on the concentrated location of high-tech firms were conducted by Keeble on the UK, Sternberg on Germany, Ciciotti on Italy, Decoster and Tabaries on France, Malecki on the USA, Frenkel on Israel, and Maggioni on a group of OECD countries. See Keeble, 1990; Sternberg, 1996; Ciciotti, 1982; Decoster and Tabaries, 1986; Frenkel, 2001; Maggioni, 2002. For detailed studies on the role of innovation in regional development see e.g. Cappellin and Nijkamp, 1990; Ewers and Allesch, 1990; de Groot et al., 2004. For a recent theoretical and empirical analysis of spatial spillovers see Maier and Sedlacek, 2005.

3 Medium-high and high-tech manufacturing industries correspond to employment in chemicals (NACE24), machinery (NACE29), office equipment (NACE30), electrical equipment (NACE31), telecommunications and related equipment (NACE32), precision instruments (NACE33), automobiles (NACE34) and aerospace and other transport (NACE35); KIS include water transport (NACE 61), air transport (NACE 62), post and telecommunications (NACE64), financial intermediation (NACE 65), insurance and pension funding (NACE 66), activities auxiliary to financial intermediation (NACE 67), real estate activities (NACE 70), renting of machinery and equipment (NACE 71), computer and related activities (NACE72), research and development (NACE73) and other business activities (NACE 74).

4 Source of the data is Eurostat.

5 See also Capello et al. (2012) for investigation of regional knowledge-intensive service specialization.

6 The definitions of 'agglomerated', 'urban' and 'rural' are as follows. Agglomerated regions are defined as those with a city of more than 300,000 inhabitants and a population density of more than 300 inhabitants per square kilometre, or a population density between 150 and 300 inhabitants per square kilometre. Urban regions are defined as those with a city of between 150,000 and 300,000 inhabitants and a population density of between 150 and 300 inhabitants per square kilometre (or a smaller population density – 100 and 150 inhabitants per square kilometre with a bigger centre of more than 300,000). Rural regions have a population density lower than 100 per square kilometre and a centre of more than 125,000 inhabitants, or a population density lower than 100 per square kilometre with a centre of fewer than 125,000.

7 These statements refer to the region-specific rates of change plotted in Maps 2.5 and 2.6; data are available from the authors upon request.

8 The associated p-value is equal to 0.28.

9 In this case the Pearson's correlation index equals 0.05 for non-TARs, and 0.10 for TARs, in both cases however with no statistical significance.

3   Scientific regions

Alessandra Colombelli, Marta Foddi,
and Raffaele Paci

3.1. Introduction[1]

Since the Lisbon Agenda in 2000, Europe has pledged to become the most advanced knowledge economy in the world, relying specifically on the increase and strengthening of its human capital and technological endowments. This strategy is in line with the economic literature that has widely proved the positive impact of knowledge, embedded in both human and technological capital, on economic growth and productivity. However, the recent enlargement process of the European Union, which has brought on stage new players characterized by a low average level of knowledge-related activity and introduced a huge degree of internal territorial disparity, raises the question of how to reduce high inequalities among regions. Economic geography theoretical models have indeed shown that unequal levels of economic growth across regions may emerge as a result of knowledge accumulation and learning processes. Due to increasing returns to knowledge, if one region gets ahead by chance in the innovation process it tends to stay ahead and even increase its lead (Arthur, 1994). Within this line of reasoning, the goal of building a knowledge economy in Europe might actually generate an increase in territorial inequalities.

In order to cope with this problem, policies seeking to ease the process of integration and cohesion, on the one hand, and to expand the opportunities for innovation, on the other hand, tend to focus on the process of knowledge generation, diffusion and absorption. This is in line with the economic literature showing that knowledge spillovers are localised and mainly occur between neighbouring regions as a result of spatial decay effects. Knowledge spillovers, in turn, have a positive impact on the growth and productivity of neighbouring regions. However, the magnitude of this effect depends on the receiver's capacity to absorb knowledge spilling over from other regions (Cohen and Levinthal, 1990). Recent empirical literature in the field of regional economics has shown that regions with a larger stock of knowledge are more able to absorb new knowledge with respect to regions that do not perform any knowledge-generating activity (Maurseth and Verspagen, 2002; Paci and Marrocu, 2013).

Following these arguments, the purpose of this chapter is to propose a classification of the regions based on their knowledge endowment which will allow the identification of the most scientific regions in Europe and examination of their main territorial features. This functional classification adds to the sectoral and relational ones presented, respectively, in Chapters 2 and 4.

Mapping the geographical distribution of knowledge in the enlarged Europe is useful from a policy perspective. We propose a workable definition of scientific regions based on the two main pillars of the knowledge economy: human capital and technological activities. Scientific regions are defined as the areas which show values above the EU average for both dimensions. The rationale behind this choice is clearly shown by the literature: by representing a complex and multifaceted process composed by input and output elements, these two elements are able to capture both the creation of new knowledge within a region and the capacity of the local firms to absorb knowledge spilling from the internal and external economies.

Different indicators for human capital and technological activities are used to identify the scientific regions. This approach also allows us to provide a unique classification of all European regions in four groups, based on their relative knowledge performance. Moreover, as a robustness check of the previous taxonomy, we perform a cluster analysis based on several indicators of human capital and technology. As in the other chapters, our contribution is based on a broad data set which includes 287 NUTS2 regions belonging to EU27 countries and the four EFTA countries (Iceland, Liechtenstein, Norway and Switzerland).

The remainder of the chapter is organized as follows. Starting with a brief overview of the literature, Section 3.2 defines the conceptual framework of our empirical analysis. Human capital and technological indicators are presented, respectively, in Sections 3.3 and 3.4. Section 3.5 presents and discusses the identification of scientific regions while in Section 3.6 we present a robustness exercise based on a cluster analysis. Section 3.7 concludes with some general remarks on the main findings.

3.2. A brief survey of the literature

Knowledge is crucial for economic growth. Since the endogenous growth theory development, economic geography and regional economics have focused on the spatial dimension of this phenomenon and have demonstrated that barriers to the diffusion and absorption of knowledge, in turn leading to differences in the stock of knowledge, can explain the differential growth rates among regions. The debate on the spatial dimension of knowledge diffusion has evolved through different steps based on the defining characteristics attributed to knowledge (see Döring and Schnellenbach, 2006; Antonelli, 2008; Camagni and Capello, 2009). Since the works by Arrow (1962a) and Nelson (1959), knowledge has been firstly regarded as a public good. The basic idea behind this assumption is that knowledge may spill over instantaneously through the whole economy and it is freely available to individuals; as such, it cannot be the source of differences in regional productivity. Subsequently, knowledge has been considered as a quasi-proprietary good (Nelson and Winter, 1982). In this view, a fraction of the knowledge created and accumulated by individuals within firms can be appropriated and protected. From this perspective, knowledge can diffuse but only to a limited extent. In particular, it has a limited spatial range. This is particularly true in the case of tacit knowledge, while codified knowledge can diffuse also over great distances. Finally, the literature has shifted towards the concept of knowledge as a collective process. This approach focuses on external knowledge, generated by interactions among the diverse economic agents (Griliches, 1992; David, 1993; Cooke, 2002a). Interrelations and local networks among economic agents are now considered vital for the generation, diffusion and absorption of new knowledge. Knowledge can indeed be transferred and disseminated among different actors in the economic system. The spillovers of knowledge generate positive externalities by stimulating innovation activities and productivity.

Since the diffusion of knowledge depends on knowledge accumulated in the past and on the absorptive capacity of the receiving regions, the existence of barriers to the diffusion of knowledge has emphasized the importance of investments in technological activities and human capital formation. Thus, technological activities and human capital – the two main pillars at the base of the scientific regions definition – have become the object of flourishing strands of the literature at the regional level.

As far as the first pillar of our approach is concerned, which is the set of technological activities, the appreciation of the role of knowledge spillovers and knowledge externalities in the area of regional science has emphasized the importance of advanced tasks like research efforts (R&D expenditure, patenting activities) for regional economic development. Indeed, the innovation process requires exploring the kind of activities that denote a deliberate and active effort to search for new technical and organizational solutions, new products and processes. The main economic agents involved in this process are R&D professional laboratories in private firms, and research institutes and universities in the public domain. In this line of thought, regions hosting large and well-known scientific institutions have become the object of a new field of enquiry known as 'institutional approach' in regional economics. In this area, concepts like Regional Innovation Systems (Cooke et al., 1997; Braczyk et al., 1998) and Triple Helix (Etzkowitz and Leydesdorff, 1997, 2000) emphasize the active role of territorial actors within regional development dynamics and give relevance to the institutional foundations of regions' competitive advantage in the areas of education and research and development. These institutional approaches argue that differences in economic behaviours and outcomes are primarily related to differences in institutions (Hodgson, 1988, 1998; Whitley, 1992, 2003; Saxenian, 1994; Gertler, 1997).

Many empirical works have analysed regional differences in the distribution of research and innovative activities and have investigated the process of knowledge creation and diffusion within and across regions. These empirical studies are based on knowledge input and output indicators like R&D expenditure, patents statistics and innovation counts. A first strand of the literature has focused on pure knowledge spillovers and proved that they are geographically bounded (Audretsch and Feldman, 1996; Baptista and Swann, 1998; Acs et al., 2002). In this line of research, a number of empirical contributions have investigated the role of universities in the process of knowledge spillovers (Jaffe, 1989; Anselin et al., 1997; Audretsch and Feldman, 1996) and found strong evidence in favour of a significant positive correlation between firms' concentration and university location (Varga, 2000; Audretsch and Lehmann, 2005). A second strand of the literature has attempted to investigate the main general mechanisms of the process of creation and diffusion of inventive knowledge rather than just looking for localized knowledge spillovers. Many of these studies have been applied to the US case (Varga et al., 2005; Carlino et al., 2007), but also to Europe (Bottazzi and Peri, 2003; Greunz, 2003; Moreno et al., 2005a; Rodríguez-Pose and Crescenzi, 2008; Tappeiner et al., 2008; Acosta et al., 2009; Marrocu et al., 2012b) and OECD countries (Usai, 2011). All in all, these contributions find that technological spillovers, both pure and pecuniary, may exist within and across regions and have shed light on the role of geographical distance in the economics of knowledge transmission. Moreover, this strand of the literature has suggested that knowledge spillovers may also be affected by cognitive, social, organizational, and institutional distance, as suggested by Torre and Rallet (2005) and Boschma (2005).

A further set of empirical literature has attempted to distinguish between Marshallian externalities and Jacobian externalities and has focused on the regional differences in the patterns of specialisation and diversification of innovation. In the case of US metropolitan areas, Feldman and Audretsch (1999) find that there is no evidence of specialization externalities, while diversity externalities are at work. However, these results have been somewhat disputed by several analyses based on European data (for example, Paci and Usai, 1999, 2000; Massard and Riou, 2002; Greunz, 2003; and Moreno et al., 2006), suggesting a notable difference in the functioning of the local innovation systems in the United States and Europe.

As far as the second pillar is concerned, since Solow's (1957) contribution, the literature has emphasized the positive role of human capital, measured, for example, by means of a well-educated labour force, university research staff or graduate students, on productivity level and growth. Two main approaches have been applied. The first approach was developed by Mankiw et al. (1992), who extended the Solow growth model by explicitly introducing human capital as an ordinary input in the production function. An alternative approach was introduced by the endogenous growth models (Lucas, 1988; Romer, 1989) that directly related human capital to the adoption of technology and underlined the positive interaction between knowledge, capabilities and innovative ability. On a parallel basis, the seminal paper by Cohen and Levinthal (1990) on the firm's absorptive capacity gave rise to a strand of the literature aimed at understanding key characteristics of firms, regions and countries that make it easier to absorb external knowledge in an economically efficient manner. In this line of reasoning, human capital is not just a precondition for enhancing the growth capabilities of regions or countries, but rather it provides the stock of accumulated knowledge that allows a region to identify and utilize knowledge from outside.

A recent and wide body of empirical literature has been developed in order to verify these theoretical predictions at the regional level of analysis. For example,

Rauch (1993) finds that at the regional level a higher availability of well-educated labour forces represents an advantage for the localization of innovative firms, thus promoting local productivity. For the case of EU27 regions, Marrocu and Paci (2012) show that the presence of university graduates, working in creative occupations, enhances the regional economic performance. Bronzini and Piselli (2009) assess the role of technological knowledge, as measured by the stock of R&D capital, the human capital, and the stock of public infrastructure, in enhancing the levels of Total Factor Productivity (TFP) of Italian regions over the period 1980–2001. They show that there exists a long-run equilibrium between productivity level and the three kinds of capital, and that human capital turns out to have the strongest impact on productivity. Dettori et al. (2011), who worked on a sample of 199 European regions over the period 1985–2006, provide robust evidence on the role played by intangible factors like human capital, social capital and technological capital on TFP levels, thus enhancing economic efficiency and social cohesion. Abreu et al. (2008), using UK firm-level data, investigate how absorptive capacity at the firm level impacts on regional variations in innovation performance, showing that, in order to be effective, innovations require an appropriate endowment of human capital.

3.3. Human capital indicators

As mentioned in the introduction to this chapter, we describe the human capital endowment in a region by means of both input and output indicators (Table 3.1). As input indicator we use the percentage of population employed in the education sector, assumed as a proxy of the regional effort to create and promote new knowledge and human capital activities. As output indicator, we use the share of the population that has attained at least a university degree. Furthermore, we include the amount of funding per capita received by a region in the activities of the 5th Framework Programmes (FP) as a proxy for the quality of the human capital and technological activities conducted in the region and the diffusion of knowledge through cooperation. Indeed, as FP calls are very competitive and involve partners from different countries, the amount of funding granted can be used as an indicator for the presence of high-quality scientists who are active at the international level.

For each indicator we present in Tables 3.2, 3.3 and 3.4 the average values, the coefficient of variation and the Moran index, respectively; moreover, we include maps showing the spatial distribution of our indicators (see Maps 3.1–3.3). In the statistical description of the indicators, we use two different classifications for the regions of Europe: the first is 'institutional', classifying a region with respect to the country of membership while the second one is more functional and it is based on the eligible areas under the Convergence Objective and the European Competitiveness and Employment Objective (Cohesion Policy 2007–2013).[2]

Table 3.2 presents average values for the human capital indicators. If we consider the whole sample of regions, we observe that on average 3.24% of the population is employed in the education sector where the highest average value

Table 3.1 Data sources and definitions

Knowledge variables		Weights	Measurement unit	Description	Sources	Years
Human capital	Employees in education	1/3	Percentage	Percentage of population employed in the NACE education sector	CRENoS elaborations on Eurostat data	2005–2007
	Tertiary education	1/3	Percentage	Percentage of population aged 15 and over by highest level of education attained		2005–2007
	5th FP funding	1/3	Thousands of Euro per 1000 POP	Funding over population divided by 1000	CRENoS elaboration on CORDIS data	1998–2002
	R&D expenditure	1/4	Millions of Euro per 1000 POP	Millions of Euro spent per RD activities over population divided by 1000	CRENoS elaboration on Eurostat, ISTAT and Institut National de la Statistique et des Études Économiques data	2006–2007
Technological activities	R&D personnel	1/4	Percentage	Head count employment in R&D over employment		2006–2007
	Number of patents	1/4	Patents per 1000 POP	Number of patents released at NUTS2 over population divided by 1000	CRENoS elaboration on OECD REGPAT database	2005–2006
	Number of high-tech patents	1/4	Patents high-tech per capita	Number of patents per million population in high-tech IPC sectors		2005–2006
Other variables:						
Population		POP	Thousands	Total population at 1st January	Eurostat	2005–2007
Employment		EMP	Thousands	Head count employment aged 15 and over	Eurostat	2006–2007

Note: IPC = International Patent Classification

Table 3.2 Human capital indicators. Average values for selected samples

	Whole sample	Countries			EU Regions		
		EU15	EU12	EFTA	Convergence	Transition	Competitive
Employees in education (% pop)	3.24	3.24	2.87	4.27	2.84	3.10	3.37
Tertiary education (% pop)	12.37	12.88	9.34	16.41	9.21	12.66	13.61
Project funding per 1000 pop (thousands of euro)	22.27	24.31	7.13	47.89	6.94	15.25	28.99

Table 3.3 Human capital indicators. Coefficient of variation for selected samples

	Whole sample	Countries			EU Regions		
		EU15	EU12	EFTA	Convergence	Transition	Competitive
Employees in education (% pop)	0.26	0.26	0.21	0.13	0.19	0.26	0.26
Tertiary education (% pop)	0.36	0.35	0.41	0.19	0.39	0.44	0.30
Project funding per 1000 pop (thousands of euro)	1.19	1.08	1.61	0.82	1.55	1.01	0.96

Table 3.4 Human capital indicators. Moran (standardized distance). Whole sample

	I	*z*	*p-value*
Employees in education (% pop)	0.144	28.725	0
Tertiary education (% pop)	0.129	25.86	0
Project funding per 1000 pop (thousands of euro)	0.065	13.47	0

is presented by regions belonging to EFTA countries (4.27%) and competitive regions (3.37%). Lower values are shown by transition regions (3.10%), convergence regions (2.84%) and regions belonging to New Entrant countries (2.87%). As for the percentage of population that has attained a university degree, the average value for the whole sample is equal to 12.3% and again the highest average value is presented by regions that belong to EFTA countries (16.4%), followed by competitive regions (13.6%) and regions that belong to EU15 countries (12.9%). As far as the 5th FP funding is concerned, on average regions in our sample receive 22.2 thousands euro per 1000 population where competitive regions, regions belonging to EFTA countries and EU15 countries show the highest average values (respectively 29.0, 47.9 and 24.3 thousands euro per 1000 population) while lowest average values are shown by convergence regions and regions belonging to New Entrant countries (respectively 6.9 and 7.1 thousands euro per 1000 population).

In Table 3.3 we can observe the values of the variation coefficient of the regional distribution, a measure of the dispersion of data around the mean. In the case of the percentage of employees in the education sector, the range of variation is small in absolute terms as shown by the coefficient of variation value equal to 0.26. In the case of tertiary education, it is equal to 0.36, slightly higher than for the previous variable. The coefficient is higher than for the previous variables and equal to 1.19 for the 5th FP funding, stressing a greater distance between low and high values.

The Moran Index presented in Table 3.4 shows strong evidence of geographical pattern of the values distribution and the presence of spatial association for the whole sample of indicators.

The spatial distribution of employees in the education sector can be observed in Map 3.1. As the map clearly shows, regions characterized by the highest values are mainly concentrated in northern countries. The highest class includes also two Belgian regions (Prov. Brabant Wallon and Prov. Namur), a Dutch region (Utrecht) and two British regions (Oxfordshire and Essex), where important universities are located. Moreover, most of the Swiss regions are also included in the top class together with few regions belonging to New Entrant countries: Estonia, Lithuania, Zahodna Slovenija (Slovenia) and Bratislavský kraj (Slovakia). The sample of regions included in the second and third class are less geographically concentrated. Finally, the lowest class of values includes regions belonging mainly to central and southern countries where the most represented countries are Austria, Germany, Spain, France, Greece, Italy and Romania.

Looking at the map for tertiary education (Map 3.2), a well-defined geographical pattern appears for the values distribution. The presence of spatial association of

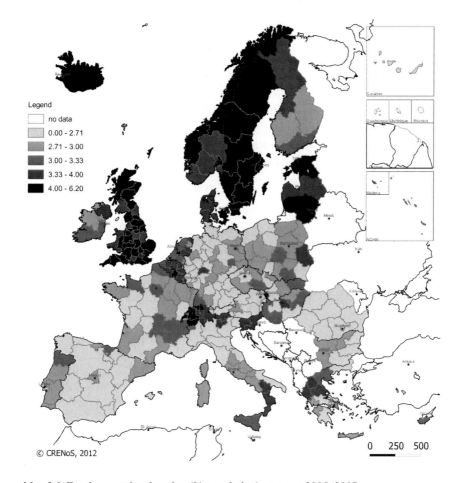

Map 3.1 Employment in education (% population), average 2005–2007

the values is confirmed by the Moran Index value (0.14) that is highly statistically significant. As in the previous map, regions that show highest values are mainly concentrated in the northern countries but there are some exceptions, for instance Spanish northern regions, Swiss regions, Bulgarian regions, Cyprus. It is interesting to notice that in the top class there are several capital cities, like the regions where Brussels, Sofia, Madrid, Paris, London, Stockholm, Helsinki, Amsterdam and Prague are located. In the second- and third-highest classes, ranging between 11% and 16%, there are again regions belonging mainly to northern countries but also some important administrative regions belonging to New Entrant countries (for instance, the regions where the capital cities Budapest, Warsaw and Bucharest are located and also Lithuania and Latvia). In the lowest two classes, where

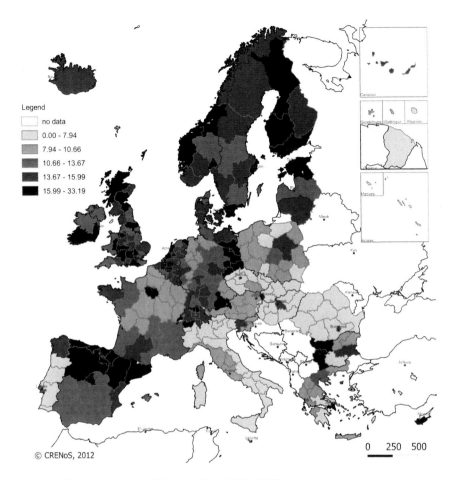

Map 3.2 Tertiary education (% population), 2005–2007

the percentage of graduates is lower than 10.6%, 71 out of 113 regions belong to EU15 countries. Furthermore, most regions included in the lowest two classes are convergence regions that, indeed, show the lowest average value with a percentage of graduates equal to 9.2%.

Map 3.3 shows the spatial distribution of values for the variable which proxies the quality of the human capital in the region and the diffusion of knowledge through cooperation: the involvement of each region in the activities of the 5th FPs, measured by funding per 1000 population. Again, regions characterized by the highest values, ranging between 18 and 207 thousands of euro per 1000 population, are mainly localized on the northern and central territories. Furthermore, regions from the rest of Europe, mainly characterized by a high population density and hosting important administrative cities, are also included within these samples.

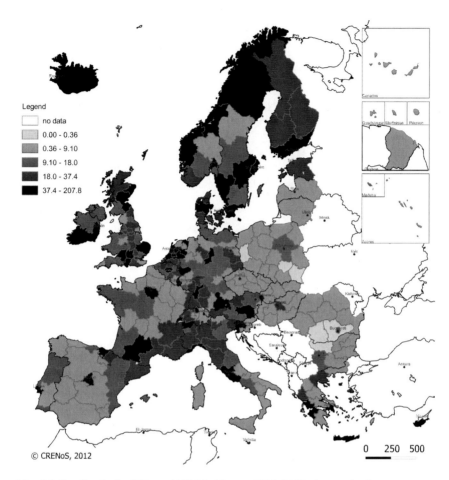

Map 3.3 Funding in the 5FP per 1000 inhabitants, 1998–2002, thousands of euro

Among them we find, for instance, Prague, Budapest, Estonia, Spanish regions including the Madrid region, and the most important Italian regions. Among the darkest-coloured regions are almost all Greek regions. Regions included in the third and fourth class, ranging between 7.9 and 13.6 thousands of euro, are not so spatially concentrated as regions in the first two classes. However, we can see that they mainly belong to EU15 countries and most of them are competitive regions. Unlike the previous subsample, the regions in this group are mostly rural regions, where the population density is lower. The majority of regions included in the lowest class belong to New Entrant countries and are convergence regions. Summing up, again the map reveals a spatial concentration of high and low values that is confirmed by the Moran index (0.065), highly statistically significant.

3.4. Technological indicators

In this section we present the regional endowment of technological activities measured by means of both input and output indicators. As an input variable, we employ R&D expenditures (millions of euro) per 1000 inhabitants and the percentage of employees in R&D over total employment. To measure the inventive activities we rely upon patent counts including two complementary measures: the total number of patents released in a region in all sectors and the number of patents for the subsample of high-tech sectors. These output indicators are expected to measure the return resulting from the technological activity of the firms and can be used as a proxy for R&D effectiveness.

Similarly to what we did for the human capital indicators, the first table for the technological indicators (Table 3.5) presents average values for different groups of regions. The whole sample average for R&D expenditure is equal to 0.44 millions of euro (per 1000 inhabitants). The average value for competitive and EFTA regions (respectively 0.60, 1.09) is again higher than the same value for convergence, transition and New Entrant regions (respectively 0.09, 0.18 and 0.07 millions of euro per 1000 inhabitants). As far as the percentage of employees in the R&D sectors over total employment is concerned, we find an average value for the whole sample of European regions of 1.46%. Again, the highest average value is shown by regions belonging to EFTA countries and competitive regions (respectively 2.35% and 1.76%). The lowest average value is presented by regions belonging to New Entrant countries (0.86%). For output variables, we consider the number of patents for all sectors and for the high-tech sectors per million inhabitants. For the first variable, the whole sample average value is equal to 103.2 patents. Higher values are shown by regions belonging to EFTA countries (210.6), EU15 countries (120.2) and competitive regions (153.1). The lowest average value is observed for regions belonging to New Entrant countries (7.2). In the case of high-tech patents, the ranking for the sample of regions is slightly different: the highest average value is shown by competitive regions (20.4 patents per million inhabitants), followed by regions belonging to EFTA countries (18.61). Average values lower than the whole sample average, equal to 13.12, are observed for regions belonging to New Entrant countries (0.85), convergence and transition regions (respectively 1.52 and 3.46).

Table 3.6 presents the coefficient of variation. If we consider the whole sample, we can observe that the highest value is shown by high-tech patents, stressing large differences within the distribution as emerged also in the previous table. Furthermore, if we look at each single indicator for all the different samples, again high-tech patents show the highest coefficient of variation, signalling a great heterogeneity in its spatial distribution.

The Moran index shown in Table 3.7 confirms the strong geographical pattern also for technological indicators as revealed by Maps 3.4–3.7.

In the case of R&D expenditure (Map 3.4), a clear spatial pattern emerges: the darkest-coloured regions are concentrated on the Scandinavian regions, southern UK regions and territories located in the centre of Europe. More specifically,

Table 3.5 Technological indicators. Average values for selected samples

	Whole sample	Countries			EU Regions		
		EU5	EU12	EFTA	Convergence	Transition	Competitive
R&D expenditure per 1000 inhabitants (millions of euro)	0.44	0.49	0.07	1.09	0.09	0.18	0.6
R&D personnel (% employment)	1.46	1.56	0.88	2.35	0.86	1.09	1.76
Number of patents per million inhabitants (all sectors)	103.2	120.2	7.2	210.6	11.8	32.9	153.1
Number of patents per million inhabitants (high-tech sectors)	13.12	15.9	0.85	18.61	1.52	3.46	20.4

Table 3.6 Technological indicators. Coefficient of variation for selected samples

	Whole sample	Countries			EU Regions		
		EU15	EU12	EFTA	Convergence	Transition	Competitive
R&D expenditure per 1000 inhabitants (millions of euro)	1.07	0.92	1.52	0.49	1.39	0.67	0.78
R&D personnel (% employment)	0.65	0.59	0.9	0.4	0.62	0.56	0.56
Number of patents per million inhabitants (all sectors)	1.25	1.05	1.61	0.89	1.99	1.1	0.85
Number of patents per million inhabitants (high-tech sectors)	1.74	1.56	1.67	1.07	2.7	1.38	1.34

Table 3.7 Technological indicators. Moran (standardized distance). Whole sample

	I	*z*	*p-value*
R&D expenditure per 1000 inhabitants (millions of euro)	0.091	18.391	0
R&D personnel (% employment)	0.026	5.791	0
Number of patents per 1000 inhabitants (all sectors)	0.156	31.168	0
Number of patents per million inhabitants (high-tech sectors)	0.056	11.882	0

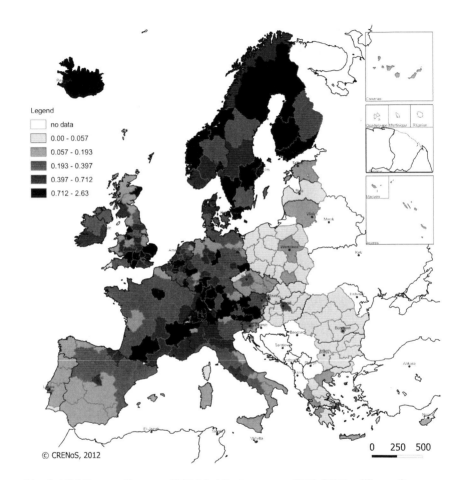

© CRENoS, 2012

Map 3.4 R&D expenditure per 1000 inhabitants, average 2006–2007, millions of euro

regions belonging to the highest two classes, ranging between 0.39 and 2.63 million euro per 1000 population, mainly belong to EU15 countries and EFTA countries. Furthermore, most of them are competitive regions. Also regions included in the third and fourth classes mainly belong to countries located in the north and centre but there are some exceptions like Czech, Slovak, Romanian, Poland,

Slovenian, Spanish, Greek, Italian and Portuguese regions and also Estonia, Lithuania and Malta. Most regions included in the lowest class, ranging between 0.002 and 0.06 million euro per 1000 population, are strongly concentrated in the eastern territories. Mainly they are convergence regions and belong to New Entrants. Among them, there are also overseas territories (i.e. Spanish Ciudad Autónoma de Ceuta and Ciudad Autónoma de Melilla), islands and peripheral territories characterized by other specialization than technological activity (i.e. the French island of Corsica, Greek regions, the Portuguese Algarve and the UK Cornwall and Isles of Scilly). Most of them are also defined as rural territories.

Map 3.5 shows the spatial distribution of values for the percentage of R&D personnel over total employment. The map shows a less marked spatial pattern than for the previous indicators. Although regions belonging to the lowest classes are

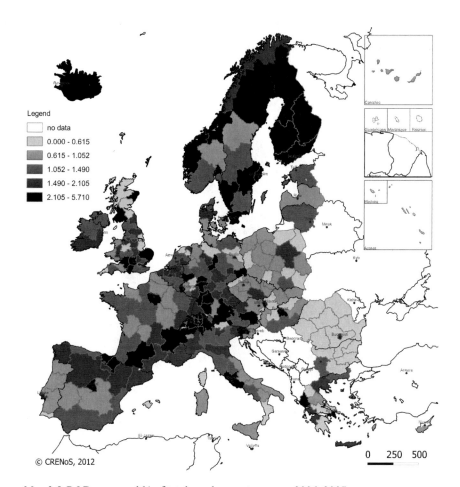

Map 3.5 R&D personnel % of total employment, average 2006–2007

mainly localized in the eastern part of the continent, there are some pale-coloured territories also in the north, for example British, Dutch and German regions. The highest two classes include mainly competitive regions and regions that belong to the EU15 countries; it is important to remark that a large number of regions in these classes are characterised by a high population density.

In Maps 3.6 and 3.7 we display the spatial distribution of patent counts including two complementary measures: the total number of per capita (1000 inhabitants) patents released in the region in all economic sectors (average 2005–2006) (Map 3.6) and the number of per capita patents for the subsample of high-tech sectors (Map 3.7). In Map 3.6 the high spatial concentration, with respect to the previous maps, is also confirmed by the visual inspection of the map which reveals a well-defined territorial pattern. Regions in the highest classes are highly concentrated in the central European territories. As one moves towards peripheral

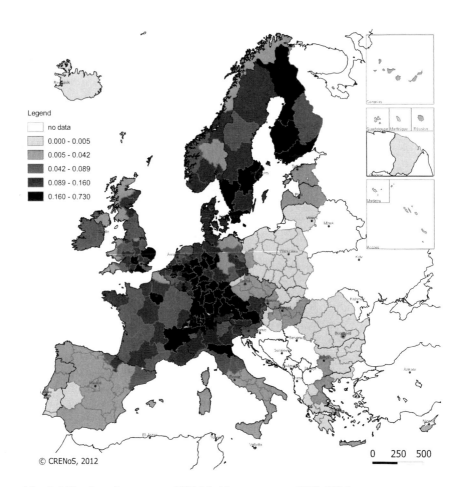

Map 3.6 Number of patents per 1000 inhabitants, average 2005–2006

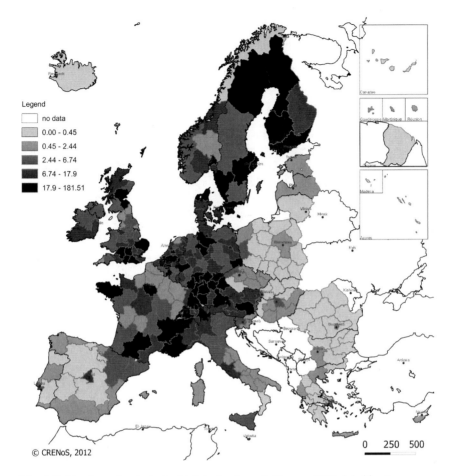

Map 3.7 Number of patents in high-technology fields per 1000 inhabitants, average 2005–2006

areas, the colours get lighter. The highest two classes (ranging between 0.089 and 0.730), are formed by territories belonging to Austria, Belgium, Switzerland, Denmark, Spain, Finland, France, Italy, Luxemburg, Netherlands, Norway, Sweden, United Kingdom and above all Germany, with most of its regions. There are only two transition regions and two convergence regions in this class. There are no regions belonging to New Entrant countries. If we distinguish among rural, urban, agglomerated regions and regions where huge cities are located, a large number of territories included in the first two classes are urban regions. The lowest class includes mainly convergence and rural regions. These territories are mainly located in the eastern part of Europe.

In Map 3.7 we can observe the map of the distribution of high-technology patents, which is very similar to the one observed for total patents. Highest values are concentrated in the north and centre of the continent. Regions included in the two highest classes, ranging between 6.74 and 181.51, are mainly competitive urban regions belonging to EU15 and EFTA countries. Regions included in the third and fourth class, ranging between 0.45 and 6.74, are mainly rural areas that are not geographically concentrated. Regions included in the lowest class, ranging between 0 and 2.71, are mainly concentrated in the eastern countries.

3.5. The scientific regions in Europe

In this section we use the indicators of technological activities and human capital previously described in order to identify the group of scientific regions in Europe, selecting those regions which exhibit a value above the European average for both dimensions. To this aim we will develop a synthetic indicator that provides the rankings of the regions according to their scientific knowledge performance.

As described in the previous sections, we measure the human capital dimension by means of the following indicators:

- the percentage of population employed in the education sector;
- the share of population that has attained at least a university degree;
- funding per capita for the activities of the 5th Framework Programme.

Similarly, the technological activity dimension is measured by:

- the R&D expenditure per capita;
- the percentage of employees in R&D;
- the number of patents per capita for all sectors;
- the number of patents per capita for the subsample of high-tech sectors.

As a preliminary step, in order to detect the degree of association among these indicators, we calculate the correlation coefficient by distinguishing between human capital and technological knowledge indicators (Tables 3.8 and 3.9). With the human capital indicators, we have always positive coefficients: the highest value is

Table 3.8 Correlation coefficients for human capital indicators (standardized values)

	Tertiary education	Employees in education	5th FP funding
Tertiary education (TE)	1.00		
Employees in education (EMPL)	0.50	1.00	
5th FP funding (5FP)	0.60	0.35	1.00

Table 3.9 Correlation coefficients for technological indicators (standardized values)

	PAT	PATHT	RDE	RDP
Number of patents (all sectors) (PAT)	1.00			
Number of patents (high-tech sectors)(PATHT)	0.75	1.00		
R&D expenditure (RDE)	0.73	0.67	1.00	
R&D personnel (RDP)	0.49	0.52	0.82	1.00

shown by the correlation between tertiary education and 5th FP funds (0.60). This value stresses the strong relationship between the indicators assumed to measure the human capital endowment of a region from a 'quantity' and a 'quality' perspective.

Also in the case of knowledge indicators, we always have positive coefficients. We obtain high correlation coefficients, as expected, when we look at R&D expenditure and R&D personnel (0.82) and total number of patents compared to the number of high-tech patents (0.75). Also the coefficient for the total number of patents and R&D expenditure is quite high (0.73). All in all, we can conclude that positive signs suggest that all the indicators for human capital and scientific knowledge activity are measuring a similar phenomenon. At the same time, the magnitude of coefficients suggests that they are measuring it in a complementary way, making our analysis more complete.

Then, we develop a synthetic measure for each of the two dimensions by standardizing the simple indicators around the European average (imposed equal to zero) and by constraining the distribution within the range –1 and 1, following the methodology used in the Regional Innovation Scoreboard (RIS) (Hollanders et al., 2009a).[3] In this way we no longer have the problem of different units of measurement (and this allows us to add the various indicators) and we solve the problem of outliers. At this point, we can build the two synthetic measures by imposing the same weight on each simple indicator: 1/3 for each human capital indicator and 1/4 for each technological activity indicator.[4]

Finally, we define the scientific regions as the group of European regions which shows a value greater than zero for both indicators. Regions showing positive values for human capital but negative for technological activity are labelled *human-capital-intensive regions*. On the contrary, regions characterized by values greater than zero for technological activity and less than zero for the human capital indicator are indicated as *technologically intensive regions*. Finally, regions showing negative values for both indicators are defined as *regions with no specialisation in knowledge activities*. The four groups of regions are depicted in Figure 3.1.

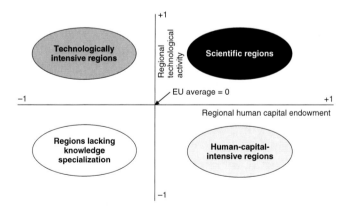

Figure 3.1 Typology of regions according to technological activity and human capital endowment

In Figure 3.2 we present the scatter of regions with respect to the two dimensions of human capital and technological activity. We can observe 74 scientific regions, 30 technologically-intensive regions and 52 human-capital-intensive regions. It is worth remarking that the highest number of European regions (126) is concentrated in the quadrant where we identify regions with no specialisation in knowledge activities.

In Table 3.10 we report for each of group of regions the average values of the human capital and technological activity composite indicators. As expected, the scientific regions show positive values above the European average set equal to zero for both indicators. In the case of technologically-intensive regions and human-capital-intensive regions, the two indicators present opposite signs and the positive one signals their main specialisation. The regions with no specialisation in knowledge activities present negative values, below the whole sample average, for both synthetic indicators.

In Table 3.11 we present the ranking for the 74 scientific regions based on the value of the synthetic indicator described in the previous paragraph. Among the

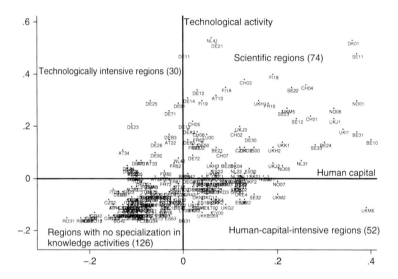

Figure 3.2 Scatter plot of scientific regions in Europe

Table 3.10 Typology of scientific regions. Average values of normalised variables

	Human capital	Technological activity
Scientific regions	0.138	0.171
Technologically intensive regions	−0.072	0.081
Human-capital-intensive regions	0.077	−0.054
Regions with no specialization in knowledge activities	−0.094	−0.096

Note: Synthetic indicators have been obtained by standardizing the simple indicators around the European average imposed equal to zero and by constraining the distribution within the range −1 and 1, following the methodology used in the Regional Innovation Scoreboard (Hollanders et al., 2009a).

Table 3.11 Ranking of the scientific regions

Code	Region Name	Synthetic Indicator	Code	Region Name	Synthetic Indicator
DK01	Hovedstaden	0.89	UKD2	Cheshire	0.25
SE11	Stockholm	0.85	CZ01	Praha	0.25
NO01	Oslo og Akershus	0.67	CH05	Ostschweiz	0.25
CH04	Zürich	0.62	LU00	Luxembourg	0.22
NL41	Noord Brabant	0.59	CH06	Zentralschweiz	0.22
NO06	Trøndelag	0.59	DE13	Freiburg	0.21
FI18	Etelä Suomi	0.59	BE21	Prov. Antwerpen	0.20
SE22	Sydsverige	0.58	ES21	Pais Vasco	0.19
DE21	Oberbayern	0.58	DEA2	Köln	0.19
BE31	Brabant Wallon	0.55	FR62	Midi-Pyrénées	0.19
UKJ1	Berkshire. Bucks. Oxfordshire	0.55	ES30	Comunidad de Madrid	0.18
BE10	Région de Bruxelles	0.55	CH07	Ticino	0.18
UKI1	Inner London	0.53	DK04	Midtjylland	0.18
CH03	Nordwestschweiz	0.51	DE50	Bremen	0.17
CH01	Région lémanique	0.51	SK01	Bratislavský kraj	0.17
UKM5	North Eastern Scotland	0.49	NL32	Noord Holland	0.17
DE11	Stuttgart	0.48	DED2	Dresden	0.17
SE23	Västsverige	0.47	DE60	Hamburg	0.16
SE12	Östra Mellansverige	0.47	FR71	Rhône Alpes	0.16
UKH1	East Anglia	0.47	BE23	Prov. Oost Vlaanderen	0.16
FR10	Île de France	0.47	NL11	Groningen	0.15
BE24	Prov. Vlaams Brabant	0.45	UKF2	Leicestershire. Rutland. Northants	0.15
FI1A	Pohjois Suomi	0.45	NL22	Gelderland	0.14
SE33	Övre Norrland	0.41	NL33	Zuid Holland	0.13
AT13	Wien	0.39	SI02	Zahodna Slovenija	0.13
DE12	Karlsruhe	0.36	UKH3	Essex	0.12
UKK1	Gloucestershire. Wiltshire. Bristol	0.35	UKG1	Herefordshire. Worcestershire. Warks	0.12
FI19	Länsi Suomi	0.34	DE72	Gießen	0.12
NL31	Utrecht	0.32	ES22	Comunidad Foral de Navarra	0.12
DE14	Tübingen	0.32	UKF1	Derbyshire and Nottinghamshire	0.09
UKJ3	Hampshire and Isle of Wight	0.32	UKM3	South Western Scotland	0.09
UKH2	Bedfordshire. Hertfordshire	0.31	NO03	Sør-Østlandet	0.07
DE30	Berlin	0.30	BE22	Prov. Limburg	0.06
CH02	Espace Mittelland	0.29	DK05	Nordjylland	0.05
IS00	Iceland	0.27	FI13	Itä Suomi	0.03
NO05	Vestlandet	0.26	FR42	Alsace	0.03
UKJ2	Surrey. East. West Sussex	0.25	DEG0	Thüringen	0.01

top ten scientific regions in Europe we find Hovedstaden (Denmark), Stockholm (Sweden), Oslo og Akershus (Norway), Zurich (Switzerland), Noord Brabant (Netherlands), Trøndelag (Norway), Etelä Suomi (Finland), Sydsverige (Sweden) and Brabant Wallon (Belgium). Thus, Scandinavian countries are largely represented in the highest part of the ranking as most regions in these countries are included in the group of scientific regions: for Denmark 3 out of 5 regions, Finland 4 out of 5, Norway 4 out of 7, and 5 out of 8 for Sweden. Notice that all the Swiss regions and most Belgian regions are listed. Among the scientific regions there are also 12 (out of 39) German regions, 6 regions belonging to Netherlands and 14 (out of 37) British regions. Moreover, there are regions where capital cities are located: the Wien region for Austria, Prague for the Czech Republic, and the Madrid and Paris regions. We can also observe that scientific regions are mostly regions belonging to EU15 countries and EFTA countries, as expected. But we also notice the presence of some regions belonging to New Entrants: Prague (Czech Republic), Zahodna Slovenija (Slovenia) and Bratislavskýkraj (Slovakia). Finally, it is also important to stress that Italy is the only large industrialised country with no regions included in this group.

Map 3.8 shows the spatial distributions of the four categories of regions. Scientific regions are mainly concentrated in the centre and the north of Europe and this spatial pattern is confirmed by the Morax index results presented in Table 3.12.

This result is very similar to that presented in the RIS (2009) where regions belonging to the 'highest innovative' classes are mainly located in the same territories. On the other hand, we can observe that regions with no specialization in knowledge activities are mainly located on the peripheral territories of Europe and also in this case our results are in line with the RIS (2009) (Hollanders et al., 2009a). Finally, technological-intensive regions are concentrated on territories characterized by a manufacturing productive specialization (i.e. Northern Italy, German regions) and, as expected, human-capital-intensive regions are mainly in the northern part of Europe.

In general, the map shows a strong spatial pattern supporting the thesis of the presence of geographically bounded knowledge spillovers (Audretsch and Feldman, 1996; Baptista and Swann, 1998; Acs et al., 2002). The spatial pattern is confirmed by Moran statistics (Table 3.12), positive and highly significant for both specifications.

3.6. A robustness check: cluster analysis

As a robustness test we use a cluster analysis to determine the natural groupings (or clusters) of our observations based on the set of seven simple indicators used in the previous sections. This kind of analysis has been widely used in the literature on knowledge and innovation (see, among others, Evangelista et al. 2001; Roelandt and den Hertog, 1998; Padmore and Gibson, 1998).

There are several types of cluster analysis, each having specific methods and allowing for a variety of distance measures for determining the similarity or dissimilarity among observations. In this chapter we use the *partition method* which breaks the observations into a distinct number of groups by creating an iterative

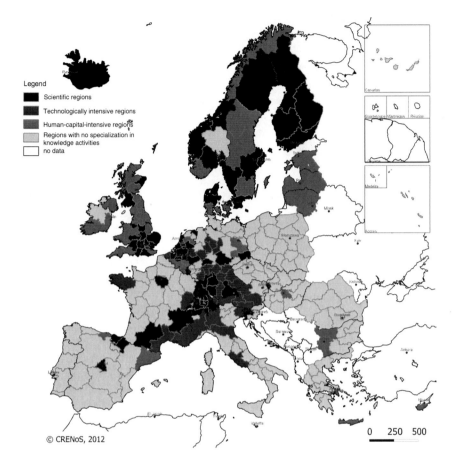

Map 3.8 Scientific regions

Table 3.12 Typology of scientific regions, Moran index

Inverse distance matrix (row standardized)

Variable	I	Mean	St. Dev.	Z	p-value
Scientific regions	0.052	−0.004	0.005	10.208	0.000

Inverse of squared matrix (row standardized)

Variable	I	Mean	St. Dev.	Z	p-value
Scientific regions	0.160	−0.004	0.019	8.459	0.000

process during which each observation is assigned to the group whose mean is closest. The iterative process ends when no observation changes group.

To enable comparisons with the previous taxonomy, we impose four groups and use the same standardized variables described above.

The average values for the indicators of technological activity and human capital in each class are presented in Table 3.13. The regions in Class 1 show the highest average values for all variables and thus we can associate this cluster to the scientific regions typology. Class 2 regions are related to the technological-intensive regions group since they show relatively higher values for the technological indicators and, similarly, Class 3 regions are associated with the human-capital-intensive regions. Finally, Class 4, which shows the lowest values for both human capital and technological indicators, is related to the group labelled regions with no specialisation in knowledge activities.

Map 3.9 shows that the distribution of regions among the four classes is quite similar to that obtained previously for scientific regions. Indeed the correlation index between the two taxonomies is quite high and equal to 0.81. We can observe that all Class 1 regions are scientific regions and they are located in central Europe, in the Scandinavian countries and UK. Finally, the fourth class includes mostly the regions with no specialisation in knowledge activities (125 regions over 142) but also two human capital regions and eight technological-intensive regions. It is important to note that no scientific regions fall into this fourth class.

3.7. Conclusions

Intangible assets, such as human capital and technological activity, are recognised as the key factors in determining the competitiveness of firms and territories, especially among the industrialised countries. Therefore much effort should be devoted to defining and measuring these elements and to assessing how they influence the regional economic performance.

Table 3.13 Average values for each cluster class

	Class 1 (close to SR)	Class 2 (close to TIR)	Class 3 (close to HKR)	Class 4 (close to RNS)
Employees in education (EMPL)	4.01	2.78	4.02	2.78
Tertiary education (TE)	18.24	12.59	15.55	9.53
5th FP funding (5FP)	73.41	23.77	27.11	9.09
R&D expenditure (RDE)	1.50	0.73	0.46	0.15
R&D personnel (RDP)	3.29	1.99	1.65	0.89
Number of patents (all sectors) (PAT)	311.43	272.06	79.87	37.61
Number of patents (high-tech sectors) (PATHT)	58.44	28.49	9.26	3.07

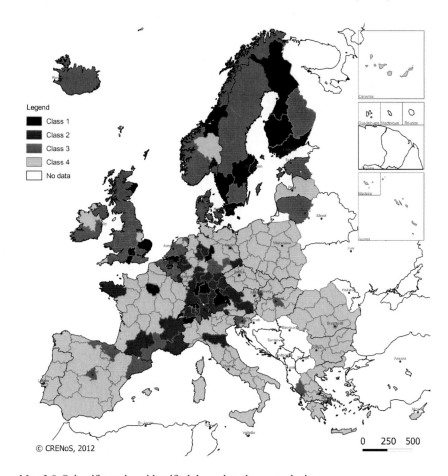

Map 3.9 Scientific regions identified through a cluster analysis

The aim of this chapter is to develop a classification of the regions based on a functional approach where the two main pillars of the knowledge economy – human capital and technological activities – have been used to identify the scientific regions in Europe and to examine their main territorial features.

These two factors are able to capture not only the creation of new knowledge within the region, but also the capacity of the local firms to absorb knowledge spilling from internal and external economies.

The human capital endowment in a region has been expressed by means of both input and output indicators. Among the former is the share of population employed in the education sector, which measures the regional effort to create a new flow of human capital. Among the latter, we have used the share of population with a university degree and participation in the EU 5th FP, which measure human capital quality and knowledge diffusion through international technological cooperation. The regional level of technological activities has been described by input indicators (R&D expenditure and employees) and output measures (total number of patents granted and patents in high-tech sectors). The first set of indicators shows the amount of resources invested in technological activities while the second can be used as a measure of their effectiveness.

All variables confirm the presence of huge differences among the European regions, with a clear spatial divide between western vs eastern regions and northern vs southern regions. It is interesting to remark that all indicators show the presence of spatial dependence, thus signalling that a knowledge spillover process with spatial features is taking place in Europe.

On the basis of these seven indicators we compute two synthetic measures for human capital and technological activity by standardizing the simple indicators around the European average. The intersection of the two indicators allows us to identify four areas and to define the following taxonomy for the European regions:

- *scientific regions*: both indicators above the European average (74 regions);
- *human-capital-intensive regions*: human capital above and technological activity below the average (52 regions);
- *technologically intensive regions*: technological activity above and human capital below the average (30 regions);
- *regions with no specialisation in knowledge activities*: both indicators below the European average (126 regions).

We have remarked that the scientific regions represent less than one quarter of all European regions and are spatially concentrated. More specifically, the vast majority of the scientific regions belong to the EU15 member states in the Scandinavian area and other core countries like Belgium, the Netherlands, Germany, the UK and also Switzerland. Moreover these key functions are often located in the capital cities both in the western (Paris, Madrid, Wien) and in the new accession eastern countries (Praha, Bratislava, Ljubljana). On the contrary, most of the European regions, mainly those located in southern and eastern Europe, do not show any specialization in knowledge activities.

These results suggest the presence of a strong core–periphery pattern in the geographical distribution of the scientific functions in Europe. This outcome indicates the need of specific place-based policies for the generation, diffusion and absorption of knowledge in order to favour the process of integration and cohesion of these territories. Clearly, the functional approach proposed in this chapter is just one of the various dimensions necessary to properly assess the regional pattern of the knowledge economy in Europe. Therefore our results need to be complemented with the analysis of other important elements like the inter-regional knowledge spillovers connected to the relational approach, which are examined in Chapter 4.

Notes

1 The research leading to these results has received funding from the EU ESPON applied KIT project – Knowledge, Innovation, Territory (ESPON KIT, 2012). We also acknowledge funding from the Regione Autonoma della Sardegna, L.R.7/2007 (European Social Fund 2007–2013, 'Promotion of research and technological innovation in Sardinia'). We would like to thank Matteo Bellinzas, Barbara Dettori and Giuseppe Onano for their assistance in preparing the database.

2 Convergence regions are defined as eligible areas under the Convergence objective within the 2007–2013 Cohesion Policy programming period, transition regions are defined as phasing-in and phasing-out areas within the 2007–2013 Cohesion Policy programming period, and competitive regions are defined as eligible areas under the European and Competitiveness and Employment Objective within the 2007–2013 Cohesion Policy programming period. Further details on this classification are available at http://ec.europa.eu/regional_policy/atlas2007/index_en.htm.

3 Rescaled value = $[(x_i) - \min(x_{1-n})]/(\max(x_{1-n}) - \min(x_{1-n}))$. For positive and negative outliers and small countries where the value of the relative value is above the maximum score or below the minimum score, the rescaled value is set respectively equal to 1 (or −1).

4 Since the choice of the weights is arbitrary, we have done extensive simulations with different weights structures, but the classification of the scientific regions remains quite stable. Therefore we have preferred to adopt a distribution with equal weights.

4 Knowledge networking regions

*Ernest Miguélez, Rosina Moreno
and Jordi Suriñach*

4.1. Introduction[1]

Agents do not create in isolation. Indeed, the production of innovation relies on the recombination of existing knowledge and ideas. Employees within a firm and across its different departments create and recombine ideas through a process of collective learning that is structured within the organization (Lorenz, 1996; March, 1991). Organizations produce innovations by combining existing knowledge that goes beyond the limits of their boundaries. In short, firms turn to external sources of ideas (Rosenkopf and Almedia, 2003) and their ability to recombine and exploit such knowledge is pivotal in boosting their competitive advantage (Dosi, 1988; Singh and Agrawal, 2011).

Recognition of the critical role of knowledge flows, knowledge diffusion and knowledge recombination dates back to the well-known Marshallian externalities. Endogenous growth models (Grossman and Helpman, 1991a; Lucas, 1988; Romer, 1990) put knowledge spillovers again at the forefront of the mainstream research agenda. During the nineties, empirical analysis from the geography of innovation (Feldman, 1994; Feldman and Audretsch, 1999; Jaffe 1986, 1989; Jaffe et al., 1993) and new economic geography models (Martin and Ottaviano, 1999) emphasized the localized pattern of knowledge spillovers and their role in explaining both the high spatial concentration of economic activity and spatial differences in economic growth.

Recently, scholars have started to claim that excessively close actors may have little to exchange after a certain number of interactions (Boschma and Frenken, 2010). Indeed, the production of ideas requires the combination of different, complementary pieces of knowledge to be most effective. However, at some point, co-located agents may start to combine and recombine local knowledge that eventually becomes redundant and less valuable. As a result, processes of lock-in may begin to occur (Arthur, 1989; David, 1985). Conversely, firms looking for external sources of knowledge that lie beyond their own boundaries may find that the knowledge they require is available beyond the boundaries of the region (Bergman and Maier, 2009). Hence, if there are strong internal connections between firms within a given region, but weak external connections to other sources of knowledge, 'there is the risk of localism, which implies that a regional economy is unable to acquire and master external knowledge and is hence likely to be less innovative' (Fratesi and Senn, 2009, p.17).

We build our empirical strategy on this idea and develop a method that tries to quantify to what extent actors in regions can access sources of knowledge that lie beyond the confines of their cluster. This puts regions in a better strategic position to potentially use extra-regional ideas in the production of innovations. In so doing, we expect to increase our understanding of why some regional economies become locked into non-dynamic development paths, whilst others seem able to reinvent themselves continuously (Martin and Sunley, 2006).

Thus, the aim of this chapter is to provide a map of the penetration of the knowledge-based economy in the European regions, when this is defined in relational terms, i.e. by looking at a region's capacity to engage into cross-regional knowledge relationships. Both the sector-based and the function-based approaches (Chapters 2 and 3 respectively) to the knowledge-based economy provide a sound, but only partial, characterization of the phenomenon under study. Therefore, a rather different approach should be utilised, a cognitive one, stressing the relational, cultural and psychological elements that define the preconditions for knowledge creation, development, transmission and diffusion.

In sum, the present chapter describes a method for constructing a synthetic indicator able to identify the regions in the best (and worst) positions to access sources of knowledge from beyond their boundaries. To the best of our knowledge, little attention has been paid to this issue from a policymaking perspective (e.g. the Regional Innovation Scoreboard, 2009). To do this, we feed from various research streams, and we survey and discuss the most recent conceptual and empirical contributions. On the basis of this review, we conceptually model the ways in which organizations and other actors in regions access external-to-the-region pieces of knowledge. We suggest that two different regimes are at work: (1) informal interactions and unintentional relations arising from serendipitous encounters between actors who lie in close spatial proximity; and (2) formal, intentional relations based on coordinated and well-defined linkages between actors who might, or might not, be in close spatial proximity. Hence, we characterize regions in terms of the ways in which they can potentially access external knowledge. In short, our research will provide a method for quantifying regions' exposure to external knowledge through these two patterns. Afterwards, we also provide a thorough descriptive analysis of the computed indicators, and suggest exploratory hypotheses on the relationships between our measures and several metrics of regional economic performance.

On the basis of the proposed method, we aim to develop a typology of regions according to their position in the two dimensions above-mentioned: regions in a superior position to build informal connections with the outside world, but lacking formal, intentional linkages (*clustering regions*); regions with numerous formal relations but potentially few informal connections (*globalizing regions*); regions that do not have an advantageous positions in either of these two dimensions (*non-interactive regions*); and finally, regions with values above the mean in both indices (*knowledge networking regions*). We apply our approach to a group of

NUTS2 regions in 31 European countries (EU27 plus Iceland, Liechtenstein, Norway and Switzerland).

The outline of the chapter is as follows. Section 4.2 reviews some relevant conceptual and empirical studies on the idea that agents access external-to-the-region knowledge to avoid regional lock-in. In this section, we bring together dispersed, but related, literature. Section 4.3 develops in more detail our conceptual relational model of connectivity through the two dimensions outlined above, and examines in depth the concept of knowledge networking regions. Section 4.4 describes the empirical approach taken here. Section 4.5 summarizes some remarkable findings and Section 4.6 presents conclusions and policy implications.

4.2. Literature review

Most geography of innovation scholars have reiterated that the role of physical proximity in enhancing knowledge creation is critical to understanding the uneven distribution of economic and innovation activities across space, as well as the major spatial differences in growth rates across regions, even within the same country. To recap, empirical studies in the geography of innovation (Feldman, 1994; Feldman and Audretsch, 1999; Jaffe 1986, 1989; Jaffe et al., 1993) and economic geography (Martin and Ottaviano, 1999) literature have established that knowledge produced by a firm is only partially appropriated by the producer itself, whereas part of this knowledge spills over to other firms and institutions, reducing in this way innovation costs of these other organisations, as shown by endogenous growth models (Lucas, 1988; Romer, 1986, 1990). Face-to-face interactions between employees (Allen, 1977; Krugman, 1991b), frequent meetings, monitoring of competitors (Porter, 1990), spin-offs, trust building (Glaeser et al., 2002) and the like, which are essential to the effective exchange of ideas, have been indistinctly taken to explain the mechanisms by which knowledge spills over as an externality. Due to the nature of these mechanisms and the highly contextual features of the knowledge that is transferred, knowledge barters are assumed to occur among members of a co-located community and, therefore, knowledge is considered to be spatially sticky.

However, an increasing number of academics have called into question the widely accepted assumption that knowledge flows are so localized. This assumption, they argue, might have limited our understanding of the ways in which knowledge flows across space (Coe and Bunnell, 2003). Certainly, recent empirical evidence casts doubts on the orthodox viewpoint outlined above. Hence, some studies have started to explore the influence of extra-local knowledge sources on firms' innovative performance, though the results are ambiguous. For instance, in their analysis of the Boston biotech community, Owen-Smith and Powell (2004) showed that while membership to local networks, rather than centrality within these networks, was a conduit to better company performance, central positions in geographically dispersed networks increased firms' patent volume. Thus, 'being situated at the intersection of numerous formal pipelines enhances firm-level knowledge outputs' (op. cit., p. 16). Gittelman (2007) suggested that geographical proximity matters for innovation, but opportunities for learning by interacting also exist beyond regions' boundaries in the case of US biotech firms. Indeed, she estimated that distant research teams received more citations of their output than teams formed in closer proximity. In parallel, Gertler and Levite (2005) found that the most successful Canadian biotech firms are externally oriented. Thus, patenting Canadian biotech firms are more likely to have foreign partners in their collaborative projects than their non-patenting counterparts. This suggests that the best places for biotech innovators are not only those with a strong 'local buzz', but also regions that are well connected extra-locally. In a similar vein, Rosenkopf and Almedia (2003) convincingly argued that, in spite of the larger pools of knowledge available at local level, firms need to search for knowledge sources beyond their geographical and technological vicinity as the distant context may offer particularly useful ideas and insights for recombination. Using data on patents, citations, inter-firm alliances and labour mobility, the aforementioned authors evaluated various knowledge inflows at different spatial scales. Despite their claims, the positive effects of distant relationships (in the form of alliances and mobility) were not supported by the data.

This empirical evidence goes hand in hand with an increasing number of claims from prominent academics who have raised concerns in this area. Thus, several scholars have lately stressed the need for firms to network with extra-local knowledge pools to overcome potential situations of regional 'entropic death', 'lock-in' or 'over-embeddedness' (Boschma, 2005; Camagni, 1991; Grabher, 1993; Uzzi, 1996). These claims have contributed to a lively current debate among research streams about the conditions in which tacit knowledge can be transmitted at a distance and go beyond a region's confines, as well as the extent of such transmission. Indeed, it has been argued that two very close actors may have little knowledge to exchange and that innovative production usually requires the combination of dissimilar, but related, complementary knowledge (Boschma and Frenken, 2010; Boschma and Iammarino, 2009). Thus, as time passes and local interactions lead to the combination and recombination of the same pieces of knowledge, organizations end up stuck in strong social structures that tend to resist social change (Boschma and Frenken, 2010; Morrison et al., 2011) and prevent them from recognizing opportunities in new markets and technologies (Lambooy and Boschma, 2001).

Truly dynamic regions in the era of the knowledge economy are therefore characterized not only by dense local learning and interaction, but also by the ability to identify and establish inter-regional and international connections to outside sources of ideas (Gertler and Levitte, 2005; Maskell et al., 2006). Thus, they introduce knowledge variation into the regional economy, which can prevent the region from entering non-dynamic development paths. In sum, regions that host globally connected organizations end up being more successful than others (Bergman and Maier, 2009).

Following on from part of these theoretical and empirical contributions, Bathelt et al. (2004) envisage a conceptual model that is concerned with the coexistence between a vibrant 'local buzz' and a number of 'pipelines' that provide access to relevant pools of knowledge outside the 'buzz'. These authors hint at the fact that in reality firms build pipelines to benefit from knowledge hotspots around the world, and do not build their knowledge stock solely from local interactions (Bahlmann et al., 2008). The logic in Bathelt's et al. (2004) study implies that[2]: (1) new (tacit) knowledge is created around the globe and firms that can access it through global pipelines gain competitive advantage; (2) this knowledge acquired from abroad may spill over or be transferred within the local cluster through the local network of a firm or individual; consequently (3) there is a kind of trade-off between 'a too much inward-looking and a too much outward-looking' structure of grabbing knowledge (Bathelt et al., 2004, p. 46); and (4) there are limits to the number of pipelines a firm can manage at the same time, and therefore it is better to have several firms managing a set of pipelines than for one large firm to manage a high, but limited, number of pipelines. In a similar vein, Maggioni et al. (2007) and Maggioni and Uberti (2011) developed an extensive research agenda based on the distinction between unintended cross-regional spatial spillovers and intentional relations based on a-spatial networks. Their logic is straightforward: knowledge is created in central organizations that tend to co-locate. Subsequently, knowledge is diffused either through a trickle-down process of spatial contagion of neighbouring regions (by means of face-to-face interactions and other 'unintended' means) or through a-spatial networks structured in the form of contractual agreements between organizations that connect clusters, irrespective of the spatial distance between them. As we will see in more detail in Section 4.3, our conceptual framework is based on these contributions, though some differences will be worth mentioning.

Within the regional science literature, the number of studies that address cross-regional relationships and their impact on economic outcomes has sharply increased in the last 25 years. A clear example is the growing number of papers that apply spatial econometric techniques at regional level. These papers have been more or less concerned with estimating cross-regional knowledge externalities in knowledge production function (KPF) frameworks (Acs et al., 1994; Anselin et al., 1997; Bottazzi and Peri, 2003). Indeed, as stated by prominent scholars, there is no reason to assume that knowledge stops flowing because of regional borders (Audretsch and Feldman, 2004; Krugman, 1991a). Therefore, spatial econometric techniques and the spatial weight matrix have notably improved the way such externalities are measured (Autant-Bernard and Massard, 2009).

In spite of these and other contributions, the literature on cross-regional knowledge diffusion and regional innovation is relatively scant, apart from studies on the purely spatial approach. Likewise, supra-national organizations' policy reports on regional innovation do not tend to consider that extra-regional linkages are part of the regional innovation performance, either from an input or output perspective. For instance, the latest Regional Innovation Scoreboard (2009) takes into account a number of regional innovation indicators, such as human capital, R&D expenditure, ICT penetration, employment in high technologies and patents (Hollanders et al., 2009a). However, it does not include indicators concerning a region's degree of openness to external sources of knowledge, in neighbouring or distant regions, that may have a definite impact on regional innovative output and, subsequently, on economic development.[3] By means of principal component analysis, the Regional Innovation Monitor (EC, 2011a) produces a typology of innovative regions using several indicators, including public and private R&D, patents, and population with tertiary education. None of these indicators appraise a region's capacity to access and use external knowledge in its innovation processes. Similar approaches are followed by the Global Innovation Index (INSEAD, 2011), the OECD (Marsan and Maguire, 2011) and Navarro et al. (2009). Only recently, in its annual assessment of the performance of regions (OECD, 2009), the OECD included co-patenting with external-to-the-region inventors as an indicator of knowledge sharing.

In consequence, we believe that the approaches that are currently used to assess the knowledge performance of regions are far too simplistic. Our research tries to fill this gap by proposing a method for computing a composite indicator that evaluates the extent to which regions can access external pieces of knowledge and information, either by a process of informal barters between agents located in neighbouring regions or by means of formal linkages with outsiders. Subsequently, our strategy will provide a taxonomy of regions that is based on the mechanisms for accessing external knowledge: formal versus informal interactions.

4.3. Conceptual approach: the knowledge networking region

The above review helps us to build a conceptual framework for the 'knowledge networking region' notion, which we develop in the present section. Again, our primary aim in this chapter was to develop a simple method for appraising the external dimension of regional knowledge production. In doing so, we obtain an instrument for classifying regions into different tiers, according to their capacity to access external sources of knowledge and innovation. To achieve this, we distinguish between two ways in which regional agents access external knowledge. As outlined above, the approach chosen at this stage resembles that of Bathelt et al. (2004) and Maggioni et al. (2007). Thus, actors access external knowledge pools by means of two distinct patterns, i.e.

- an informal, non-intentional, serendipitous pattern of knowledge interactions that take place between agents located in spatial proximity; and
- a formal, intentional, and conscious pattern of linkage formation between actors, irrespective of their geographical location.

Below, these two patterns are illustrated in detail. Our distinction has nothing to do with the usual classifications, such as *tacit* (assimilated to informal) vs *codified* (assimilated to formal) knowledge. The tacit property has been widely advocated as the reason why knowledge of this type is easily transmitted by means of face-to-face contacts, and therefore co-location is required (Breschi and Lissoni, 2001a, b). However, several authors stress that even when knowledge is totally codified, what is required is a tacit understanding of the message that is transmitted, which is a property of the epistemic community and may have little to do with the territory in which the knowledge is produced (Breschi and Lissoni, 2001a, b; Steinmueller, 2000). Our attention is totally focused on the dichotomy between informal/formal mechanisms, rather than whether the linkages are in neighbouring regions or not. In this way, we allow for cross-regional formal knowledge flows between contiguous regions. Finally, among the formal cross-regional linkages considered, we include collaborations between actors, as in many previous studies. However, we also include geographical mobility of highly-skilled labour and access to codified knowledge located outside the region. Bearing this in mind, we will now describe in detail the logic behind each of the patterns of regional capacity to access external knowledge.

4.3.1. *Informal pattern of knowledge diffusion*

Co-location brings people together, facilitates contacts for information and enhances the exchange of knowledge. In this case, the producer of a given piece of knowledge cannot internalize all its effects and part of it spills over to other agents, who do not compensate the initial producer. These kinds of knowledge flows occur via informal face-to-face interactions, monitoring of competitors, advisor–student relationships, and so on. Just being in a location is enough to contribute to and benefit from continuous flows of information and updates, gossip, news, rumours, and recommendations (Bathelt et al., 2004; Gertler, 1995).

Empirical studies tend to confirm that knowledge externalities are geographically bound, in which no other forms of proximity are necessarily involved. The transfer of knowledge takes place without explicit coordination between agents. Thus, firms near knowledge sources show better innovative performance than firms located elsewhere (Audretsch and Feldman, 1996). In many instances, the administrative boundaries of a region do not coincide with the boundaries of the 'local buzz'. When the sender and the receiver of the externality are not located (sometimes by chance) in the same region, spillovers across regions occur.

As already stated, the spatial economics and econometrics literature has long dealt with the estimation of cross-regional knowledge externalities in a KPF framework (Acs et al., 1994; Anselin et al., 1997, among many others). For instance, well-known studies on Europe have estimated the spatial scope of knowledge spillovers to be around 250–300 km (Bottazzi and Peri, 2003; Moreno et al., 2005b).[4]

Needless to say, the informal pattern of interaction described here does not measure knowledge externalities *per se*. In fact, knowledge spillovers are invisible (Krugman, 1991a), although they may sometimes leave a paper trail (Jaffe et al., 1993). The variables chosen in our analysis only let us assess the extent to which each region is well positioned to endorse informal interactions and serendipitous encounters that may encourage knowledge diffusion between actors of neighbouring regions. What is actually measured, as in the literature, is the potential for localized spillovers (D'Este and Iammarino, 2010). Whether or not knowledge indeed flows across regions is an interesting question, which goes beyond the scope of the present analysis.[5] The following variables could be used to proxy the advantageous position of regions that may receive knowledge flows from informal interactions:

- R&D expenditure in neighbouring regions: R&D is well established as being the greatest source of new knowledge (Arrow, 1962b) and a source of spatial informal knowledge exchanges through pure externalities (Jaffe, 1986 and 1989). Thus, cross-regional R&D externalities have been widely investigated (Anselin et al., 1997; Bode, 2004; Bottazzi and Peri, 2003).
- Patent applications in neighbouring regions: patent applications have been used as an indicator of R&D productivity at regional level. Therefore, patent applications in neighbouring regions can be used as an indicator of potential informal access to new knowledge from knowledge outputs (Autant-Bernard and LeSage, 2011).
- Human capital in neighbouring regions: theoretical and empirical contributions have shown the existence of human capital externalities (Lucas, 1988; Moretti, 2004; Rauch, 1993), arguing that skilled individuals tend to be more productive when they are surrounded by their peers. Though studies regarding cross-regional informal flows from human capital stocks are less preponderant, human capital externalities may well go beyond the boundaries of the administrative region.

4.3.2. *Formal pattern of knowledge exchange*

In recent years, several authors have pointed out that, even at close spatial proximity, knowledge flows are not automatically received just by 'being there', as previous literature tends to assume. Rather, knowledge flows follow specific transmission channels, which are mainly based on market interactions (Breschi and Lissoni, 2001a, b). In some instances, actors look for external-to-the-firm pieces of knowledge in knowledge pools that lie beyond the boundaries of their own region. Thus, some members of a region can activate linkages with these pools. As reviewed in Section 4.2, such linkages are pivotal to access external pieces of ideas and information that would otherwise not be available for the local cluster.

Naturally, a large number of connections between agents and external sources of knowledge does not ensure that the knowledge will enter and spread into the region. Ultimately, this will depend on the absorptive capacity of the agents of a given region (Cohen and Levinthal, 1990) and, more importantly, on whether or not these agents are willing to share their knowledge within the 'local buzz'. If the connected agents behave as external stars (Morrison et al., 2011), then the region as a whole will not benefit from their external connections.

Like Bathelt et al. (2004) and Maggioni et al. (2007), we believe that alliances between organizations are critical to build 'pipelines' with outsiders. However, as in Boschma et al. (2009), we extend the formation of external linkages to the issue of the geographical mobility of knowledge workers who embody tacit knowledge (see also Coe and Bunnell, 2003; Rosenkopf and Almedia, 2003). The capacity of particular agents to connect with external sources of codified knowledge is also considered. In sum, the following measures may proxy for these formal linkages:

- Cross-regional co-patents. Networks of inventors are a source of potential knowledge flows, as individuals connected within a collaborative framework are more willing to learn from each other than isolated inventors (Breschi and Lissoni, 2004 and 2009; Cowan and Jonard, 2004; Gomes-Casseres et al., 2006; Singh, 2005).
- Inflows of inventors. Mobility may also favour knowledge diffusion. The movement of skilled individuals across locations contributes to knowledge mobilization throughout the space. Skilled workers take their knowledge with them and share it in a workplace with their new employer and colleagues. In return, they acquire knowledge from their new colleagues and, in general, promote new combinations of knowledge (Laudel, 2003; Trippl and Maier 2010).
- Citations made to outside-the-region patents. We use this proxy as it indicates the extent to which regional actors rely on already codified sources of knowledge that go beyond regional boundaries. Patent citations have been used widely in the related literature to measure the scope of knowledge flows (Jaffe et al., 1993, Peri, 2005).

4.3.3. A simple typology

In short, up to six variables (three for each regime) are assembled to approximate the extent to which a region can take advantage of cross-regional knowledge diffusion.

The computation of the two sub-indices will shed some light on each region's specialization pattern, in terms of its level of connectivity with external knowledge. Combinations of regions' specialization in one regime or the other will produce the following typology:

- *Clustering regions*: regions showing higher-than-average values for potential informal linkages but lower-than-average values for formal linkages.
- *Globalizing regions*: regions characterized by lower-than-average values for informal linkages but higher-than-average values for formal linkages.
- *Non-interactive regions*: regions showing lower-than-average values for both indicators.
- *Knowledge networking regions*: regions showing higher-than-average values for both synthetic indicators: informal and formal linkages.

Figure 4.1 graphically summarizes the suggested typology. In a nutshell, knowledge networking regions are regions that are in a relatively advantageous position to receive and access external pools of knowledge through the two patterns illustrated in the previous sections.

4.4. Empirical approach

Below we summarize a few empirical practicalities resulting from applying the method outlined in the previous section to a group of 287 NUTS2 regions

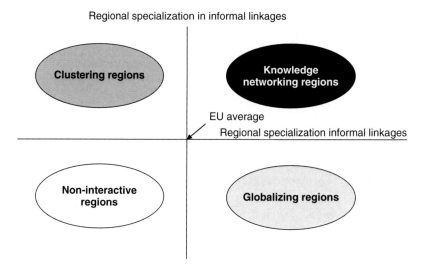

Figure 4.1 Typology of regions according to the type of linkages to external sources of knowledge

belonging to 31 European countries (EU27 plus Iceland, Liechtenstein, Norway and Switzerland).

4.4.1. Variables construction

With respect to the construction of the indicator of a region's capacity to access knowledge through informal interactions we consider the following variables:

- R&D expenditure in neighbouring regions (R&D expenditure weighted by a predefined spatial weight matrix): average value of R&D expenditure in the neighbouring regions.
- Patent applications in neighbouring regions (patent applications weighted by a predefined spatial weight matrix): average value of patent applications in the neighbouring regions.
- Human capital in neighbouring regions (population aged 15 and over with tertiary education over the total population, weighted by a predefined spatial weight matrix): average value of human capital in the neighbouring regions.

The spatial weight matrix taken from the spatial econometrics toolkit will help us to construct this sub-indicator. This is a non-stochastic square matrix that captures an ad hoc intensity of the interdependencies between each couple of regions, where $W = \{w_{ij}\}$, leading to a definition of 'neighbouring'. The most usual definition of neighbouring is first-order physical contiguity; that is, if two regions share the same administrative border $w_{ij} = 1$, and $w_{ij} = 0$ otherwise. In this chapter, we use a more complex version of this matrix, which takes the physical distance between regions' centroids, instead of contiguity, as a neighbouring criterion and introduces strong spatial decay, giving far more importance to short-distance neighbours than to long-distance neighbours. Concretely, we define $w_{ij} = \exp(-0.01d_{ij})$, where d_{ij} is the Euclidean distance, in kilometres, between the centroids of region i and region j. Following Bottazzi and Peri (2003), a cut-off of 300 km is introduced.[6]

The proxies used to construct the indicator that captures formal interactions include:

- Co-patents with other regions: the valued degree centrality of cross-regional co-patents. The number of patents co-authored with inventors from outside the region. When a patent involves inventors whose addresses are in different regions, we assume that cross-regional collaborations took place. We 'full-count' all the collaborations across regions, irrespective of the number of inventors reported in each patent. For each patent with multiple inventors, all possible pairs of regions *ij* were created.
- Inflows of skilled workers: valued in-degree centrality of cross-regional inflows of inventors. Number of inflows of inventors from other regions. A 'mobile' inventor is broadly defined as an individual who moves across different regions, irrespective of whether the focal individual changes his employer or not. Mobility is computed through observed changes in the inventor's region of residence, as reported in the patent documents.[7] Admittedly, in this manner we only capture mobility if the inventor applies for a patent before or after a move, which probably underestimates real mobility. We compute the movement in time between the origin and the destination patent, but only if there is a maximum lapse of 5 years between them.
- Cross-regional patent citations: valued in-degree centrality of cross-regional patent citations. Number of citations made to patents of other regions.

The socio-matrix, taken from social network analysis (SNA), is used to build the variables that make up this indicator. This is a tabular representation in matrix form that measures social relationships between the members of a network. Networks are formed by actors, or nodes (regions in our case), which are connected to one another by means of relations or ties. These connections form relationships between nodes that can be represented in the socio-matrix, whose elements capture the intensity of the relationship between nodes i and j. Relations in a network might be undirected when the relationships are symmetric, or directed when the direction of the relation between a given pair of points does matter. Additionally, the relations between nodes might be binary (1 when a relationship exists, and 0 otherwise) or valued (the intensity of the relationship matters and numerical values are 'attached' to each of the lines). One of the most important point measures in SNA is that of degree centrality. The aim is to detect the most central (i.e. the most popular) actor within the structure. This is defined as simply the number of incumbent linkages that a given node has. When networks are directed, the degree centrality may include separately in-degree centrality (the number of edges directed to the vertex) and out-degree centrality (the number of edges that the vertex directs to other vertices).

Using the different variables suggested and the corresponding instruments, we compute a single measure that allows us to assert whether or not a given region is a knowledge networking region. In addition, we obtain a composite indicator for the formal linkages dimension and another for informal linkages.

Both synthetic indicators corresponding to each dimension are developed following the procedure used in the Regional Innovation Scoreboard (Hollanders et al., 2009a). Specifically, since the indicator variables we are using for the two different categories of linkages can be highly volatile and have skewed data distributions (where most regions show low performance levels and a few regions show exceptionally high performance levels), data will be modified firstly using a square root transformation. Secondly, based on the square root values, rescaled values are obtained by subtracting the minimum value and then dividing by the difference between the maximum and minimum value. The maximum rescaled score is thus equal to 1 and the minimum rescaled score is equal to 0.[8] For each kind of linkage (informal and formal) a composite indicator (KNR: knowledge networking region) is calculated as the unweighted average of the rescaled scores for all indicators within the respective dimension.

4.4.2. Data sources

The raw data corresponding to informal knowledge diffusion variables (R&D expenditure, patents, and human capital) were assembled by CRENoS, using manifold data sources: Eurostat, OECD REGPAT database, ISTAT and the Institut National de la Statistique et des Études Économiques. A summary of data sources can be found in Table 4.1, where the time span considered for each variable is also reported.

The data source for the formal knowledge exchange variables was the OECD REGPAT database (January 2010 edition). The OECD citations database (January 2010 edition) was used for the cross-regional citations. A socio-matrix was built for each of the variables, and degree centrality (or in-degree centrality) measures were calculated.

Population data from Eurostat was used to normalize all six measures to the size of the region (see Table 4.1 again).

We are completely aware of the caveats of using patent data in economic analysis. For instance, it is well known that not all inventions are patented, they do not have the same economic impact, and not all patented inventions are commercially exploitable (Griliches, 1991). Additionally, it is known that firms frequently patent for strategic reasons, to build up a patent portfolio to improve their position in negotiations or their technological reputation (Verspagen and Schoenmakers, 2004). Equally, the socio-matrices that were built reflect, to some extent, either the knowledge capacity of regions, the degree of decentralization of knowledge activity in the different national states, or the different industry specializations of

Table 4.1 Description of the variables used for the synthetic indicators

Variable	Description	Sources	Years considered	Weight
VARIABLES USED FOR THE CONSTRUCTION OF THE SYNTHETIC INDICATOR ON INFORMAL LINKAGES				
R&D expenditure per capita in the neighbouring regions	Average value of the millions of euros spent on R&D activities over population in the closest neighbouring regions: $w_{ij} = \exp(-0.01 \cdot d_{ij})$, cut-off 300 km	Compiled by CRENoS using Eurostat, ISTAT and Institut National de la Statistique et des Études Économiques	2006–2007	1/3
Patent activity per capita in the neighbouring regions	Average number of patents released over population in the closest neighbouring regions: $w_{ij} = \exp(-0.01 \cdot d_{ij})$, cut-off 300 km	Compiled by CRENoS using the OECD REGPAT database	2005–2006	1/3
Human capital in the neighbouring regions	Percentage of population aged 15 and over with tertiary education in the closest neighbours: $w_{ij} = \exp(-0.01 \cdot d_{ij})$, cut-off 300 km	Compiled by CRENoS using Eurostat	2005–2007	1/3
VARIABLES USED FOR THE CONSTRUCTION OF THE SYNTHETIC INDICATOR ON FORMAL LINKAGES				
Co-patents per capita	Number of patent co-authored with inventors from outside the region over population	Compiled by AQR using the OECD REGPAT database	2002–2004	1/3
Inflows of inventors per capita	Number of inflows of inventors coming from other regions over population	Compiled by AQR using the OECD REGPAT database	2002–2004	1/3
Cross-regional citations per capita	Number of citations made to patents from other regions over population	Compiled by CRENoS using the OECD REGPAT and citations database	2002–2004	1/3

regions, which in turn determine the regional propensity to apply for patents (pharmaceuticals and biotech firms have an above average patent propensity).[9] Bearing these shortcomings in mind, we still find the empirical analysis worthwhile.

4.5. Results

4.5.1. Descriptive statistics

We built both sub-indicators using the procedure described above, and a composite indicator, as the sum of the two sub-indicators, that is, the informal linkages indicator and the formal linkages indicator. This section provides a descriptive overview of the composite indicator computed, as well as the two sub-indicators. Table 4.2 provides few descriptive measures of the three indicators. As can be seen from that table, the level of inequality of the formal linkages indicators is larger than for the case of its informal linkages counterpart.

Table 4.3 further explores differences between the three indexes by breaking down into different group of regions. The first set of columns computes averages and the second set coefficients of variation. This table reveals few interesting insights. For the three indicators, the EU15 countries show higher average values and more homogeneity (lower dispersion). However, the differences between country groups are more accentuated for the case of the formal linkages indicator than for the case of informal linkages. On their side, regions of the EFTA countries (Iceland, Lichtenstein, Norway and Switzerland) show systematically larger average values of the three indexes.

Table 4.4 summarizes few descriptive figures of our synthetic indicator, broken down by country. Again, Switzerland, Lichtenstein, Germany, Belgium and Denmark, in this precise order, lead the ranking in terms of average values of the indicators.

Table 4.5 shows the top ten and bottom ten regions according to the KNR composite indicator computed. As expected, the top ten ranking is mainly filled by Swiss and German regions, the German region of Freiburg having the largest value for the indicator, followed by two Swiss regions – Zurich and Nordwestschweiz. On the opposite side, those regions from the south and south-east of Europe take most of the positions of the bottom ten ranking – most of them corresponding to isolated or remote territories.

Table 4.2 Descriptive statistics for the synthetic index and sub-indicators

	Obs.	Mean	Std. Dev.	Min.	Max.	Co. var.	Gini	Theil
Sub-indicator informal linkages	287	0.48	0.23	0	0.99	0.48	0.27	0.15
Sub-indicator formal linkages	287	0.38	0.28	0	1.00	0.73	0.42	0.30
Synthetic indicator: KNR	287	0.86	0.47	0	1.87	0.55	0.32	0.17

Note: KNR = knowledge networking regions

Table 4.3 Average values and coefficient of variation for the synthetic index and sub-indicators, by country groups

	Average values				Coefficient of variation			
		Countries				Countries		
	EU average	EU15	EU12	EFTA	EU average	EU15	EU12	EFTA
Sub-indicator informal linkages	0.48	0.52	0.28	0.63	0.48	0.41	0.50	0.52
Sub-indicator formal linkages	0.38	0.44	0.10	0.58	0.73	0.59	1.28	0.49
Synthetic indicator: KNR	0.86	0.96	0.38	1.21	0.55	0.45	0.59	0.46

Table 4.4 Descriptive statistics for KNR synthetic indicator, by country

Country name	Observations	Average	Standard dev.	Min.	Max.
Austria	9	1.17	0.13	1.05	1.50
Belgium	11	1.31	0.21	1.01	1.67
Bulgaria	6	0.29	0.06	0.23	0.35
Switzerland	7	1.64	0.18	1.34	1.84
Cyprus	1	0.08	—	0.08	0.08
Czech Republic	8	0.60	0.10	0.45	0.73
Germany	39	1.42	0.26	0.95	1.87
Denmark	5	1.28	0.32	1.01	1.70
Estonia	1	0.91	—	0.91	0.91
Spain	19	0.51	0.27	0.03	0.91
Finland	5	0.98	0.49	0.36	1.66
France	26	0.82	0.33	0.15	1.50
Greece	13	0.31	0.09	0.12	0.43
Hungary	7	0.42	0.08	0.34	0.52
Ireland	2	0.82	0.24	0.65	0.99
Iceland	1	0.14	—	0.14	0.14
Italy	21	0.70	0.26	0.29	1.25
Liechtenstein	1	1.62	—	1.62	1.62
Lithuania	1	0.23	—	0.23	0.23
Luxembourg	1	1.16	—	1.16	1.16
Latvia	1	0.49	—	0.49	0.49
Malta	1	0.37	—	0.37	0.37
Netherlands	12	1.17	0.20	0.91	1.60
Norway	7	0.87	0.43	0.20	1.48
Poland	16	0.26	0.06	0.17	0.38
Portugal	7	0.29	0.18	0.00	0.47
Romania	8	0.19	0.10	0.07	0.35
Sweden	8	1.14	0.42	0.43	1.72
Slovenia	2	1.09	0.12	1.00	1.18
Slovakia	4	0.44	0.17	0.27	0.67
United Kingdom	37	1.01	0.22	0.53	1.44

The following figures explore the relationship of our main index, the knowledge networking region composite indicator, with several measures of regional socio-economic features, such as local endowments and economic performance. Figures 4.2 and 4.3 look at local knowledge endowments and their relationship with our composite index. Figure 4.2 plot the per capita R&D expenditures of regions against our index. The figure confirms a positive strong relationship between the two variables, which is even more pronounced for the largest values of the index (from 0.75 on).

Figure 4.3 mimics the former analysis, but assessing the role played by regional human capital endowments in enhancing the networking features of regions with out-of-the-region agents. Although the relationship is not as strong as before (lower correlation and R-squared than in Figure 4.2), still there seems to be a positive and fairly marked relationship between human capital at the level of regions and the regions' ability/potential to access external sources of knowledge.

Table 4.5 Knowledge-networking regions – Top and bottom ten regions

Position	Region code	Region name	Country	KNR
		Top regions		
1	DE13	Freiburg	Deutschland	1.87
2	CH04	Zürich	Schweiz/Suisse/Svizzera	1.84
3	CH03	Nordwestschweiz	Schweiz/Suisse/Svizzera	1.84
4	DE14	Tübingen	Deutschland	1.83
5	DE12	Karlsruhe	Deutschland	1.82
6	DE11	Stuttgart	Deutschland	1.78
7	DE71	Darmstadt	Deutschland	1.75
8	DEB3	RheinhessenPfalz	Deutschland	1.74
9	CH06	Zentralschweiz	Schweiz/Suisse/Svizzera	1.73
10	SE12	Östra Mellansverige	Sverige	1.72
		Bottom regions		
278	GR41	Voreio Aigaio	Ellada	0.12
279	PT30	Região Autónoma da Madeira	Portugal	0.12
280	RO22	SudEst	Romania	0.11
281	ES53	Illes Balears	España	0.11
282	RO11	NordVest	Romania	0.10
283	CY00	Cyprus	Kypros / Kibris	0.08
284	RO21	NordEst	Romania	0.07
285	ES64	Ciudad Autónoma de Melilla	España	0.06
286	ES70	Canarias	España	0.03
287	PT20	Região Autónoma dos Açores	Portugal	0.00

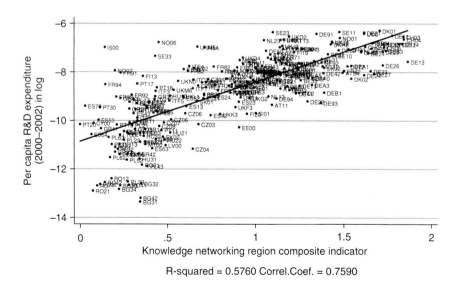

R-squared = 0.5760 Correl.Coef. = 0.7590

Figure 4.2 R&D expenditure and the knowledge networking region composite indicator

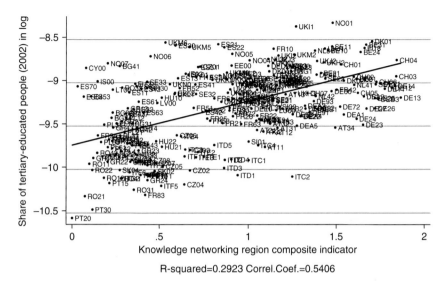

Figure 4.3 Human capital and the knowledge networking region composite indicator

Figure 4.4 clearly shows a strong positive relationship between our composite index and subsequent per capita GDP levels (average 2005–2007). The correlation is, however, stronger for larger levels of our index (larger than 0.5) than for the lower tail of the distribution. From this figure we learn that, all else being equal, highly connected regions tend to show larger levels of GDP. Obviously, we do

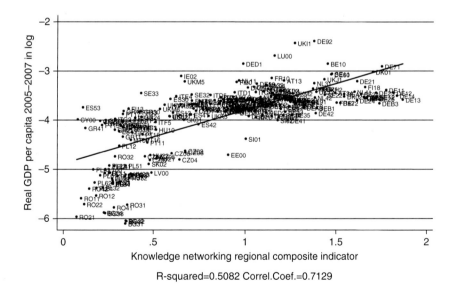

Figure 4.4 GDP level and the knowledge networking regional composite indicator

not claim any causal relationship between the two variables – nor the direction of this causality – as we did not do it for the previous bivariate relationship analysed. However, the strong association between these two variables is notorious and deserves further research.

4.5.2. A typology of European regions

Figure 4.5 shows the scatter plot of the sub-indicators that were computed. Clearly, a strong positive relationship arose, as the correlation coefficient is 0.73. Note that the majority of the regions were either *non-interactive* (113) or knowledge networking regions (118). Meanwhile, only 41 regions were clustering regions, and 15 were globalizing regions. Clearly, there seems to be a relationship between both sub-indices. We believe that this relationship is not accidental. The question of whether or not there is a causal relationship between the two sub-indices or the direction of this causality is interesting but goes beyond the scope of the present analysis.

In Map 4.1 we depict the spatial distribution of the four categories of regions considered. A short description of each type of region is given below, based on Figures 4.1 and 4.5.

Clustering regions. We obtained that 41 regions out of 287 can be labelled as clustering regions. These are regions that are located in relatively close proximity to other highly innovative regions (in terms of R&D, patents and human capital) and therefore can potentially receive informal knowledge flows governed by

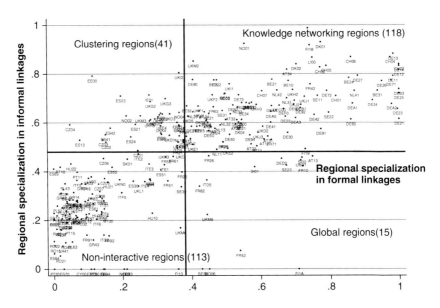

Figure 4.5 A scatter plot of regions according to the intensity of formal and informal linkages

physical distance. However, and more importantly, these regions lack a critical number of formal, intentional knowledge linkages with external sources of knowledge. Amongst them, we identified regions in the centre of Spain and the north of Italy, some French regions close to Paris and Germany, some regions in the north and west of England, part of Ireland, and the regions of Southern Norway. To sum up, the clustering regions seem to belong to the EU15 and are close to core regions that are both informally and formally specialized. Broadly speaking, they are low-to-medium technologically advanced regions that, by happy chance, are located physically near to knowledge poles and are therefore dragged into innovative activities by their innovative neighbours.

Globalizing regions. We computed that 15 regions out of 287 were labelled as globalizing regions. These regions are well connected by formal linkages to external areas, in spite of being relatively physically isolated from other innovative regions. Broadly speaking, these regions tend to perform notably better than clustering regions in terms of knowledge creation. The list includes one German region (Dresden), four French regions (Île de France, Bourgogne, Provence-Alpes-Côte d'Azur and Bretagne), two British regions (East Anglia and North Eastern Scotland), Emilia Romana in Italy, Trondelag in Norway, Wien in Austria, Pohjois Suomi in Finland, 2 Swedish regions (Vaestsverige and Örve Norrland) and two Slovenian regions (Zahodna Slovenija and Vzhodna Slovenija). Two of these 15 regions contain important capital cities, e.g. Paris and Wien. This kind of region acts more intensely as a regional knowledge hub, since it is connected to external knowledge sources by means of formal relations, and enables actors in nearby regions to access knowledge by means of a contagious process of informal interactions. This is particularly true for the two aforementioned capitals.

Non-interactive regions. We obtained that 113 regions out of 287 were non-interactive regions. These regions, which lack potential access to external knowledge by means of formal and informal linkages, are mainly those belonging to the new entrant countries and some specific regions in southern European countries (all of Portugal and Greece, most of Spain except the central area and the south of Italy).

Knowledge networking regions. Networking regions are concentrated in the centre of Europe as well as in the Scandinavian countries. These regions are physically located close to high-performing regions, so they are potentially in an advantageous position to benefit from informal knowledge-diffusion mechanisms. However, they also act as knowledge hubs that are formally connected to external knowledge pools. As we can see, this sub-sample consists of 118 regions out of 287, which are mostly located in Germany, the Netherlands, Belgium, Denmark, Southern Sweden, Southern Finland, Switzerland, Northern Italy, South East England and part of France. Therefore, apart from three Northern Italian regions, no other region in southern or eastern Europe appears on the list. This supports a clear core–periphery pattern in the geographical distribution of the regions that in one way or another rely on external sources of knowledge. Therefore, broadly speaking, knowledge networking regions are those that are better positioned to benefit more from spatial knowledge diffusion, through different regimes and at different spatial scales, and from the construction of the European Research Area.

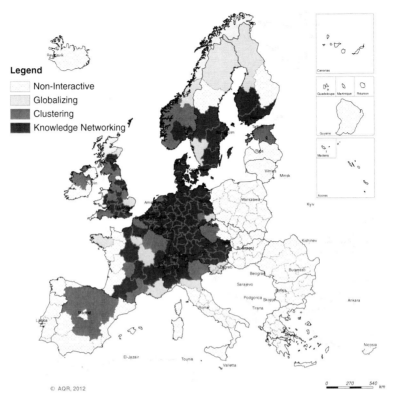

Map 4.1 Knowledge networking regions

4.6. Concluding remarks and policy implications

In the previous sections, we described a detailed method to construct a composite indicator and two sub-indices that examine the ways in which actors in regions may access external-to-the-region pools of different and complementary knowledge. In motivating our approach, we extensively surveyed an instrumental list of theoretical and empirical studies across different disciplines and sub-disciplines. These studies have more or less dealt with the mechanisms through which knowledge diffuses, especially across space and between different locations. Based on our method, we also provided a typology of regions that captures their diversity in terms of their degree of openness to external sources of knowledge. Finally, the NUTS2 regions of 31 European countries were used to apply our novel approach and derive preliminary conclusions and policy implications from the results.

In spite of increasing evidence of the role of knowledge diffusion across different geographical areas and the importance of this phenomenon for regional knowledge creation, our review showed that mainstream research and policymakers barely consider this issue when they assess the innovative performance of cities, regions or countries. We believe that connections to external sources of knowledge are as important for regions as their scientific and technological base, and policies that specifically focus on this issue might be required. For years, regional policy programmes have aimed to strengthen the local cluster knowledge base and its social preconditions for further knowledge creation (Rodríguez-Pose and Crescenzi, 2008). Here, we call into question this narrow approach and propose that the external dimension of regions is also relevant. Since this dimension has been quietly overlooked so far, policymakers lack a critical pillar for the development of regional innovation systems. As stressed in Bathelt et al. (2004), the 'local buzz' basically takes care of itself, whilst external linkages specifically require institutional and infrastructure support. The present inquiry was an attempt to open up a future research agenda within the literature to improve our understanding of the external dimension of regional innovation systems and consequently develop a battery of policies on this issue.

Next, our empirical approach provided a typology of four distinct types of regions according to their degree of openness to external sources of knowledge, as well as their specialization in the different ways in which actors in these regions may access external knowledge, that is, formal and informal linkages. This diversity of regions suggests that specific policies should be applied to each type of region, not only according to their innovative performance and social preconditions, but also according to the ways in which they connect with outsiders. This typology also translates into a ranking, which could serve as a guideline for regions to identify other areas with similar development conditions that have achieved a better rank and whose best practices could serve as a benchmark for implementing similar policies elsewhere.

Finally, our study also provides elements that could help firms' localization policies. As stressed in Gertler and Levitte (2005), firms' location decisions are influenced by the endogenous characteristics of regions and by opportunities to benefit from linkages worldwide, through which they can access manifold knowledge pools.

Notes

1 Part of this work was carried out while Ernest Miguélez was visiting the Rotman School of Management at the University of Toronto (Toronto, Canada). The use of the School's facilities is gratefully acknowledged. Roberta Capello and Camilla Lenzi provided insights on earlier versions of this chapter, which were of great help. Some of the data used in this chapter were compiled by CRENoS and by Politecnico di Milano. We also acknowledge financial support from the Ministerio de Ciencia e Innovación (Ernest Miguelez and Rosina Moreno, grant number ECO2011-30260-C03-03; Jordi Suriñach grant number ECO-12678) and the EU ESPON 2013 applied project KIT Knowledge, Innovation, Territory. The usual disclaimers apply.
2 Please note that in their model they allow the scope of the 'local buzz' to go beyond the limits of the administrative region into neighbouring regions that might totally or partially belong to this same 'buzz'. In contrast, 'pipelines' are established with actors located at a distance. Moreover, whereas information inflows within the 'local buzz' do not require a major effort as they are more or less automatically received, the construction

of 'pipelines' requires a conscious, intentional commitment to identify potential partners and build formal relations.

3 For further criticisms on the Regional Innovation Scoreboard, see Chapter 7.

4 These estimations imply that spillovers are very likely to cross administrative borders, even at the level of NUTS2 regions and in countries in which this aggregation level translates into large regions, such as Spain.

5 Yet, the ability of actors within regions to absorb, understand and take advantage of incoming spillovers might also be dependent on their absorptive capacity (Cohen and Levinthal, 1990).

6 Other distance decays have been tried, such as 0.02, 0.03, 0.04, 0.05, 0.06, 0.07, 0.08, 0.09, and 0.10.

7 Note that a single ID for each inventor and anyone else involved is missing. Hence, to compile the mobility history of inventors, we need to identify them individually by name and surname, as well as via other useful information contained in the patent document. Data cleaning and parsing, name matching, and name disambiguation are the different stages undertaken to single out who is who in these patents; see Miguélez and Gómez-Miguélez (2011).

8 To determine the maximum and minimum scores in the normalization process, we exclude outliers. Positive outliers are identified as values that are higher than the average plus two times the standard deviation. Negative outliers are identified as values that are lower than the average minus two times the standard deviation.

9 See Ter Wall and Boschma (2009) for a discussion of additional shortcomings of using patents in regional analysis, and Lenzi's (2010) awareness of the use of inventors' mobility identified through patents.

5 The knowledge–innovation nexus in European regions

Roberta Capello and Camilla Lenzi

5.1. Introduction

The previous chapters have provided a description of the diffusion of the knowledge-based economy in Europe according to three different approaches: an industrial approach (Chapter 2), a functional approach (Chapter 3) and a relational approach (Chapter 4). As discussed in Chapter 1, in fact, the knowledge-based economy does not have a single definition and can assume different forms that sometimes complement and sometimes substitute each other. In particular, the knowledge-based economy has been measured through either the presence of high-tech manufacturing and service sectors, or through the presence of scientific activities (human capital and research activities), or through the capacity of a region to cooperate – intentionally or unintentionally – with other regions. Accordingly, three typologies of *knowledge-based regions* have been empirically identified: technologically-advanced regions, scientific regions, and knowledge networking regions.

This chapter adds to previous ones by considering the ability of regions to transform knowledge and inventions into innovation and to become innovation-driven economies. To measure the penetration of the innovation-driven economy across European regions, several indicators of different types of innovations are considered here. To the best of our knowledge, this is the first time that innovation spatial trends have been described at such a fine regional disaggregation for the entire European territory and by taking such a large variety of innovation types into account. To date, similar exercises have been prevented mostly, but not exclusively, by the paucity and/or low quality of available innovation data. In this regard, this chapter takes a step forward by presenting original data on innovation spatial patterns for 262 NUTS2 regions of the 27 EU member states.

In our opinion, the distinction between knowledge and innovation is an advancement not only from the empirical and methodological points of view but also from the conceptual one. In fact, this distinction directly questions the widely adopted knowledge–innovation equivalence that interprets knowledge and innovation as necessarily overlapping processes at the spatial level; a conceptual ambiguity which is clearly manifest in the widespread use of knowledge indicators such as R&D or patent intensity as proxies for innovation outputs.

However, knowledge and innovation are not necessarily overlapping processes; nor are they necessarily sequential at the local level. They can mix in space in a variety of ways: the geography of knowledge and the geography of innovation may or may not match according to the availability at the local level of specific enabling mechanisms that allow the translation of new knowledge into commercially viable innovations. In our opinion, this is for two main reasons. Firstly, factors that enhance the creation and implementation of new knowledge can be quite different from the factors which stimulate innovation, and regions may exhibit larger endowments of either the former or the latter. Secondly, locally created knowledge does not automatically or necessarily turn into local innovation; or, conversely, local innovation does not inevitably arise from locally produced knowledge – as also indicated in Chapter 1. More generally, there may be regions with weak internal knowledge creation capacity but which are able to leverage upon external knowledge sources and to develop innovation. In short, regions can exhibit different advantages and specializations in different phases of the innovation process.

Overall, this suggests that the knowledge–innovation nexus is far from straightforward at the regional level. The availability of indicators measuring both knowledge and innovation separately allows deeper exploration of the complex pathways from knowledge to innovation across space, and this is precisely the ultimate goal of this chapter.

To achieve this goal, the chapter is organized as follows. Section 5.2 offers a broad and inclusive description of knowledge-based regions in Europe according to all definitions and dimensions considered in the previous chapters and their possible combinations. Section 5.3 presents regional innovation data collection and elaboration while Section 5.4 describes innovation spatial trends for a large variety of innovation indicators. Section 5.5 addresses the knowledge–innovation nexus and shows that the geography of knowledge and the geography of innovation do not necessarily match. This important and counter-intuitive result holds regardless of the adopted definition of knowledge-based economy and the knowledge dimensions considered. Lastly, Section 5.6 offers some concluding remarks and raises the research questions stemming from these empirical findings that are addressed in the next chapters.

5.2. The penetration of the knowledge-based economy across European regions

The empirical results presented in the previous chapters have described different diffusion patterns of the knowledge economy, according to the different definitions used. The definitions of the sector and functional approaches provide a more selective geographical pattern of the knowledge economy than does the relation approach.

The sectoral approach indicates that the geography of high-tech sectors in Europe is indeed highly concentrated, although some peripheral regions and regions with capital cities in New Member Countries do play a major role. The productive fabric of Europe shows a remarkable concentration of technology, related either to advanced manufacturing or services activities or to both. However, while specialization in manufacturing high-tech seems to be much more diffused in the European space, specialization in knowledge-intensive service industries displays impressive concentration rates (Chapter 2).

Similarly, all research activity indicators used for defining scientific regions constantly record a remarkable degree of spatial concentration, and the largest category of regions has no specialisation in research and knowledge activities. In fact, a very small number of regions in Europe (i.e. 30 regions) is able to achieve 3% of R&D expenditures on GDP, with only two regions able to achieve and overcome this threshold in the period 2000–2007 (namely, the Dutch Noord-Brabant and North Eastern Scotland in the UK) and a few regions losing this status (namely, the French Île de France, the Dutch Flevoland, the Germans Köln and Münster) (Maps 5.1–5.3). On the other hand, the share of R&D expenditures on GDP is lower than 1% in most regions (the two first classes in Maps 5.1–5.3), although

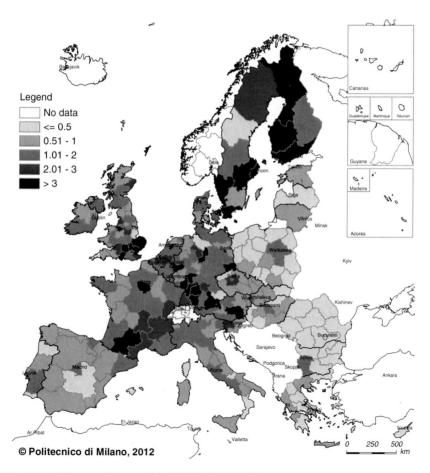

Map 5.1 R&D expenditures as % of GDP (2000–2002)

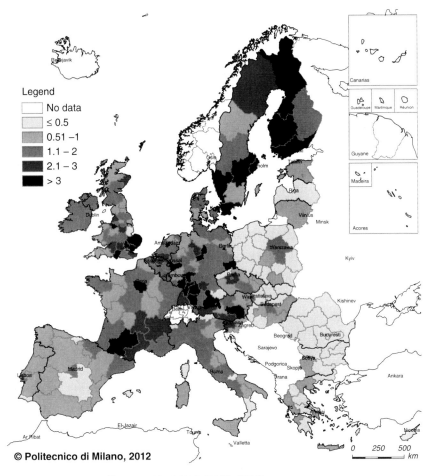

Map 5.2 R&D expenditures as % of GDP (2002–2004)

the situation seems to improve slightly over time (respectively, 130 regions out of 262 in the period 2000–2002, 127 regions out of 262 in the period 2002–2004, and 114 regions out of 262 in the period 2006–2007).

This evidence once again testifies that the smart growth called for by the Europe 2020 Agenda, with the achievement of 3% of the EU's GDP invested in (public and private) R&D/innovation is still an ambitious aim.

Differently, a relatively high number of regions belong to the category of *knowledge networking regions* (113), a much larger group than TAR and scientific regions. This finding is rather important and indicates that external sources of knowledge, in the form of spatial spillovers or intentional knowledge exchanges, constitute a common channel for local knowledge accumulation, even more common than the internal production of knowledge.

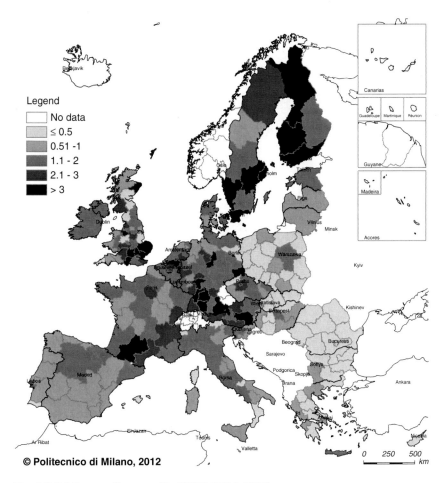

Map 5.3 R&D expenditures as % of GDP (2006–2007)

As discussed above, these different definitions of the knowledge-based economy can complement, overlap or, rather, substitute each other. Accordingly, Map 5.4 furnishes a broad and inclusive description of knowledge-based regions in Europe by presenting an integrated picture encompassing all definitions considered in the previous chapters and their possible combinations.

The picture appears very fragmented, with a substantial number of regions being only networking ones, and mainly located in the central part of Europe. Only three technologically advanced regions host scientific functions (Dresden, Vestlandet and Bratislava), while most of the technologically advanced islands are both scientific and networking regions. In general, scientific regions are also networking regions, which testifies that knowledge accumulation within a region also requires networking activity for the acquisition of external knowledge.

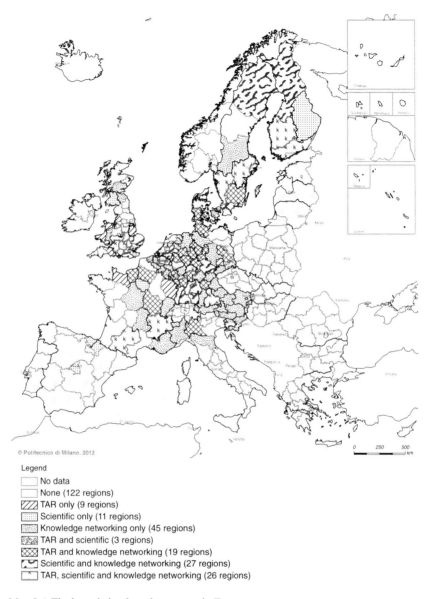

Legend

- No data
- None (122 regions)
- TAR only (9 regions)
- Scientific only (11 regions)
- Knowledge networking only (45 regions)
- TAR and scientific (3 regions)
- TAR and knowledge networking (19 regions)
- Scientific and knowledge networking (27 regions)
- TAR, scientific and knowledge networking (26 regions)

Map 5.4 The knowledge-based economy in Europe

Impressively, a very large number of European regions, mainly in Eastern countries and in the southern peripheral countries, are below the EU average for any process of high-tech specialisation, knowledge creation, and knowledge acquisition. Therefore, regardless of the definition of knowledge-based economy adopted, the knowledge economy in Europe seems to be still in its infancy. The knowledge production fabric in Europe is highly selective, whereas the largest majority of European regions cannot be classified as knowledge-based according to any of the definitions proposed.

Interestingly, Table 5.1 shows that metropolitan settings seem to favour the development of the knowledge-based economy, since most of the knowledge-based regions (regardless of their definition) are located in agglomerated areas.[1] This confirms that cities are loci conducive to knowledge creation and, more generally, creative activities (Carlino et al., 2007) – as suggested by the incubator hypothesis (Leone and Struyk, 1976) and its recent refinements (Duranton and Puga, 2001). In fact, the share of agglomerated knowledge-based regions (38.5%, Table 5.1) is greater than the share of agglomerated regions at the EU level (26.7%, Table 5.1).

The disproportionate concentration of knowledge-based regions in EU15 countries (89.2%, Table 5.1) and competitive regions (79.2%, Table 5.1) detected in the previous chapters is further confirmed; and this holds regardless of the definition of knowledge-based economy adopted (Table 5.1).[2] Overall, therefore, the knowledge-based economy appears highly concentrated and selective in spatial terms. The unbalanced development of the knowledge-based economy across the European space raises concerns and, possibly, warnings on the political terrain and interesting questions on the scientific one.

In the normative domain, these results pose a challenge concerning the future steps and policy actions needed to make Europe and its regions grow smartly and become increasingly competitive in international markets, as proposed by the Lisbon Agenda in 2000 and relaunched by the Europe 2020 policy strategy. Importantly, this questions the opportunity, applicability and validity of 'one-size-fits-all' research and innovation policy aims and tools for all regions.

On scientific terrain, the marginally differentiated employment and GDP growth patterns in knowledge-based versus non-knowledge-based regions (Table 5.1) question the idea that locally created knowledge per se can justify local innovative and economic performance and that knowledge is the main discriminating element in economic and social performance. In fact, as Table 5.1 shows, knowledge-based regions do not seem to enjoy sizeable employment and GDP growth advantages (3.2% and 3.4% respectively) with respect to non-knowledge-based regions (4.3% and 3.8% respectively); indeed, ANOVA tests implemented on the two variables employment growth (2005–2007) and GDP growth (2005–2007) do not reveal any statistically significant difference across the eight different groups of knowledge-based regions.[3]

To open the 'black box' of the complex knowledge–innovation–performance nexus, we proceed gradually. We start by exploring regions' ability to transform knowledge and inventions into innovation and to become innovation-driven economies, and by addressing the articulated knowledge and innovation relationship and its territorial roots. The next sections of this chapter are dedicated to this purpose.

Table 5.1 Share of knowledge-based vs. non knowledge-based regions by settlement structure, typology and average employment and GDP growth rates 2005–2007

	Number of regions	Agglomerated	EU15	EU12	Convergence	Transition	Competitive	Employment growth (2005–2007)	GDP growth (2005–2007)
Non-knowledge-based regions	122	18.8	66.3	33.6	49.1	11.4	39.3	4.3	3.8
Knowledge-based regions of which:	140	38.5	89.2	10.8	13.	7.8	79.2	3.2	3.4
Only TAR	9	44.4	88.8	11.1	11.1	11.1	77.7	2.9	3.2
Only SCIENTIFIC	11	45.4	81.8	18.1	9.0	9.0	81.8	2.7	3.3
Only NETWORKING	45	20.0	88.8	11.1	15.5	8.8	77.7	3.1	3.4
TAR and SCIENTIFIC	3	33.3	100.0	0.0	33.3	0.0	66.6	4.7	3.3
TAR and NETWORK.	19	36.8	94.7	5.2	5.2	10.5	84.2	4.1	3.0
SCIENTIFIC and NET.	27	44.4	88.8	11.1	18.5	3.7	77.7	3.5	3.9
TAR, SCIEN. And NET.	26	61.5	88.4	11.5	11.5	7.6	80.7	2.6	3.5
TAR	57	45.6	96.4	3.5	5.2	3.5	91.2	2.9	2.9
Non-TAR	205	24.8	73.6	26.3	37.0	11.2	52.2	3.9	3.8
SCIENTIFIC	62	58.0	95.1	4.8	4.8	1.6	93.5	3.5	3.5
Non-SCIENTIFIC	200	20.5	73.5	26.5	38.0	12.0	50.5	3.8	3.6
NETWORKING	113	38.0	98.2	1.7	4.4	5.3	91.1	3.3	3.2
Non-NETWORKING	149	22.8	63.7	36.2	49.6	12.7	37.5	4.0	3.9
EU	262	26.7	78.6	21.3	30.1	9.5	60.3	3.7	3.6

5.3. Assessment of the innovative performances of European regions: data availability and measurement issues

5.3.1. Data availability and the Community Innovation Survey

The fundamental importance of innovation in contemporary economies is not generally matched by the quality of data and/or their widespread diffusion. The Community Innovation Survey (henceforth, CIS) is one of the best attempts to measure technological and non-technological innovative activities, although it still presents problems that are not negligible, especially for spatial analyses.[4] CIS is structured as a micro-survey, and it is designed to obtain information on innovation activities within enterprises with ten or more employees, as well as various aspects of the innovation process, such as the effects of innovation, the sources of information used, the costs and the obstacles to innovation, and other relevant topics.

Data are collected on a regular basis and six waves have so far been implemented; the first one was carried out in 1992, the last one made available is the 2008 wave. The first CIS (CIS1) was a pilot exercise conducted in 1993, while the second survey (CIS2) was carried out in 1997/1998, except in Greece and Ireland, where it was launched in 1999. The third survey (CIS3) was implemented in 2000/2001 in most of the participating countries. The CIS4 was launched in 2005, based on the reference period 2004, with the observation period 2002 to 2004. The fifth survey, CIS 2006, was launched in 2007, based on the reference period 2006, with the observation period 2004 to 2006. The last survey, CIS 2008, was launched in 2009, based on the reference period 2008, with the observation period 2006 to 2008.

CIS covers EU Member States, EU Candidate Countries, Iceland and Norway. Country coverage, however, differs among the different waves. CIS3 was run in the 25 EU Member States, Candidate Countries, Iceland and Norway. CIS4 was run in the 27 EU Member States, Candidate Countries, Iceland and Norway. CIS2006 and CIS2008 were run in the 27 EU Member States, Candidate Countries, and Norway. However, participating countries are free not to release some information, which may thus appear as confidential in the Eurostat database and may therefore not be available (e.g. some UK and Iceland data for CIS4).

Eurostat, in fact, reports that the confidentiality of CIS data is flagged by Member States. In order to ensure comparability across countries, Eurostat, in close cooperation with the EU Member States, has developed a standard core questionnaire starting with CIS3 data collection, with an accompanying set of definitions and methodological recommendations. Responsibility for the survey at the national level lies, in most cases, with the National Statistical Office or a national Ministry. Eurostat collects aggregated data and micro-data from participating countries.

However, problems of comparability across waves represent a rather awkward issue. Different waves may, in fact, have different sectoral coverage. For example, CIS3 has a sectoral coverage different from that of CIS4 and of CIS2006. Moreover, CIS2008 uses the NACE Rev.2 classification of economic activities,

whereas previous waves were based on the NACE Rev.1.1 classification of economic activities. This limits the scope of comparisons across waves to comparison
between CIS4 and CIS2006.

The enterprises surveyed are classified by type of innovation activity according to the following definitions. Innovation is defined as a new or significantly
improved product (good or service) introduced into the market or the introduction
within an enterprise of a new or significantly improved process. Innovations are
based on the results of new technological developments, new combinations of
existing technology, or the utilization of other knowledge acquired by the enterprise. Innovations may be developed by the innovating enterprise or by another
enterprise. However, pure selling innovations wholly produced and developed by
other enterprises are not included as innovation activities. Innovations should be
new to the enterprise concerned. In the case of product innovations, these do not
necessarily have to be new to the market; and in the case of process innovations,
the enterprise does not necessarily have to be the first one to have introduced the
process.

Product innovations are defined as new or significantly improved goods and/or
services with respect to their fundamental characteristics, technical specifications,
incorporated software or other non-material components, intended uses, or user-
friendliness. Changes of a solely aesthetic nature and the pure sale of product innovations wholly produced and developed by other enterprises are not included.

Process innovations are defined as new or significantly improved production
technologies or new or significantly improved methods of supplying services and
delivering products. The outcome of such innovations should be significant with
respect to the level of output, quality of products (goods or services) or costs of
production and distribution. Purely organizational or managerial changes are not
included.

In more detail, Eurostat makes available the data on firms that introduce only
product innovations, firms that introduce only process innovations, and firms that
introduce both product and process innovations. This sharper distinction is in our
option better suited to capturing the different sets of functions and capabilities
necessary to complete these different types of innovation and introduce them into
the market.

It is important to clarify that a subsample of product innovators consists of
'only product innovators', i.e. those that introduce product innovations without
introducing process innovations. Likewise, a subsample of process innovators
consists of 'only process innovators', i.e. those that introduce process innovations
without introducing product innovations. Table 5.2 clarifies this distinction. The
third category is composed of innovators that introduce both product and process
innovations. The three categories together represent the largest group of innovators: those that introduce product and/or process innovations.[5]

The last category of innovators consists of those firms that introduce marketing
and/or organizational (i.e. non-technological) innovations into one of their markets. The purpose of this category is to better capture innovation processes in services. Marketing innovation is defined as the introduction of 'Significant changes

to the design or packaging of a good or service' or 'New or significantly changed sales or distribution methods, such as internet sales, franchising, direct sales or distribution licenses'. An organisational innovation is defined as the introduction of either 'New or significantly improved knowledge management systems to better use or exchange information, knowledge and skills within your enterprise', 'A major change to the organisation of work within your enterprise, such as changes in the management structure or integrating different departments or activities' or 'New or significant changes in your relations with other firms or public institutions, such as through alliances, partnerships, outsourcing or sub-contracting'.

Unfortunately, Eurostat provides data at NUTS0 level only (and only for those participating countries allowing data release) and there are limited official sources of CIS data at the regional level (NUTS2 or NUTS1). The main reason for this is that CIS data are unequally stratified across space. Since in some EU countries data are not stratified at NUTS2 level, such spatial detail is not publicly made available. Moreover, firm micro-data are made anonymous and geo-referentiation is not released for confidentiality reasons. However, regional data may be issued by some National Statistical Offices. This is the case of Italy, Romania, Czech Republic, and the UK.

Unfortunately, information from these sources is not consistent and directly comparable. In fact, the types of innovation covered may differ and the weighting procedures are not necessarily harmonized or are still awaiting approval by Eurostat. For instance, the UK provides information on product innovators and process innovators whereas Italy only provides information on 'only product innovators' and 'only process innovations'. This seriously hampers the use of these data in a comparative perspective. Regional data are also available from the Annex to the Methodology Report of the Regional Innovation Scoreboard (RIS) but only for the largest category of technological innovators, i.e. product and/or process innovators, and for a selected group of countries.

Table 5.3 lists European countries participating in CIS4 according to the NUTS level of data availability, as reported in RIS Methodology Report (2009)

Table 5.2 Definition of product innovation and process innovation in the CIS survey

		Product innovation	
		Yes	*No*
Process innovation	Yes	Product and process innovation	Only process innovation
	No	Only product innovation	—

Table 5.3 Geographical coverage of CIS4 by European countries

Geographical coverage	*European countries*
NUTS0	DE, DK, IE, NL, SE
NUTS1	AT, BE, BG, FR, UK
NUTS2	CY, CZ, EE, ES, FI, HU, GR, IT, LT, LU, LV, MT, NO, PL, PT, RO, SI, SK

(Hollanders et al., 2009b). The NUTS level of data availability also indicates the regional level used for stratification of the sample to which the questionnaire was administered. As mentioned above, this information confirms that CIS data are not representative at the same regional level in all countries.

5.3.2. *NUTS2 data estimation methodology*

The lack of innovation data at the regional level has been a rather severe limitation preventing analyses on the diffusion of innovation activities across space and their economic impact. The analysis reported in what follows sought to fill this gap by developing a robust methodology with which to estimate regional (i.e. NUTS2) CIS data.

Regional data (i.e. NUTS2 level) were estimated starting from the national data (i.e. NUTS0 level) available from Eurostat in order to ensure comparability across countries. To this end, weights were applied to redistribute the NUTS0 data of the CIS4 wave at NUTS2 level. Application of the exercise to previous waves was not feasible because the CIS1-CIS3 waves were based on a different industrial stratification which impeded possible comparison with next waves. The use of later waves was not useful; reasonable time lags between the innovation variables and the pre-crisis economic performance data (e.g. GDP growth until 2007) were necessary and precluded the use of more recent waves (like the CIS2006, which covers the 2004–2006 period).

The methodology applied followed two steps. Firstly, the regional respondents sample was estimated by redistributing the NUTS0 value according to the regional employment share. Secondly, the regional sample of only product innovators, only process innovators, product and process innovators, and marketing and/or organizational innovators was estimated using different weights according to the different types of innovations. All weights were computed as regional shares of national values of the selected variables. The weights were intended to capture both a functional and an industrial dimension linked to innovation. As in the case of knowledge creation (Chapters 2 and 3), also innovation activities may depend on an industrial as well as a functional specialization of the region. One way to consider the two dimensions was to look at the share of occupations as regards the functions, and at the industrial specialization as regards the sectors. In the absence of any a priori assumption on the differing relevance of the functional vs the industrial dimension, equal importance was attributed to the selected weights, as presented in Table 5.4.

The choice of the weights was based on logical expectations. Product innovation was expected to occur to a greater extent in regions with larger endowments of advanced high-tech sectors, such as electrical and electronic equipment manufacturing (share of employment in the sector DL according to Nace Rev.1.1 classification), and advanced functions such as R&D (i.e. share of scientists) (Table 5.4). The definition used for high-tech sectors was restricted to advanced manufacturing sectors, since these sectors were expected to generate product innovation more intensively. Sectors that can deploy product innovation were not included.

Table 5.4 Selected weights for the estimation of the different types of innovation at NUTS2 level

Type of innovation	Weights
Only product	*Functional dimension* % of science and engineering occupations (1999–2001 average value; ISCO 2-digit code 21) *Industrial dimension* % employment in high-tech (NACE Rev1.1 2-digit sector DL, 2002)
Only process	*Functional dimension* % share of science and engineering associate professionals (1999–2001 average value; ISCO 2-digit codes 31), and % of administrative and of commercial managers and production and specialised services managers (1999–2001 average value; ISCO 2-digit codes 12 and 13, respectively) *Industrial dimension* % employment in manufacturing (NACE Rev1.1 1-digit sectors C-D-E; 1999–2002 average value)
Product and process	*Functional dimension* % science and engineering occupations, % of science and engineering associate professionals, % of administrative and of commercial managers and production and specialised services managers *Industrial dimension* % employment in high-tech, % employment in manufacturing
Marketing and/or organizational	*Functional dimension* % of administrative and of commercial managers and production and specialised services managers (1999–2001 average value; ISCO 12 and 13) *Industrial dimension* % employment in private services (NACE Rev1.1 1-digit sectors G-J-K-I 2000–2002 average value)

Process innovation was expected to take place to a greater extent in regions with larger endowments of manufacturing sectors in which new production technologies or methods for producing goods could be introduced (share of employment in manufacturing) and a larger share of functions closely involved in production process implementation and monitoring (i.e. share of technicians and managers) (Table 5.4).

Product and process innovation was expected to occur to a greater extent in regions characterised by both a larger endowment of advanced high-tech sectors, such as electrical and electronic equipment manufacturing (share of employment in the sector DL according to Nace Rev.1.1 classification), and advanced functions such as R&D (i.e. share of scientists) as well as a larger endowment of manufacturing sectors in which new production technologies or methods for producing goods could be introduced (share of employment in manufacturing) and a larger share of functions closely involved in production process implementation and monitoring (i.e. share of technicians and managers) (Table 5.4).

Marketing and/or managerial innovation was expected to occur to a greater extent in regions with larger endowments of the service sector (share of employment in private services), and a larger share of managerial functions (i.e. share of managers) (Table 5.4).

To check the robustness and consistency of our estimates, a series of benchmark exercises were implemented. In detail, three types of tests were conducted: on the equality of means, on the equality of standard deviation, and of Kolmogorof-Smirnoff, to assess whether our estimates diverged from the original sample distribution.

Two sets of comparisons were performed. Firstly, our estimates were compared to the share of only product innovators, the share of only process innovators, and the share of product and process innovators with regional data from National Statistical Offices. These latter were rescaled at the national value available from Eurostat, since the national figures available from Eurostat and National Statistical Offices could differ according to different strata weighting procedures. The tests could be implemented only on a limited set of countries, namely Italy, Romania and the Czech Republic, which publicly release these data on their National Statistical Offices' websites.

Secondly, to support our estimates further, we used data on product and/or process innovators from RIS. In particular, we compared our estimates of product and/or process innovators, obtained as the sum of the first three categories of innovators (i.e. only product innovators, only process innovators, product and process innovators), with RIS data. The tests could be implemented only on those countries whose data are available in the annex to the RIS methodology report.

Nevertheless, some problems of comparability remained. For example, the France NUTS0 data available from RIS on the share of product and/or process innovators are different from the France NUTS0 data available from Eurostat (in particular, the former is smaller than the latter), which may have affected the mean value of our estimates. As regards marketing and/or organizational innovation, the standardized benchmark values available from RIS 2009 report were used. The tests could be implemented only on those countries whose data are available in the annex to the RIS methodology report.

Table 5.5 summarizes the results of these tests. Overall, they indicate that our estimates do not statistically differ in their mean, standard deviation and distribution from the official data released either by National Statistical Offices or by RIS. Although for some countries, the tests indicate that either the mean or the standard deviation can be statistically different, the output of the Kolmogorov-Smirnoff test lends support to our estimates and indicates that the distribution of the original sample does not statistically differ from that of our estimates. Moreover, our estimation methodology made it possible to mitigate the above-mentioned problem of CIS sample non-representativeness at the regional level for two main reasons. Firstly, our estimates were derived from national level data. Because the weights used to estimate CIS data at NUTS2 level are representative at the regional level, this can lessen the representativeness issue. Secondly, they were highly consistent with regional level data for countries in which the sample is stratified at both

Table 5.5 Consistency tests of NUTS2 innovation data estimates

Country	Type of innovation	Mean estimates	Mean benchmark estimates	Mean difference	Std. Dev. Difference	Kolmogorov-Smirnoff test (different distribution)
	Product only					
IT*		4.41	4.53	N.S.	N.S.	Not significant; p-value equals 0.94.
RO*		1.95	1.69	N.S.	> ; p<0.05	
	Process only					
IT*		14.27	14.00	N.S.	N.S.	Not significant; p-value equals 0.95.
RO*		4.72	4.82	N.S.	> ; p<0.01	
	Product and process					
CZ*		14.48	14.38	N.S.	< ; p<0.05	Not significant; p-value equals 0.98.
IT*		8.90	9.01	N.S.	N.S.	
RO*		13.87	13.15	N.S.	< ; p< 0.01	
	Product and/or process					
AT[§]		49.03	50.03	N.S.	N.S.	Not significant; p-value equals 0.98.
BE[§]		42.37	46.61	N.S.	N.S.	
BG[§]		15.03	15.21	N.S.	N.S.	
CZ[§]		37.03	36.05	N.S.	N.S.	
ES[§]		29.97	29.06	N.S.	> ; p<0.01	
FI[§]		34.45	34.52	N.S.	N.S.	
FR[§]		27.55	24.37	N.S.	> ; p<0.01	
IT[§]		31.77	32.21	N.S.	N.S.	
PL[§]		23.07	22.56	N.S.	N.S.	

Table 5.5 Continued

Country	Mean estimates	Mean benchmark estimates	Mean difference	Std. Dev. Difference	Kolmogorov-Smirnoff test (different distribution)
Type of innovation					
PT§	39.40	38.95	N.S.	N.S.	
RO§	20.18	17.74	N.S.	N.S.	
SI§	34.11	23.85	>;p<0.05	N.S.	
SK§	22.43	20.01	N.S.	N.S.	
IT*	31.77	27.59	N.S.	N.S.	
RO*	20.18	20.54	N.S.	N.S.	
Marketing and organizational					
AT§	80.52	80.52	N.S.	N.S.	Not significant; p-value equals 0.51.
BE§	80.33	70.36	N.S.	N.S.	
BG§	0.76	0.94	N.S.	N.S.	
CZ§	54.83	54.23	N.S.	N.S.	
ES§	35.72	32.53	>;p<0.05	N.S.	
FI§	69.13	72.81	N.S.	N.S.	
FR§	55.78	56.04	N.S.	>;p<0.05	
IT§	49.12	51.39	N.S.	N.S.	
PL§	26.88	27.43	N.S.	N.S.	
PT§	64.49	67.43	N.S.	N.S.	
RO§	33.71	32.10	N.S.	N.S.	
SI§	54.35	54.28	N.S.	N.S.	
SK§	19.65	18.15	>;p<0.05	>;p<0.05	

Source: Capello et al. (2012)

Note: N.S. = Not significant.

* Source of data used as benchmark: National Statistical Offices.
§ Source of data used as benchmark: Regional Innovation Scoreboard 2006.

the sectoral and the regional level, such as Italy. Lastly, NUTS2 CIS data for all EU27 countries are not available from official sources, and previous exercises implemented for the DG Industry and DG Regio (Hollanders et al., 2009a) elaborated and used a dedicated estimation strategy to derive regional innovation data. Despite using a different methodology, our results are reasonably consistent with previous estimates.

Unfortunately, this methodology was not feasible for the UK, which does not allow Eurostat to publicly release innovation data. In particular, Eurostat does not provide NUTS0 data on the UK for the following variables: only product innovation; only process innovation; product and process innovation; product and/or process innovation; marketing and/or organizational innovation. However, the Department of Trade and Industry (DTI) provides information on the share of firms introducing product innovation, on the one hand, and on the share of firms introducing process innovation, on the other. As discussed above, however, these figures are comparable to only a limited degree with the data on only product innovation and only process innovation available for the other countries (see Table 5.2 above).

To estimate product and/or process innovation the shares of product innovation and of process innovation were summed. Unfortunately, this carried the risk of double counting (and overestimation) since both categories include also firms performing both product and process innovation. The national share of innovative firms was derived from DTI documents. This share was applied to the Eurostat national CIS sample and, by applying regional weights to this figure, the number of innovative firms in each region was obtained.

Next, the denominator (i.e. the total number of firms in the regional CIS sample) was obtained by splitting the national CIS sample according to regional employment shares. Finally, the ratio was calculated between these two values and the regional share of innovative firms finally obtained. We used a similar procedure to estimate the share of firms introducing marketing and/or organizational innovations. Given the combination of different sources of NUTS0 innovation data, the UK estimates might have proved slightly more problematic than estimates of other countries.

5.3.3. CIS limitations

CIS is definitely an innovative action in many respects because, for the first time, it has made it possible to collect internationally comparable direct measures of innovative activities at a highly disaggregated level of analysis that, in turn, has created a wide range of research opportunities in recent years (Smith, 2005; Thurieaux et al., 2000; Fagerberg et al. 2012).

Despite these merits and the increasing worldwide development and use of similar innovation surveys based on the *Oslo Manual* such as CIS (Hong et al., 2012), CIS has been much criticized. Like other surveys, it is based on self-reported evaluations of respondents that, in some circumstances, may affect the reliability of the answers provided and cannot rule out human errors/bias and risks of low response rates. In particular, overconfidence in innovation capacities may lead to overestimation of innovative activities and bias in the final innovation figures. Moreover, CIS still seems better suited to manufacturing sectors than to services; in fact, despite increasing attempts to monitor organizational and managerial changes, CIS is somewhat unbalanced towards technological change (i.e. product and process innovations).

However, the use of CIS can be defended on several grounds. Firstly, it is the only source of direct innovation measures available at the European level, collected on a regular basis, according to standard procedures, as defined by the *Oslo Manual*. Secondly, the quality and reliability of CIS data have increased over time and, more generally, the entire survey process, from the definition and construction of the questionnaire to the collection methodologies and workability of the survey itself, has been subject to reflection, criticism and debate – much more than so any other indicator (Arundel et al., 1997). Thirdly, and more importantly from the conceptual point of view, direct measures of innovation, although questionable because of low representativeness, show several advantages over indirect measures of innovation like R&D and patent statistics: namely, strong linkages with innovation and relatively lower large firm bias.

The actual exploitation of this important source of data is, however, hampered by numerous comparability problems, as discussed in Section 5.3.1, whose relevance is further magnified in the present case by the use of CIS data at the regional level. In fact, on moving to the regional level, CIS is affected by two specific problems. Firstly, because administration of the survey is implemented at the national level, and by National Statistics Offices, not all countries stratify the sample at the same regional level. Secondly, even if a regional sample stratification is adopted, non-representativeness bias may persist for small regions (Hollanders et al., 2009b).

Notwithstanding the doubts concerning the CIS data, the exercise presented here can be defended. In fact, despite the use of a different methodology, the results obtained are consistent with previous estimates implemented for the DG Industry and DG Regio (Hollanders et al., 2009a and 2009b) (Table 5.5). The consistency captured by all robustness tests is a sufficiently strong scientific basis to claim that a proxy for innovation is available. This is information vital for the next step in our conceptual reasoning.

5.4. The diffusion of innovation across European regions

5.4.1. *The geographical diffusion of product innovation only*

The share of firms introducing product innovation only is presented in Map 5.5.[6] Spatial concentration characterizes product innovation (Moran's I = 0.43, p-value <0.01), the core of product innovative activities in Europe being carried out in German, Scandinavian, and British regions, with a few notable exceptions outside those areas.[7] In general, in countries where product innovation is high, concentration seems pronounced. Spatial concentration of product innovation also strongly characterizes countries with low product innovation rates. This is the case in Portu-

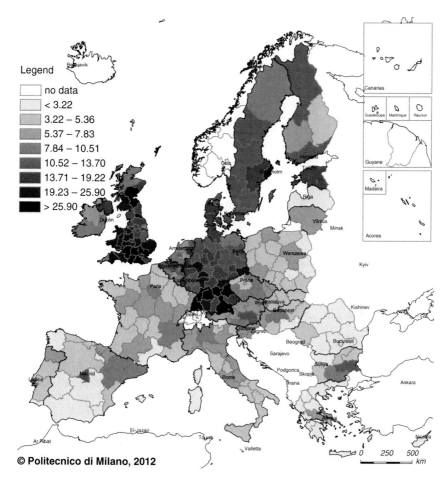

Map 5.5 Share of firms introducing product innovation only

Source Capello et al. (2012)

gal, where Lisbon is the only area with some product innovation activity, in Spain, with Madrid, Barcelona and a few Pyrenean regions, in Greece, and in some EU12 countries. Italy is an exception to this pattern, since several regions in the northern and central part of the country display similar product innovation rates.

Spatial patterns characterize the variable not only across countries but also within them. In fact, capital regions tend to display higher product innovation rates, with some exceptions consisting of regions which also register consistent innovation performance despite not hosting the capital city (e.g. Rhône-Alps and Midi-Pyrénées in France). EU15 regions tend on average to innovate more – and significantly so – than EU12 ones in all types of innovation activities (Table 5.6). The same applies to denser regions, while rural regions display a relatively lower

Table 5.6 Share of innovative firms by innovation type and regional typology

Typology of regions	Product	Process	Product and process	Product and/ or process	Marketing and/or organizational
AGGLOMERATED	14.69	11.95	15.95	40.72	28.12
EU15	11.84	12.13	15.78	38.62	28.15
EU12	5.11	7.08	12.01	24.19	18.05
CONVERGENCE	5.46	8.18	12.36	25.94	20.63
TRANSITION	6.75	11.7	15.48	33.81	27.5
COMPETITIVE	13.43	12.38	16.21	40.61	28.53
EU	10.4	11.05	14.97	35.54	25.99

Source: Adapted from Capello et al. (2012)

product innovation rate. Similarly, competitive regions outperform the others in terms of product innovation.

5.4.2. The geographical diffusion of process innovation only

A second important dimension of innovative activities concerns the introduction of new production and manufacturing methods, i.e. process innovation, which is presented in Map 5.6.[8] In general, process innovation exhibits a relatively more dispersed pattern than product innovation, although it is still highly concentrated (Moran's I = 0.43, p-value <0.01). Countries like Portugal, Spain, France, Germany, and the UK do not display a remarkable concentration of process innovation within their boundaries. The spatial variance of this variable is lower than the variance of product innovation. This finding points to a more evenly distributed process innovation propensity across space. This is also confirmed in EU12 countries that are unexpectedly characterized by relatively more homogeneous spatial trends.

Similarly to product innovation, process innovation takes place more frequently in densely populated regions and in metropolitan areas, and it is characterized by a EU15–EU12 dichotomy, in that the average process innovation rate is 5% higher in EU15 regions than in EU12 regions (Table 5.6).

Given the softer nature of process innovation, however, the process innovation rate is on average higher than the product innovation rate. Overall, process innovation displays a 1% point higher average value than product innovation. In particular, to be stressed is that process innovation displays on average higher values in southern European countries (namely, Cyprus, Spain, France, Greece, Italy, Malta, and Portugal) than in the rest of the Europe, by about two percentage points.

Overall, product and process innovation display remarkable levels of covariation. In fact, regions with high levels of product innovation also have high levels of process innovation. Notable exceptions are southern European countries – Spain, Greece, Italy, and Portugal – where relatively weak performances in terms of product innovation are matched by superior performances in process innovation.

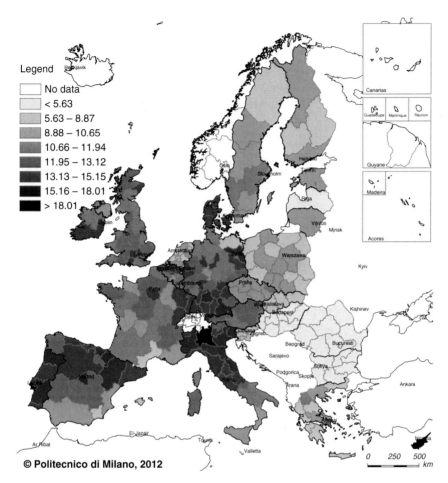

Map 5.6 Share of firms introducing process innovation only

Source Capello et al. (2012)

5.4.3. The geographical diffusion of product and process innovation

The share of firms introducing simultaneously both product and process innovation is shown in Map 5.7. These regions are the most innovative ones, i.e. those innovating in product and process innovation simultaneously. The pattern of this variable shows remarkable country effects and high concentration (Moran's $I = 0.31$, p-value<0.01), with clusters of high innovativeness in Ireland, Finland, Sweden, Germany, and Austria. Some regions in relatively more peripheral European countries (namely, Greece and Portugal) achieve remarkable performances on this variable while at the same time recording low levels of product or process innovation, as well as relatively lower performances on knowledge indicators, as discussed in Chapters 3 and 4.

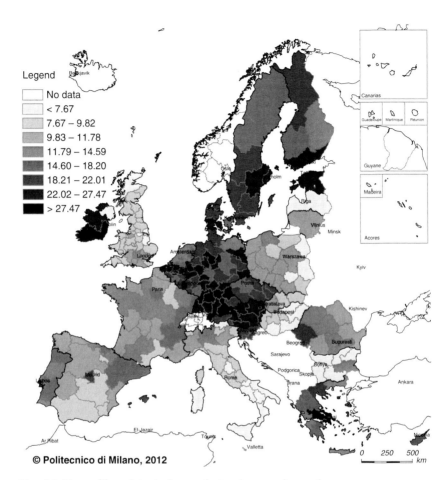

Legend

	No data
	< 7.67
	7.67 – 9.82
	9.83 – 11.78
	11.79 – 14.59
	14.60 – 18.20
	18.21 – 22.01
	22.02 – 27.47
	> 27.47

© Politecnico di Milano, 2012

Map 5.7 Share of firms introducing product and process innovation

On the other hand, the UK and Italy show rather low values along this innovation dimension, and this statement holds on average true for most regions in these two countries. In the UK, notable exceptions are Berkshire, Buckinghamshire and Oxfordshire, Surrey, East and West Sussex, Hampshire and the Isle of Wight, and Gloucestershire, Wiltshire and the Bristol and Bath area. Interestingly, EU12 countries display a relatively dispersed product and process innovation rate, especially in Romania and Poland, the latter recording a relatively better performance for the capital region and for most regions on the border with Germany.

5.4.4. *The geographical diffusion of product and/or process innovation*

The last indicator of technological innovation refers to the share of firms introducing product and/or process innovation (Map 5.8). This is the most inclusive

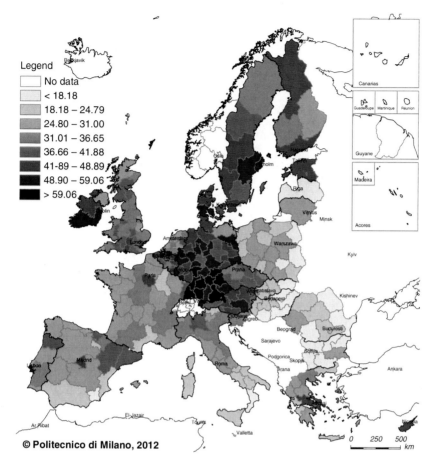

Map 5.8 Share of firms introducing product and/or process innovation

category of innovators in that it encompasses all previous ones. Therefore, this variable should yield, although in a somewhat blurred manner, an overall picture of innovative activities in Europe.

Spatial patterns for this variable closely resemble those displayed by the variables 'product innovation' and 'product and process innovation'. As a result, product and/or process innovation records remarkable levels of concentration (Moran's I = 0.36, p-value<0.01), with the bulk of innovative activities taking place in the strongest EU15 countries (namely, Germany, the UK and Ireland, the Scandinavian countries) with a few but relevant exceptions represented by some capital or metropolitan regions and single-region countries outside the core (Madrid, Lisbon, Île-de-France, Lombardy, Athens, Estonia, and Cyprus).

Similarly to the other types of innovations, product and/or process innovation tends to be concentrated in EU15, agglomerated and competitive regions, although the innovation gap with EU12, more peripheral and, relatively, lagging regions seems to be narrower according to this more inclusive definition of innovation (Table 5.6).

5.4.5. *The geographical diffusion of marketing and organizational innovation*

A quite different innovation dimension is provided by marketing and/or organizational innovation. This captures non-technological innovative activities, as detailed in the previous section. The share of firms introducing marketing and/or organizational innovations is displayed in Map 5.9. This highlights a significant concentration of marketing and/or organizational innovation (Moran's I = 0.36, p-value <0.01), especially in regions in EU15 countries, and with particularly high

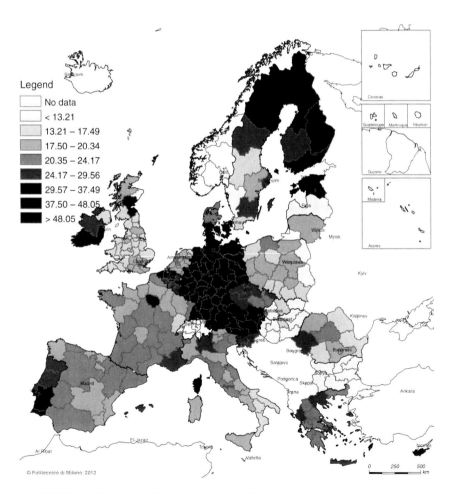

Map 5.9 Share of firms introducing marketing and/or organizational innovation

values in German and Austrian regions. However, the spatial distribution of this soft form of innovation seems much more even across the European space.

Spatial patterns characterize marketing and/or organizational innovation, with a consistently higher tendency to introduce such changes in capital regions, in higher density regions, and in regions with large cities, suggesting that their diversified and creative environments can sustain innovative behaviours. EU12 regions innovate in marketing and/or organization to a lesser extent than EU15 regions, on average by about nine percentage points (Table 5.6). Similar patterns affect Nordic and Mediterranean regions, the latter innovating less by about five percentage points.

Interestingly, marketing and/or organizational innovation is not disjoint from product and/or process innovation. In fact, pure correlation between marketing and/or organizational innovation, on the one hand, and product and/or process innovation on the other, is remarkably high (equal to 0.71 and significant at all conventional levels).

Overall, competitive, agglomerated and EU15 regions significantly outperform the other groups of regions across all innovation dimensions. Interestingly, transition regions show potential for closing the innovation gap with innovation leaders, even though the rates of product-innovation-only and process-innovation-only are below the EU average. In fact, their product and process innovation rate is slightly above the EU average and their marketing and/or organizational innovation rate is almost two percentage points above the EU average. By contrast, convergence and EU12 regions are still far from closing the innovation gap because their innovation rate is considerably below the EU average across all innovation dimensions.

5.5. The knowledge–innovation nexus at regional level

The availability of innovation data makes it possible to assess the ability of regions to transform knowledge and inventions into commercial innovations and to become innovation-driven economies. In particular, comparison between innovation data and the typologies of knowledge-based regions derived in Chapters 2, 3 and 4 yields information on the extent to which innovative activities relate to the region being classified as a knowledge-based economy.

To aid understanding of the interplay between knowledge intensity and innovation spatial trends, Table 5.7 presents the share of innovative firms by type of innovation and the different types of knowledge-based regions.

As expected, the largest difference is between knowledge-based regions and the others. The former show a higher innovation performance regardless of the definition of innovation adopted. There are very limited and statistically non-significant differences among knowledge-based regions. Although scientific regions register a high innovation rate, they are not significantly more innovative than TARs or networking regions. This holds across all types of innovative activities: product innovation only, process innovation only, and product and/or process innovation. Although differences are almost negligible, Table 5.7 shows a slightly higher product innovation rate for TARs, a slightly higher process innovation rate for

Table 5.7 Share of innovative firms by type of innovation and knowledge-based regions

Typology of regions	Product	Process	Product and process	Product and/or process	Marketing and/or organizational
Non knowledge-based	6.68	10.62	12.57	29.35	21.55
Knowledge-based					
of which:	13.64	11.43	17.07	40.94	29.86
only TAR	14.05	11.49	12.12	35.03	24.68
only scientific	13.55	11.85	14.06	37.26	23.88
only networking	12.35	11.32	17.17	39.59	29.73
TAR and scient.	14.45	10.89	19.44	44.79	27.28
TAR and network.	14.62	12.25	21.19	47.47	41.35
Scien. and netw.	13.94	10.67	16.96	41.11	28.21
TAR, scient. and netw.	14.64	11.68	16.7	41.47	28.02
ANOVA p-value	n.s.	n.s.	$p<0.05$	n.s.	$p<0.01$

Note: ANOVA implemented on knowledge-based types of regions only; n.s. = not significant.

TARs, and a slightly higher product and/or process innovation rate for networking regions. In the case of marketing and organizational innovation as well, TARs and networking regions outperform scientific regions.

This is confirmed by ANOVA tests implemented on the different types of innovative activities for the knowledge-based regions. Contrary to expectations, the results of the ANOVA tests corroborate that there are no statistical differences in product innovation, process innovation and product and/or process innovation activities among the different types of knowledge-based regions. Technologically advanced regions, or scientific regions, where the highest high-tech sector specialization and R&D/GDP ratio are concentrated, do not register statistically higher innovation rates; on the contrary, they perform as well as the networking regions in terms of innovation.

In the case where the ANOVA test is significant – namely product and process innovation – another unexpected result emerges: the significance is due to a decisive difference between TARs only, on the one hand, and TARs and networking regions on the other – the former unexpectedly registering the lowest share of product and process innovation, and the latter registering the highest, which evidences the importance of a networking attitude also for regions that develop their own knowledge.

Similarly, the significance of the ANOVA test on marketing and/or organizational innovation is mostly due to a significant difference between TARs and networking regions and all the other types of regions.

All in all, the simple analysis presented in Table 5.7 yields counter-intuitive results: regions with the highest R&D and scientific activities do not innovate the most compared with other types of knowledge-based regions. Although scientific regions register a high innovation rate, they are not significantly more innovative than TARs or networking ones – which suggests that only a few regions follow a pattern of innovation that goes straightforwardly from R&D to innovation.

This finding suggests that knowledge and innovation are not necessarily overlapping processes in space; nor are they necessarily sequential and intertwined at the local level: from an empirical point of view, the geography of knowledge does not automatically match the geography of innovation (Capello and Lenzi, 2013a).

There are various explanations for this finding. Firstly, factors that enhance the creation and implementation of new knowledge may be quite different from the factors that stimulate innovation, and regions may exhibit larger endowments of either the former or the latter. Secondly, several regions innovate on the basis of external knowledge acquired through networking with leading regions, and of specific know-how in local application sectors. Firms and individuals that lead in inventive activity are not necessarily also leaders in innovation or in the diffusion of new technologies – as discussed in the introductory chapter. More in general, there may be regions with weak internal knowledge creation capacity but which are able to leverage on external knowledge sources – for example by networking – so as to develop innovation. In short, regions can exhibit different advantages and specializations at different stages of the innovation process.

A simple taxonomy can help better to capture these different attitudes towards knowledge and innovation and modes of integrating them across regions. Regions, in fact, can be classified according to their positioning in terms of knowledge and innovation activities with respect to the European average (Figure 5.1). Accordingly, one can identify regions with a knowledge and innovation intensity that is greater than the EU average: these can be defined as *knowledge-based innovative regions*. By contrast, there may be regions where a knowledge intensity above the European average does not match an innovation outcome higher than the European average, meaning that the locally produced knowledge is not fully exploited at the local level to achieve higher innovative performances, and that there may

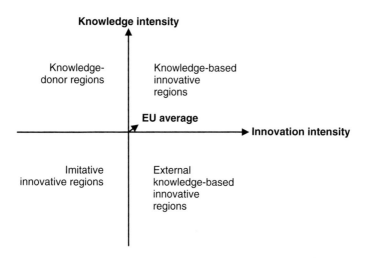

Figure 5.1 A proposed taxonomy

be some knowledge leakages or inefficiencies in the use of the locally created knowledge. Therefore, these regions can be defined as *knowledge-donor regions*. On the other hand, there may be regions able to achieve innovative performances above the European average although their local knowledge endowment is below the average. These regions are therefore very successful and efficient in the use of local knowledge and in accessing external knowledge sources to achieve above-average innovative performances. Consequently, these regions can be defined as *external knowledge-based innovative regions*. Lastly, there may be regions with a knowledge and innovation intensity below the European average in which the locally available knowledge base may be sufficient for the limited innovative outputs, or, possibly, innovation occurs through imitation of innovations developed elsewhere. These regions can accordingly be defined as *imitative innovative regions* (Figure 5.1).

This simple classification can provide a useful framework in which to read the differing propensities for knowledge and innovation among regions and, more importantly, the different modes of mixing and performing them.

Two crucial indicators can be used to capture the knowledge and innovation intensity of European regions. The first can be measured as the share of R&D expenditures (both private and public) on GDP; the second as the share of firms introducing product and/or process innovations in a region.

As discussed in Chapter 3 and Section 5.2, the Lisbon Agenda, reinforced by the Europe 2020 Strategy, has declared the importance of research and innovation to guarantee competitive and smart growth in Europe, and it has set a specific target for R&D expenditures, which should be increased to 3% of GDP. Section 5.2 has also shown that R&D expenditures on GDP in Europe vary markedly across regions, ranging from values lower than 0.5% to values of more than 6%, with a very small number of regions in Europe achieving (and exceeding) the 3% R&D expenditures on GDP target, and a very high number of regions with R&D on GDP below 0.5%. Moreover, R&D expenditures are highly concentrated in space and mostly clustered in Scandinavian countries, southern UK and central Europe, with the exception of the French region of Midi-Pyrénées.

By contrast, Map 5.8, which shows the share of firms with product and/or process innovations, points to an innovation pattern more pervasive than that of R&D expenditures on GDP, despite remarkable levels of concentration.

Importantly, comparison between the two indicators suggests that the ranking of R&D expenditures on GDP and the ranking of the share of firms with product and/or process innovation do not always coincide. Although the correlation coefficient between R&D and innovation is slightly above 0.5, and statistically significant at conventional levels, there are several regions with above-European average innovation performances but below-European average R&D expenditures, or the other way round. In fact, by applying the taxonomy set out above, we can classify European regions into four groups according to their knowledge and innovation performances with respect to the European average. Map 5.10 shows the four groups of innovative regions according to the existence of internal or external sources of knowledge.

Interestingly, 25% of regions (i.e. 66 out of 262) can be classified as *knowledge-based innovative regions* with both knowledge and innovation intensity higher than the European average. Somewhat counter-intuitively, almost 20% of regions (51 out of 262) show an above-average innovative profile, which, however, does not match an above-average knowledge profile. These regions can be accordingly classified as *external knowledge-based innovative regions*. Only a small group (11% of regions, i.e. 30 out of 262) shows an above-average knowledge intensity but a below-average innovation intensity, and are therefore classified as *knowledge-donor regions*. Lastly, the largest group of regions (almost 44% of them, i.e. 115 out of 262) are *imitative innovative regions*, with both knowledge and innovation intensities below the EU average. The size of this last group once again confirms the embryonic stage of development reached by the so-called knowledge-based economy in Europe. In fact, this group closely reflects the

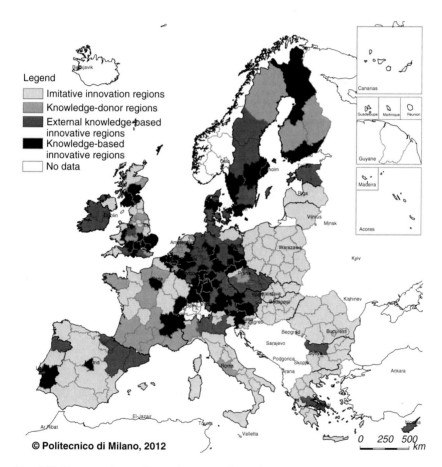

Map 5.10 European innovative regions according to knowledge sources

Source: Capello and Lenzi (2012a)

composition and size of the set of regions not classified as TAR or as scientific or networking regions.

Table 5.8 also shows that the four groups statistically and significantly differ in their average knowledge and innovation behaviours, as confirmed by the significance level of the ANOVA p-value for the R&D and innovation variables. Even more strikingly, more knowledge-intensive regions (i.e. *knowledge-based innovative regions* and *knowledge-donor regions*) do not outperform the others in terms of employment growth and, especially, GDP growth. This somewhat unexpected and puzzling empirical finding not only questions the simplistic view that knowledge equates with innovation and economic growth but also confirms that only some regions exhibit a pattern that goes from *R&D to innovation*, and that there is greater heterogeneity among regions in the modes in which knowledge and innovation activities are performed and mixed in space.

All these results suggest that the pathways from knowledge to innovation are highly heterogeneous across space and that European regions innovate in different ways. Some regions are able to produce their internal knowledge, translate knowledge into innovation, and obtain the maximum efficiency and effectiveness from innovation adoption (the so-called 'linear model'). There are other regions able to innovate by acquiring the knowledge required from other regions. Finally, there are regions able to innovate through creative imitation of already-existing innovation.

Legitimate questions ensue from these results: how do regions innovate without R&D? What are the innovation modes when R&D, and formal knowledge in general, are not available at the local level?

The conceptual and empirical distinction between knowledge and innovation and the observation of their uneven and, in some cases, disjoint spatial distribution pave the way to a framework interpreting not just a single phase of the innovation process but the *different modes of performing the different phases of the innovation process* (Chapter 6). Our expectation is that the individual phases of the innovation process are supported by different local conditions and are linked to specific context characteristics.

The conceptual elaboration and the empirical investigation of the different combinations of context conditions and innovation modes will lead to identification of *territorial patterns of innovation*. This is the task of the analyses described in the second part of the book.

5.7. Conclusions

The complex knowledge–innovation nexus has been approached in this chapter by using several indicators of different types of innovations to measure the penetration of the innovation-driven economy across European regions.

To the best of our knowledge, this is a conceptual and empirical novelty. From the conceptual point of view, it marks a departure from most of the existing conceptual approaches to innovation processes in space. These approaches either focus on one specific phase of the innovation process itself (often interpreted as

Table 5.8 Mean values by group of regions and in EU and ANOVA test statistical significance (p-value)

Variable	Knowledge-based innovative regions	External knowledge-based innovative regions	Knowledge-donor regions	Imitative innovative regions	EU average	p-value
R&D (average 2000–2002)	2.77	0.86	2.16	0.59	1.37	<0.01
Innovation (2002–2004)	49.02	44.20	31.14	25.11	35.54	<0.01
GDP growth rate (2005–2007)	3.41	3.46	3.01	4.03	3.64	<0.05
Employment growth rate (2005–2007)	3.70	3.97	2.74	4.01	3.78	n.s.
Number of observations	66 (25%)	51 (20%)	30 (11%)	115 (44%)	262	n.a.

Note: n.a. = not applicable.

the crucial one and mostly understood as knowledge creation or knowledge diffusion only) or interpret knowledge and innovation as overlapping (frequently synonymous) processes, assuming that knowledge created locally inevitably leads to local innovation, or, conversely, that local innovation is exclusively due to local knowledge availability.

From the empirical point of view, this has been one of the first attempts to present original data on a variety of innovative activities at NUTS2 level for the entire European space. This effort has been to date impaired by several technical difficulties, and a lack of good quality and comparable data. Our estimation methodology, fully consistent with previous official efforts in this direction and robust to a broad array of consistency checks, is therefore an important advance in empirically describing the geography of innovation in Europe.

Important messages can be drawn from this chapter, and they raise further interesting research questions. Firstly, the spatial distribution of knowledge-creation activities is closely concentrated in a handful of regions. Knowledge creation is in fact highly selective and only a minority of regions can be defined as knowledge-based. This result is of great importance for the current policy debate on how to make Europe become a knowledge-based economy and achieve smart growth, especially in light of the increasing international competitive pressure from emerging countries. Comparison of the spatial patterns of research and scientific activities with the US and some emerging countries, namely India and China, is therefore needed to understand whether this is specific to Europe alone, or whether it is a characteristic that Europe shares with these countries. If this is the case, it would support the view that achievement of a critical mass is fundamental for scientific activities, especially in countries that are relatively less rich, with limited funds to be devoted to R&D. These aspects will all be addressed in Chapter 11.

Secondly, and contrary to what is generally believed, although knowledge and innovation are, on average, highly correlated, the data show a discrepancy between knowledge and innovation at the spatial level: that is, the geography of knowledge does not always match the geography of innovation. Whereas knowledge-based regions outperform the others in terms of innovative activities, one would have expected the regions with the highest R&D and scientific activities in general to be the most innovative. In contrast, our empirical results show that although scientific regions record a high innovation rate, they are not significantly more innovative than TARs or networking regions. In short, only a few regions show a pattern that goes straightforwardly from R&D to innovation: regions may be able to innovate even without R&D and formal knowledge being locally available. This is also confirmed by the observation that several regions (i.e. about 20%) are able to achieve innovative performances above the European average although their local knowledge endowment is below the European average. These regions, defined as external knowledge-based innovative regions, are very successful and efficient in the use of local knowledge and in accessing external knowledge sources to achieve above-average innovative performances.

All this suggests that different modes of performing innovation exist. A region can innovate by exploiting the knowledge that it produces; it can innovate by using knowledge from outside the region; it can innovate by imitating innovation that is produced elsewhere. Our expectation is that these modes of innovation vary according to each region's territorial context conditions. Chapters 6 and 7, in the second part of the book, will be devoted respectively to elaborating conceptually and detecting empirically *territorial patterns of innovation* across European regions.

Notes

1 Agglomerated regions are defined as regions with a city of more than 300,000 inhabitants and a population density of more than 300 inhabitants per square kilometre, or a population density between 150 and 300 inhabitants per square kilometre.
2 Convergence regions are defined as eligible areas under the Convergence objective within the 2007–2013 Cohesion Policy programming period. Transition regions are defined as phasing-in and phasing-out areas within the 2007–2013 Cohesion Policy programming period. Competitive regions are defined as eligible areas under the European and Competitiveness and Employment Objective within the 2007–2013 Cohesion Policy programming period. Further details on this classification are available at http://ec.europa.eu/regional_policy/atlas2007/index_en.htm.
3 All types of regions are included in the ANOVA.
4 Information on CIS micro-data can be retrieved at the Eurostat portal http://epp.eurostat.ec.europa.eu/portal/page/portal/microdata/cis.
5 This distinction makes comparisons among CIS NUTS2 data from National Statistical Offices even more complex. In fact, as will be discussed in more detail below, some countries make CIS NUTS2 data publicly available; but, unfortunately, they refer to different categories of innovators, which eventually prevents their use in a comparative perspective.
6 The question originally administered to interviewees was 'During the three years 2002 to 2004, did your enterprise introduce new or significantly improved goods or services?'.
7 The relatively high value of Moran's I for all innovation types is in part due to our estimation strategy, based on national values.
8 The question originally administered to interviewees was 'During the three years 2002 to 2004, did your enterprise introduce new or significantly improved methods of manufacturing or producing goods or services?'.

Part II

Territorial patterns of innovation and regional dynamics in Europe

6 Territorial patterns of innovation

Roberta Capello

6.1. Introduction

The scientific debate on the role of knowledge and innovation as strategic elements behind the competitiveness of regions and countries has always strongly supported the policy frame put forward by the Lisbon Agenda (EC, 2000) and by the Europe 2020 Agenda (EC, 2010a), both aiming at increasing R&D expenditure over GDP up to 3% in Europe.

The interpretative approach adopted in the 1980s stressed the importance of pervasive and horizontal functions like R&D and high education in the process of knowledge creation and innovation diffusion. Scientific regions, hosting large and well-known scientific institutions, were studied deeply, and relationships between these institutions and the industrial fabric were analysed, with some disappointments in regard to an expected but not often visible direct linkage (MacDonald, 1987; Massey et al., 1992; Monk et al., 1988; Storey and Tether, 1998). Indicators of R&D input (like public and private research investment and personnel) and, increasingly, indicators of R&D output (like patenting activities) were used in order to understand the commitment of firms and territories to knowledge, understood as a necessary long-term precondition for continuing innovation (Dasgupta and Stiglitz, 1980; Antonelli, 1989; Griliches, 1990). This approach equated knowledge with scientific research, on the assumption that the presence of local knowledge produced by research centres and universities was a necessary and sufficient condition for increasing the innovation capacities of local firms fed by local spillovers.

The difficulties encountered in achieving the Lisbon Agenda goal stimulated reflections on the need for a new innovation policy style and scope by a group of scholars, who stressed the need to replace a thematically/regionally neutral and generic innovation policy – a 'one-size-fits-all approach' – with a policy built on the smart specialization of R&D activities in different regions and on exploitation of the advantages stemming from specialized R&D concentration (EC, 2008; Foray, 2009).

These arguments seem rather persuasive. A smart specialization is a way out of the thematically/regionally neutral and generic orientation of R&D funding investments. Core regions can be seen as the natural places for general purpose technologies, which can achieve a critical mass of scientists and knowledge able to achieve increasing returns to R&D, giving 'peripheral' regions the role of co-inventors of applications in their technological domain (Foray, 2009). On this logic, R&D funding investments become targeted in a thematic and regional sense; general purpose technological R&D investments find their most efficient destination in core regions, while R&D funding in specific innovation applications is allocated to peripheral regions, each of them fulfilling a specific role based on its comparative advantage in a knowledge production hierarchy (Pontikakis et al., 2009).

Starting from these recent reflections, there is space for development of a further conceptual framework of analysis on the reasons for the failure of the Lisbon strategy and on possible new innovation policy styles. Required in particular is a new conceptual framework on the determinants of innovation capability at regional level that goes beyond some simplified assumptions that still accompany the most recent analyses. In particular, the ideas of a simple equation between knowledge and scientific research, of a simple core–periphery dichotomy in R&D activities, of R&D expenditure as the only way to boost innovation processes, require some additional thinking in a new conceptual framework able to overcome these limits and to drive normative interventions towards *thematically/regionally focused innovation policies*.

These conceptual reflections find an additional support in the empirical results obtained in the first part of the volume; empirical evidence calls for a conceptual distinction between knowledge and innovation, and for a specific attention to spatial heterogeneity in the mix between knowledge and innovation and in the capacity to exploit them to achieve higher paces of economic growth.

The discussion starts from the assumption that the presence of advanced sectors and advanced functions like R&D and higher education are special features of only *some of the possible innovation paths* and, although they are important, they cannot be considered as necessary or sufficient preconditions for innovation. Furthermore, the emphasis on interaction *per se* among the different actors of knowledge development as the crucial factor in knowledge creation and diffusion is again not completely satisfactory.

Instead, all the valid scientific contributions produced in the field of knowledge creation (e.g. Dasgupta and Stiglitz, 1980; Antonelli, 1989; Griliches, 1990) and of knowledge spillovers (e.g. Acs et al., 1994; Audretsch and Feldman, 1996; Anselin et al., 2000; Paci and Usai, 2009) can form the basis for a new conceptual framework aimed at interpreting the different patterns of territorial innovation, defined as a combination of *context conditions* and *specific modes of performing the different phases* of the innovation process.

This chapter enters the well-documented literature on knowledge, innovation and regional growth by proposing a new conceptual approach to reading knowledge and innovation potentials at the regional level. This conceptual approach stresses the complex interplay between the phases of the innovation process and the spatial context or territorial conditions behind them by claiming that knowledge and innovation are not necessarily overlapping processes in space nor necessarily sequential at the local level. Its novelty rests on the capacity of interpreting not only a single phase of the innovation process, but the *different modes of performing the different phases of the innovation process*, built on the presence/absence of the *context conditions* that support knowledge creation, knowledge attraction and innovation.

This approach directly questions the much-diffused knowledge–innovation–performance equivalence interpreting knowledge, innovation and economic growth as necessarily overlapping processes at the spatial level. Indeed, most of the literature takes for granted that locally created knowledge unavoidably leads to local innovation and local innovation takes place because of local knowledge availability. Similarly, productivity increases are expected when creative efforts, learning processes, and an interactive and cooperative atmosphere characterize the local economy. Differently, the distinction between the knowledge and innovation stages paves the ground to a conceptual framework interpreting not only a single phase of the innovation process, but the *different modes of performing the different phases of the innovation process*, leading to the identification of different territorial patterns of innovation.

Through a review of the existing literature, the chapter moves to the limits of the existing approaches (Section 6.2), and to the presentation of our conceptual framework (Sections 6.3–6.6), which finds an operational application to the European regions in Chapter 7.

6.2. Theoretical achievements in regional innovation approaches

Innovation diffusion at regional level first attracted the interest of regional economists and geographers at the end of the 1960s, when the neoclassical paradigm, to the effect that innovation is 'manna from heaven', equally distributed among firms and in space, was questioned. These approaches viewed innovation as an exogenous event that propagates through specific territorial channels to generate positive impacts on a local area from outside. Analyses should therefore examine the territorial routes whereby innovation reaches a particular area; routes formalized in models of the spatial diffusion of innovation, whose main feature consists in the epidemic nature of diffusion. The pure likelihood of contact between people who have already adopted an innovation and its potential adopters explains innovation diffusion in this model, which implicitly assumes that every potential adopter has the same opportunity to adopt the innovation, and that spatial variations in adoption are due solely to information flows that spread territorially at different times (Hägerstrand, 1967) (Table 6.1). According to this approach, information means innovation, and innovation means higher economic performance in a natural and undisputed short circuit. The role of space in this theory is that of spatial friction to information flows. The latter arise naturally in large cities and then propagate through cities at the lower level of the urban hierarchy thanks to infrastructures and economic flows.

The idea that the spatial diffusion of innovation is influenced less by geographic distance among adopters than by economic distance has been introduced into the model of spatial innovation by economists: the amount of productive activity in an

Table 6.1 Alternative approaches to knowledge and innovation studies

	Innovation diffusion	Innovation creation	Knowledge creation		Knowledge diffusion	
			Functional approach	Cognitive approach	Spatial approach	Evolutionary approach
Aim of the theory	Identification of the spatial channels supporting innovation diffusion	Identification of the reasons for local innovation creation	Identification of the reasons for local knowledge creation	Identification of the reasons for local knowledge creation	Identification of the reasons for local knowledge diffusion	
Knowledge-innovation linkage	Information-adoption short circuit	Invention-innovation short circuit	Spin-offs, spatial spillovers	Collective learning, local synergies Entrepreneurship	Spin-offs, spatial spillovers	Common cognitive codes
From innovation to performance	Adoption-performance linkage	Radical innovation, Schumpeterian profits	Technological breakthrough, royalties on patents	Continuing innovation, productivity increases	Knowledge-performance linkage	
Location regions	Regions along the urban hierarchy	Advanced regions	Scientific regions	Milieux innovateurs, learning regions	Networking regions	
Role of space	Barrier to information diffusion	Proximity economies, specialisation advantages	Agglomeration economies	Uncertainty reduction, relational capital	Proximity economies	
Period	End of the 1960s and 1970s	Middle of the 1980s	End of the 1980s and 1990s	End of the 1980s and 1990s	Middle of the 1990s onwards	Middle of the 2000s

Key references	Hägerstrand, 1952; Griliches, 1957; Mansfield, 1961; Metcalfe, 1981; Camagni, 1985; Capello, 1988	Malecki, 1980; Saxenian, 1994	MacDonald, 1987; Massey et al. 1992; Monk et al., 1988; Storey and Tether, 1998	Camagni, 1991; Perrin, 1995; Keeble and Wilkinson, 1999; Capello 1999; Cappellin, 2003a; Lundvall and Johnson, 1994	Acs et al., 1994; Audretsch and Feldman, 1996; Anselin et al., 2000	Boschma, 2005; Rallet and Torre, 1995; Capello, 2009

Source: Capello (2012)

area, and the latter's levels of income, consumption and investment, can straightforwardly explain the greater receptiveness of an adoption area (Griliches, 1957; Mansfield, 1961; Metcalfe, 1981). Moreover, empirical analyses developed more recently in different technological trajectories, namely robotics' and ICT's development, bear witness to the importance of the stage of economic development for interpreting technological penetration rates, speed of adoption, and the historic moment of first adoption (Camagni, 1985; Capello, 1988).

When the need for an endogenous approach to regional innovation was felt, the conditions for innovation creation came to the fore as a second stage of reflection. In this literature, innovation was interpreted as being produced by high-tech goods or services, on the assumption that there is an immediate link between invention and innovation within individual firms (or their territories) operating in advanced sectors. R&D facilities, in fact, are strictly linked to production facilities, while firms tend to cluster into high-tech districts in order to take advantage of all sorts of proximity externalities. According to this approach, the mere presence of high-tech sectors was a condition for a region to innovate. The spatial conditions behind local innovation were empirically identified. Externalities arising from the presence of advanced education facilities were invoked to explain innovation capacity; but international accessibility, advanced urban atmosphere, and traditional industrial competencies under reorientation were also suggested (Malecki, 1980; Saxenian, 1994).

When many knowledge-based advances were actually achieved by 'traditional' sectors – such as textiles and car production – in their path towards rejuvenation, it became evident that the 'sector-based' approach was not sufficient; knowledge creation became the main aspect of scientific interest. Conceptual efforts were made to explain the different regional capacities in generating knowledge.

A first wave of studies mainly interpreted the capacity of a region to create knowledge thanks to the presence of pervasive and horizontal functions like R&D and higher education (MacDonald, 1987; Massey et al., 1992; Monk et al., 1988; Storey and Tether, 1998). The link between knowledge creation and innovation was interpreted as resulting from a sort of division of labour between R&D/higher education facilities, on the one hand, and innovating firms on the other. Their interaction produced academic spin-offs or knowledge spillovers flowing from the former to the latter, and subject to strong distance decay effects (Acs et al., 1994; Audretsch and Feldman, 1996; Anselin et al., 2000).

At the beginning of the 1990s, knowledge creation was studied from a different perspective whereby the degree of knowledge creation by regions was mainly their cognitive capability (Foray, 2000). The stress was on the role of interaction, synergy and cooperation among local actors as the main source of collective learning processes, and therefore of knowledge creation. Areas, local milieux as they are called, were pointed to as the loci for the construction of knowledge (Camagni, 1991; Perrin, 1995; Keeble and Wilkinson, 1999 and 2000; Capello 1999; Cappellin, 2003a) through network relations (long-distance, selective relationships), interaction, creativity and recombination capability, nourished by spatial proximity and atmosphere effects.

The 'learning' region was also identified as the place where such cognitive processes play a crucial role, combining existing but dispersed know-how, interpretations of market needs, information flows with intellectual artifacts such as theories and models, and allowing the exchange of experiences and cooperation (Lundvall and Johnson, 1994).

Therefore, in the 1990s and early 2000s, the two approaches to knowledge creation were set aside, leaving space for a debate on how knowledge spreads at the local level. Spatial proximity was first seen as the main factor explaining the channels through which knowledge spreads. In a certain sense resuming the original contributions on innovation diffusion made in the 1960s, the pure likelihood of contact between a knowledge creator (an R&D laboratory) and a potential recipient (a firm, a university, another R&D centre) was seen as the main vehicle of knowledge transmission, in a pure epidemic logic (Acs et al., 1994; Audretsch and Feldman, 1996; Anselin et al., 2000). The theory of technological spillovers developed in the 1990s linked the spatial concentration of innovative activities with the increasing returns that concentrated location generates on those innovative activities themselves. According to this theory, cross-fertilizations, dynamic interactions between customers and suppliers, synergies between research centres and local production units occur within circumscribed geographical areas like highly specialized metropolitan areas. They do so as the result of the rapid exchange of information and transmission of tacit knowledge made possible by face-to-face encounters. In a concentrated location, the beneficial effects of a firm's research and development activities are not confined within the boundaries of firms; they 'spill over' into the surrounding environment, to the advantage of innovative activity by other firms. A large number of empirical analyses, mainly econometric, successfully measured the technological spillovers and the knowledge advantages enjoyed by spatially concentrated firms. Space is purely geographical in this approach, a physical distance among actors, a pure physical container of spillover effects which come about, according to the epidemiological logic adopted, simply as a result of contacts among actors, whose probability of occurring increases in a limited geographical area.

The simplicity of this approach soon became evident, and a large debate arose on the need to enrich spatial proximity with cognitive aspects able to differentiate the absorptive capacity of different actors within a region. Knowledge creation and innovation, it was argued, are in fact cumulative and localized outcomes of search (Antonelli, 1989); as a result, the cognitive base of actors and organization and their potential for learning differ substantially. Different concepts of proximity, from social, to institutional, cultural and cognitive proximities, were added as interpretative elements in knowledge spillovers, enriching the conceptual tools interpreting knowledge diffusion (Boschma, 2005; Rallet and Torre, 1995; Capello, 2009b).

These approaches are all interesting *per se*, and over time they have furnished a rich scientific apparatus for analysis of how knowledge and innovation take place in space. Testifying to their richness are the multiple scientific paradigms on which they draw – economic geography, the evolutionary theory of innovation, neo-Schumpeterian theories on local development, evolutionary geography.

However, they have a feature in common which represents the limits of current scientific know-how on local knowledge and innovation. All these theories consider *one particular phase* of the innovation process, often interpreted as the crucial one, whether knowledge creation, innovation creation, innovation diffusion or knowledge diffusion. Some theories even interpret knowledge and innovation as coinciding processes, taking for granted that if knowledge is created locally, this inevitably leads to innovation; or if innovation takes place, this is due to local knowledge availability. A similar short circuit is assumed between knowledge/ innovation and performance, with the expectation of a productivity increase in all cases in which a creative effort, a learning process, and an interactive and cooperative atmosphere characterize the local economy.

Instead, factors that enhance the implementation of new knowledge may be quite different from the factors which stimulate invention and innovation. Invention, innovation and diffusion are not necessarily intertwined, not even at the local level. The firms and individuals leading an invention are not necessarily also leaders in innovation or in the widespread diffusion of new technologies. The real world is full of examples of this kind: the fax machine, first developed in Germany, was turned into a product successful worldwide by Japanese companies. Similarly, the anti-lock brake system (ABS) was invented by US car makers but became prominent primarily due to German automotive suppliers (Licht, 2009).

Moreover, it is by no means always the case that technological catching-up shows a positive correlation with economic convergence; the strong economic growth performance of Eastern countries up to 2008 was certainly not related to knowledge economy growth, as these countries (and their regions) witnessed no technological catching-up in those years. Regional economic growth is weakly related to different scientific indicators, both of input (R&D) and of output (patenting activity). This has been demonstrated by a simple correlation run on a sample of 287 NUTS2 regions in Europe between regional GDP growth in the years 2006–2008 and R&D on GDP in 2006–2007, which showed a negative (and significant) value (–0.33); the value of the correlation index remained negative and significant (–0.23) when the correlation was measured between regional growth in the years 2006–2008 and patents per capita in a period of 2005–2006.

All this suggests that innovation can be the result of different patterns, different modes of performing each phase of the innovation process. The variety of innovation modes explains the failure of a 'one-size-fits-all' policy for innovation, like the thematically/regionally neutral and generic R&D incentives expected to develop a knowledge economy everywhere. On the contrary, innovation modes typical of each specific area have to be identified so that *ad hoc* and targeted innovation policies can be devised.

6.3. Territorial patterns of innovation: a proposed definition and a framework

The paradigmatic leap in interpreting regional innovation processes today consists in the capacity to build – on the single approaches developed for the interpretation of knowledge and innovation – a conceptual framework interpreting, *not one single phase of the innovation process* – either knowledge or innovation creation or knowledge or innovation diffusion, but the *different modes of performing the different phases of the innovation process*, highlighting the context conditions that accompany each innovation pattern. Thus considered is a 'multiple-solution model of innovation' where innovation builds on internal knowledge, or where local creativity allows, despite the lack of local knowledge, an innovative application thanks to knowledge developed elsewhere and acquired via scientific linkages, or where innovation is made possible by imitation of innovations developed outside the region (Capello, 2012).

The concept of territorial patterns of innovation is proposed and defined as a combination of *territorial specificities (context conditions)* that lie behind *different modes of performing the different phases of the innovation process*. In particular *'territorial patterns of innovation'* consist in spatial breakdowns of variants of the knowledge → invention → innovation → development logical path built on the presence/absence of territorial preconditions for knowledge creation, knowledge attraction, and innovation.

The concept of territorial patterns of innovation therefore lies on a logical sequence between knowledge, innovation and economic performance as in the abstract but consistent 'linear model of innovation' – even if heavily criticized as unrealistic and rooted in the idea of a rational and orderly innovation process (Edgerton, 2005). In fact, we strongly believe that: i) in many cases scientific advance is a major source of innovation, as the ICT paradigm and trajectory indicate; ii) an alternative model of full complexity, where 'everything depends on everything else', does not help in conceptualizing and interpreting the systemic, dynamic and interactive nature of innovation; iii) self-reinforcing feedbacks from innovation to knowledge and from economic growth to innovation and knowledge play an important role in innovation processes. The impact of science on innovation does not merely reside in the creation of new opportunities to be exploited by firms, but rather in increasing productivity of, and returns to, R&D through the solution of technical problems, elimination of research directions that have proven wrong and the provision of new research technologies (Nelson, 1959; Mowery and Rosenberg, 1998; Malerba, 2004; Balconi et al., 2010). We therefore strongly support the concept of a 'spatially diversified, phase-linear, multiple-solution model of innovation', in which the single patterns represent a linearization, or a partial-block-linearization, of an innovation process where feedbacks, spatial interconnections and non-linearities play a prominent role.

By stressing complex interplays between phases of the innovation process and spatial context or territorial conditions, the concept of 'patterns of innovation' adds three new elements with respect to the previous theoretical approaches. First of all, it disentangles knowledge from innovation, addressing the two as different (and subsequent) phases of an innovation process, each phase calling for specific local elements for its development, and having a different location depending on the presence of the factors that support their development. This approach departs from the assumption of an invention–innovation short circuit taking place inside individual firms (or their territories) operating on advanced sectors, as well as an immediate interaction between R&D/higher education facilities on the one hand and innovating firms on the other, thanks to spatial proximity.

Secondly, the new concept calls for the identification of the context conditions, both internal and external to the region, that support the different innovation phases; these context conditions become integral in the definition of a territorial pattern of innovation. In this sense, the approach does not look for special territorial capabilities that allow territories (in general) to exploit single innovation and knowledge phases. An integrated conceptual framework like this one identifies the local conditions that guarantee: a) the shift from local knowledge to innovation; b) the acquisition of external knowledge to innovate locally; c) the acquisition of external innovation for imitation with different degrees of creativity. It builds on both the different modes of performing innovation and the context conditions that guarantee the different phases of the innovation process. The conceptual effort required, therefore, is to identify the combination of context conditions that accompany each phase of the innovation process, and give rise to alternative patterns of innovation.

The third new element concerns the overcoming of a purely geographic concept of proximity to interpret inter-regional knowledge spillovers, moving towards a concept of 'cross-regional cognitive proximity'. This concept links knowledge spillovers to the presence of a common technological domain inside which cumulative search processes and inventions can be performed through inter-regional cooperation (Boschma, 2005; Capello and Caragliu, 2012).

The well-established literature presented in Table 6.1 helps in two respects. Firstly, being a 'spatial innovation and knowledge literature', it identifies the different context conditions that accompany each phase of the innovation process. Secondly, the existing literature helps in choosing the most interesting combinations between innovation modes and territorial elements. The literature, in fact, strongly emphasizes processes of, and territorial elements associated with: (i) local knowledge creation and knowledge spillover (the 'R' of R&D); (ii) external knowledge acquisition (the 'D' of R&D); (iii) pure innovation imitation. For this reason, among all possible combinations between innovation modes and territorial elements, the 'archetype' ones may be indicated in the following, each of which reflecting a specific piece of literature on knowledge and innovation in space:

a)   *an endogenous innovation pattern in a scientific network*, where local conditions fully support the creation of knowledge, its local diffusion and transformation into innovation and its widespread local adoption. Given the complex nature of knowledge creation nowadays, this pattern is expected to show a tight interplay among regions in the form of international scientific networks. From the conceptual point of view this advanced pattern is the one considered by most of the existing literature dealing with knowledge and innovation creation and diffusion (Camagni, 1991; Audretsch and Feldman, 1996; Boschma 2005; Capello, 2009b);

b)   *a creative application pattern*, characterized by the presence of creative economic actors interested and curious enough to look for knowledge outside the region – given the scarcity of local knowledge – and creative enough to apply external knowledge to local innovation needs. This approach is conceptually built on the literature on regional innovation adoption/adaptation, as also proposed by the smart specialization approach (Foray, 2009; EC, 2010b);

c)   *an imitative innovation pattern*, where the actors base their innovation capacity on imitative processes, that can take place with different degrees of adaptation of an already existing innovation. This pattern is based on the literature dealing with innovation diffusion (Hägerstrand, 1952; Capello, 1988).

Conceptually speaking, these three patterns represent by and large the different ways in which knowledge and innovation can take place in a regional economy. The three patterns of innovation have some novelties with respect to what is suggested in the literature. Concerning the endogenous innovation pattern in a scientific network, it departs from the idea that knowledge exchange is only influenced by pure spatial proximity and proposes that the capacity to access and to benefit from knowledge created elsewhere depends on the degree to which two regions are cognitively proximate, i.e. if they enjoy a complementary set of skills and competences pertaining to a common knowledge base (Capello and Caragliu, 2012), moving at the cross-regional level the concept of related variety defined by Boschma (Boschma, 2005). The cognitive proximity between regions explains their degree of virtual connection and, consequently, the knowledge potential that regions may benefit from.

The novelty of the creative application pattern rests on its break with the general belief embedded in most of the literature that knowledge equates to innovation and that if knowledge is locally available, this will automatically lead to local innovation. This is not always the case and leads to a break from the general belief that if knowledge spreads from other areas into the region, the latter is able to absorb it according to the degree of local absorptive capacity measured through existing formal knowledge. In this approach, the capacity of a region to innovate through external knowledge acquisition is made dependent on territorial creativity, embedded in local culture and in tacit knowledge. The next sections present in details the three patterns of innovation mentioned above.

6.4. The endogenous innovation pattern in a scientific network

A first and straightforward territorial pattern of innovation is an endogenous one referring to a situation in which a region is endowed with local conditions for knowledge creation and for turning knowledge into innovation, so as to guarantee a productivity increase and regional growth. This model relies on specific *internal context conditions* that explain knowledge creation and diffusion, as well as innovation by looking at the internal structural conditions of a region (Figure 6.1).

Knowledge creation is in general dependent on an urban environment where material and non-material elements supporting scientific knowledge find a natural location. Table 6.2 summarizes the main elements identified as the sources of knowledge creation. These are material and non-material, stemming from

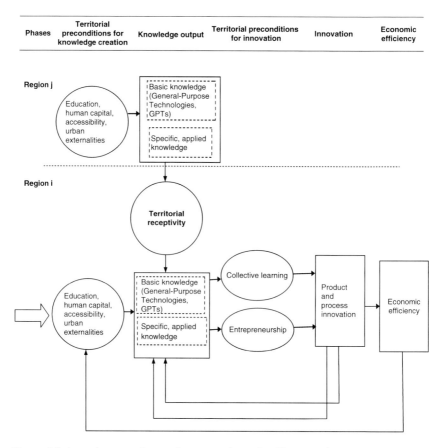

Figure 6.1 An endogenous innovation pattern in a scientific network

Source: Capello (2012)

indivisibility and synergies, i.e. from agglomeration and proximity – the two elements characterizing urban environments:

- urban size per se (McCann, 2004), especially concerning the creation of large human capital pools and wide labour markets (Lucas, 1988; Glaeser, 1998);
- diversity, concerning the variety of activities and the possibility for specializations in thin subsectors and specific productions, thanks to the size of the overall urban market (Jacobs, 1969 and 1984; Quigley, 1998);
- contacts and interactions allowing face-to-face encounters which reduce transaction costs (Scott and Angel, 1987; Storper and Scott, 1995);
- synergies due to proximity, complementarity and trust (Camagni, 1991 and 1999); in more formalized models, these same effects stem from the complexity of the urban system (Haken, 1993);

Table 6.2 Urban elements and knowledge creation

	Sources of urban increasing returns	
Types of elements supporting knowledge	*Indivisibility (agglomeration)*	*Synergy (proximity)*
Material elements	– Fixed social capital – High-level functions	– City as a node of national and international transport networks
Non-material elements	– Large markets of inputs – Large market of qualified human capital – Diversified productive systems – Creative capital accumulation	– High availability of information – R&D and higher education integration – Transcoding system of knowledge and information

Source: Capello (2012)

- reduced risks of unemployment for households, thanks to the thick and diverse urban labour market (Veltz, 1993);
- trans-territorial linkages emerging from the international gateway role of large cities, which is particularly crucial in a globalising world (Sassen, 1994).

The literature has not confined itself to identification of territorial factors in knowledge creation. Study has been made of the *territorial elements* that explain the capacity of a region to use its knowledge for innovative activities. In particular, creativity and recombination capability to translate basic or applied scientific knowledge into innovative applications require a relational space where functional and hierarchical economic and social interactions are embedded in a geographical space. Geographical proximity (agglomeration economies, district economies) and cognitive proximity (shared behavioural codes, common culture, mutual trust and sense of belonging) guarantee the *socioeconomic and geographical substrate* on which collective learning processes can be incorporated, mainly due to two main processes (Camagni and Capello, 2002):

- high mobility of professionals and skilled labour – between firms but internally to the local labour market defined by the district or the city, where this mobility is maximal); and
- intense cooperative relations among local actors, and in particular customer–supplier relationships in production, design, research, and finally knowledge creation.

The translation of knowledge into innovation is facilitated by interaction and cooperation, by the reduction of uncertainty (especially concerning the behaviour of competitors and partners), of information asymmetries (thus reducing mutual suspicion among partners) and of the probability of opportunistic behaviour under the threat of social sanctioning (Camagni, 1991 and 2004) – all of which are elements confirmed by many regional economics schools (Bellet et al., 1993; Rallet and Torre, 1995; Cappellin, 2003b).

The foregoing discussion on the role of territorial variables and the centrality of local conditions should not be taken as suggesting a return to an anti-historical localism or territorial autarchy. On the contrary, local milieux should be perfectly accessible, open and receptive to external flows of information, knowledge, technologies, organisational and cognitive models, and always ready to combine local knowledge and external knowledge anew. What is really meant by referring to the importance of local territories is the fact that, while some important production factors like financial capital, general information, consolidated technologies and codified knowledge are today readily available virtually everywhere, the ability to organize these 'pervasive' factors into continuously innovative production processes and products is by no means pervasive and generalized, but instead exists selectively only in some places where tacit knowledge is continuously created, exchanged and utilized, and business ideas find their way to real markets (Camagni and Capello, 2009).

In this respect, the knowledge filter theory of entrepreneurship put forward by Acs and Audretsch envisages an explicit link between knowledge and entrepreneurship within the spatial context, where entrepreneurs are interpreted as the innovative adopters of new knowledge (Acs et al. 2004). This theory posits that investments in knowledge by incumbent firms and research organizations such as universities will generate entrepreneurial (innovation) opportunities because not all of the new knowledge will be pursued and commercialized by the incumbent firms. The knowledge filter refers to the extent that new knowledge remains uncommercialized by the organization creating that knowledge. These residual ideas are those that generate the opportunity for entrepreneurship. The interesting aspect of this theory is that the capabilities of economic agents within the region to access and absorb the knowledge and ultimately utilize it to generate entrepreneurial activity is no longer assumed to be invariant with respect to geographic space, contrary to what has always been thought. In particular, diversified areas, in which differences among people that foster differing appraisals of a given information set, thereby resulting in different appraisals of any new idea, are expected to gain more from new knowledge.

Notwithstanding the internal capacities to generate knowledge, given the complex and systemic nature of knowledge and innovation, in most cases regions reinforce and complement their internal knowledge with external knowledge through diffusive, mostly unintentional, knowledge patterns based on spatial proximity ('spatial linkages') subject to strong distance decay effects, and/or through intentional relations based on a-spatial networks or non-spatially mediated channels ('a-spatial linkages') that may take place at both short and long distances according to the organization of forms of transfer and exchange of information and knowledge different from the pure spatial proximity (on this issue, see also Chapter 4).

An innovation pattern of this kind can be labelled '*endogenous innovation pattern in a scientific network*'. In the face of a territorial pattern of innovation of this kind, the natural innovation policy aim is to achieve the maximum return to R&D investments; an aim which emphasizes the importance of a specialization in R&D at European level that guarantees the achievement of a critical mass of researchers, equipment and R&D resources. This critical mass is interpreted as crucial to attaining the desired goal, for research work to become effective, and to achieve an acceptable research performance (Table 6.3).

Based on the indivisibility rule associated with research activities in general, and with general purpose technologies in particular, the idea of a smart specialization in R&D activity has pervaded the innovation economic debate, with a call for a spatial concentration of research activities enabling agglomeration processes to occur and giving rise to centres of excellence. This can only be done within an integrated research space where knowledge is exchanged within a solid and

Table 6.3 Characteristics of the different territorial innovation patterns

Innovation patterns	Endogenous innovation pattern in a scientific network	Creative application pattern	Imitative innovation pattern
Characteristics			
Knowledge/ technology	Basic, general purpose technologies	Applied technologies	Imitation
Role of the region in the innovation process	Active role	Active role	Passive role
Outcome of the interregional cooperation	Knowledge creation	Creative innovation application	Innovation diffusion
Territorial preconditions behind the inter-regional flows of knowledge and innovation	Territorial receptivity	Territorial creativity	Territorial attractiveness
Natural regional context associated to the innovation pattern	Metropolitan regions	Second ranking urban regions	Catching-up regions
Innovation policy aims	Maximum return to R&D investment	Maximum return to co-inventing applications	Maximum return to imitation

Source: Capello (2012)

efficient network among centres of excellence that become regions specialized in the basic inventions. A region exhibiting 'an endogenous innovation pattern in a scientific network' can become one of these centres; the specialization of each centre in general purpose technology research activities can become a policy mission.

The innovative model in this territorial innovation pattern is a typical supply-driven model; from scientific activities, from an invention, the subsequent co-invention of applications leads to a number of innovations mainly by inventors and co-inventors of applications.

The condition for a region to acquire knowledge from outside its boundaries can be regarded as *territorial receptivity* (Table 6.4), broadly defined as the capability of the region to interpret and use external knowledge for complementary research and science advances, a capacity embedded in local culture and in tacit knowledge rather than in formal knowledge à la Cohen and Levinthal (1990). More specifically, territorial receptivity is made up of different aspects according to the nature of knowledge and its diffusion. If a modern view of knowledge is adopted, learning and interaction processes are put at the forefront, and knowledge is considered to be complex semi-public or cooperative. Its diffusion follows largely unpredictable creative processes. Knowledge creation and learning often depend on combining diverse, complementary capabilities of heterogeneous agents.

Given these characteristics, receptivity is first of all dependent on a *relational capability* required to ensure that a region is in general made up of individuals, firms and institutions oriented towards cooperation and synergy, nourished by trust and sense of belonging, in order to guarantee collective and interactive learning processes.

Moreover, spatial proximity facilitates the overcoming of spatial friction, and the exchange of knowledge, mainly tacit knowledge, seems to be subject to strong distance decay effects. Spatial proximity to a region may therefore be another component of receptivity. However, this kind of proximity is not enough. The

Table 6.4 Preconditions for the inter-regional exchange of knowledge and innovation

	Territorial Receptivity	*Territorial Creativity*	*Territorial Attractiveness*
Preconditions to receive	Relational capacity	Openness to innovation, creativity	Limited labour costs
Preconditions to exploit external knowledge	Cross-regional cognitive proximity	Technological proximity	Income differentials
Channels for achieving external knowledge	Scientific networks Co-patenting Migration of inventors	Participation in industrial associations and in formal and informal clubs	Foreign direct investments

Source: Capello (2012)

complexity of science and knowledge evolution, together with the bounded rationality which generates cognitive constraints on actors, induces economic agents to search in close proximity to their existing knowledge base, which provides opportunities and sets constraints for further improvement (Boschma, 2005). Knowledge evolution therefore takes place in a cumulative way, localized around a technological paradigm, in cooperation among actors with a strong complementarity within a set of shared competences. Extending Boschma's concept of 'related variety' from the intra-regional to the inter-regional level, a third component of territorial receptivity is a cross-regional cognitive proximity. This is necessary for one region to acquire knowledge from another, and to understand and use it in a creative way (Table 6.4). In our conceptual approach, two regions are cognitively proximate if they enjoy a complementary set of skills and competences pertaining to a common knowledge base (Capello and Caragliu, 2012).

All these features are more easily found in metropolitan areas. The latter are the main sites of innovative activity, the 'incubators' of new knowledge: cities are the principal centres of research, given their large pools of expertise, and the availability of advanced services (finance and insurance) ready to carry the risk of any innovative activity. The fuel for a continuing knowledge and innovation process in cities consists in the density of external, particularly international, linkages maintained and developed by individuals, groups, associations, firms and institutions – what is increasingly called 'relational capital' (Camagni, 1999) – coupled with a large diversity of competences on which complementary knowledge can find common cognitive ground.

6.5. The creative application pattern

The reality also shows that some regions are latecomers and mainly users of general purpose, basic technologies; experience shows that being a latecomer in core technologies has serious implications that are long-lasting and difficult to reverse. Foremost, technological leaders are enabled to expand into new science and technology fields and create the conditions for reiteration such processes in further emerging science and technology areas.

However, reality is full of examples in which invention and innovation are not intertwined. The linkage between basic knowledge and innovation is therefore in many cases not evident, and there are many regions in which innovation takes place on the basis of basic knowledge acquired from outside and of specific know-how in local, application sectors. In this case, innovation activity stems from a merging between general purpose technology knowledge deriving from networking with leading regions and local specialized knowledge in the region (Figure 6.2). In this pattern, a particular case consists of investments in the 'co-invention of applications' – that is, development of applications in one or several important domains of the regional economy – without embarking on expensive basic R&D activities with an insufficient critical mass of human and financial resources (Foray, 2009; Foray et al., 2009).

In this innovation pattern, regions must develop an original and unique

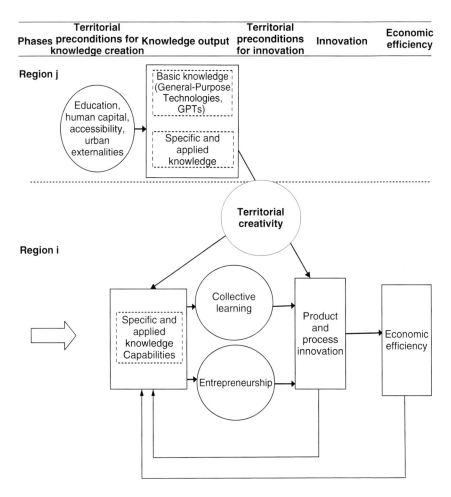

Phases	Territorial preconditions for knowledge creation	Knowledge output	Territorial preconditions for innovation	Innovation	Economic efficiency

Figure 6.2 A creative application pattern

Source: Capello (2012)

knowledge domain based on their productive vocations; therefore regions must discover the research and innovation areas in which they can hope to excel. This discovery is made by firms which have to achieve combinations between technologies and various elements of the value chain, and construct very different and unpredicted specific niches of competitive advantage. In this sense, this innovation pattern is supply-driven, in that it depends on the creativity and recombination capability of potential innovating firms which – thanks to their internal specific knowledge – identify a gap in a possible application of general purpose technologies, and devote their creative efforts to closing that gap.

This does not necessarily mean that regions must specialize in one or a few knowledge domains. In an innovation pattern like this one, the evolutionary trajectories of innovation can either be specialized or can progress by means of the evolution of 'platforms' combining many technologies. But they can also be the result of differentiated technological fields in which local firms operate. The features shared by all these possible forms in which this innovation pattern can take place is that the move from invention to innovation resides in creativity, recombination capability, ability to identify at the same time new needs and the right basic technology of local actors, and the ability to recombine local knowledge and external knowledge anew. In this sense, the innovation process results from an active role by collective actors in a region, especially potential innovators/adopters, which leads to innovation creation despite the lack of ability in knowledge creation.

The maximum return to R&D investments is not the natural policy aim of this pattern; the innovation policy aim in this case is the maximum return to co-inventing application (the typical Schumpeterian profits), which depends closely on the ability of regions to change rapidly in response to external stimuli (such as the emergence of a new technology). In other words, it depends on the ability to promote 'shifting' from old to new uses.

The networking activity between scientific core regions in which basic knowledge is created and co-innovating application regions finds an economic rationale in the dynamic feedback loops that link invention to application. Invention gives rise to the co-invention of applications which in their turn increase the return on subsequent inventions. When this virtuous cycle takes place, a long-term dynamic develops, consisting of large-scale investments in R&D whose social and private marginal rates of return reach high levels. Myriads of economically important innovations result from the co-invention of applications, and the amount of application co-invention increases the size of the general technology market and improves the economic return on invention activities relating to it (Foray, 2009).

The territorial conditions necessary for this innovation pattern to occur are linked to the concept of *territorial creativity* (Table 6.3). This consists of entrepreneurs able to access and absorb the knowledge produced in the world and ultimately utilize it to invent co-applications; this can more easily happen in a context open to innovation which nourishes itself with external knowledge useful for its local purposes and needs. Likely to interact in this kind of innovative pattern are regions with similar technological vocations. Participation in industrial associations and/or the exploitation of external experts are the channels through which knowledge flows into the region (Table 6.4).

Regions in which this innovation pattern finds a natural location are the second-ranking urban regions characterized by high accessibility to metropolitan leading regions, with a local labour market fed by human capital in general formed in first-ranking urban areas (Table 6.3). But it is also the case of highly specialized areas, like local districts, where specialized knowledge cumulates over time and where the need for technological jumps is often resolved by merging specific local competences with new basic knowledge from outside through what has been labelled 'trans-territorial networking' (Camagni, 1991). In the milieu innovation theory, these networking capabilities have always been thought of as ways to feed local specialized knowledge with technological novelties at the frontier, to jump on a new technological paradigm – something which is impossible to achieve only by cumulating specialized technological knowledge inside the area. This latter carries the inevitable risk of locking the area into a technological pattern with no possible way out.

6.6. The imitative innovation pattern

Another innovation pattern which can be envisaged is an imitative innovation pattern, this being a situation in which a region innovates because it receives innovation from outside. This is more an adoption innovation pattern, where technological developments at the local level result from a region's passive attitude – in terms of invention, knowledge creation and innovation generation – which is fed by external actors of innovation already developed elsewhere (Figure 6.3).

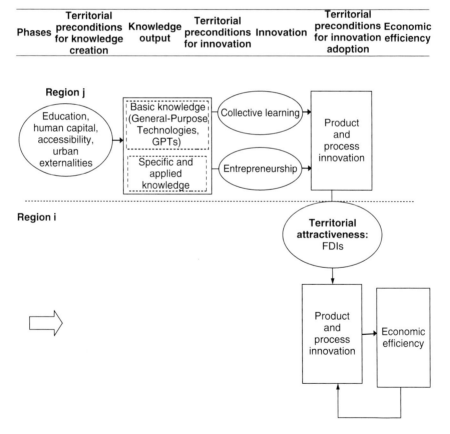

Figure 6.3 An imitative innovation pattern

Source: Capello (2012)

Product, process, managerial, and organizational innovation embedded in large multinationals can be the channel through which innovation is brought into catching-up regions (Table 6.4). *Territorial attractiveness* is the precondition for regions to acquire external innovation (Table 6.3); a large final market (market seeking) and/or labour cost competitiveness (efficiency seeking) are the preconditions to become attractive areas for foreigner direct investments (Dunning, 2001 and 2009; Cantwell, 2009). Regions exchanging innovation through foreign direct investments are regions with strong income differentials.

This imitative pattern is not necessarily the least productive and efficient innovation pattern; regions can be creative and rapid in the imitation phase if they deepen and improve productivity in existing uses, adapt existing uses to the specific local needs, adjust products to local market interests, and forge innovation processes on local productive needs. Regions can also be more passive and imitate innovation from outside as conceived elsewhere.

The right innovation policy for this pattern has nothing to do with efficiency in R&D activities, or in supporting co-inventing applications. In this case, policy actions must be devoted to achieving the maximum return to imitation, and this aim is accomplished through creative adaptation of already-existing innovation, i.e. through adoption processes driven by creative ideas on how already existing innovation can be adapted to respond to local needs.

Imitative innovation patterns are typical of the Eastern countries that, over the past two decades, have shown a decisive economic performance mainly based on foreigner direct investments, and all the innovative capacity brought about by multinationals. The efficiency of this innovation pattern may be high, giving rise to strong positive feedback loops from growth to innovation through higher financial resources to invest in the innovation process. The high rate of growth may produce higher living standards and a higher quality of life in these countries. The ways in which innovation is attracted from outside the region may evolve in a second stage towards other channels, like the mobility of inventors, whose determinants are economic growth potentials, expected high wages, and high quality-of-life potential.

6.7. Conclusions

The main idea put forward by this chapter is that the pathways towards innovation and modernization are differentiated among regions according to local specificities, and that this differentiation explains why a single overall strategy is likely to be unsuited to providing the right stimuli and incentives in the different contexts.

The chapter has moved away from the idea that R&D equals knowledge and that knowledge equals innovation. The distinction between (i) the process of invention in general purpose, basic technology, pervading different sectors horizontally once invention has turned into an innovation, and (ii) the process of inventing an application of basic knowledge in a specific sector innovating in new products and new market niches is vital for understanding current patterns of innovation. This becomes even more important if we consider that the factors which stimulate new knowledge, invention, innovation and diffusion differ.

Invention and innovation are not necessarily intertwined and this gives rise, even at the local level, to very different and multifaceted situations. Some regions have the capacity to go through all phases of the 'linear model' from knowledge creation to innovation and growth, with all the feedback that can be foreseen from growth to knowledge and innovation. Other regions reinforce this 'linear model' by exchanging knowledge with other regions to gain complementary assets through a scientific network. There is, however, a completely different situation in which regions innovate by combining their creative thinking with basic knowledge accumulated in other regions to develop co-inventing applications. Finally, another territorial innovation pattern consists of the situation in which regions innovate by creative imitation of innovation developed elsewhere.

All these innovation patterns are the result of specific context conditions that support one innovation pattern more than another. Required to enter scientific networks is territorial receptivity, defined as the capability of the region to exploit external knowledge for complementary research and science advances, a capacity embedded in local culture and in tacit knowledge rather than in formal knowledge like the absorptive capacity concept Cohen and Levinthal suggest: cognitive proximity, understood à la Boschma as the presence in a region of complementary knowledge within competences shared with another region. Territorial creativity is a sine qua non for a region to exploit external knowledge in order to launch internal innovation processes driven by an entrepreneurial process of discovery. Territorial attractiveness is the local condition for imitating innovation from outside.

More importantly, what emerges clearly from this approach is that each territorial innovation pattern calls for specific ad hoc innovation policy goals: the maximum return to R&D investment can be the right goal for a region specialized in knowledge creation, but it cannot at the same time be the right policy goal for regions that innovate by exploiting external knowledge, or for regions that imitate innovation processes. For the former, the ad hoc policy goal is the maximum return to co-inventing applications, which happens when the region promotes changes in response to external stimuli (such as the emergence of a new technology). A maximum return to imitation, pushing towards creative imitation, is instead the right policy aim for regions that rely on external innovation processes. Each region must be able to discover its territorial innovation pattern, and only through the awareness of the original and unique territorial innovation pattern can a region hope to excel in exploiting innovation efficiency.

There is no pattern that is by definition superior to the others in terms of the efficiency and effectiveness of innovation on growth; on the contrary, each territorial pattern may provide an efficient use of research and innovation activities generating growth. This impression will be proved empirically in Chapters 8 to 10.

In order to analyse the efficiency of the territorial patterns of innovation, there is a need to identify the conceptual patterns in the real world; a taxonomy of innovative regions based on this conceptual approach is extremely useful if ad hoc policy interventions have to be developed. This is the subject matter of the next chapter.

7 Territorial patterns of innovation

Evidence from European regions

Roberta Capello and Camilla Lenzi

7.1. Introduction

The conceptual framework of 'territorial patterns of innovation' proposed in the previous chapter represents a step forward in the conceptual elaboration of innovation processes at the local level, since it clearly stresses the complexity and diversity of regional modes of innovation. Moreover, it sets the conceptual background for the empirical identification of these patterns in the real world which can be at the basis of the elaboration of a new taxonomy of innovative regions; an exercise that proves useful for developing ad hoc innovation policies, as suggested by the regional – place-based – approach (Barca, 2009) without incurring the unrealistic situation of developing one policy for each region.

Taxonomies on 'innovative regions' have already been proposed. In general, most of them seek to identify similarities among regions in terms of their knowledge bases. The most recent OECD taxonomy is no exception in this respect (OECD, 2010), since it groups European regions according to their intensity of knowledge, identifying the knowledge regions, the industrial production zones, and the non-S&T-driven regions.

However, taxonomies on innovative regions based only on local knowledge production intensity are somewhat misleading, since they neglect the wider heterogeneity of innovation attitudes across regions by assuming a knowledge–innovation equivalence in space, and they lack interpretations of how the different phases of the innovation process develop, mix and combine with specific context conditions at the local level.

Building on the conceptual framework set out in Chapter 6, therefore, the aim of this chapter is to offer a new and sound taxonomy of European regions able to interpret the different combinations of context (local) conditions and modes of performing the different phases of the innovation process, by identifying the different territorial patterns of innovation in Europe.

To achieve this goal, the rest of the chapter is organized as follows. The next section comments on the existing taxonomies of European regions and identifies the main limits which the taxonomy that we propose intends to overcome. Section 7.3 presents our data set and the indicators developed to derive and to describe territorial patterns of innovation in European regions. Section 7.4 reports and comments on the results of a cluster analysis implemented with the aim of deriving a new taxonomy of innovative regions in Europe. Interestingly, this cluster analysis detects an even more fragmented variety than conceptually envisaged. Importantly, by relying on the intensity of both *knowledge and innovation*, it gainsays the general belief that knowledge equates with innovation. Moreover, the groups of regions identified in the taxonomy prove to be characterized by specific *territorial conditions* that can be associated with the different modes of innovation. Section 7.5 discusses the main findings from a multinomial regression model used to contrast the different patterns of innovation detected in Section 7.4 according to some distinctive features, the purpose being to strengthen our descriptive results further. Section 7.6 concludes and argues for the importance of such a typology for understanding the heterogeneity across the European space of economic performance reactions to increases in knowledge and innovation intensity.

7.2. The need for a new territorial taxonomy of innovative regions

The increasing awareness and need for a shift from thematically/regionally neutral R&D and innovation policies to new thematically and/or regionally focused innovation ones requires the identification of context specificities in the knowledge-to-innovation process, in a way similar to how a 'place-based' approach is postulated for a renewed EU regional development policy (Barca, 2009). Required to achieve this goal is a conceptually and empirically sound regional innovation taxonomy to be tested on the European space.

Two crucial ingredients are necessary for the development of such a taxonomy. Firstly, a departure from the simplistic core–periphery view which proposes a simplified partitioning of the European space. This view is still current in the policy discourse, and it still shapes reflections and ideas developed within the frame of the 'smart specialization' debate (Foray, 2009; Foray et al., 2009; Giannitsis, 2009; Pontikakis et al., 2009). From this perspective, regions which specialize in high-tech sectors and are top R&D performers represent the 'core' regions, which lead the creation of new knowledge and its transformation and diffusion in the economy and can make Europe successful in international technological competition. The remaining regions can only adopt the frontier technologies developed in core regions, adapting and integrating them into their own 'knowledge domain', according to their local production specialization profiles. This approach, however, neglects the more complex and heterogeneous ways in which knowledge may be created, acquired, utilised and transformed into innovation at the regional level – as discussed in the previous chapter.

Secondly, a taxonomy must be a conceptually driven taxonomy consistent with a specific view of how knowledge and innovation take place and mix at the local level, and which, accordingly, emphasizes the context (pre)conditions supporting local innovation processes. Our goal, in fact, is to detect regional 'patterns' based on a clear conceptual definition of the different phases of any innovation process, and of the context conditions that are expected to support the different phases of that innovation process.

The existing taxonomies are unsatisfactory precisely in this regard because they are mostly data-driven rather than theoretically driven. Most of them group European regions only on the basis of their intensities of knowledge production, taking it for granted that knowledge equates with innovation while ignoring the territorial conditions behind local innovation modes. This is precisely the case of the most recent OECD taxonomy (OECD, 2010 and 2011), which identifies knowledge regions, industrial production zones, non-S&T-driven regions on the basis of R&D intensity.

An exercise of this kind is not at all isolated, and it is also well established in the academic domain. For example, Verspagen (2010) develops a 'spatial hierarchy' of innovative regions in Europe that are grouped according to both their innovative (i.e. patenting) and economic performance and sectoral specialization. Accordingly, four groups of regions are identified, namely South Europe, East Europe, West Europe and North Europe. Nevertheless, the mix among (local and external) knowledge inputs, territorially embedded elements that facilitate the creation of knowledge and innovation, and economic performance indicators prevents any great progress in departing from a strong core (West and North Europe) and a periphery (South and East Europe) pattern.[1]

When elements other than pure knowledge intensity indicators have been considered, the methodology used to identify the groups of regions has been that of mixing together (local) knowledge inputs (e.g. gross domestic R&D expenditure as a share of GDP, business R&D expenditure as a share of total R&D expenditure, patent applications per million inhabitants), territorially embedded elements that facilitate the creation of knowledge and innovation (e.g. tertiary education as a share of the labour force, population density), and economic performance indicators (e.g. GDP per capita, unemployment rate, share of employment in the primary sector, share of employment in the public sector, employment in high and medium high-tech manufacturing as a share of total manufacturing, employment in knowledge-intensive services as a share of total services, share of employment in manufacturing). This approach has no theoretical expectations other than that of linking knowledge to innovation and economic growth through some 'enabling factors'. On this simple reasoning, regional growth is expected to be the straightforward outcome of any knowledge creation activity; of any learning process taking place at the local level with the support of innovation-prone local conditions supposed to be the same in each region regardless its knowledge intensity and innovation development stage.

In this vein, Winties and Hollanders (2010) partition the European space on the basis of different indicators of sectoral specialization in high-tech and knowledge-intensive industries (on the basis of employment data), of engagement in research-intensive activities (namely, R&D expenditures and patent applications), of human resources development (namely, the population's educational attainment) as well as indicators of economic wealth and the characteristics of the labour market. Produced in this case is a description of the European territory more variegated than the one based on knowledge intensity indicators alone, but still without clear conceptual expectations as to the linkages among the different variables and the final grouping of regions.

Until very recently, a crucial hindrance to the development of taxonomies of innovative regions was the lack of innovation data at the regional level.[2] More recently, some empirical works, developed for the DG Enterprise and Industry (namely, the different editions of the Regional Innovation Scoreboard; Hollanders et al., 2009a), have proposed taxonomies of European regions that go far beyond the dichotomous typology implicit in a core–periphery pattern, and that make use of regional innovation data. The use of innovation data at the regional level is indeed a novelty introduced by these scoreboarding exercises. Interesting results are achieved by empirically departing from the knowledge–innovation equivalence typical of the previous taxonomies using knowledge indicators such as R&D or patent intensity as proxies for innovation outputs. Again, however, the methodologies implemented merge together indicators as diverse as innovation performance, knowledge inputs like R&D, sectoral structure, presence of spatial innovation enablers, with no a priori expectations on the conceptual links among the variables used, and with no clear differences among the roles played by the different local preconditions in each phase of the innovation process. Also, no attention to knowledge external to the regions is given in this taxonomy, as signalled in Chapter 4.

Importantly, none of these taxonomies has deep and rich territorial roots. Groups of regions, in fact, are derived on the basis of economic structural indicators (e.g. industrial specialization and labour market characteristics) and research propensity indicators. There is little mention of territorial structural characteristics (except for a population density indicator, mostly considered as a 'size' indicator, and human capital development indicators), and little effort is made to link the resulting partition of the European space to specific context conditions enabling knowledge and innovation processes at the local level.

The territorial innovation patterns framework makes it possible to take a step forward in the elaboration of a sound and conceptually grounded taxonomy of innovative regions that is substantially free from the limitations of the previous ones. This approach, in fact, introduces three conceptual novelties: firstly, by adopting a (spatially diversified) linear model of innovation (Chapter 6), it distinguishes the different stages of the innovation process; secondly, by breaking the knowledge–innovation–growth chain, it does not assume any straightforward positive impact of either knowledge or innovation (or both) on economic performance; thirdly, on the basis of the vast literature on knowledge and innovation processes at the local level, it posits clear expectations as to how specific regional characteristics are important in the different phases of the innovation process, giving rise to a specific local innovation pattern.

From the empirical point of view, therefore, developing a taxonomy fully consistent with such a framework requires:

1) distinguishing the knowledge and innovation stages from the empirical point of view and grouping regions according to both dimensions without expecting innovation to occur only because of the availability at the local level of knowledge and research-intensive activities. According to the discussion in Chapter 6, innovation can, in fact, successfully emerge from externally

sourced knowledge. Focusing on knowledge-related variables alone is therefore somewhat partial, and the availability of original innovation regional data is extremely helpful in this regard.

2) distinguishing the knowledge and innovation stages from their impact on a region's economic performance and, differently from previous taxonomies, keeping knowledge and innovation variables separate from economic performance indicators. This latter point is crucial for assessing the efficiency and effectiveness of each pattern of innovation for economic performance (Chapters 8 to 10).

3) associating (and reading) the partitioning of the European space obtained on the basis of regions' knowledge and innovation intensities in light of specific regional characteristics.

To achieve this goal, massive data collection and elaboration efforts are needed, and they are presented in the next section.

7.3. The data set

To identify innovation patterns across European regions, we drew on an original data set which encompasses all the elements that characterize the territorial patterns of innovation conceptually derived and described in Chapter 6, namely endogenous knowledge and innovation creation activities, external knowledge and innovation acquisition potential as well as the regional preconditions behind them.[3] Accordingly, we can group our indicators as follows:

•   knowledge and innovation creation indicators;
•   regional preconditions for knowledge and innovation creation indicators;
•   inter-regional knowledge and innovation flows and potentials (i.e. external knowledge and innovation) indicators;
•   regional preconditions necessary to benefit from external knowledge and innovation indicators.

Grouped in this way, the indicators are fully mentioned and described in Sections 7.3.1 to 7.3.4, respectively. Most of them are traditional indicators frequently used in the literature that need little clarifications; others, instead, are more innovative. Therefore, their construction and links with the literature require more detailed explanation and, accordingly, we mostly focus on them.

7.3.1. Knowledge and innovation creation indicators

Knowledge data mostly relied upon patent data available from the OECD REG-PAT database, from which we drew selected information (Table 7.1).[4]

Firstly, the size of a region's knowledge base was measured by means of a traditional indicator of the share of a region's patents in Europe in the period 1998–2001[5] as well as by the level of R&D expenditures on GDP in the period 2000–2002.

Table 7.1 Knowledge and innovation creation: indicators and measures

Indicators	Measures	Computation	Year	Source
Knowledge				
R&D	R&D expenditures	Share of R&D expenditures on GDP	Average value 2000–2002	CRENoS database
Knowledge	Share of patents	Regional share of EU total patents	Total patents in the period 1998–2001	Authors' calculation on CRENoS database
Specialization in GPTs	Index of specialization on patents in GPTs (i.e. nanotech, ICT, biotechnology)	Location quotient of regional GPT patents	Total patents in the period 1998–2001	Authors' calculation on CRENoS database
Generality	Opposite of the Herfindal index on the technological classes of forward citations	See eq. 7.1	Total patents in the period 1998–2001	Authors' calculation on CRENoS database
Originality	Opposite of the Herfindal index on the technological classes of backward citations	See eq. 7.2	Total patents in the period 1998–2001	Authors' calculation on CRENoS database
Capabilities (knowledge embedded in human capital)	Share of managers and technicians	Factor analysis on the share of production and specialized service managers and science and engineering associate professionals (ISCO codes 13 and 31, respectively)	Average value 1997–2001	European Labour Force Survey

Innovation

Product and/or process innovation	Firms introducing a new product and/or a new process in the market	Share of firms introducing product and/or process innovations	One value for the period 2002–2004	Authors' estimation on CIS (Eurostat) data
Marketing and/or organizational innovation	Firms introducing a marketing and/or an organisational innovation	Share of firms introducing marketing and/or organizational innovations	One value for the period 2002–2004	Authors' estimation on CIS (Eurostat) data
Product innovation	Firms introducing a new product in the market	Share of firms introducing a product innovation	One value for the period 2002–2004	Authors' estimation on CIS (Eurostat) data
Process innovation	Firms introducing a new process in the market	Share of firms introducing a process innovation	One value for the period 2002–2004	Authors' estimation on CIS (Eurostat) data
Product and process innovation	Firms introducing both a new product and a new process in the market	Share of firms introducing both product and process innovations	One value for the period 2002–2004	Authors' estimation on CIS (Eurostat) data

Source: Capello and Lenzi (2012a)

Note: Patent citations are here classified according to the 7 technology fields classification developed by OST (see also footnote 6 for further details).

More importantly, and differently from previous studies, we also developed a list of indicators capturing the nature and type of the knowledge created in a region – namely the degree of basic, pervasive and radical knowledge.

The degree of basic knowledge generated in a region was measured through the presence of General Purpose Technologies (GPTs) in the region. For each region *i*, we computed a technological specialization index on the basis of the number of patents applied for in GPTs. GPTs include nanotechnology, biotechnology and ICTs, as also claimed by some studies (Foray et al., 2009). We assigned patents to these technologies on the basis of their IPC codes (see also footnote 6) following the OECD classification. The focus on these technologies was motivated by the fact that they are considered to have wider applications, large adoption and diffusion potential and, ultimately, greater economic impact. Moreover, the lagged development and adoption of these technologies in Europe is considered to be one of the main causes of the European productivity gap with respect to the US (Foray et al., 2009). The specialization index was computed as the share of GPTs at regional level for the period 1998–2001 with respect to the European share of patents in GPTs.

Pervasiveness was captured through a *generality* index (Hall et al., 2001), that is, an adapted Herfindal index on the technological classes[6] of the citations received (i.e. *forward citations*) by the patents applied for in the period 1998–2001. More general and pervasive knowledge is used in a wider spectrum of diverse technological applications, and it is thus of greater technological value than more specific and targeted knowledge. In detail, this was computed as the opposite of the Herfindal index on the technological classes of forward citations ($H_{forward}$), as follows:

$$Generality = 1 - H_{forward} = 1 - \sum_{j=1}^{7} \left(\frac{cit\_forward_{ij}}{cit\_forward_i} \right)^2 \tag{7.1}$$

where $cit\_forward_{ij}$ is the number of forward citations in region *i* in technological class *j*.

Originality of the knowledge produced, i.e. the extent to which the knowledge being developed in each region is original compared to the state of the art and recombines pieces of knowledge distributed across different technical fields, was measured by means of an *originality* index (Hall et al., 2001). More original knowledge is likely to be associated with previously unexplored technological applications and with more radical inventions. This is also an adapted Herfindal index on the technological classes of the citations made (i.e. *backward citations*) by the patents applied for in the period 1998–2001 ($H_{backward}$). In detail, it was computed as the opposite of the Herfindal index on the technological classes of backward citations, as follows:

$$Originality = 1 - H_{backward} = \sum_{j=1}^{7} \left(\frac{cit\_backward_{ij}}{cit\_backward_i} \right)^2 \tag{7.2}$$

where $cit\_backward_{ij}$ is the number of backward citations in region *i* in technological class *j*.

Lastly, in order to capture the knowledge not directly linked to patent activities, and which is instead embedded in human capital available in a region in the form of *technical and managerial capabilities*, an indicator was derived from a factor analysis aimed at synthesizing the information provided by two variables, i.e. the share of production and specialized service managers, and physical and engineering science associate technicians on total employment. In fact, skilled and specialized human capital is an important repository of embedded and tacit knowledge and can identify the pool of capabilities locally available. One factor, extracted by the principal component method, is associated with the two variables (i.e. correlation greater the 0.75). The percentage of variance explained is 58.18.

We expected the three archetypical patterns identified in Chapter 6 to differ in terms of knowledge creation capacity and the nature of knowledge produced. In particular, the endogenous innovation pattern was expected to show a strong knowledge base of a pervasive and original nature. The creative application pattern was expected to have a not negligible knowledge base, although one of a relatively more applied and specific nature, as well as some degree of informal knowledge embedded in managerial and technical competencies. The third innovation pattern was expected to be relatively weaker on all these dimensions.

Innovation data were built by the authors on the basis of data from the Community Innovation Survey (CIS) Eurostat database. In particular, innovation indicators were based on national CIS4 wave figures (covering the 2002–2004 period), next developed at the NUTS2 level (see Chapter 5 for details on the methodology). As in the case of knowledge, a general indicator of the degree of innovation was the regional share of firms introducing a product and/or a process innovation.

Importantly, we distinguished between different types of innovation by making use of different questions in the CIS. This distinction is not a minor one, because different innovation strategies require a different mix of knowledge and competencies. In fact, product innovation can be associated with a technological competitiveness strategy, whereas process innovation can be associated with a price competitiveness strategy (Pianta, 2001). The former involves substantial inventive and innovative efforts intended to introduce new products and to gain market shares, if not to open new markets. The latter focuses on efficiency gains obtained thanks to technological changes such as the introduction of adjustments in the production process or the adoption of new machinery, with the ultimate goal of decreasing labour costs and/or increasing production flexibility, which may lead to market shares gains (Bogliacino and Pianta, 2010). In particular, we were able to compute the share of firms introducing only product innovations, the share of firms introducing only process innovations, the share of firms introducing product and process innovations (both types of innovation simultaneously, as well as all the first three main typologies altogether), and the share of firms introducing marketing and/or organizational innovations.

We expected the endogenous innovation pattern to show the greatest innovation potential in all respects and to be relatively more specialized in product innovation, whereas the creative application and the imitative innovation patterns would be relatively more specialized in process innovation. In fact, product innovation generally requires a larger (scientific and formal) knowledge base and larger investments in knowledge advances. In contrast, process innovation generally relates more to applied, informal and tacit knowledge.

7.3.2. Regional preconditions for knowledge and innovation creation

Indicators on the regional preconditions for knowledge creation were relatively traditional indicators proposed in the literature. Among all indicators, two were available: the degree of scientific human capital in the region, measured respectively by the share of inventors and by the share of highly educated people; and the degree of accessibility (transport infrastructure) in the region (Table 7.2). We lacked an indicator of high-level functions, like universities and research centres, for which no reliable data exist with EU27-wide coverage at NUTS2 level. The availability of a dummy capturing the size of cities in a region (the so called agglomerated regions) was of help in compensating for the lack of these data.

We expected especially the endogenous innovation pattern to exhibit a relatively larger endowment in terms of scientific human capital and a higher accessibility, also related to the likely location in urban settlements. Metropolitan areas, in fact, are the main sites of innovative activity, the 'incubators' of new knowledge; the principal centres of research are mostly located in cities, given their large pools of expertise and the availability of advanced services (finance and insurance) ready to carry the risk of any innovative activity.

As regards a region's capacity to translate knowledge into innovation, the milieux innovateurs theory and the knowledge filter theory stress the presence of collective learning and entrepreneurship as the local preconditions for knowledge to be turned into useful innovative applications. Entrepreneurship was measured as the share of self-employment, with the exclusion of wholesale and retail sectors that might create distortion in the indicator. Collective learning was indirectly measured through the degree of concentration in manufacturing sectors, the idea being that the higher the concentration in specific sectors, the higher the (unintended) exchange of knowledge among local firms, as claimed by the theory of milieux innovateurs (Camagni, 1999) and innovative clusters (Cooke, 2002a; Asheim and Coenen, 2005). We also added an indicator derived from factor analysis capturing the entrepreneurial and strategic vision of innovation as an element crucial for competitiveness and growth.

We expected especially the creative application pattern to show a larger endowment in terms of these variables because they represent the preconditions for 'smartly' and creatively adapting external knowledge to local innovation needs.

7.3.3. Inter-regional knowledge and innovation flows

Regional knowledge and innovation intensity also depend considerably on the capacity of regions to attract, absorb, recombine, and adopt knowledge and innovations sourced from other regions. Specific indicators were built to measure the

Table 7.2 Regional preconditions for knowledge and innovation creation: indicators and measures

Indicators	Measures	Computation	Year	Source
Regional preconditions for knowledge creation				
Scientific human capital	Share of inventors	Share of inventors on population	Average value 1999–2001	AQR' calculation on CRENoS database
Highly educated human capital	Share of highly educated people	Share of people aged 15 and over with tertiary education on total population	Average value 1999–2001	CRENoS on Eurostat
Accessibility	Rail and road network length by usable land	Km of rail and road network on usable land	2000	ESPON
Agglomerated regions	NUTS2 with more than 300,000 inhabitants and a population density of more than 300 inhabitants per km sq., or a population density between 150 and 300 inhabitants per km sq.	Dummy variable equal to 1 if the region is classified as agglomerated	2005	ESPON
Regional preconditions for innovation creation				
Entrepreneurship	Share of self-employment (wholesale and retail excluded)	Share of self-employed on total labour force (wholesale and retail sectors excluded)	Average value 1999–2004	Eurostat
Collective learning	Concentration in manufacturing sectors	Herfindal index on the share of employment in manufacturing subsectors[1]	Average value 1999–2001	Eurostat
Strategic vision on innovation	Perception of innovation as a relevant factor for growth	Factor analysis on Eurobarometer questions on innovation importance to economic performance[2] and broadband penetration rate	2005	Eurobarometer 63.4 and Eurostat

Source: Capello and Lenzi (2012a)

1 Six manufacturing subsectors are considered, namely: Food, beverages and tobacco; Textiles and leather; Coke, refined petroleum, nuclear fuel and chemicals; Electrical and optical equipment; Transport equipment; Other manufacturing.
2 See Annex 7.1 for the list of variables used in and details about the factor analysis.

flows of inter-regional knowledge and innovation, i.e. the external knowledge and innovation potential of a region (Table 7.3).

In particular, in order to capture the potential benefits that may accrue to each region *i* from the pool of basic (GPTs) knowledge developed by other regions (i.e. *knowledge potential*), we computed the sum of the share of all GPTs patents developed by all the N- *i* regions weighted by a measure of cognitive proximity between each pair of regions. In fact, the flows of basic knowledge are influenced to a limited extent by gravity-type behaviours, proxied by physical proximity, and much more by similar backgrounds, cognitive maps and common basic knowledge shared by two regions. For this reason, the potential acquisition of basic knowledge from other regions was weighted by the degree of cognitive proximity between pairs of regions.

Cognitive proximity among actors in a region was defined in terms of related variety, i.e. the presence of complementary knowledge within a set of shared and common knowledge (Boschma, 2005). This idea was transferred to the inter-regional level, and it was measured as the inter-regional knowledge similarity in a specific technological macro-field *i* multiplied by the interregional knowledge variety in the technological sub-fields of macro-field *i* among each pair of regions.

We in fact assumed that the capacity to absorb and to use GPTs knowledge sourced from other regions depends on what we call 'cross-regional cognitive proximity' between two regions. Two regions are in fact cognitive proximate if they have complementary sets of skills and competences pertaining to a common knowledge base (Capello and Caragliu, 2012). Two main elements must be measured to capture such proximity. First, it positively depends on two regions sharing a common knowledge base and cognitive frame in technological macro-fields. Second, it is more likely to occur when two regions are specialized in different, albeit related and complementary, technological subfields within a common knowledge base, i.e. 'cross-regional related' variety.

Common knowledge base is captured through the degree to which the distribution of patents across technological macro-fields in two regions overlap. It is the product of the share of a region's *i* patents in class d_l, i.e. p_{idl}, times the share of region's *j* patents in class d_l, i.e. p_{jdl}, summed over classes. This is discounted by the absolute difference between the share of patents in class d_l of the two regions to account for the fact that common knowledge base is likely to be higher the more similar the importance of the sector in the two regions. Common knowledge base equals 1 for regions with exactly the same distribution of patents across classes, and 0 for regions with no patents in the same classes. Complementarity within a knowledge base is measured by the difference between the share of patents in a two-digit technological classes belonging to a one-digit class in two regions. The greater the difference between the two regional shares of patents in two-digit technological classes, the higher the complementarity between regions. Two-digit are represented by the 30 technology fields of the OST classification, and one-digit by the seven OST main technological fields (see footnote 6 for further details on the OST classification).

Finally, because of the high skewness of the distribution of this variable, data

Table 7.3 Inter-regional knowledge and innovation flows: indicators and measures

Indicators	Measures	Computation	Year	Source
Inter-regional knowledge and innovation flows				
Knowledge potential	Share of patents in GPT of all other regions weighted by cognitive proximity	Sum of the share of patents of all regions, but the focal one, weighted by the cognitive proximity to the focal region	Total patents in the period 1998–2001	Authors' calculation on CRENoS database
Capability potential	Capabilities of all the other regions weighted by industrial proximity	Sum of the capabilities of all regions, but the focal one, weighted by industrial proximity to the focal region	Average value 1997–2001	European Labour Force Survey and Eurostat
Innovation potential	FDI penetration rate	Number of FDI in manufacturing on total population	Average values 2005–2007	FDI-Regio, Bocconi-ISLA
Proximity matrices				
Cross-regional cognitive proximity	Cross-regional common knowledge base in a digit-1 technological class multiplied by cross-regional knowledge complementarity in digit-2 technological sub-classes belonging to the digit-1, summed over classes	See eq. 7.3	Total patents in the period 1998–2001	Authors' calculation on CRENoS database
Industrial proximity	Cross-regional similarity in production specialization	Euclidean proximity between regional location quotients in 6 different manufacturing sectors	Average values 1998–2001	Eurostat

Source: Capello and Lenzi (2012a)

Note: Six manufacturing sub-sectors are considered, namely: Food, beverages and tobacco; Textiles and leather; Coke, refined petroleum, nuclear fuel and chemicals; Electrical and optical equipment; Transport equipment; Other manufacturing.

were transformed using a square root transformation, a methodology largely applied in the literature (Hollanders et al., 2009b).

All this is summarized in the following formula:

Cross-regional cognitive proximity =

$$\sqrt{\sum_{d1=1}^{n}\left[\frac{\left(p_{id1}\times p_{jd1}\right)}{\left(|\,p_{id1}-p_{jd1}\,|\right)}\times\left(\sum_{d2=1}^{m}\left(p_{id1}-p_{jd1}\,|\right)\right)\right]}. \qquad (7.3)$$

where n represents the number of one-digit technological classes, m the number of two-digit technological sub-classes within each n digit-1 class, p_{id2} the share of region's i patents in digit-two sub-class d_2, p_{jd2} share of region's j patents in digit-2 sub-class d_2, p_{id1} the share of region's i patents in digit-1 class d_1, p_{jd1} share of region's j patents in digit-1 class d_1.

We expected a greater knowledge potential to be associated especially with the endogenous innovation pattern, because of its stronger knowledge vocation and, accordingly, higher absorptive capacity to scout external basic knowledge and to integrate it into the local research and knowledge trajectories.

Next, in order to capture the potential benefits that may accrue to each region i from the pool of embedded knowledge available in other regions (i.e. *capability potential*), we computed the sum of the capabilities in all the N- i regions weighted by a measure of industrial proximity between each pair of regions. The exchange of capabilities is in fact higher, the closer the similarities in terms of industrial mix. In particular, industrial proximity is measured as the distance between pairs of regions in their location quotient on the basis of employment data in six manufacturing sectors. The greater this similarity, the greater the opportunity to benefit from embedded knowledge in human capital sourced from other regions, i.e. capabilities external to the region.

We expected the creative application pattern to show a greater capability potential, because of its relative specialization in more applied and less formal knowledge, frequently sourced from external regions and then rapidly adapted to local business needs.

Finally, in order to take into account the potential benefits that may accrue to each region i from the pool of innovations developed in other regions (*innovation potential*), we drew on the evidence that multinational corporations and FDIs can be considered as innovation diffusion channels and promoting learning processes (Cantwell and Iammarino, 2003; Castellani and Zanfei, 2004). We thus computed the number of FDIs in each region in the manufacturing sector and discounted it by the regional population size.

We expected this to be prominent in the imitative innovation pattern, which (in relative terms) lacks endogenous knowledge and innovation capacities and is more likely to draw on external innovation that may be imitated perhaps with some degree of elaboration and by making some adjustments to the original product concepts. As recent evidence shows, FDIs are increasingly concentrated in Central and Eastern European countries.

7.3.4. *Regional preconditions for benefitting from external knowledge and innovation*

The knowledge and innovation potentials are likely to be enhanced by specific regional preconditions for external knowledge and innovation acquisition.

Receptivity is defined as the capability of the region to exchange, to interpret and to use external knowledge for complementary research and science advances. It is therefore the precondition for a region to acquire external knowledge and to use it efficiently. To capture this relational and networking capacity, we used an indicator of the 5th framework programme funding per capita (Table 7.4).

We expected relational and networking capabilities to be especially associated with the endogenous innovation pattern. In fact, the complex and systemic nature of knowledge has increasingly made its production more dispersed. Therefore, regions need to sustain and expand their local knowledge basis by engaging in knowledge-oriented relationships and exchanges with external agents and regions. Such exchanges can be both unintentional and mediated by spatial proximity, and thus subject to strong distance decay effects, as well as selective and intentional, and mediated by forms of proximity other than pure spatial proximity (Boschma, 2005; Capello, 2009a).

Creativity is instead necessary for a region to achieve knowledge and turn it into local innovation, adding to internal specific capabilities not necessarily embedded in formal knowledge. Meant by 'creativity' is recombination capability, the ability

Table 7.4 Regional preconditions for benefiting from external knowledge and innovation: Indicators and measures

Indicators	Measures	Computation	Year	Source
Regional preconditions for external knowledge acquisition				
Receptivity	Capacity of the region to interpret and to use external knowledge (i.e. degree of networking)	Regional 5th Framework Programme funding per capita	Average value 1998–2002	Authors' calculation on CRENoS database
Creativity	Sensibility, interest and openness to innovation	Factor analysis on Eurobarometer questions on sensibility, interest and openness to innovation	2005	Eurobarometer 63.4
Regional preconditions for external innovation acquisition				
Attractiveness	Regional wage differential with respect to the EU average	$W_{EU\ average} - W_{Reg\_i}$	Average value 1999–2001	Eurostat

Source: Capello and Lenzi (2012a)

to identify new needs and the right basic technology of local actors, the ability to combine local knowledge and external knowledge anew, the ability to identify a gap in the application of existing technologies and to make creative efforts to overcome that gap. Creativity was therefore expected to be prominent especially in the creative application pattern, in which regions must identify and build a novel and unexploited knowledge basis consistent with their local productive structure. This search process is driven by firms and talented entrepreneurs that by successfully and innovatively matching new technologies and market needs can develop very different and unpredicted competitive advantages in specific market niches. This variable was measured by means of a factor analysis on the Eurobarometer questions on sensibility, interest and openness to innovation of the local population.[7]

By 'attractiveness' is meant the capacity of a region to receive innovations developed outside the region and apply it to local needs. If innovation mainly derives from advanced multinational firms, from which the local firms system can imitate managerial, organizational, product and process innovation, a good proxy for FDI attractiveness is low labour cost, measured by the region's wage differential from the European average. Accordingly, this was expected to characterize especially the imitative innovation pattern.

7.4. A taxonomy of innovative regions in Europe

A cluster analysis was performed to combine regions into groups and to identify different patterns of knowledge and innovation across regions, the aim being to describe the variety of attitudes and knowledge and innovation behaviours across European regions. The purpose of the clustering exercise was to identify similarities and differences across regions.

In particular, we performed a *k*-means cluster analysis based on the degree of knowledge and innovation in general produced by a region.[8] In our conceptual approach, in fact, knowledge and innovation take place in different stages and can mix in a variety of ways. In particular, the cluster analysis was run on two innovation variables and one knowledge intensity variable. As to the innovation variables, the share of firms introducing product and/or process innovation and the share of firms introducing marketing and/or organizational innovations were chosen, since they encompass the largest category of innovators and can thus take different innovation typologies into account. Used for the intensity of knowledge production was the indicator of the region's knowledge base size (i.e. the share of EU total patents).

This choice has a conceptual motivation. In fact, it allows emphasis on the role of endogenous knowledge and innovation creation capabilities. Our purpose, in fact, was to derive a taxonomy of knowledge and innovation potentials in European regions to then be read in light of specific territorial elements.

We considered various statistical criteria with which to identify the appropriate number of clusters to be retained, such as the relationship between within-cluster and between-cluster variance, but also the number of firms per se. The balance between the information advantages provided by expanding the number of clusters and the interpretability of the results in terms of innovation patterns supported the extraction of five clusters; each cluster included a reasonable portion of observations, so that they could be plausibly interpreted as patterns of innovation. They statistically and significantly differed in the main variables used for the clustering exercise, as the results of the ANOVA tests presented below show. Indeed, the magnitude of the F values performed on each dimension is an indication of how well the respective dimension discriminated between clusters.

Performing an ANOVA exercise on the variables presented in Tables 7.1–7.4 provided interesting additional information that made it possible to emphasise the differences among clusters in terms of key distinctive territorial preconditions for knowledge and innovation creation and acquisition. Table 7.5 synthesises the results of the ANOVA exercise and presents the mean values of the variables across the five clusters, in EU27 and (in the last column) the significance level of the ANOVA test.

The variables used for the clustering exercise reported in Table 7.5 at first sight simply provide a ranking of EU27 regions in terms of their endogenous knowledge and innovation performance from cluster 5 (the least knowledge- and innovation-intensive) to cluster 1 (the most knowledge- and innovation-intensive). However, this description may be somewhat too straightforward, and it may hide a greater variety of knowledge and innovation potentials and behaviours. The ANOVA exercise was very helpful in this regard and helps to qualify better the cluster description and identification.

In fact, careful inspection of the descriptive variables of each cluster yields an extremely rich picture in terms of cases of innovation and knowledge profiles associated with territorial preconditions for knowledge and innovation creation and acquisition.

In particular, the empirical results highlight that there exists a variety even more fragmented than that conceptually envisaged. There are two clusters that can be associated with our conceptual Pattern 1 (i.e. endogenous innovation pattern), whose difference resides in the intensity of knowledge creation, but especially in the type of knowledge created. Moreover, two patterns can be associated with Pattern 2 (i.e. creative application pattern), whose difference lies in the type of knowledge that they acquire from outside the region: one (Cluster 3) mainly looks for formal knowledge (in the form of patents in specific technologies) outside the region; the other (Cluster 4) acquires tacit knowledge, embedded in capabilities.

Interestingly, the five groups exhibit sizeable differences in the variables considered in the clustering exercise. Map 7.1 shows the five patterns, which are briefly described below in terms of their characteristics.

Cluster 1: a European science-based area
Cluster 1 consists of the regions that are the most knowledge- and innovation-intensive. Their innovative attitude is well above the EU average across all dimensions (i.e. product, process, marketing and/or organizational innovation). This couples with a very strong knowledge orientation which is more directed to GPTs than in the other cases (and above the EU average) in terms of both the

Table 7.5 Mean values by cluster and in EU and ANOVA test statistical significance (p-value)

	Imitative innovation area (5)	Smart and creative diversification area (4)	Smart technological application area (3)	Applied science area (2)	European science-based area (1)	EU average	ANOVA P-value
Number of observations	37	86	67	52	20	262	
Variables used to define the clusters							
Knowledge (%)	0.01	0.13	0.40	0.48	1.53	0.35	$p<0.01$
Product and/or process innovation (%)	18.14	27.58	38.43	46.36	63.16	35.54	$p<0.01$
Marketing and/or organisational innovation (%)	13.94	22.05	19.61	39.33	51.07	25.99	$p<0.01$
Variables used to describe the clusters							
Knowledge							
R&D (%)	0.4	1	1.71	1.81	2.56	1.37	$p<0.01$
Specialisation in GPT	0.68	0.65	0.84	0.86	0.92	0.76	$p<0.05$
Share of patents in GPT (%)	18.66	17.95	22.91	23.58	25.24	20.85	$p<0.05$
Generality	0.242	0.531	0.730	0.724	0.801	0.592	$p<0.01$
Originality	0.384	0.636	0.759	0.749	0.804	0.661	$p<0.01$
Capabilities	−0.30	0.36	−0.04	−0.29	−0.81	−0.01	$p<0.01$
Innovation							
Product innovation (%)	4.13	5.01	15.38	12.20	23.46	10.40	$p<0.01$
Process innovation (%)	5.88	10.65	12.23	12.97	13.41	11.05	$p<0.01$
Product and process innovation (%)	8.13	11.91	13.97	21.66	26.29	14.97	$p<0.01$
Regional preconditions for knowledge creation							
Scientific human capital (%)	0.001	0.005	0.013	0.018	0.034	0.01	$p<0.01$
Highly educated human capital (%)	5.38	7.97	10.77	10.91	11.24	9.12	$p<0.01$
Accessibility (%)	12.42	17.46	31.47	34.70	59.52	26.62	$p<0.01$
Agglomerated regions	4	15	30	15	13	79	not applicable

Regional preconditions for innovation creation							
Entrepreneurship (%)	14.39	14.83	10.73	9.24	8.61	12.04	$p<0.01$
Collective learning	26.10	29.07	29.13	29.50	28.86	28.75	$p<0.05$
Strategic thinking on innovation	−0.87	−0.36	−0.07	0.22	0.48	−0.14	$p<0.01$
Regional preconditions for external knowledge and innovation acquisition							
Receptivity (1000 euro per capita)	3799.39	16016.29	25015.88	30147.05	41220.50	21068	$p<0.01$
Creativity	0.39	−0.05	−0.03	−0.59	−0.96	−0.13	$p<0.01$
Attractiveness	9.45	1.54	−1.98	−2.66	−8.23	0.25	$p<0.01$
Inter-regional knowledge and innovation flows							
Knowledge potential	99.07	92.04	102.44	102.31	106.33	99.07	not significant
Capability potential	−0.91	0.07	−5.13	−49.50	−92.33	−18.60	$p<0.01$
Innovation potential	51.57	55.22	55.48	30.73	20.60	47.16	not significant
Regional stage of development							
EU12 (Dummy variable equal to 1 if the region is located in Bulgaria, Cyprus, Czech Republic, Hungary, Estonia, Latvia, Lithuania, Malta, Poland, Romania, Slovakia, Slovenia)	30	17	6	3	0	56	not applicable

Source: Capello and Lenzi (2012a)

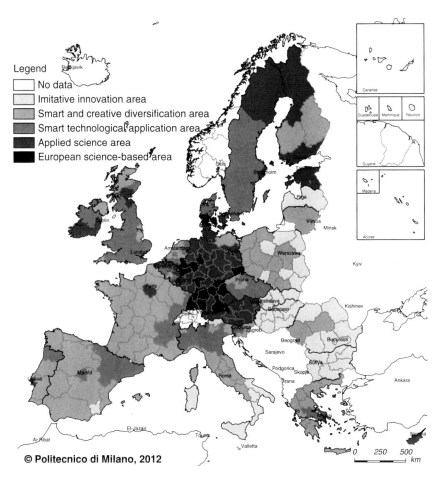

Map 7.1 Territorial patterns of innovation in Europe

Source: Capello and Lenzi (2012a)

amount of knowledge developed and specialization profile. Interestingly, this knowledge tends to be of greater generality and originality; that is, of greater technological value and more radical than the EU average. The regions in this cluster are also well endowed with the preconditions frequently associated with a greater endogenous capacity for knowledge creation, namely the presence of a highly educated population and, more importantly, the presence of scientific human capital, here measured by the share of inventors on total population. Their accessibility is also the highest (Figure 7.1), indicating that these regions probably comprise more urban and metropolitan settings (as confirmed by the variable accounting for the number of agglomerated regions), which are tradi-

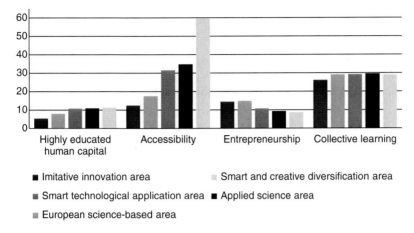

Figure 7.1 Regional preconditions for knowledge and innovation creation (shares), by cluster

Source: Capello and Lenzi (2012a)

tionally more open and fertile environments for new ideas generation (Carlino et al., 2007).

The indicators of regional preconditions for innovation creation, on the other hand, do not show the highest values across EU27. In particular, these regions are less entrepreneurial than the EU average. However, the variable accounting for collective learning shows a value comparable to the EU average and, interestingly, the regions in this cluster seem to have a more strategic attitude to the role of innovation in performance, competitiveness and economic growth. As regards the variables relative to the preconditions for knowledge and innovation acquisition, these regions outperform the others in terms of their propensity to network (i.e. receptivity) whereas they seem less creative and attractive than the EU average (Figure 7.2). Lastly, their capability and innovation potentials are below the EU average whereas their knowledge potential is above it (Figure 7.3).

Overall, these observations suggest that these regions have a strong knowledge and innovation orientation which is primarily linked to their endogenous capacity to create new knowledge and to translate it efficiently into new products and processes, as well as into managerial and/or organizational changes. This marked orientation suggests that these regions can potentially host the European science-based area and be part of what has been termed the European Research Area (Foray et al., 2009; Pontikakis et al., 2009). These regions are mostly located in Germany, with the addition of Vienna, Brussels, and Syddanmark in Denmark. It may come as a surprise that important knowledge centres like Paris, London

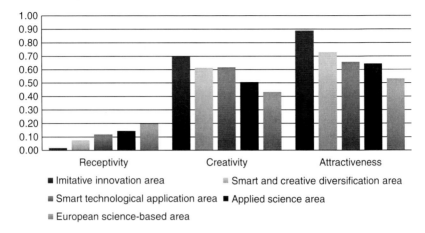

Figure 7.2 Regional preconditions for external knowledge and innovation acquisition (normalized values), by cluster

Source: Capello and Lenzi (2012a)

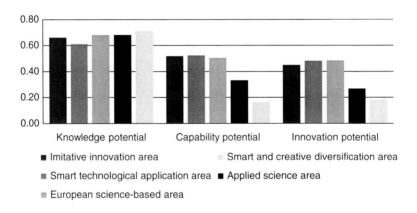

Figure 7.3 Inter-regional knowledge and innovation flows (normalized values), by cluster

Source: Capello and Lenzi (2012a)

and the Dutch Randstad regions are not included in this group (Map 7.1). In this respect, it is worth pointing out that, firstly, these regions are not among the top 20 regions in terms of total patent applications; also, they are mainly specialized in knowledge-intensive services, and thus have a lower propensity to introduce technical innovations.

Cluster 2: an applied science area

Cluster 2 includes a wider group of regions with characteristics similar to those of regions in cluster 1, although most of the variables show lower mean values. In particular, this is the case of the share of EU total patents, which is almost halved, as well as the share of scientific human capital and R&D expenditures. Interestingly, the importance of GPTs is lower both in terms of share of GPTs patents developed and in terms of specialization profile. Importantly, these regions appear more entrepreneurial, creative, attractive and with larger capability potential than regions in cluster 1, although it is below the EU average. These regions thus maintain a rather strong knowledge and innovation intensity, i.e. form a knowledge area; but, in contrast with those in cluster 1, they are less focused on GPTs, and, accordingly, more specialized in a wider spectrum of applied technologies.

Map 7.1 shows that these regions are mostly agglomerated and located in central and northern Europe, namely in Austria, Belgium, Luxembourg, France (i.e. Paris), Germany, Ireland (i.e. Dublin) Denmark, Finland and Sweden, with some notable exceptions in the East such as Prague, Cyprus and Estonia, and in the South, such as Lisbon and Attiki.

These are strong knowledge-producing regions that distinguish themselves from the European science-based area by their applied knowledge production profile. From the normative point of view, these regions can strengthen their positions by specializing in the production of applied knowledge, making use of the basic knowledge produced by the science-based area. If they do so, this group may become the Applied science area of Europe.

Cluster 3: a smart technological application area

Regions in cluster 3 are rather different from those in cluster 1. They have knowledge bases of smaller size than in the previous two clusters and a lower intensity and importance of GPTs. By contrast, they show a greater endowment of embedded knowledge in human capital (i.e. capabilities). Despite their lower knowledge intensity, they are strongly oriented to product innovation, while they are somewhat weak in terms of process innovation (although more innovative than the EU average also according to this dimension), and of marketing and/or organizational innovation.

Their weak knowledge creation is associated with low regional preconditions for knowledge and innovation creation, while their strong product innovation capacity is linked to the fact that they have more favourable preconditions for knowledge and innovation acquisition, namely creativity and attractiveness, than in the previous clusters (Figure 7.2 above).

Overall, these regions have the greatest advantage in terms of product innovation, accompanied by a high degree of knowledge potential flows and internal preconditions to translate external knowledge into innovation thanks to high creativity. These results suggest that these regions are able to translate efficiently internal and external knowledge into new specific commercial applications. Cluster 3 can easily represent our conceptual Pattern 2, the creative application pattern, where co-invention of applications results from internal creativity and external basic knowledge. It includes mostly agglomerated regions in EU15, such as the northern part of Spain and Madrid, Northern Italy, the French Alpine regions, the Netherlands, the Czech Republic, Sweden, and the UK (Map 7.1). This group can be labelled the Smart technological application area of Europe.

Cluster 4: a smart and creative diversification area

Cluster 4 exhibits some distinctive features that clearly discriminate regions in this group from the others. In particular, the knowledge and innovation variables show values below the EU average. However, these regions excel in capabilities, which suggests that the innovation activities carried out in regions belonging to this cluster, which are not negligible, mainly rely upon tacit knowledge embedded in human capital.

Moreover, regions in this cluster appear highly entrepreneurial (this variable takes the highest mean value in this cluster) and, importantly, are strongly endowed with those characteristics such as creativity and attractiveness that help to absorb and to adopt innovations developed elsewhere. Additionally, whereas the knowledge potential does not seem prominent, the capability and innovation potentials are well above the EU average. Thus, the key advantages of these regions reside in their embedded human capital and the entrepreneurial and creative attitudes that can be wisely exploited to upgrade innovative strategies.

In these regions, a different type of Pattern 2 (Chapter 6) emerges with respect to cluster 3. In these regions, internal innovation capacity is largely fed by external knowledge, as is the case for cluster 3, but the type of knowledge is neither basic nor applied formal knowledge. These regions gain significant advantages from external knowledge embedded in technical and organizational capabilities, in technicians and managers (Cooke, 2005). On the basis of the high degree of local creativity, these regions are able to take advantage of specific capabilities available in regions with similar sectoral profiles, and to innovate in different industries (Figure 7.3).

For this reason, the group of regions can be called a Smart and creative diversification area in order to highlight a possible innovative strategy associated with these regions, namely a creative and appropriate diversification of existing specialization and an upgrading of their quality. These regions are mainly located in Mediterranean countries (i.e. most of the Spanish regions, Central Italy, Greece, Portugal), in EU12 agglomerated and capital regions in Slovakia and Slovenia, Poland and the Czech Republic, few regions in northern Europe, namely in Finland, and the UK (Map 7.1).

Cluster 5: an imitative innovation area

Finally, the last group (i.e. cluster 5) can be associated with the imitative innovation pattern. In fact, it consists of regions which have rather narrow knowledge and innovation profiles and which are the worst performers in both respects. However, some key distinctive features characterize this cluster. In particular, entrepreneurship, creativity, attractiveness, capability and innovation potentials show values above the EU average. Especially, attractiveness is stronger than in the other clusters (Figure 7.3). These dimensions can be enhanced and supported creatively to embrace new adoption, imitation and innovation strategies. For this reason, this group of regions can form an Imitative innovation area in Europe. Most of these regions are rather peripheral and rural, mostly in EU12, such as all regions in Bulgaria and Hungary, Latvia, Malta, and several regions in Poland, Romania, and Slovakia, but also in Southern Italy (Map 7.1).

The high levels of creativity, entrepreneurship and collective learning in this cluster are potential assets with which to turn, from an evolutionary perspective, this area into a Smart and creative diversification area through normative intervention that helps to exploit creativity and entrepreneurship in order to increase endogenous innovation activities, and not only for imitative innovation.

7.5. The link between territorial elements and innovation patterns

In order further to support the descriptive evidence presented in Section 7.4, and to gain better understanding of the most relevant territorial elements associated with each knowledge and innovation pattern and their interplay, we compared the five clusters across some key territorial characteristics. An exercise of this kind has two additional advantages. First, it identifies the key features discriminating between clusters associated with the same conceptual archetypical pattern, namely, between clusters 1 and 2, and between clusters 3 and 4. Second, from a normative point of view, by emphasizing the crucial distinctive characteristics associated with each group of regions, it provides information on the most likely targets for policy intervention.

The nature of the dependent variable would have made estimation of an ordinal logit a more appropriate methodological choice. However, this failed to meet the parallel regression assumption, and several covariates failed to pass the Brant test assessing the parallel regression assumption at the single variable level. We therefore decided to estimate the multinomial logit model described in the text. The multinomial logit model was also preferred because it makes it possible to emphasise the differences across groups of regions in the territorial elements most likely associated with each pattern of innovation.

Therefore, we estimated the following multinomial logistic model, where the dependent variable is the probability that region i belongs to cluster j (Pr):

$$Pr(Y_i = j) = \left(\frac{exp\left(x_i \beta_j\right)}{\sum_{m=1}^{5} exp\left(x_i \beta_m\right)} \right) \; for \; j = 1, \, \dots \, , \, 5 \tag{7.4}$$

where Y_i is the dependent variable (i.e. cluster membership), x_i are case-specific regressors (including the intercept) and β_j is a vector of coefficients, which is set at zero for cluster 5, which is the base category. Therefore, coefficients will be interpreted in relative terms, i.e. in comparison with the reference category, which in Table 7.6 is cluster 5, the Imitative innovation area.

On the basis of our conceptual approach (Chapter 6) and the results of the cluster and ANOVA analyses (Section 7.4), we selected a set of independent variables able to capture some distinctive regional features associable with different knowledge and innovation attitudes and patterns. In particular, we mainly focused on regional preconditions for knowledge and innovation creation and acquisition. This choice was functional to our conceptual and empirical strategy as these can more easily become policy targets.

Before the results are discussed, it should be pointed out that the econometric model is used here for descriptive purposes in order to compare groups of regions across some key territorial elements. The set of regressions proposed and commented on what follows are to be interpreted as descriptive ones, and no causation link is assumed to run from the independent variables to the dependent ones since they are likely to be affected by endogeneity issues. Therefore, the following regression coefficients are to be interpreted as a set of partial correlation indices which help to provide a description of the elements associated with different knowledge and innovation patterns.

Comparison between the Imitative innovation area (cluster 5) and the Smart and creative diversification area (cluster 4) suggests that the key distinctive features of the latter reside in a larger pool of locally available capabilities (i.e. tacit knowledge embedded in human capital) and, moderately, in a higher level of collective learning that facilitates the circulation, socialization and re-elaboration of local knowledge. Comparison between the Imitative innovation area and the Smart technological application area (cluster 3) indicates that the latter has a significantly stronger knowledge orientation in terms of the generality of the knowledge produced as well as the capabilities and the human resources available (both scientific and highly educated human capital). Moreover, the levels of collective learning and creativity are higher in cluster 3, supporting the idea of a faster and more efficient recombination of knowledge into new products development. The Applied science area is better endowed with capabilities, scientific human capital and collective learning, but it is far less entrepreneurial than the Imitative innovation area. Lastly, the European science-based area (cluster 1) confirms its strong knowledge-intensive profile and shows greater knowledge generality, a larger scientific human capital base, a higher level of collective learning, but a lower entrepreneurial attitude. Importantly, no difference emerges among regions in the importance attached to receptivity, which suggests that all types of regions can take advantage from the learning, knowledge and innovation opportunities deriving from knowledge networks.

By changing the reference case, some additional insights can be obtained on the main distinctions among these groups of regions.[9] In particular, by setting the Smart and creative diversification area (cluster 4) as reference, its comparison with the Smart technological application area, also associated with the creative application pattern, specifies that the two clusters clearly differ in their capacity to generate internal knowledge. This is much more closely associated with the Smart technological application area, which, moreover, shows a stronger capacity to recombine internal and external knowledge via collective learning into superior innovative performance.

Table 7.6 Territorial characteristics: relevance across clusters

	Smart and creative diversification area – Cluster 4		Smart technological application area – Cluster 3		Applied science area – Cluster 2		European science-based area – Cluster 1	
	Coeff.	Std. Err.	Coeff.	Std. Err.	Coeff.	Std. Err.	Coeff.	Std. Err.
Specialization in GPT	-0.445	0.807	-0.790	1.002	-0.487	1.140	0.711	1.844
Generality	0.456	1.342	3.567**	1.820	4.145	2.097	25.937***	9.017
Capabilities	8.131***	2.453	8.870***	2.388	7.503***	2.568	1.703	5.411
Scientific human capital	6.925	4.793	11.513***	4.958	11.848***	4.999	14.006***	5.031
Highly educated human capital	6.926	10.823	20.870*	11.818	12.668	12.354	-4.442	25.077
Accessibility	2.077	4.103	3.463	4.025	4.208	4.050	4.462	4.063
Entrepreneurship	1.948	4.473	-0.144	6.246	-15.075***	7.966	-15.929	12.688
Collective learning	13.922*	7.851	21.928***	8.287	26.780***	9.003	28.309***	11.083
Strategic thinking on innovation	0.342	0.443	0.446	0.486	0.210	0.516	-0.253	0.667
Receptivity	0.000	0.000	0.000	0.000	0.000	0.000	0.000	0.000
Creativity	0.148	0.421	0.557	0.503	-0.606	0.515	-1.830**	0.728
Attractiveness	0.127	0.156	0.070	0.165	-0.089	0.168	0.290	0.181
Constant	-7.405***	2.919	-14.991***	3.427	-14.829**	3.582	-32.934***	8.996

Notes: Robust standard errors. Wald chi2(48) = 202.62; Prob > chi2 = 0.000; Log likelihood = -229.11 Pseudo $R2$ = 0.42

*** $p < 0.01$, ** $p < 0.05$, * $p < 0.1$.

Base case: Cluster 1 (Imitative innovation area).

Lastly, by setting the Applied science area (cluster 2) as reference, its comparison with the European science-based area, also associated with the endogenous innovation pattern, specifies that the two clusters clearly differ in their knowledge intensity and generality, which guarantees a superior endogenous innovative performance in the European science-based area despite a less visible creative attitude. Interestingly, the Smart technological application area (cluster 3) shows a level of knowledge intensity comparable to that of the Applied science area but differs in terms of its greater entrepreneurial and creative attitude, which sustains a relatively superior capacity for screening, selecting and absorbing the most appropriate external knowledge and turning it into new products.

Overall, this suggests that the imitative regions exhibit advantages in terms of entrepreneurship and creativity that could be strategically exploited as key assets in launching innovation upgrading policies. However, fully obtaining the benefits of these policies also requires a strong commitment to catching up with the other groups of regions, especially in terms of human capital and capability endowment. The Smart and creative diversification area regions can rely upon a stronger local knowledge base in terms of capabilities and a high level of entrepreneurship and creativity. These guarantee higher than negligible levels of innovation in all dimensions (albeit below the EU average). These elements represent their competitive advantage and should be supported by innovation policies, which, nevertheless, can also be oriented to promoting greater technological specialization and enhancing the local knowledge base and intensity so as to approach the Smart technological application regions. These latter have their greatest advantage in a rather strong knowledge intensity based on a combination of both endogenous knowledge capacity and the ability to screen, select and absorb external knowledge, and to locally recombine and adapt it via collective learning. This enables achievement of a substantial innovation performance (especially in terms of product innovation) not far from that of the applied science regions. These have a profile very similar to that of the European science-based area, albeit with a more limited knowledge and innovation intensity. They thus have the opportunity either to catch up with the European science-based area regions by investing hugely in the upgrading of their knowledge basis or to join the Smart technological application regions by initiating a process of increasing technological specialization, on the one hand, and by promoting an entrepreneurial and creative attitude on the other. Lastly, European science-based area regions can be considered the most advanced in terms of knowledge and innovation performance, and they gain this advantage from their superior knowledge base. Maintaining this status thus requires a mix of policy initiatives oriented to the promotion and support of research activities and the diffusion of scientific and technical competencies.

7.6. Conclusions

This chapter has shown that the territorial patterns of innovation conceptually elaborated in Chapter 6 do actually exist, and that they are more fragmented than expected: each archetypical pattern can in fact accommodate different behaviors.

In particular, within the knowledge creation pattern, two different innovation modes can be identified: on the one hand, there are regions specialized in basic knowledge. This has been called the European science-based area, where general purpose technology research activities can be concentrated and economies of scale in research activities exploited. On the other hand, there are regions where relatively more specific and applied knowledge is developed: these regions could be pushed towards the production of applied and, more relevantly, diversified knowledge.

Two distinct behaviors can be identified within the creative application pattern as well. On the one hand, there are regions exploiting specific formal knowledge, mostly acquired from external sources, in order to innovate. These are the regions to which the smart specialization experts refer, where the co-invention of application relies on external basic knowledge. On the other hand, there are regions exploiting external knowledge embedded in experience and in learning by doing (i.e. capabilities) consistent with specific and possibly diversified productive vocations of some areas. These regions innovate on the basis of external capabilities that, once acquired and absorbed, merge with local creativity to innovate.

The empirical results also show that the geography of innovation is much more complex than the simple core–periphery model proposed in the smart specialization debate (Foray et al., 2009) and by previous taxonomies (OECD, 2010; Vespagen, 2010). The capacity to turn knowledge and innovation into regional growth differs among regions, and the identification of regional specificities in innovation patterns is essential for building targeted normative strategies to achieve the cohesion policy goals.

This variety of innovation patterns can explain the likely failure of a 'one-size-fits-all' policy for innovation, like the thematically/regionally neutral and generic R&D incentives. The latter do not seem suitable for the widespread development of a knowledge economy. On the contrary, innovation patterns specific to each area should be identified in order to devise and implement ad hoc and targeted innovation policies based on the smart specialization concept put forward by the EU.

Necessary to move in this direction is measurement of the efficiency of each pattern of innovation in knowledge creation, in innovation diffusion and economic performance. Our impression is that none of these patterns is by definition superior to any other; on the contrary, each territorial pattern may provide an efficient use of local research and innovation activities to generate growth. Proof of this statement, however, requires empirical analysis.

The overall logic of the impact analyses is presented in Figure 7.4, with the chapters in which each issue is treated. In particular, our aim is to understand the efficiency of each territorial pattern of innovation in:

- producing new knowledge from internal knowledge inputs (Chapter 8);
- generating economic growth from knowledge inputs (R&D and human capital), in order to identify which types of regions benefit the most from

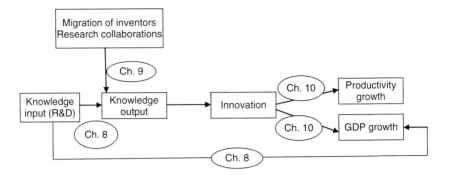

Figure 7.4 The logic of the impact analysis and related chapters

an increase in R&D, as suggested by the Lisbon and Europe 2020 Agendas (Chapter 8);
• exploiting knowledge coming from outside the region to develop the local knowledge base (Chapter 9);
• exploiting innovation to increase regional growth and to achieve higher productivity levels (Chapter 10).

The results associated with knowledge production in European regions (Chapter 8) are compared with empirical evidence on the US, China and India (Chapter 11), for which similar regional knowledge data are available. The comparison makes it possible to draw some lessons for the European regions.

Annex 7.1. **Eurobarometer Survey**
To extract the factor 'Strategic vision on innovation', we used the following questions from the Eurobarometer Survey 63.4:

• innovation simplifies everyday life (% of people mentioning this statement), Q396;
• a company that sells an innovative product or service improves the image of all its products or services (% of people mentioning this statement), Q397;
• a company which does not innovate is a company that will not survive (% of people mentioning this statement), Q398;
• innovation is essential for improving economic growth (% of people mentioning this statement), Q401;
• broadband penetration rate (% of households with broadband access) from Eurostat, Qbb.

To extract the factor 'creativity', we used the following questions from the Eurobarometer Survey 63.4:

Table A7.1 Factor loadings

Variable	Strategic vision on innovation	Creativity
Q389	0.265	**0.741**
Q390	0.205	**0.827**
Q392	0.484	**0.577**
Q394	−0.051	**0.861**
Q395	0.157	**0.670**
Q396	**0.635**	0.312
Q397	**0.813**	0.204
Q398	**0.869**	0.160
Q401	**0.880**	0.257
Qbb	**0.659**	−0.029

Source: Capello and Lenzi (2012a)

Note: Factor loadings greater than 0.55 are in bold.

- In general, to what extent are you attracted towards innovative products or services, in other words new or improved products or services? (% of people that are very or fairly attracted to new products), Q398.
- Compared to your friends and family, would you say that you tend to be more inclined to purchase innovative products or services? (% of people that are more inclined than the average to buy innovative products), Q390.
- In general, when an innovative product or service is put on the market and can replace a product or service that you already trust and regularly buy, do you quickly try the innovative product or service at least once? (% of people that easily shift consumption patterns towards innovative products), Q392.
- Innovative products or services are gadgets most of the time (% of people not mentioning this statement), Q394.
- Innovative products or services are a matter of fashion (% of people not mentioning this statement), Q395.
- The advantages of innovative products or services are often exaggerated (% of people not mentioning this statement), Q400.

We extracted the two factors by means of principal component analysis and applied a varimax rotation method with Kaiser normalization. The percentage of variance explained is 62.54. In this analysis, within each component, we considered the variables with a factor loading greater than 0.55. highlighted in bold in Table A7.1.

Notes

1 For similar taxonomies see also Muller and Nauwelaers (2005) on EU12, Navarro et al. (2009) on EU25.
2 See Chapter 5 for details on the collection and the release of innovation data at the European level and their regional disaggregation.
3 The indicators and the taxonomy obtained are also presented in Capello and Lenzi (2012a).

4 Patents were assigned to regions according to the respective inventor's residence address as available in patent documents. Fractional count is applied. The authors are grateful to Crenos – University of Cagliari (Italy) for granting access to, and use of, their patent database.

5 We are aware that this measure may be affected by size effects because bigger regions may have larger shares of total EU patents. However, this is not a major concern because the correlation coefficient between the regional share of EU patents and the share of regional patents normalized by the regional population is about 0.8.

6 Every patent is attributed to one or more technological classes according to the International Patent Classification (IPC). We reclassified patents according to a 30 technological fields classification that aggregates all IPC codes into 30 technological fields, and then into seven main technological fields. This is a technology-oriented classification, jointly elaborated by Fraunhofer Gesellschaft-ISI (Karlsruhe), Institut National de la Propriété Industrielle (INPI, Paris) and Observatoire des Sciences and des Techniques (OST, Paris). To compute the generality and the originality indexes, we used the seven-class classification.

7 See Annex 7.1 for the list of variables used and details about the factor analysis.

8 We opted for the k-means approach because, in the literature, it is preferred to hierarchical approaches (Afifi et al., 2004).

9 Estimates are not reported but are available upon request.

8 Knowledge, human capital and regional performance

Marta Foddi, Emanuela Marrocu,
Raffaele Paci and Stefano Usai

8.1. Introduction

Theoretical and applied economists no longer consider regional growth to be entirely dependent on traditional production factors endowment, such as physical capital and labour. Increasingly, regional growth is thought to be related to the presence of local intangible resources such as knowledge, innovative capacity and competence.

Following this line of thought, policymakers at the European Union (EC, 2011b) have set several initiatives which devote particular attention to the process of creation of such intangibles. In particular, the Europe 2020 Agenda has confirmed the previous Lisbon Strategy's goal to make Europe more competitive through knowledge and technological change. Moreover, high levels of regional heterogeneity in terms of knowledge creation and absorption have motivated a special attention to the territorial dimension of this phenomenon.

Our main aim is, consequently, to provide some further evidence on the process of knowledge accumulation and diffusion and its influence on economic growth at the regional level within the analytical settings offered in Chapter 7. The study is carried out for the whole sample of 287 regions in 31 countries in Europe (see the list of regions in Chapter 1) and it is also intended as the empirical starting point for a what-if kind of analysis on the potential impact of policies which aim at attaining the goals of the Europe 2020 strategy.

We firstly analyse the main factors influencing the innovation process and, in a second step, how the innovation process affects economic growth. We pursue this aim by adopting parametric and non-parametric methods to investigate both production and knowledge creation processes at regional level. More specifically, the analysis is based on regression models, in particular spatial econometric ones, and on data envelopment analysis (DEA). While regression models are particularly suited to measuring central tendencies of a given phenomenon, DEA is more adequate for benchmarking analysis as it permits us to identify the best-performing units within a given set of entities. The DEA approach will allow us to single out the specific characteristics of each region and to determine how far they are, in relative terms, from the most efficient areas. This can offer an assessment of the potential productive gains not yet achieved by inefficient regions. The two methods may provide, in general, different indications on the same object of analysis, therefore we employ both of them in a complementary guise in order to gain wider and different insights on the European regional economic performance.

The first part of the analysis is devoted to the investigation of the impact of intangible assets on the innovative capacity of a region. We present results for a knowledge production function where, in addition to the traditional R&D input, we also include the human capital endowment and other economic and institutional variables which characterize the regional environment. Moreover, the model is specifically parameterized to account for spatial technological spillovers. This allows us to distinguish the effects due to the internal determinants of a given region from those received in the form of positive externalities from neighbouring territories.

In the second part of this chapter, the analysis focuses on the measurement of the effects of the knowledge factors (that is, technological and human capital) on regional output by estimating a spatial Cobb-Douglas production function. The spatial econometric setting is adopted in order to assess at the same time the contribution of each region's internal capability, represented by intangible as well as traditional tangible inputs, and the role of inter-regional spillovers.

The remainder of the chapter is organized as follows. Section 8.2 provides a brief description of the methodological tools adopted to study the economic performance of European regions in terms of both new knowledge creation and productivity. Section 8.3 presents and discusses the results related to the spatial knowledge production function, while section 8.4 reports the production function estimation findings. Section 8.5 concludes by offering some general remarks.

8.2. Methodological issues

In this section we present a brief description of the methodological tools adopted to analyse the economic performance of the European regions in terms of productivity and of new knowledge creation. For both knowledge and production, the study is based on regression models, in particular spatial econometric ones, and on DEA.

The regression parametric method is well known and in what follows we only discuss the distinctive features of the spatial specifications. More details are given about the DEA methodology, a non-parametric method (Farrell, 1957) based on mathematical programming techniques, which has rarely been applied at the regional level. In general, the two methods offer different perspectives of analysis on the same phenomenon[1], so in this study we employ both as complementary techniques to gain diverse insights on the European regional economic performance. As a matter of fact, with the regression model we derive an estimate of the average behaviour of the phenomenon under examination, while with the DEA we identify the best-performing units (regions in our case) among a set of entities whose common objective is to convert multiple inputs into output. The best performance is characterized in terms of 'technical' efficiency[2], so that the best-performing units define the efficient frontier, which 'envelopes' all the other units. These latter units are then evaluated by calculating their relative efficiency in terms of distance from the frontier.

This crucial difference between the regression method and the DEA can be easily appreciated by considering Figure 8.1: the frontier is defined by only one unit (B), the most efficient one, which represent a benchmark for all the other less efficient units; the regression line, as it captures the central tendency, passes through all the data points, regardless of their level of efficiency.

8.2.1 Spatial econometric models

Spatial econometrics is, according to Anselin (1988), the collection of techniques which deal with the peculiarities caused by space in the statistical analysis of territorial units, such as regions. Spatial econometrics is, in other words, a subfield of econometrics that deals with the treatment of spatial interaction (spatial dependence) and spatial structure (spatial heterogeneity) in regression models. Spatial dependence may be caused by different kinds of spatial spillovers, while heteroskedasticity could easily result from the inherent heterogeneity in the setting of spatial units. Two models are used as standard in order to correct for spatial dependence and are proposed in the following sections: the Spatial Error Model (SEM) and the Spatial Autoregressive Model (SAR).[3] These two spatial specifications, in their panel version applied to 287 European regions, are reported below:

$$\text{Spatial error model: } y_{it} = \beta X_{it} + \varepsilon_{it} \text{ with } \varepsilon_{it} = \lambda W \varepsilon_{it} + u_{it} \tag{8.1}$$

$$\text{Spatial autoregressive model: } y_{it} = \beta X_{it} + \rho W y_{i} + u_{it} \tag{8.2}$$

where i refers to regions and t to periods, y is the dependent variable, X is a set of explanatory variables, u is a i.i.d error process and W is the matrix of spatial weights used to describe the geographical interconnectivity among the regions. In

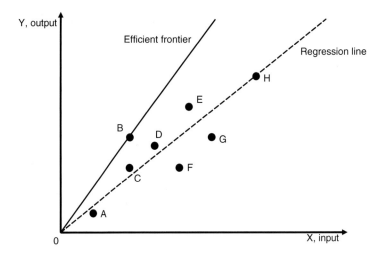

Figure 8.1 Regression model vs DEA

our case each entry of W is the inverse of the distance between any two regions in the sample; note that in all the estimations and testing procedures the W matrix is max-eigenvalue normalized.

The spatial error model, on the one hand, is a linear specification with a spatially autocorrelated error, which only requires the tackling of such a correlation in order to ensure efficiency of the estimators. The autoregressive model, on the other hand, comprises an additional term (the spatially averaged value of all-other regions' dependent variable values), which explicitly captures possible cross-border externalities in the form of production or knowledge spillovers. Given the presence of the spatially lagged term the usual interpretation of the coefficients as partial derivatives does not hold and the effect on y of a unit change in the x regressor is given by the sum of a direct effect (due to a change in a given region's regressor plus feedbacks loops) and an indirect or spillover effect (due to a change in the other regions' regressor). Both specifications are estimated by applying the Maximum Likelihood estimation method.

8.2.2 Data envelopment analysis

DEA is a widely used quantitative tool for measuring and evaluating the performance of entities involved in an ample range of activities and contexts, such as firms, hospitals, universities, cities, regions and countries (see Cook and Seiford, 2009, for a thorough review, from the pioneering contributions to the latest advances and applications). Thanks to its high flexibility, DEA has proved successful in identifying various sources of inefficiency, in particular in studying benchmarking practices. As a matter of fact, DEA does not require a specific functional form for the relation linking inputs to outputs and it is capable of handling multiple inputs and outputs, expressed in different units of measurement, as long as they are the same for all the decision-making units (DMUs).

Following Coelli (1996) and Cooper et al. (2007), the approach based on the DEA method is illustrated in Figure 8.2, where we report the same units of

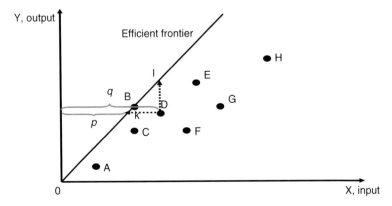

Figure 8.2 DEA-CCR model, one input-one output

Figure 8.1, which are labelled from A to H. The model is known as DEA-CCR after Charnes, Cooper and Rhodes (1978). In this case constant return to scale (CRS) are assumed and for simplicity only one input and one output are considered. As a result, on the basis of the available empirical information, the frontier is identified, as before, by DMU B, which is fully efficient. According to Cooper et al. (2007) a DMU is said to be fully (100%) efficient if the performance of any other DMU shows that no inputs or outputs of the efficient unit can be improved without worsening some of its other inputs or outputs. Note that this notion refers to 'technical' efficiency and it does not require a priori information on prices or weights accounting for the relative importance of inputs or outputs.

Focusing on DMU D, its efficiency is given by the ratio p/q; this means that, assuming for instance a ratio of 0.75, D could still produce the same level of output if it reduced all inputs proportionally by 25%. This way DMU D would be projected horizontally towards the efficient frontier. Under the assumption of CRS, the same efficiency gain would be obtained by a vertical projection, in this case with the same input amount DMU D could produce a level of output 33% ($1/0.75$ $= 1.33$) greater than the previously produced one. DMU B is called the benchmark or reference unit for DMU D. In the former case we have an input-oriented measure of efficiency, while in the latter case the measure is output-oriented. Note that under the assumption of CRS the two orientations identify the same frontier and the same set of efficient DMUs; only the measures associated with the inefficient DMU can be different. Note also that in the case of DMU D efficiency can be achieved by each movement in the area K-D-I (Figure 8.2).

More formally, to get an efficiency measure (h) for all the units included in the sample it is necessary to solve a nonlinear programming model. Consider a set of n DMUs, with each DMU i ($i = 1, ... n$) using m inputs, x_{ij} ($j = 1, ... m$) to get r ($r = 1, ... s$) outputs y_{ir}; following Charnes et al. (1979) this amounts to solving the following maximization problem for each DMU; considering DMU_0:

$$max\ h_0\left(u,v\right) = \sum_{r=1}^{s} u_r y_{0r} \bigg/ \sum_{j=1}^{m} v_j x_{0j} \ \ s.t. \ \sum_{r=1}^{s} u_r y_{0r} - \sum_{j=1}^{m} v_j x_{0j} \leq 0 \ \ for\ all\ i,\ with$$

$$u_r, v_j \geq 0\ for\ all\ r, j \tag{8.3}$$

the additional constraint $\sum_{j=1}^{m} v_j x_{0j} = 1$ ensures that an infinite number of solutions is ruled out.

This is known as the *multiplier* ratio-form of DEA, since the ratio of outputs to inputs is used to measure the efficiency of a DMU with respect to all other DMUs. When the output to inputs ratio is maximized, the model is referred to as an input-oriented model; conversely, we have an output-oriented model when the ratio is inverted and a minimization problem is solved.

The solution of the problem requires finding optimal values for the weights u and v such that the technical efficiency of DMU_0 is maximized, subject to the constraints that the efficiency measures of all the other DMUs are less or equal to unity. Note that the weights may change from one DMU to the other as their magnitude reflects how highly an item (input or output) is evaluated with respect to the others.

The last model is also known as the 'Farrell model' and it can only provide measures of 'weak' efficiency as it does not account for the presence of possible non-zero input or output slacks. The case of *weak* efficiency arises when the frontier is piece-wise linear so that once an inefficient DMU is projected on a straight part of it, further gains may be achieved moving towards a kinked part. Nonetheless, the importance of slacks has been somehow overstated as they are often due to the very small dimension of the sample; with a large number of DMUs the frontier line becomes smoother so that straight traits become less likely to appear. As a result, we devote limited attention to slack measures, as the size of our sample – 287 regions – is reasonably large.

Since the assumption of CRS is rarely attainable in real-world situations, as it requires that each DMU operates at an optimal scale, in our analysis we adopt the Varying Return to Scale (VRS) variant of the DEA (Model DEA-BCC, Banker et al., 1984). It allows us to envelop the data more tightly so that technical efficiency measures are always greater than or equal to the ones obtained under the assumption of CRS. The aim is to isolate 'pure' technical inefficiency from 'scale' inefficiency. Operationally this is done by carrying out both a CRS and VRS DEA; if for a given DMU there is a difference in the technical scores, this is interpreted as evidence of scale inefficiency. This is illustrated in Figure 8.3, where for simplicity there is only one input and one output, and where we report both the CRS and the VRS frontiers. For DMU F, under CRS and adopting an input orientation, the technical inefficiency is measured by the segment FFc, while assuming VRS the technical inefficiency would be just FFv so that the difference, FcFv, is entirely due to scale inefficiency. In order to acquire information on whether a DMU is scale-inefficient, because it operates along the increasing or the decreasing trait of the VRS frontier, one needs to solve an additional DEA problem, which returns a Non-Increasing Return to Scale (NIRS) frontier (the narrow continuous line in Figure 8.3). For a given DMU, if the NIRS technical score is different

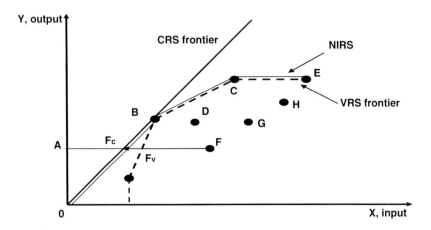

Figure 8.3 DEA-BCC model

from the VRS one, then that DMU is facing increasing returns to scale (as is the case for DMU F); conversely a DMU is operating along the decreasing returns part of the frontier when the technical scores are the same for both NIRS and VRS frontiers. In our analysis we present and discuss technical efficiency scores of the European regions devoid of the scale effects under the assumption of VRS.

In the next two sections the two methodologies described above (spatial econometric techniques and data envelopment analysis) are applied – first, to the study of regional knowledge production, and secondly to the analysis of regional economic performance.

8.3. The production of new knowledge

In this section we present the analysis aimed at investigating the returns of R&D expenditures and human capital on regional new knowledge production. The analysis is carried out by employing both parametric and non-parametric methods. The former is based on the theoretical framework of the Knowledge Production Function (KPF) (Griliches, 1979) where, in addition to the traditional R&D input, we also include the human capital endowment (Usai, 2011) and other economic and institutional phenomena at the regional level (Crescenzi et al., 2007). In light of several previous contributions (Greunz, 2003; Moreno et al., 2005b; Autant-Bernard and LeSage, 2011; Marrocu et al., 2012b) we adopt an empirical spatial specification in order to assess the presence and the intensity of geographical technological spillovers. The non-parametric DEA, on the other hand, permits us to single out the best practices among the European regions (or typologies of territories) in performing innovation activities and to identify those less efficient at converting R&D investments and human capital into the creation of new knowledge.

8.3.1 Spatial econometric analysis

The dependent variable in our KPF model is proxied by the patenting activity at the regional level. We consider a four-period panel, where each period comprises three years according to a moving average structure: 2002–04, 2003–05, 2004–06, 2005–07. Consequently, the values of the dependent variable are computed for each region as three-year averages of the number of patent applications to the European Patent Office (EPO) (*patents*).[4] This allows us to deal with a small number of zero-value observations and, at the same time, to get a less volatile, more reliable, picture of the innovation dynamics in Europe. As is well known, the production of knowledge, represented by an invention formalized through a patent application, is characterized by a delay with respect to investment in R&D (Jaffe, 1986 and 1989). Therefore, the explanatory variables are included with a lag of two years with respect to the initial year of the four periods considered (i.e. 2000 for $t = 1$, 2002 for $t = 2$ and so on). A detailed description of all variables along with the data sources is reported in Table 8.1.

Following a well-established literature on KPF estimation, we consider the expenditure in R&D as one of the main determinants of the knowledge production

Table 8.1 Variables description and sources

Variables	Description	Measurement unit	Source
Patents	EPO patent applications per priority year and residence region of inventors	Number	CRENoS elaboration on OECD REGPAT database
R&D expenditure	Total intramural R&D expenditure	Millions of euro	Eurostat
Human capital	Economically active population with tertiary education attainment – 15 years and over	Number of people	Eurostat
Population	Number of resident people at 1st January	Number of people	Eurostat
GDP	Gross Domestic Product	Millions of euro	Eurostat
Capital	Fixed stock of capital	Millions of euro	CRENoS elaborations on Cambridge Econometrics data
Employment	Number of employees – 15 years and over	Thousands	Eurostat
Investments	Gross fixed capital formation	Millions of euro	Eurostat

Note: All variables are defined for the period 2000–2007

activity. However, some authors (Cohen and Levinthal, 1990) have emphasized that the effectiveness of such an investment depends crucially on the absorptive capacity of a territory, which, in turn, is linked to the availability of highly skilled human capital. For this reason, we augment the traditional KPF model by including also the human capital endowment. The log-linearized version of the basic model is thus formalized as follows:

$$patents_{it} = \alpha + \beta_1 r \ \& \ d_{it} + \beta_2 hk_{it} + \beta_3 pop_{it} + \varepsilon_{it} \tag{8.4}$$

where $i = 1, \ldots 287$ and t as explained above; lower letters indicate log-transformed variables. For R&D we consider the total intramural expenditure in millions of euro, while the human capital (hk) endowment is represented by the number of economically active individuals with at least a tertiary education degree (ISCED 5–6).[5] In equation (8.4) we also include the resident population (*pop*) as a control variable to account for the relative dimension of the regions and the presence of potential local externalities due to agglomeration.

The econometric results are reported in Table 8.2. In the first two columns we present two non-spatial specifications, which allow us to test for the presence of spatial dependence. The first column reports the simplest version of the baseline model, which includes a common constant, whilst in the second column we include country dummies in order to account for diverse institutional factors, which, when overlooked, may induce spatial dependence. According to the robust

Table 8.2 Spatial knowledge production function: estimates

Dependent variable: patents

	1	2	3	4	5
Model	Pooled	Pooled	SEM	SAR	SAR
Estimation method	OLS	OLS	ML	ML	ML
R&D	1.102 *** (34.155)	0.495*** (8.624)	0.418*** (7.828)	0.430*** (8.011)	
Human capital	0.300*** (2.776)	0.699*** (4.115)	0.648*** (3.999)	0.629*** (3.985)	0.582*** (3.593)
R&D* Imitative innovation					0.360*** (5.725)
R&D* Smart and creative diversification					0.469*** (8.252)
R&D* Smart technological application					0.476*** (8.600)
R&D* Applied science					0.423*** (7.440)
R&D* European science-based					0.414*** (7.544)
Population	0.023 (0.224)	0.367* (2.237)	0.442*** (2.825)	0.447*** (2.926)	0.463*** (2.974)
Spatial autocorrelation coefficient – λ		0.968*** (85.423)			
Spatial autoregressive coefficient – ρ				0.500*** (12.177)	0.422*** (9.139)
Constant	Yes	Yes	No	No	No
Country dummies	No	Yes	Yes	Yes	Yes
Adj. R^2	0.739	0.825			
Square Corr. (actual fitted values)			0.455	0.847	0.850

Table 8.2 Continued

Dependent variable: patents

	1	2	3	4	5
Model	*Pooled*	*Pooled*	*SEM*	*SAR*	*SAR*
Estimation method	OLS	OLS	ML	ML	ML
Diagnostics					
Robust LM test – No spatial lag	17.1				
p-value	0.000				
Robust LM test – No spatial error	1187				
p-value	0.000				
LM test – No spatial error	56.043				
P-value	0.000				

Notes: Panel observations N*T = 1148; T = 4, N = 287
For the definition of the five groups of regions see Chapter 7
For spatial models and tests the weight matrix is the max-eigenvalue normalized matrix of inverse distance in kilometres
Asymptotic t-statistics in parenthesis; significance: *** 1%; ** 5%; * 10%

LM tests (bottom panel of Table 8.2), we find evidence of spatial dependence in both specifications. For this reason, in the subsequent three models we propose the estimation of spatial specifications starting from the model (2) with country dummies. The SEM model (3) exhibits significant coefficients for all the variables included; human capital, with an estimated coefficient of 0.65, outperforms R&D, which has a coefficient equal to 0.42, in enhancing the innovation activity at the regional level in Europe. Moreover, the spatial autoregressive coefficient of the error term turns out to be highly significant and sizeable, signalling the importance of spatial correlation among regions. In the case of the knowledge creation process, therefore, it is reasonable to argue that such a dependence may be attributable to the presence of spillovers, which cross the borders according to the varying degrees of proximity among regions.

Although we are aware that the notion of proximity cannot be limited to the simple spatial one, as it includes also technological and organizational dimensions (Boschma, 2005; Marrocu et al., 2011), in this study we assume that geographical vicinity is an adequate proxy to capture the interconnectivity among regions which makes possible the existence of spillovers. Since the SEM specification eliminates spatial dependence by construction, we test its relevance more explicitly within the SAR specification. SAR estimation results are reported in the last two columns of Table 8.2, while the direct, indirect and total effects are presented in Table 8.3. Focusing on specification (4), all the estimated coefficients are significant and the spatial autocorrelation parameter (equal to 0.50) indicates the relevance of positive externalities coming from neighbouring areas: other things being equal in terms of R&D and human capital, the closer a region to the most innovative areas, the higher the benefit in terms of new knowledge creation. It is important to observe that these externalities may have quite a different nature: for example, they may be related to pure technological spillovers which do not necessarily involve formal and voluntary exchanges between agents, or to pecuniary externalities which are bound to be related to market transactions (Krugman, 1991b). Note also that model (4) returns a higher value for the squared correlation (0.85) between actual and fitted values which implies that the goodness-of-fit of the SAR model is better than that of the SEM model.

The analysis of specification (4) is further elaborated in Table 8.3 where we report direct, indirect and total effects of both R&D and human capital on patenting activity[6]. We recall that the direct effect is mainly due to a change in a region's own endowments, while the indirect effect is generated by a change in the other regions' factors; the total effect is the sum of the direct and indirect effects and it represents the long-run average increase in patents due to a change in a given productive factor, once all the regional interactions have taken place across space and over time.

For model (4) the internal factors yield approximately 55% of the total effect, innovation spillovers are thus quite sizeable as they account for the remaining 45%. More specifically, an increase of 1% in human capital induces an increase of 1.14% in patent activity, while the same increase in R&D expenditure produces a variation in patents equal to 0.81%. To assess what such elasticities entail in

Table 8.3 Effects of human capital and R&D on patents

from Table 8.2 SAR models	4			5		
	Direct	*Indirect*	*Total*	*Direct*	*Indirect*	*Total*
R&D	0.436	0.371	0.808			
Human capital	0.617	0.524	1.141	0.583	0.368	0.951
R&D* Imitative innovation				0.362	0.229	0.591
R&D* Smart and creative diversification				0.471	0.297	0.768
R&D* Smart technological application				0.479	0.301	0.780
R&D* Applied science				0.426	0.268	0.694
R&D* European science-based				0.416	0.262	0.678

Note: The estimated effects are all significant at the 1% level

terms of the creation of new patents, a simple what-if analysis can be carried out: if the human capital endowment increases by 10%, so that the European 2007 average of around 215 thousands graduate people per region increases to 236 thousands, this would entail the production of 21.1 additional patents (regional average being equal to 184.5 in 2007), 11.4 of which are due to internal efforts and 9.7 result from regional spillovers. A similar scenario can be envisaged for R&D: an increase of 10% in the 2007 regional average level of 845 million euro[7], keeping constant the human capital endowment, would lead to the patenting of 14.9 inventions per region, 8 of them as the result of the internal investment in research activities and the remaining 6.9 produced thanks to the knowledge interactions with the neighbouring regions. It is worth remarking that such considerable spillover effects are strongly related to the endowment of highly skilled human capital, which enhances the absorptive capacity and the ability to exploit knowledge flows moving along the regional innovation networks.

The effects derived from model (4) for the main determinants of innovative capacity, R&D and human capital, can be considered as average estimates for the whole of Europe, since we constrain their coefficients to be the same across all regions. Given the well-known heterogeneity which characterizes the European territories, we, then, attempt to assess whether the effects discussed so far may change significantly when we allow for varying coefficients at the regional level. Given the usual degrees of freedom problem, we suggest tackling this heterogeneity by dividing the 287 regions into five groups on the basis of the taxonomy proposed in Chapter 7. The five mutually exclusive groups of regions are identified according to their propensity to innovate: the most innovative regions are those in the European science-based area, followed by regions in Applied science, Smart technological application, Smart and creative diversification and Imitative innovation groups. For each group we construct a binary variable which is interacted with the R&D investment level.

We focus on R&D since this is the knowledge input that is more likely to feature changing effects across regions due to the different institutional settings and the varying absorptive capacity at territorial level. The most parsimonious model including the five interactive R&D terms is reported in column (5) of Table 8.2. All the coefficients exhibit the expected positive sign and are highly significant; furthermore, we note that the coefficient of human capital proves robust with respect to the inclusion of the five new regressors for R&D. Since the new variables contain specific territorial information, the spatial autocorrelation coefficient becomes smaller with respect to the one obtained from the simpler model (4).

Human capital is confirmed as the most effective input in determining patenting activity, its total elasticity of 0.95 is remarkably higher than the one associated with R&D in all the different areas considered. The latter exhibits the highest elasticity for the areas of Smart technological application and of Smart and creative diversification (0.78 and 0.77, respectively), while the lowest value is shown by the Imitative innovation group (0.59). These results suggest that the R&D expenditure effort has its largest impact on knowledge production in those regions with strong orientation towards product innovation but for which the endowment of knowledge and innovation variables is smaller than the EU average. This result confirms that the knowledge endowment relies upon tacit knowledge and that it is embedded into human capital, entrepreneurial and creative attitudes. Moreover, if we look at Map 8.1, where we observe the spatial distribution of these values, we see that the lowest R&D coefficient, the one associated with the imitative group, refers mainly to the eastern part of Europe where most New Entrant countries are located. As a result, we conclude that R&D expenditure is least effective in those regions with the lowest propensity to innovate. On the contrary, for the other four groups we observe a clear pattern of diminishing returns to scale in knowledge production: regions with the highest endowments of R&D show a lower return for the marginal unit of each input employed, while regions in the two 'smart' groups appear to enjoy higher returns.

Finally, we focus on the estimated effects reported in the last three columns of Table 8.3, where we find further evidence supporting the relevant role played by knowledge spillovers; as a matter of fact, on average the indirect effects account for a substantial proportion (nearly 40%) of the overall effect.

8.3.2 *Data envelopment analysis*

Following Cullinane et al. (2004), in carrying out the data envelopment analysis to investigate the innovative performance of European regions we adopt the output-oriented approach, as it is more suitable when the analysis serves as the basis for defining planning and policy strategies, which is commonly the case for geographical units, such as regions or countries. On the other hand, the input orientation is more adequate when operational and managerial objectives are involved. For the European regions included in our sample, the assessment of technical efficiency is carried out by allowing for VRS.[8]

The application of non-parametric methods to the study of regional economic performance is still quite rare, especially in the case of regional innovation systems' performance. The only partial exception is the study by Zabala-Iturriagagoitia

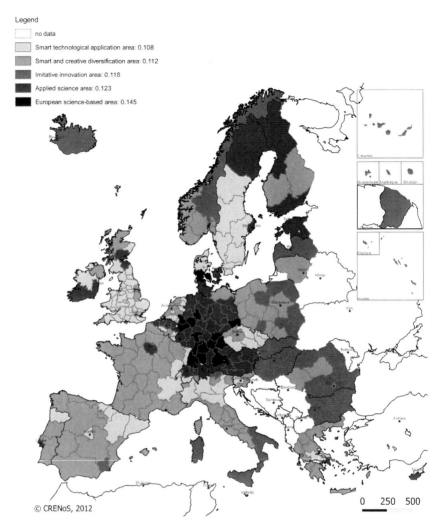

Legend
☐ no data
▨ Smart technological application area: 0.108
▨ Smart and creative diversification area: 0.112
▨ Imitative innovation area: 0.118
▨ Applied science area: 0.123
■ European science-based area: 0.145

0   250   500

© CRENoS, 2012

Map 8.1 Elasticity of knowledge production to R&D by territorial patterns of innovation (average 2000–2007)

et al. (2007) who aim at measuring European regional innovation efficiency through DEA. However, the usual output variable in the KPF setting – that is, patents – is considered as input here, while regional GDP per capita is used as the dependent variable. This makes the contribution analogous to a growth accounting study rather than a KPF analysis. To the best of our knowledge the only studies which closely follow the standard regional KPF model are Roman (2010) and Foddi and Usai (2013).[9] The former analyses local innovation performance, measured by patents, with reference to the limited local context of 14 regions of

Bulgaria and Romania. The latter applies the DEA methodology to 271 European regions in 29 countries in order to assess their efficiency in the use of internal and external inputs for the production of new knowledge.

We follow this last contribution by enlarging the sample of countries and regions to 31 and 287 respectively, and by focusing on the taxonomy of regions suggested above. Results are reported in Maps 8.2 and 8.3 which show the regional distribution of the efficiency measures for the knowledge production calculated for the initial (2000) and final (2007) years of our analysis. Fully efficient regions, in terms of converting R&D and human capital inputs into patents, have a technical efficiency score of 100; these are the best-performing areas in innovation activity and therefore they define the production possibility frontier. Comparing the two maps the overall picture does not seem to change appreciably, this is obviously due to the fact that an eight-year period is too limited in time for the pattern of

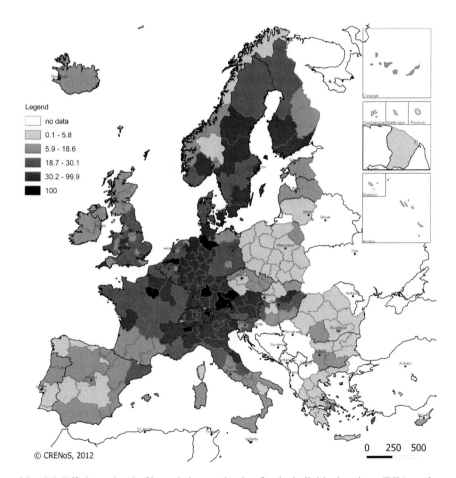

Map 8.2 Efficiency level of knowledge production for the individual regions (DEA methodology, 2000)

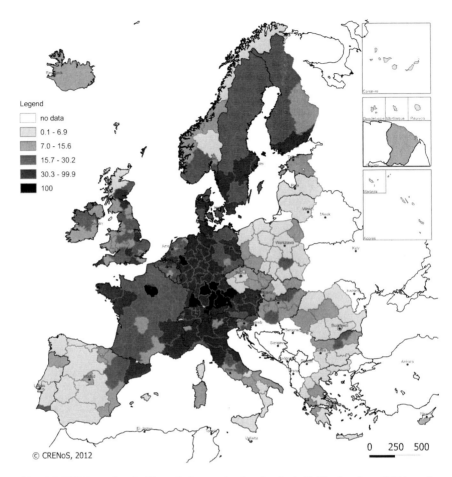

Map 8.3 Efficiency level of knowledge production for the individual regions (DEA methodology, 2007)

the knowledge creation process to change; it is well known that such a process is quite persistent as it requires considerable efforts on the investment side, both for R&D expenditure and, especially, for human capital, whose economic returns and effects occur completely only over long-run horizons.

Focusing on the maps, the group of the most efficient territories exhibits a great deal of heterogeneity. The majority of the efficient regions are located in the central and strategic areas of the continent, as is the case for Île de France, Stuttgart or the Dutch Noord-Brabant. However, due to the particular features of the DEA methodology, which selects efficient units also at a low scale, we find high-efficiency scores also in small and peripheral regions (such as Åland). The most efficient regions are followed by a group of German and Northern Italian regions, which are quite close to the frontier as they show high technical scores. By contrast, the lowest scores are shown by regions located in European peripheral areas, especially in the new accession countries. This analysis confirms the presence of a dualistic – centre vs periphery – pattern in the innovation activity. This calls for specific policies, which should target the latter group of regions, in order to support them – not necessarily with additional resources – rather, with the provision of organizational and structural assistance. This is expected to enable them to exploit all the potential of their relatively abundant inputs in delivering higher levels of knowledge output, which in turn is expected to ensure better long-run economic performance.

In Table 8.4, we extend the implementation of the taxonomy proposed above by looking at the differences in the average efficiency of the five groups of regions. We found that, as expected, the highest efficiency is found in the European science-based area, followed by regions in the Applied science area. The least efficient areas, on the contrary, are the Smart and creative diversification and the Imitative innovation clusters. Moreover, we find that while the average efficiency is increasing in the top clusters, it is either stagnating or decreasing in the bottom clusters. This is a signal of a process of divergence in the efficiency in the knowledge production process across groups of regions in Europe.

8.4. The economic production

The aim of this section is to assess whether knowledge factors, such as technological and human capital, exert a relevant role on regional output levels in addition to the traditional inputs such as physical capital and labour units. There is a long tradition of studies, starting with Lucas (1988), Mankiw et al. (1992) and Benhabib and Spiegel (1994), which assign a central role to human capital in the economic growth process. Likewise, technological capital and knowledge stock have been directly included as inputs in the production function at the firm level by Griliches (1979) in the so-called knowledge-capital model. Audretsch and Feldman (2004) provide a comprehensive review of the subsequent contributions which have extended and generalised this model.

Other intangible elements have been also examined by the literature under various complementary approaches. Some authors have highlighted the role of social capital as a growth driving factor since a high level of social capital in a certain area facilitates cooperation among agents, reduces transaction costs and supports

Table 8.4 Average efficiency in knowledge production

	2000	*2007*
European science-based	0.554	0.686
Applied science	0.402	0.428
Smart technological application	0.263	0.249
Smart and creative diversification	0.166	0.159
Imitative innovation	0.107	0.073

knowledge diffusion (Beugelsdijk and van Schaik, 2005; Dettori et al., 2011). Crescenzi and Rodríguez-Pose (2009 and Chapter 11 of this book) resort to the concept of 'social filter' to assemble the main socioeconomic features of the local environment in a unique indicator and thus assess their joint effect on economic outcomes. Finally, Paci and Marrocu (2013), within a similar setting, provide an interesting investigation to test different impacts of intangible factors at different development stages or with respect to diverse specialization patterns.

Similarly to the previous analysis, we employ a parametric method by estimating a spatial Cobb-Douglas production function and the non-parametric DEA method to measure the efficiency performance. For both methodologies, we consider the level of GDP as the output variable and employment, physical and human capital and R&D expenditure as the main determinants of production levels.

8.4.1 Spatial econometric analysis

The empirical model is represented by a log-linearized Cobb-Douglas production function as formalized in (8.5):

$$gdp_{it} = \alpha + \beta_1 k_{it} + \beta_2 l_{it} + \beta_3 r\&d_{it} + \beta_4 hk_{it} + \varepsilon_{it} \tag{8.5}$$

where $i = 1, \ldots 287$ regions and $t = 2000–2007$. The production level (gdp) is represented by GDP (millions of euro); the labour factor (l) is measured by the number of employees aged 15 years or over; the physical capital endowment (k) is calculated with the perpetual inventory method starting from investments data over the period 1980–2000; research and development ($r\&d$) effort is measured by the total intramural R&D expenditure (millions of euro); human capital (hk) is the share of economically active individuals with at least a tertiary education degree (ISCED 5–6) in total resident population; and lower-case letters indicate log-transformed variables. Finally we include a complete set of country dummies to account for institutional factors as much as for other non-measurable determinants specific for each nation. In order to take into account the commonly found geographical association across regions, our analysis is carried out within the spatial panel econometric framework.

The results of the production function estimation are presented in Table 8.5; we follow the same empirical strategy as for the KFP, we start our investigation by estimating two non-spatial specifications for the basic model (common constant, country dummies, columns 1–2 of Table 8.5), which allow us to test for the presence of spatial dependence. To partly control for endogeneity we have also estimated the basic specification augmented with country dummies with one- and two-year lags for the production factors; results are very similar and, as a consequence, we prefer to exploit the full temporal set of information. As the evidence provided by the LM tests (bottom panel of Table 8.5) confirms a considerable degree of spatial autocorrelation we focus the discussion on the main results obtained from the spatial specifications (columns 3–5);

The simple SEM model (3) exhibits significant coefficients for all the variables included. Labour and human capital show the highest coefficient (respectively

Table 8.5 Spatial production function: estimates

Dependent variable: GDP

Model	1	2	3	4	5
Estimation method	Pooled OLS	Pooled OLS	SEM ML	SAR ML	SAR ML
Capital	0.017 ** (1.967)	0.045 *** (5.277)	0.028 *** (3.376)	0.035 *** (4.128)	0.043 *** (5.136)
Employment (labour)	0.396 *** (33.58)	0.756 *** (57.040)	0.775 *** (61.824)	0.757 *** (58.208)	0.764 *** (59.621)
R&D	0.414 *** (60.256)	0.130 *** (18.605)	0.129 *** (19.747)	0.131 *** (19.178)	
Human capital	0.028 (1.397)	0.313 *** (16.428)	0.235 *** (12.069)	0.297 *** (15.759)	0.300 *** (16.021)
R&D* Imitative innovation					0.118 *** (15.181)
R&D* Smart and creative diversification					0.112 *** (15.927)
R&D* Smart technological application					0.108 *** (15.666)
R&D* Applied science					0.123 *** (17.382)
R&D* European science-based					0.145 *** (21.249)
Spatial autocorrelation coefficient – λ			0.942 *** (65.013)		
Spatial autoregressive coefficient – ρ				0.0191 *** (7.206)	0.022 *** (7.435)
Constant	Yes	Yes	No	No	No
Country dummies	No	Yes	Yes	Yes	Yes

Table 8.5 Continued

Dependent variable: GDP

	1	2	3	4	5
Model	*Pooled*	*Pooled*	*SEM*	*SAR*	*SAR*
Estimation method	OLS	OLS	ML	ML	ML
Adj. R²	0.912	0.971			
Square Corr. (actual fitted values)			0.952	0.972	0.973
Diagnostics					
Robust LM test – No spatial lag	5.39				
p-value	0.020				
Robust LM test – No spatial error	689				
p-value	0.000				
LM test – No spatial error		645.89			
p-value		0.000			

Notes: Panel observations N*T = 2296; T = 8, N = 287
For the definition of the five groups of regions see Chapter 7.
For spatial models and tests the weight matrix is the max-eigenvalue normalized matrix of inverse distance in kilometres
Asymptotic t-statistics in parenthesis; significance: *** 1%; ** 5%; * 10%

0.78 and 0.24). Moreover, also in this case human capital outperforms R&D (0.13) in enhancing regional output once the contribution of other traditional inputs is accounted for. Similarly to the knowledge production function estimation, the spatial autoregressive coefficient of the error term turns out to be highly significant and sizeable, signalling geographical dependence among neighbouring regions. Since this is likely to arise as a result of regional interactions, the SAR specification is believed to be more adequate to explicitly account for such interactions, especially when they occur in the form of production spillovers.

In column (4) we report results for the first SAR specification and we observe that all input coefficients are highly significant and exhibit the expected positive sign. Since our major interest is in the role of R&D and human capital in driving the level of production, we mainly focus on the evidence provided on such intangible assets when discussing the results. The relative magnitude of direct, indirect and total effects (Table 8.6) highlights that in the case of the overall production a prominent role is played by the internal regional endowments; spillovers, although significantly present, have a much smaller impact than was the case for the knowledge production process.

The human capital total elasticity is more than twice that found for R&D expenditure (0.30 and 0.13, respectively) confirming the great economic potential of a region endowed with a highly skilled labour force: a 10% increase in the share of graduate people would entail a 3% increase in total GDP, keeping constant the level of the other inputs.

Model (5) in Table 8.5 reports the results obtained when R&D is allowed to have varying effects according to the distinctive territorial innovation pattern proposed in Chapter 7. It is worth remarking that, as noted previously for the KPF, the coefficient of human capital is very robust with respect to the inclusion of the five interactive terms.

In the case of model (5), as we expected, the highest elasticity total values (see Table 8.6) occur for the pre-eminent groups in innovation activity, that is European science-based and Applied science territories (respectively 0.15 and 0.13). While, on average, a 10% increase in R&D yields up to a 1.5% increase in

Table 8.6 Effects of human capital and R&D on GDP

from Table 8.5 SAR models	4			5		
	Direct	Indirect	Total	Direct	Indirect	Total
R&D	0.131	0.002	0.133			
Human capital	0.297	0.005	0.302	0.300	0.006	0.306
R&D* Imitative innovation				0.118	0.002	0.120
R&D* Smart and creative diversification				0.113	0.002	0.115
R&D* Smart technological application				0.109	0.002	0.111
R&D* Applied science				0.123	0.002	0.126
R&D* European science-based				0.145	0.003	0.148

Note: The estimated effects are all significant at the 1% level

regional production, this is not the case across all types of regions. In fact, R&D is more efficiently used (i.e. shows a greater elasticity) in those regions which invest considerably in R&D, that is, those territories belonging to the European science-based area. By contrast, regions characterised by low levels of R&D spending have little benefit from further investments in R&D, their elasticity of production to R&D being below the European average. The lowest coefficient is shown by the Smart technological application group (0.11), which consists of regions with a strong orientation towards product innovation but which are somehow weaker in terms of process innovation.

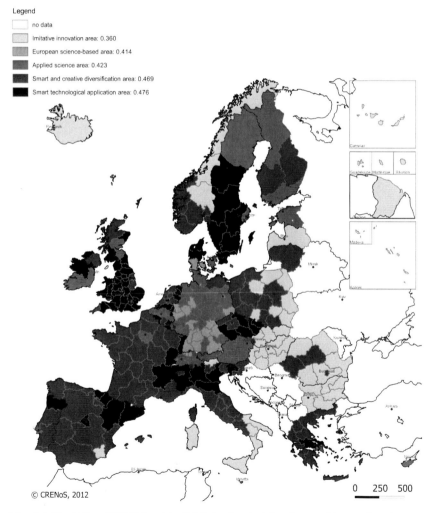

Map 8.4 Elasticity of GDP level to R&D by territorial patterns of innovation (average 2000–2007)

The results are reported in Map 8.4, where we can observe that regions with the highest R&D elasticity values are mainly located in the centre of Europe.

Overall, for the case of R&D production impacts we find evidence of limited heterogeneity; the total effects are estimated in the range 0.15–0.11, so that the most robust result remains related to the fact that human capital is at least twice as effective as R&D expenditure.

8.4.2 Data envelopment analysis

In this final section we carry out an output-oriented data envelopment analysis also for production, under the assumption of VRS. The analysis is based on the comparison of the technical efficiency scores in the initial and final year of the period under investigation, in order to unveil possible changes in the ability of the European territories to efficiently exploit their resources.

There are few previous DEA studies at the regional level in Europe. In fact, earlier regional studies using DEA have mainly estimated efficiency and technical change for regions within a single country, rather than across countries, such as Canaleta et al. (2003) for the Spanish regions, and Maffezzoli (2006), who studies convergence across Italian regions. A wider perspective has been suggested by Enflo and Hjertstrand (2009) and Filippetti and Peyrache (2012) who have studied labour productivity dynamics across 67 Western European regions and across 211 European regions in 18 countries over the period 1995–2007, respectively. We, therefore, further enlarge their analysis to 31 countries and 287 regions even though we deal with the shorter time period from 2000 to 2007.

Results of the 2000 efficiency levels are depicted in Map 8.5, whilst Map 8.6 reproduces results for the frontier in 2007. The production frontier in 2000 is defined by 27 regions, which exhibit a high degree of heterogeneity in terms of demographic characteristics and geographical location. More specifically, the efficient regions group comprises both small- and low-population-density regions, mostly located in peripheral areas (Ciudad Autónoma de Ceuta, Illes Balears, Corse, Malta, Åland or Valle d'Aosta) and large, densely populated central regions, such as Île de France, and Inner and Outer London. This apparently contradictory picture is expected with the DEA methodology, since it selects efficient units at all possible scales and may therefore reveal high-efficiency scores also for small and peripheral regions. Nonetheless, the least efficient territories are, like the case of KPF, mostly located in the Eastern Europe.

In 2007, Map 8.6 shows quite a different picture, with a general efficiency gain signalled by the number of efficient regions on the frontier increasing from 27 to 32. The spatial distribution of the efficiency scores, however, exhibits a higher degree of dispersion as darker areas now emerge also in Central-Eastern countries, especially in Poland and even in Romania. In general, this analysis points out that the relative average efficiency level has improved for all European regions over the last decade. As a matter of fact, in 2000 the farthest region from the frontier had an efficiency score of 0.20 while in 2007 this value went up to 0.34. These results confirm Filipetti and Peyrache (2012) who find that there has been overall

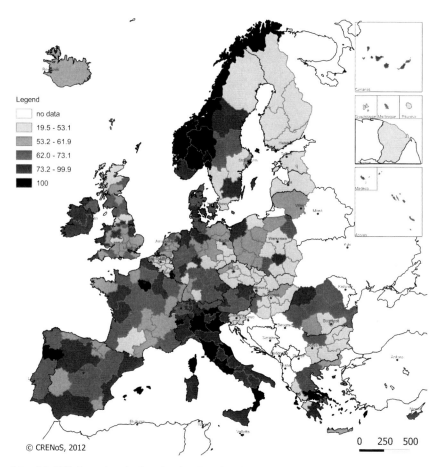

Map 8.5 Efficiency level of production function for the individual regions (DEA methodology, 2000)

convergence in labour productivity growth, driven by capital accumulation and
exogenous technical change. Further, they argue that the lack of convergence of
some backward regions is mainly due to a shortage of endogenous technological
capabilities.

In Table 8.7, we present the average efficiency levels for the five territorial
groups previously discussed. First of all, we confirm that there is lower heterogeneity in terms of production efficiency with respect to the knowledge efficiency
examined in Table 8.4. Most importantly, the ranking, which was very stable in
the knowledge production, is very unsteady for production efficiency. Finally,
we find that the most efficient clusters are the Smart and creative diversification
regions in 2000 and the Imitative innovation area in 2007, which were the least

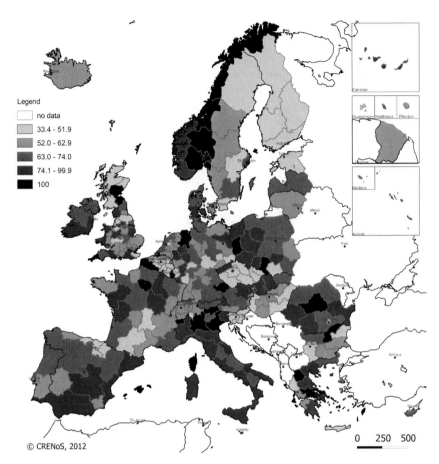

Map 8.6 Efficiency level of production function for the individual regions (DEA methodology, 2007)

Table 8.7 Average efficiency in economic production

	2000	2007
European science-based	0.698	0.658
Applied science	0.633	0.638
Smart technological application	0.636	0.723
Smart and creative diversification	0.704	0.617
Imitative innovation	0.641	0.727

efficient in knowledge production. These contrasting evidences underline that the capacity of a certain region (or a cluster of regions) to be efficient in the process of knowledge creation does not necessarily imply a similarly efficient performance when the production function is considered.

8.5. Conclusions

The main purpose of this chapter is to investigate the functioning of the knowledge economy at the regional level in Europe. In particular, we assess the impact of intangible assets, such as human capital and R&D activities, on regional economic performances, which is proxied by inventive activity and by production levels. We also evaluate whether this impact is significantly different among regions on the whole and in particular with respect to the characteristics of their innovation behaviour, which is synthesized in the taxonomy of the territorial pattern of innovation developed in Chapter 7. Finally, we investigate the presence of phenomena of spatial dependence across regions, arising from knowledge and technological externalities which go beyond regional borders.

As far as the returns of R&D expenditure and human capital on regional innovative capacity are concerned, we find robust evidence of the strong role played by these inputs in fostering innovation and knowledge creation. Most importantly, the presence of a qualified and skilled labour force proves to be a crucial factor, even more than direct investment in R&D. The estimated impacts exhibit a high degree of heterogeneity across individual regions and across territorial clusters. Results also reveal the presence of a significant spatial association which generates spillovers in the innovation activity.

Results from the DEA provide evidence of a dualistic (centre vs periphery) pattern in the regional innovation activities, with the most efficient territories located in the most central or economically strategic areas of the continent. Conversely, the lowest efficiency scores are shown by regions located in European peripheral areas, especially in the new accession countries.

As far as the analysis of the regional production function is concerned, the importance of intangible assets is confirmed. The implementation of econometric techniques permits the conclusion that the variables measuring knowledge and innovation are significantly related to regional economic performance. Moreover, the relative prevalence of the effects of human capital with respect to R&D is corroborated, providing important indications about public policies to foster regional economic growth. The importance of cross-border externalities is also substantiated, signalling that regional growth is influenced by external factors in addition to the internal ones. This implies that investments in intangible assets are also required within a region, in order to build an adequate absorptive capacity to exploit knowledge coming from other regions and countries. Finally, both econometric and data envelopment analyses suggest the presence of a high level of heterogeneity across regions in terms of the impact of intangible factors and in terms of efficiency levels in the use of productive resources. Such differences apply also to the classification of the territorial patterns of innovation.

In general, the efficiency ranking of the knowledge production function shows a much higher heterogeneity with respect to the production function. We conclude that for backward regions reaching efficiency in the creation of knowledge is much more difficult than obtaining efficient performances on the production side. This might help explain why we observe a convergence process in the production performances across regions but not in the knowledge production. Cohesion strategies in Europe should therefore aim at supporting the knowledge creation and diffusion processes as well as, or even more than, the production performances.

Notes

1 A comprehensive review of different methodologies to assess economic growth and productivity can be found in Del Gatto et al. (2011).
2 When data on costs and prices are available the DEA method also allows measurement of allocative efficiency, which is informative for productive units such as firms or hospitals, but is less appropriate for regions.
3 For a comprehensive description of spatial models and related specifications, estimation and testing issues refer to Le Sage and Pace (2009) and Elhorst (2010).
4 EPO applications are associated with regions on the basis of the inventors' addresses. If there are multiple inventors, the application is divided equally among all their respective regions (fractional counting), avoiding thus double counting.
5 A general overview of the territorial pattern of human capital and R&D in the enlarged Europe is reported in Chapter 3.
6 The effects are estimated by using the Matlab code recently made available by J. P. Elhorst for the case of spatial static panel data models (http://www.regroningen.nl/elhorst/).
7 Keeping constant the 2007 GDP level, a 10% rise in R&D increases the average R&D/GDP share from 1.86% to 2.05%.
8 The DEAP software by Coelli (1996) is used throughout the analysis.
9 Analogous KPF models have been, nonetheless, implemented in some studies which investigate knowledge production at the national level as in Wang (2007), Wang and Huang (2007) and Sharma and Thomas (2008) who have recently followed the pioneering contribution by Rousseau and Rousseau (1998).

9 Knowledge flows and regional knowledge creation

Ernest Miguélez, Rosina Moreno and Jordi Suriñach

9.1 Introduction

The goal of this chapter is to analyse the contribution made by research networks and the labour and geographical mobility of inventors to the process of knowledge creation. To this end, we extend the typical regional Knowledge Production Function (KPF, hereafter) to include such features of the local labour market, which are likely to explain the spatial heterogeneity in patent production across 287 European regions, in a multivariate econometric model. In this way, we can measure the elasticity of new knowledge to intra-regional and extra-regional knowledge flows. To the best of our knowledge, the contribution of these features to spatial differences in regional innovation is still poorly understood.

This chapter builds upon the long tradition of the regional KPF within the geography of innovation literature (Audretsch and Feldman, 2004), and try to take on board the multiple criticisms this approach has received, both from a methodological viewpoint, as well as from an interpretative perspective. Specifically, our motivation is based upon two strands of criticisms. On the one side, we take on board those claims against the linear perspective of regional innovation production, which states that all kind of R&D efforts will systematically lead to a larger number of inventions. We argue that this argument overlooks the importance of a set of factors that actually account for how innovation is generated at the regional level (Rodríguez-Pose and Crescenzi, 2008). Hence, we aim to estimate disproportionate levels of patent production that are attributable to the aforementioned features – mobility and networks, above and beyond regional R&D endowments and other control variables. On the other side, we take into account those criticisms to the localization of knowledge diffusion and claim that, indeed, 'being there' is not enough to access private pools of knowledge within regions. Rather, knowledge diffuses within the region by means of structured and defined channels, such as networks and labour mobility of human capital, whose spatial distribution explains a non-negligible part of patent production heterogeneity across regions.

The second part of the chapter focuses its attention on the external dimension of regional knowledge production. As has been argued in the literature, we claim that cross-regional research networks and movements of skilled workers across regions act as the main channels through which knowledge is transferred throughout the space (Fratesi and Senn, 2009). As stated by Bathelt et al. (2004) and Owen-Smith and Powell (2004), firms in regions build 'pipelines' in the form of alliances to benefit from knowledge hotspots around the world. In a similar vein, as Breschi et al. (2010) put it, 'knowledge always travels along with people who master it. If those people move away from where they originally learnt, researched, and delivered their inventions, knowledge will diffuse in space. Otherwise, access to it will remain constrained in bounded locations'. In consequence 'crucial extra-regional exchanges of knowledge take place beyond firm networks, in particular through the migratory patterns of different types of mobile individuals embodying tacit knowledge' (Coe and Bunnell, 2003). With these ideas in mind, we examine in detail the role of external-to-the-region research alliances in the likelihood of patenting at the regional level, as well as the influence exerted by the geographical mobility patterns of knowledge workers.

The motivation of the present inquiry is also strongly based on latest policy developments at the European level. That is to say, our study perfectly fits the rationale around the smart specialization strategy, recently launched by the European Commission (Foray et al., 2009). As McCann and Ortega-Argilés (2011) recently put it, in order to work out how the smart specialization concept could be applied to regional policy, the concepts of *embeddedness* of the local networks and the local labour force, as well as the idea of *connectedness* to global knowledge hotspots, by means of learning-linkages in the form of cross-regional alliances and spatial mobility of human capital, are pivotal. To the best of our knowledge, few empirical analyses have tried to give empirical content to the conceptual rationale behind the smart specialization strategy, and therefore we aim to fill in this gap.

Contrary to what is customary in this literature, we make use of a longitudinal data set and estimate a fixed-effects model which allows us to control for a number of unobservable time-invariant confounders that might bias our results if not included. We extend previous empirical works by including a large sample of 287 regions of 31 European countries. In addition, by drawing on patent data and computerized algorithms to identify individual inventors, a large data set of individuals containing information regarding their personal address(es), their patenting history, the owners of their patents, and the co-authors of their patents, among other details, was constructed. To the best of our knowledge, very few studies have examined the influence of these features on regional innovation and therefore it constitutes a main contribution of the present analysis.

The rest of the chapter is organized as follows. Section 9.2 reviews the literature on knowledge diffusion, space, and innovation, as well as inventor networking and mobility, and their relationship with the former phenomena. Section 9.3 presents a testable empirical model. Section 9.4 presents the data; whilst Section 9.5 includes the results. Finally, Section 9.6 presents the conclusions and identifies certain limitations in the approach.

9.2 Theoretical and empirical background

The KPF has been widely used to empirically test the relationship between technological inputs (such as R&D and human capital investments) and knowledge outputs. First used in the seminal studies of Griliches (1979) and Hausman et al. (1984) at the firm level, this framework was subsequently extended by Jaffe (1986, 1989) to the regional level. The regional setting was claimed to be more apposite to appraise the aforementioned relationships, since it better takes on board potential direct and indirect effects of R&D and human capital efforts of firms and institutions on firms' innovation rates. Among other things, this approach was strongly based on the belief that knowledge – especially that of a tacit nature – is difficult to appropriate in its totality by its creator and therefore may spill over to third parties, on the one hand; and on the evidence that knowledge spills over, but its diffusive patterns are subjected to strong spatial decays (Jaffe et al., 1993). This logic chain gave rise during the nineties, and does so to the present day, to a flourishing literature claiming that, by being co-located and sharing the same geographical space, agents are exposed to a ceaseless number of information flows, knowledge transfers and learning opportunities that take place continuously in both organized and accidental meetings (Bathelt et al., 2004). That is to say, knowledge flows are more or less automatically received by those who share the same physical space (op. cit.).

The first set of criticisms stems from the evidence that the passage from R&D efforts to innovation is not always straightforward. As Rodríguez-Pose (1999) puts it, different social and institutional local conditions may lead to marked spatial differences in the returns to innovation (Rodríguez-Pose, 1999). In spite of the widespread wisdom of technology as the engine of economic growth (Romer, 1986, 1990), the relationship between innovation efforts and knowledge outputs is far from being linear and overlooks the importance of a set of factors that actually account for how innovation is generated at the regional level (Rodríguez-Pose and Crescenzi, 2008). Rather, countries and regions do enormously differ in their socioeconomic background, which may explain a sizeable part of the spatial heterogeneity in patent production, above and beyond local R&D and human capital endowments. It follows from this appreciation that certain features of the local labour market for inventors, such as their job-to-job mobility, as well as the configuration of their networks of research collaboration, may influence regional innovation rates.

A parallel strand of criticisms relates to the widespread logic chain of the localized knowledge spillovers story. During the nineties, empirical analysis from the geography of innovation (Feldman and Audretsch, 1999; Jaffe 1986, 1989; Jaffe et al., 1993) and new economic geography models (Martin and Ottaviano, 1999) indicated the localized pattern of knowledge spillovers and their role in explaining both the high spatial concentration of economic activity as well as marked spatial differences in economic growth. Central to this reasoning is the assumption that corporate and public R&D investment spills over to third parties in the form of an externality, but 'the ability to receive knowledge spillovers is influenced by distance from the knowledge source' (Audretsch and Feldman, 1996, p. 630). After all, 'intellectual breakthroughs must cross hallways and streets more easily than oceans and continents' (Glaeser et al., 1992, p. 1127).

Against this widely accepted tradition, some studies consistently argue that co-location is not a sufficient condition for accessing private pools of local knowledge, but the active participation in meaningful networks such as the collaboration patterns between inventors and their job-to-job mobility across firms and institutions. As Zucker et al. (1998) or Breschi and Lissoni (2009) put it, in the absence of large levels of local labour mobility of super-skilled labour and research networks of formal collaboration, informal linkages and serendipitous encounters explain only a relatively minor part of the localization of knowledge flows. Thus, knowledge flows might be a powerful agglomeration force and might basically occur at the regional level – not in the form of a spillover, but through well-regulated knowledge exchanges deliberated on a market basis (Breschi and Lissoni, 2001b). As far as we know, few quantitative studies have attempted to disentangle the effect of these features as mechanisms of local knowledge diffusion and innovation.

Broadly speaking, the literature on collaborative research networks, and their impact on knowledge diffusion and innovation, has expanded greatly in recent years.[1] This is particularly true in the case of networks of co-inventors thanks to the availability of relevant data (co-patent data). Part of this literature has been devoted to explaining the determinants of these collaborative patterns (Hoekman et al., 2009; Maggioni and Uberti, 2008), while a further important line has focused on networks as mechanisms for inter-regional R&D spillovers (Kroll, 2009; Ponds et al., 2007, 2010), and, in particular, networks as the means by which knowledge diffuses between individuals and across firms (Breschi and Lissoni, 2004, 2006; 2009; Gomes-Casseres et al., 2006; Singh, 2005).

Singh (2005) finds strong evidence in the US that the existence of interpersonal ties in the form of co-patents increases the probability of knowledge flows, as measured by patent citations. Singh claims that geography matters especially because interpersonal networks tend to be regional in nature (op. cit.). Similar results are found by Breschi and Lissoni (2004) for Italy. In the same line, recent findings by Breschi and Lissoni (2009), using patent applications to the European Patent Office (EPO), similarly suggest that networking activity across firms is in large part responsible for the localisation of knowledge flows, indicating that the residual effect of non-market externalities is not as great as was previously believed.

All these studies stress the importance of networks as knowledge transmission, and hence, creation mechanisms. Co-location and shared space are reported as being neither necessary nor sufficient for knowledge flows, but rather it is social distance, or social connectivity, which appears to be critical for the effective diffusion of knowledge (Boschma, 2005). If this were to be the case, the features of the inventors' network structure at any given location should play a significant role in regional knowledge outcomes. In this sense, a number of macro-level empirical analyses have recently been conducted in a knowledge production function framework by Bettencourt et al. (2007a and 2007b), Fleming et al. (2007) and Lobo and Strumsky (2008) for the case of US metropolitan statistical areas. These studies have shown that the agglomeration of inventors is much more critical in explaining regional innovation rates than structural properties of inventors' networks, such as the 'small world' configuration – which combines low average path length among individuals in a network and high levels of clustering coefficient, and which has

214 Ernest Miguélez, Rosina Moreno and Jordi Suriñach

been identified to be innovation-prone (Watts and Strogatz, 1998; Cowan and Jonard, 2004). Breschi and Lenzi (2011), by contrast, find 'small world' properties to be positively correlated with a city's rates of innovation. The present chapter's aim is rather different, though, since it does not attempt to appraise 'small world' properties' influence on European regional innovation, but the general degree of connectivity through networks of research collaboration as well as the strength of these networks.

Similarly, earlier studies have examined how the labour mobility of inventors acts as a key mechanism in the diffusion of knowledge (Almeida and Kogut, 1999; Rosenkopf and Almeida, 2003; Saxenian, 1994). One strand of this literature has shown the relationship between mobility and the flow of knowledge as measured by patent citations, as well as the knowledge gain by a firm hiring an inventor from another firm. For example, in a pioneering study, Almeida and Kogut (1999) show that inter-firm mobility of patent holders in the semiconductor industry of the US influences the local transfer of knowledge across firms. Similar findings are reported in the aforementioned study conducted by Breschi and Lissoni (2009) for US inventors in selected technological fields making patent applications to the EPO. In a similar vein, Agrawal et al. (2006) stress the idea that once inventors leave their workplace, they will maintain interpersonal ties with their former colleagues which can translate into a citation of their work by these co-workers. In addition, several studies (Crespi et al., 2007; Corredoria and Rosenkopf, 2006; Kim et al. 2006; Singh and Agrawal, 2009; Song et al., 2003) have stressed the role of mobility insofar as it increases the hiring firm's use of a hired inventor's prior knowledge.

Parallel to these studies, another line of research has studied mobility by focusing its attention on inventors' performance itself. For instance, mobility–productivity relationships have been studied by Hoisl (2007 and 2009) for German, by Lenzi (2009) for Italian, and by Shalem and Trajtenberg (2008) for Israeli inventors. Broadly speaking, it has been shown that mobility may in fact enhance productivity (Hoisl, 2007), although results in that direction are not as robust as one would expect (Shalem and Trajtenberg, 2008), which has been attributed to what have been identified as the short-term costs of mobility.

If an individual's knowledge output increases on moving and the new host firms acquire more knowledge and are more efficient in their knowledge activities, the innovative capacity of a region as a whole should increase as the degree of inventors' mobility rises across firms within a region. To the best of our knowledge, there have been few empirical attempts at quantifying how this feature of the local labour market for inventors – in other words, the degree of job-to-job mobility of inventors – impacts on regional knowledge outcomes, and as such constitutes one of the main contributions of this chapter.

The second part of this chapter aims to put to the forefront an important debate within the geography of innovation literature that has emerged recently; that is, the role of external knowledge linkages in the process of regional knowledge creation. Indeed, an increasing number of academics have called into question the widely accepted assumption that knowledge flows are localized.

This assumption, they argue, might have limited our understanding of the ways in which knowledge flows across space (Coe and Bunnell, 2003). Certainly, recent empirical evidence casts doubts on the orthodox viewpoint outlined above and some studies have extensively explored the influence of extra-local knowledge sources on firms' knowledge performance and knowledge acquisition (Owen-Smith and Powell, 2004; Gittelman, 2007; Gertler and Levite, 2005; Rosenkopf and Almedia, 2003; Simonen and McCann, 2008; Boschma et al., 2009).

Besides, several scholars have lately stressed the need for firms to network with extra-local knowledge pools to overcome potential situations of regional 'entropic death', 'lock-in' or 'over-embeddedness' (Boschma, 2005; Camagni, 1991; Grabher, 1993). These claims have contributed to a lively current debate among research streams about the conditions in which tacit knowledge can be transmitted at a distance and go beyond a region's confines, as well as the extent of such transmission. Indeed, it has been argued that two very close actors may have little knowledge to exchange whereas innovative production usually requires the combination of dissimilar, but related, complementary knowledge (Boschma and Frenken, 2010; Boschma and Iammarino, 2009).[2] Thus, as time passes and local interactions lead to the combination and recombination of the same pieces of knowledge, organizations end up stuck in strong social structures that tend to resist social change (Boschma and Frenken, 2010; Morrison et al., 2011) and prevent them from recognizing opportunities in new markets and technologies (Lambooy and Boschma, 2001). Thus,

> distant contexts can be a source of novel ideas and expert insights useful for innovation processes (. . .). Firms therefore develop global pipelines not only to exchange products or services, but also in order to benefit from outside knowledge inputs and growth impulse.
>
> (Maskell et al., 2006, p. 998)

This way, the analysis of the role of extra-regional formal linkages in the process of knowledge creation is the second main contribution of this chapter.

9.3 Research design

In order to meet the goals identified in the previous sections, the KPF framework at the regional level is used. For the sake of simplicity, the local/non-local dimensions are analysed separately and the multivariate analysis is divided into two parts. Thus, we first suggest an empirical model where local mobility and networks are included as main explanatory variables under scrutiny. In the second part, extra-regional linkages are included as regressors.

Our point of departure is the simplest specification of this model:

$$Y = f(RD, HK, Z), \qquad\qquad (9.1)$$

where Y is the knowledge output of a given region, which depends on regional R&D expenditures (RD) as well as the stock of human capital (HK). To capture a variety of returns that might affect knowledge outcomes, Z are a number of time-variant controls that account for specific features of the region i at time t. Among them, the level of inventors' labour mobility within a given region, as well as the scale and density of its collaborative research networks are included. Population of the regions (POP) is also included in order to control for size and market potential. As is customary in the related literature, it is assumed that the KPF follows a multiplicative functional form:

$$Y_{it} = e^{\theta} RD_{it}^{\beta} HK_{it}^{\gamma} POP_{it}^{\rho} Z_{it}^{\alpha} e^{\delta_i}, \tag{9.2}$$

where e^{θ} is a constant term capturing the impact of all common factors affecting knowledge. In additional, e^{δ_i} stands for 287 regional time-invariant fixed-effects, that allow us to capture unobserved time-invariant heterogeneity that might significantly bias our estimates if they were not considered. In particular, we refer to institutional features that may affect knowledge, technology-oriented regional policies, inherited skills of the local community, prestige of research and higher education institutions, inherited knowledge culture, social capital and, in general, all the historical path-dependent features that may significantly affect spatial differences in knowledge rates.

9.3.1. Labour mobility, research networks and knowledge

In the present chapter, social network analysis (SNA) tools are employed to investigate empirically the quantitative relationship between inventors' collaborations and levels of inventiveness.[3] We are interested in measuring some particular aspects of inventors' networks. First of all, we will measure the scale of these networks, i.e. whether a greater number of social ties are beneficial for inventive intensity. A positive effect on creativity is expected. Second, the extent of the local network is also of interest, i.e. whether a large number of local inventors involved in co-inventions is beneficial for regional knowledge. Finally, we are concerned with the strength of the inventors' community ties, measured as the network density. The naïve, expected effect of density on innovation is positive. However, we should bear in mind Granovetter's (1985) warning that overly strong interpersonal ties might well hamper innovation because, at some point, the information flowing across those ties becomes redundant and less valuable. In consequence, the scale and extent of research networks, as well as their intensity within the region, are included as additional regressors. Besides, the degree of labour mobility within the region is also included. Thus,

$$Z_{it} = g(MOB_{it}, DEGREE_{it}, CONN_{it}, DENS_{it}, X_{it}) \tag{9.3}$$

where *MOB* is the measure of mobility, *DEGREE* stands for the average degree centrality of skilled workers, that is, the average 'popularity' of inventors in regions, *CONN* stands for the overall connectivity of the local network, i.e. the inclusiveness of the local network, and *DENS* is a measure of the density of the regional network. Finally, *X* controls for the existence of specialization and concentration economies. Assuming that (9.3) also follows a multiplicative functional form and inserting it into the logarithmic transformation of (9.2) yields to:

$$ln\ Y_{it} = \theta + \beta\ ln\ RD_{it-1} + \gamma\ ln\ HK_{it-1} + \rho\ POP_{it-1} + \omega_1 MOB_{it-1} +$$
$$\omega_2\ ln\ DEGREE_{it-1} + \omega_3\ CONN_{it-1} + \omega_4\ ln\ DENS_{it-1} + \omega_n\ ln\ X_{it-1} + \delta_i + \varepsilon_{it} \quad (9.4)$$

Note that the subscript *t–1* is now introduced in all the explanatory variables in order to make clear that they have been time-lagged one period in order to lessen endogeneity problems. Section 9.4 includes further details regarding the construction of all the variables used in the present analysis and a brief summary is provided in Annex 9.1.

9.3.2. *Spatial heterogeneity of labour mobility and networks impacts on knowledge*

As labour mobility and research networks are assumed to be a fundamental factor in the creation of knowledge, an unequal distribution of such mechanisms in the territory could be a cause of regional differences in knowledge levels and economic development in general. Knowledge can therefore be considered to be a causal factor in regional disparities. As a consequence, it can be thought that policies aimed at encouraging the mobility of highly skilled workers or enhancing participation in research networks (as promoted by the European Commission through Marie Curie programmes or the Framework Programmes) in less productive regions can constitute a key factor in the creation of knowledge and development, or at least a necessary condition for it. However, the effectiveness of this policy depends in large part on each region's capacity to give returns to labour mobility and the participation in research networks. One would expect these returns to be homogeneous in all regions if they were also homogeneous in other aspects, such as industrial mix, and propensity to generate and adopt innovations and technological specialization, among others. When this is not the case, returns to labour mobility and research networks may differ between regions. Any appraisal of the value of this policy as a tool for use in regional development would therefore be particularly useful if information about the regional distribution of such returns were available.

The aim of this subsection is to analyse the existence of regional variations in the returns to labour mobility and networking. In such a case, we could conclude that development policies based on stimulating these mechanisms of knowledge diffusion could differ in their effectiveness according to local conditions. In order to do it, we obtain different elasticities according to the different territorial patterns of innovation in the European regions (developed in Chapter 7): European science-based area, Applied science area, Smart technological specialization area, Smart and creative diversification area and Imitative innovation area.

9.3.3. *Labour mobility, networks and knowledge diffusion*

We turn now to investigate the specific role of our foci variables, not only as a knowledge creation mechanism, but also as knowledge diffusion mechanisms. It is commonplace in the related literature that close network links should prove more useful in transferring complex knowledge (Cowan and Jonard, 2004), especially that with a high component of 'tacitness' (Singh, 2005). Similarly, individuals connected within a collaborative framework are more willing to learn from each other than is the case with isolated inventors. Additionally, participating in networks reduces the degree of uncertainty and provides fast access to different kinds of knowledge. All this would signal to the fact that belonging to a research network may imply higher returns of knowledge endowments, such as R&D and human capital investments, on regional innovation.

On the other hand, mobility may favour knowledge diffusion as well. Knowledge, especially that of a tacit nature, is mostly embedded in individuals. Moving themselves means moving the knowledge capital they accumulate. Their movement across firms must therefore contribute to knowledge exchange between firms (Boschma et al., 2009). Skilled workers take their knowledge with them and share it in a new workplace with their new colleagues, at the same time as they provide their new employer with this knowledge. In return, they acquire new knowledge from their new colleagues, establish new links and social networks for future collaborations based on trust and, in general, promote new combinations of knowledge (Laudel, 2003; Trippl and Maier 2007). Therefore, the return obtained from the investments in R&D and human capital may increase with the level of mobile workers.

To address this issue, we allow now the coefficient of both R&D and human capital in equation (9.4) to be a function of a constant part, which can be identified as the direct impact on knowledge, and an additional element which is a function of one of the characteristics of the local labour market (we are reluctant to include the resulting interactions in the same equation in order to minimize collinearity problems). Thus,

$$\beta = \lambda_0 + \lambda_1 F_{it-1} \text{ and } \gamma = \tau_0 + \tau_1 F_{it-1} \tag{9.5}$$

where F stands for each of the variables included in the main model, that is, labour mobility, two measures of research networks, and network density. Therefore, (9.4) includes now interaction effects between R&D and each of the four foci variables in the main model, running four different estimations for each of the interactions included, as well as interactions between human capital and again our four variables under analysis:

$$
\begin{aligned}
ln\,Y_{it} &= \theta + \lambda_0\,ln\,RD_{it-1} + \lambda_1\,(F_{it-1}\,ln\,RD_{it-1}) + \tau_0\,ln\,HK_{it-1} \\
&+ \tau_1\,(F_{it-1}\,ln\,HK_{it-1}) + \rho\,ln\,POP_{it-1} + \omega_1\,MOB_{it-1} + \omega_2\,ln\,DEGREE_{it-1} \\
&+ \omega_3\,CONN_{it-1} + \omega_4\,ln\,DENS_{it-1} + \omega_n\,ln\,X_{it-1} + \delta_i + \varepsilon_{it}
\end{aligned}
\tag{9.6}
$$

9.3.4. *Cross-regional collaborations and inter-regional mobility*

As stated in the previous section, a second aim of this chapter is the analysis of extra-local linkages, in the form of skilled labour mobility and spatial networks, on the knowledge performance of European regions. Regions are not isolated entities that do not interact with the rest of the world; rather, an increasing number of studies have identified that firms in regions source their knowledge more and more often in non-local knowledge interactions.

First, as has been stated elsewhere, local knowledge diffusion is favoured by the labour mobility of skilled workers (Breschi and Lissoni, 2009; Almeida and Kogut, 1997, 1999). However, to the extent that knowledge travels along with people who master it (Breschi et al., 2010), what happens when highly skilled individuals move in the space? Geographical mobility of knowledge workers has been regarded to be a source of knowledge diffusion across areas and, on top, is responsible for the recombination of previously unconnected pieces of knowledge that may lead to increased knowledge rates. In order to analyse the role of skilled geographical mobility on the knowledge performance of regions, we correlate two different measures proxying inflows of skilled migration with regional patent production. Again, within the KPF framework, where typical knowledge inputs, as well as structural controls, are included as regressors, the rate of incoming skilled individuals, as well as the net rate, are included among the r.h.s. variables, running two different models in order to avoid collinearity problems. Positive and significant coefficients are expected for both variables.

Recently, several authors have pinpointed outward migration of skilled individuals as an alternative source of knowledge flows and interactions back to the home location of the skilled employee who has left, reversing the 'brain drain' phenomenon into 'brain gain' or 'brain circulation' (Saxenian, 2006). Thus, for instance, Agrawal et al. (2006) and Oettl and Agrawal (2008) report disproportionate knowledge flows from inventors leaving a region or a country back to their former colleagues. Kerr (2008) and Agrawal et al. (2008, 2011) do likewise and estimate disproportionate knowledge flows from ethnic inventors in the US to their origin countries, stressing the role of diasporas in accessing frontier knowledge. Following these ideas, we also test the role of the gross migration rate (inflows plus outflows) of skilled individuals, as well as the outward migration rate, as patent production predictors in regions.

Next, we also hypothesize that the more inventors collaborate with fellow inventors outside the region, the greater are the returns on knowledge. As in the case of geographical mobile inventors, spatial networks formation is also likely to be conducive to knowledge diffusion, knowledge recombination and innovation. At the level of European regions, Ponds et al. (2010) and Maggioni et al. (2007) show the importance of cross-regional networks to the process of knowledge diffusion. Following these ideas, we conjecture that higher amounts of patents co-authored with fellow inventors outside the region are expected to explain spatial differences in innovation.

9.4 Data

In order to meet the goals identified in previous sections, the KPF is estimated for 287 NUTS2 European regions of 31 countries (EU27 plus Iceland, Liechtenstein, Norway and Switzerland, as detailed in Table 1.1 in Chapter 1). Thanks to data availability, we are in a position to estimate a panel fixed-effects model of six periods (2001 to 2006). Again, the use of longitudinal data and the inclusion of fixed effects in our regressions allow us to improve previous estimates in a KPF framework, to the extent that these fixed effects account for a number of time-invariant unobservable characteristics of the regions that might bias our results if not included.

Next, knowledge is measured by patent applications (PAT), a variable widely used in the literature to proxy knowledge outcomes. As is well known, this proxy presents serious caveats since not all inventions are patented, nor do they all have the same economic impact, as they are not all commercially exploitable (Griliches, 1991). In spite of these shortcomings, patent data have proved useful for proxying inventiveness as they present minimal standards of novelty, originality and potential profits, and as such are a good proxy for economically profitable ideas (Bottazzi and Peri, 2003). Patent data come from the KIT database, collected from the OECD REGPAT database. Since these data are prone to exhibit lumpiness from year to year, we have averaged out patent figures. Thus, a three-year moving average is computed for every observation, thereby mitigating the effects of annual fluctuations in this variable, especially in those less populated areas.

As for the explanatory variables, R&D expenditures data also come from the KIT project and again figures are averaged out from the same reason. Specifically, all the data were collected from Eurostat and some National Statistical Offices, with some elaboration for regions in specific countries (Belgium, Switzerland, Greece, Netherlands). Human capital (HK) is measured as the absolute population with tertiary education (population aged 15 and over by ISCED level of education attained) and is extracted again from the KIT records, collected from Eurostat. Annual figures are considered in this case. Both variables, as well as the remaining regressors, are time-lagged one period in order to lessen endogeneity problems. Thus, for instance, the average R&D expenditures in time t are computed using data from t–3 to t–1, whereas data from t–1 is used to compute human capital figures in the t period. Population data is computed used a single (lagged) year as well, and retrieved from Eurostat databases.

The data for constructing the mobility and network variables are based on individual inventor information retrieved from EPO patents, taken from the REGPAT database (January 2010 edition). However, in spite of the vast amount of information contained in patent documents, a single ID for each inventor and anyone else is missing. In order to draw the mobility and networking history of inventors, it is necessary to identify them individually by name and surname, as well as via the other useful details contained in the patent document. The method chosen for identifying the inventors is therefore of the utmost importance in studies of this nature. In line with a growing number of researchers in the field, we apply several algorithms squeezing patent data information for singling out individual inventors (Miguélez and Gómez-Miguélez, 2011).

Once each inventor has been assigned an individual identification, mobility and network data can be calculated for each region. In line with related studies (Schilling and Phelps, 2007; Breschi and Lenzi, 2011), a one-year lagged five-year moving window is adopted to compute all the mobility and network variables, as well as for the case of the control variables. Thus, mobility or network measures of the period t include data from t–5 to t–1.

A 'mobile' inventor is broadly defined as an individual who moves across different organisations offering his/her services (Breschi and Lissoni, 2009). Therefore, mobility can refer either to the concept of labour mobility as it is understood in its strictest sense (an employee leaving a firm to take up a position in a new one), or to that demonstrated by consultants, freelance workers, university inventors, and the like. We assume that both constitute sources of knowledge flows to the extent that in both instances knowledge is transferred from former employers or customers to new ones. Mobility is then proxied as the share of mobile inventors to the absolute number of inventors per region, as is usually done in the labour literature.

The design of the network variables is built upon the theory of SNA. Thus, the inventors form the nodes in the network, and these are grouped via edges or ties (in this instance, co-patents) into different components.

Two different, though complementary, variables measure the scale of network connectivity among inventors in regions. Average degree centrality is calculated by averaging out the degree centrality of the nodes (inventors) by region. The degree centrality of a node is the number of linkages it has to other nodes. That is to say, it measures how well connected, how popular, is each of the nodes. Thus, it measures the extent to which inventors in regions are prone, on average, to be connected with other inventors through networks of research collaboration. On its side, connectivity goes a little bit further and tries to take on board the scope of the local network by computing the share of inventors with at least one tie in the form of a co-patent. That is, the number of connected nodes of the whole network minus the number of isolated nodes, as a proportion of the total number of nodes (inclusiveness, in SNA terms). Formally,

$$CONN_{it} = \frac{Q_{it} - NQ_{it}}{Q_{it}} \tag{9.7}$$

where Q_{it} stands for the total number of inventors in region i and time t, and NQ_{it} stands for the number of isolated inventors.

The strength of these ties is proxied by the network density, which is the number of ties between inventors within the region divided by the possible number of ties within that region. Formally,

$$DENS_{it} = \frac{T_{it}}{Q_{it}(Q_{it} - 1)/2} \tag{9.8}$$

where T_{it} stands for the number of edges (ties) within a given region, and Q_{it} is again the total number of inventors within that region. As stressed earlier, the expected effect (be it positive or negative) of knowledge density is not so clear a priori.

As regards the variables proxying meaningful linkages across regions, the one-year lagged five-year moving window criteria is also adopted. The Net Migration Rate (NMR) is computed as the inflows minus outflows of inventors to the current number of inventors, for each time window. The Inward Migration Rate (IMR) corresponds only to the inflows of inventors to the current number of inventors, whereas the Outward Migration Rate (OMR) computes the outflows of inventors to the current number of inventors, again within each time window. Finally, Gross Migration Rate (GMR) measures inflows plus outflows of inventors to the current number of inventors. Importantly, spatial mobility is computed through observed changes in the reported region of residence by the inventor in patent documents. Note also that we compute each movement in-between the origin and the destination patent, but only if there is a maximum lapse of five years between them. Otherwise, the exact move date is too uncertain.

Cross-regional networks of research collaboration are computed as the sum of local patents, fractional count, co-authored with inventors from outside, to the total number of inventors of the region, within each five-year time window. Extra-regional inventors include both European and non-European ones.

As explained in the methodological section, several variables were also included in our regressions to control for other regional time-variant features that may affect spatial differences in patent production. Thus, a specialization index and a concentration index of industries constructed using patents from 30 IPC[4] technological sectors – OST subdivision – are also included, in order to control for the influence of specialization and concentration economies on innovation (Feldman and Audretsch, 1999). To calculate the technological specialization index, we employ the following formula

$$SpIn_{it} = \frac{1}{2}\sum_j \left| \frac{PAT_{ijt}}{PAT_{it}} - \frac{PAT_{Cjt}}{PAT_{Ct}} \right|, \tag{9.9}$$

where PAT is the number of patents in each region i for each sector j, expressed as a difference for the whole sample of regions (C). The concentration index is built as follows:

$$ConIn_{it} = \sum_{jt} (PAT_{ijt}/PAT_{jt})^2. \tag{9.10}$$

Three additional controls capture differences in technological content across regions: the shares of biotechnology (BIOTECH), organic chemistry (CHEM), and pharmaceuticals (PHARMA) in their patenting activity, according to the IPC classification – since these three sectors tend to be more research-intensive.[5, 6]

9.5 Results of the econometric specifications

9.5.1 Results on the role of research networks and labour mobility on knowledge: Evidence on the direct impact

Column (1) of Table 9.1 presents the results of the fixed effect estimation of the KPF once labour mobility of inventors as well as the scale and density of the research networks in which they participate are included as additional variables. In principle, the coefficients can be interpreted as elasticities, since the variables in the regression are either expressed in natural logarithmic form or as in percentage terms: the proportional increase in patenting activity in response to a 1% increase in a given explanatory variable. Note also that Hausman tests (Hausman, 1978) have also been computed for all the models and the null hypothesis that individual effects are uncorrelated with the independent variables is always rejected, so the fixed-effects (FE) model is preferred to the expense of the random effects.

Some results are worth highlighting. In general, the KPF holds in the European regional case for the period under consideration. The elasticity of patents with respect to R&D expenditures when the FE estimation is carried out presents a significant value of 0.19, which is in line with the value obtained in the literature, although in the lower limit. In fact, the elasticity goes from 0.2 to 0.9 in the USA (Jaffe, 1989; Acs et al., 1994; Anselin et al., 1997), and from 0.24 to 0.8 in the European case (Bottazzi and Peri, 2003; Moreno et al., 2005a). It should be noted that with respect to these previous contributions we exploit a more disaggregated and updated database for the European regions, covering more countries and in a panel data set. In fact, our parameter resembles more the ones obtained in the study by Moreno et al. (2005a), with an elasticity of 0.25, where a vector of control variables are included, as in our case. Additionally, the human capital parameter is, in general, strongly significant and with the expected positive sign, with similar values to those reported elsewhere in the literature when a similar indicator is used (as in Bottazi and Peri, 2003, with values between 0.4 and 0.5).

The foci variables of this study are also significant. Labour mobility, for example, is significant at 1%, presenting a parameter of 0.01, whilst the relationship between the scale of the networks and knowledge is always positive and strongly significant – no matter whether it is proxied through the average degree centrality or the connectivity measure. Thus, we can conclude that collaborative research networks of inventors boost regional knowledge capability and that the mobility of inventors within the local labour market of a region enhances knowledge intensity. In addition, network density shows a significant negative impact on knowledge intensity, which bestows credibility to Granovetter's (1985) arguments about weak ties and knowledge. In other words, it seems that, in the European case, strong personal ties hamper knowledge once the information flowing becomes redundant. Finally, we must say that the results are robust to the inclusion of a large number of time-variant controls. In this sense, although among the control variables only the share of patents in biotechnology has a significant and negative parameter, we have decided to leave all of them in the regression. However, once they are discarded the main results on the foci variables remain.

Table 9.1 Baseline estimations. Regional networks and regional mobility

Dep. var.: ln(patents)$_t^{‡}$	(1)	(2)	(3)	(4)	(5)
	FE	FE	FE	FE	FE
ln(RD)$_{t-1}$	0.19***	0.20***	0.16**	0.19**	0.40***
	(0.07)	(0.07)	(0.07)	(0.07)	(0.13)
ln(HK)$_{t-1}$	0.50***	0.50***	0.46***	0.50***	0.50***
	(0.10)	(0.10)	(0.10)	(0.10)	(0.10)
ln(POP)$_{t-1}$	−0.19	−0.16	−0.45	−0.19	−0.02
	(0.81)	(0.82)	(0.81)	(0.81)	(0.82)
Mobility$_{t-1}$	0.01***	0.01*	0.01***	0.01***	0.01***
	(0.00)	(0.01)	(0.00)	(0.00)	(0.00)
ln(Average degree)$_{t-1}^{‡}$	0.04*	0.04*	−0.13***	0.04*	0.04*
	(0.02)	(0.02)	(0.05)	(0.02)	(0.02)
(Connectivity degree)$_{t-1}$	0.02***	0.02***	0.01***	0.02***	0.02***
	(0.00)	(0.00)	(0.00)	(0.00)	(0.00)
ln(Network density)$_{t-1}^{‡}$	−0.18***	−0.18***	−0.17***	−0.18***	−0.32***
	(0.04)	(0.04)	(0.04)	(0.04)	(0.08)
ln(SpecIn)$_{t-1}^{‡}$	0.02	0.02	0.00	0.02	0.03
	(0.11)	(0.11)	(0.11)	(0.11)	(0.11)
ln(ConIn)$_{t-1}^{‡}$	−0.03	−0.03	−0.04	−0.03	−0.03
	(0.03)	(0.03)	(0.03)	(0.03)	(0.03)
(% Chemistry)$_{t-1}$	−0.00	−0.00	−0.00	−0.00	−0.00
	(0.00)	(0.00)	(0.00)	(0.00)	(0.00)
(% Biotechnology)$_{t-1}$	−0.01***	−0.01***	−0.01***	−0.01***	−0.01***
	(0.00)	(0.00)	(0.00)	(0.00)	(0.00)
(% Pharmaceuticals)$_{t-1}$	0.00	0.00	0.00	0.00	0.00
	(0.00)	(0.00)	(0.00)	(0.00)	(0.00)
ln(RD)$_{t-1}$ * (Mobility)$_{t-1}$		−0.00			
		(0.00)			

	(1)	(2)	(3)	(4)	(5)
ln(RD)$_{t-1}$ * ln(Average degree)$_{t-1}$					
ln(RD)$_{t-1}$ * (Connectivity degree)$_{t-1}$			0.06*** (0.02)	0.00 (0.00)	
ln(RD)$_{t-1}$ * ln(Network density)$_{t-1}$					0.05* (0.03)
Constant	1.56 (11.21)	1.10 (11.26)	5.42 (11.20)	1.58 (11.23)	−1.34 (11.31)
Observations	1,722	1,722	1,722	1,722	1,722
Number of regions	287	287	287	287	287
R2 within	0.1408	0.1409	0.1500	0.1408	0.1429
R2 between	0.7706	0.7639	0.7686	0.7704	0.7019
R2 overall	0.7474	0.7415	0.7421	0.7472	0.6830

Notes: *** p<0.01, ** p<0.05, * p<0.1. Standard errors in parentheses. ‡ We added 0.01 to these variables before the logarithmic transformation.

In short, the empirical analyses undertaken here support the hypotheses concerning the importance of labour mobility and networks in the local labour market for the creation of regional knowledge. However, several extensions to this initial approach can now be made.

9.5.2. Results on the indirect impact of labour mobility and research networks

As discussed in the research design section, there are theoretical arguments supporting the existence of indirect effects of networking and labour mobility due to knowledge diffusion. As a consequence, belonging to a research network would imply higher returns to the investments made in R&D and human capital, whereas their returns would also increase with the level of mobile workers.

The results provided in columns (2) to (5) of Table 9.1 give insights with respect to these hypotheses through the introduction of cross-effects between these two variables (labour mobility and networks) and R&D.

Specifically, we do obtain that regions with higher number of individuals connected within a research network (measured through the average degree centrality measure) may obtain higher returns to R&D investments, probably due to the fact that its inventors are more prone to learning from each other, with faster access to new and complementary knowledge. However, when the cross-effect is computed with the index of connectivity degree, no significant parameter is obtained. Additionally, it seems that the density of the network does not imply a reduction of the R&D return, so that we can conclude that even with highly dense networks, researchers belonging to networks may obtain higher returns from the investments made in innovation than in the case of isolated inventors.

However, the parameter for the cross-effect between R&D and labour mobility is not significant. We have, therefore, not obtained evidence that in regions with high levels of mobile workers, the investment made in R&D is more profitable that in those with lower levels of labour mobility.

We now turn to analysing the reinforcing effects of networks and mobility on human capital investments returns on patent production. Results provided in Table 9.2 offer similar conclusions to the ones above. What is more, all the interactions between human capital and our four focal variables are positive and significant, indicating the importance of these features to enhance human capital externalities in regions and their impact on local inventiveness levels.

9.5.3. Results on the regional heterogeneity in the returns to mobility and networking

The results for the whole of the European regions mask substantial regional variations in the returns to innovation with respect to mobility and networking. In order to analyse this variability of the elasticity, we turn now to the variation in the return to labour mobility and networking according to the typology of territorial patterns of innovation (Chapter 7). First of all, we must say that we have tested

Table 9.2 Baseline estimations. Interaction with human capital only

Dep. var.: $\ln(patents)_t^{\ddagger}$	(1)	(2)	(3)	(4)
	FE	FE	FE	FE
$\ln(RD)_{t-1}$	0.17**	0.14**	0.22***	0.17**
	(0.07)	(0.07)	(0.07)	(0.07)
$\ln(HK)_{t-1}$	0.46***	0.45***	0.62***	1.28***
	(0.10)	(0.10)	(0.11)	(0.20)
$\ln(POP)_{t-1}$	−0.08	−0.36	−0.19	−0.17
	(0.82)	(0.81)	(0.81)	(0.81)
Mobility$_{t-1}$	−0.01	0.00	0.01***	0.00
	(0.01)	(0.00)	(0.00)	(0.00)
$\ln$(Average degree)$_{t-1}^{\ddagger}$	0.03	−0.33***	0.03	0.05**
	(0.02)	(0.08)	(0.02)	(0.02)
(Connectivity degree)$_{t-1}$	0.02***	0.01***	0.04***	0.01***
	(0.00)	(0.00)	(0.01)	(0.00)
$\ln$(Network density)$_{t-1}^{\ddagger}$	−0.19***	−0.19***	−0.18***	−0.94***
	(0.04)	(0.04)	(0.04)	(0.18)
$\ln(SpecIn)_{t-1}^{\ddagger}$	0.03	0.00	0.04	−0.03
	(0.11)	(0.11)	(0.11)	(0.11)
$\ln(ConIn)_{t-1}^{\ddagger}$	−0.03	−0.01	−0.03	−0.02
	(0.03)	(0.03)	(0.03)	(0.03)
(% Chemistry)$_{t-1}$	−0.00	−0.00	−0.00	−0.00
	(0.00)	(0.00)	(0.00)	(0.00)
(% Biotechnology)$_{t-1}$	−0.01***	−0.01***	−0.01***	−0.01***
	(0.00)	(0.00)	(0.00)	(0.00)
(% Pharmaceuticals)$_{t-1}$	0.00	0.00	0.00	0.00
	(0.00)	(0.00)	(0.00)	(0.00)
$\ln(HK)_{t-1}$ * Mobility$_{t-1}$	0.00*			
	(0.00)			
$\ln(HK)_{t-1}$ * $\ln$(Average degree)$_{t-1}$		0.10***		
		(0.02)		
$\ln(HK)_{t-1}$ * (Connectivity degree)$_{t-1}$			0.01**	
			(0.00)	
$\ln(HK)_{t-1}$ * $\ln$(Network density)$_{t-1}$				0.18***
				(0.04)
Constant	0.11	4.47	0.93	−1.54
	(11.23)	(11.15)	(11.19)	(11.16)
Observations	1,722	1,722	1,722	1,722
Number of regions	287	287	287	287
R2 within	0.1427	0.1528	0.1440	0.1523
R2 between	0.7353	0.7080	0.7919	0.7168
R2 overall	0.7148	0.6813	0.7691	0.6941

Notes: *** $p<0.01$, ** $p<0.05$, * $p<0.1$. Standard errors in parentheses. ‡ We added 0.01 to these variables before the logarithmic transformation.

the equality of the coefficients for the different groups of regions. Specifically, we have done it through the use of Wald tests for the linear hypothesis of equality between the elasticity values of patenting to each one of our foci variables across the different territorial patterns of innovation. The results are provided in Tables 9.3 to 9.6, pointing in almost all cases to the rejection of the null; that is, indicating that the elasticities differ across categories.

Table 9.3 Wald tests of the linear hypothesis of differences between the elasticity values of patenting to mobility across the different territorial patterns of innovation

	1	2	3	4	5
Imitative innovation area					
Smart and creative diversification area	34.29***				
Smart technological application area	70.32***	19.98***			
Applied science area	139.80***	83.30***	26.78***		
European science-based area	116.79***	72.12***	33.37***	3.58*	

Note: (1) Imitative innovation area; (2) Smart and creative diversification area; (3) Smart technological application area; (4) Applied science area; (5) European science-based area.

Table 9.4 Wald tests of the linear hypothesis of differences between the elasticity values of patenting to degree centrality across the different territorial patterns of innovation

	1	2	3	4	5
Imitative innovation area					
Smart and creative diversification area	0.37				
Smart technological application area	20.86***	33.33***			
Applied science area	79.24***	114.52***	24.61***		
European science-based area	73.18***	96.14***	29.83***	2.19	

Note: (1) Imitative innovation area; (2) Smart and creative diversification area; (3) Smart technological application area; (4) Applied science area; (5) European science-based area.

Table 9.5 Wald tests of the linear hypothesis of differences between the elasticity values of patenting to connectivity across the different territorial patterns of innovation

	1	2	3	4	5
Imitative innovation area					
Smart and creative diversification area	1.42				
Smart technological application area	14.02***	13.00***			
Applied science area	40.73***	48.69***	14.81***		
European science-based area	60.01***	69.55***	37.57***	9.57***	

Note: (1) Imitative innovation area; (2) Smart and creative diversification area; (3) Smart technological application area; (4) Applied science area; (5) European science-based area.

Table 9.6 Wald tests of the linear hypothesis of differences between the elasticity values of patenting to network density across the different territorial patterns of innovation

	1	2	3	4	5
Imitative innovation area					
Smart and creative diversification area	95.13***				
Smart technological application area	162.14***	37.10***			
Applied science area	251.06***	112.50***	24.74***		
European science-based area	219.38***	107.53***	41.37***	6.97***	

Note: (1) Imitative innovation area; (2) Smart and creative diversification area; (3) Smart technological application area; (4) Applied science area; (5) European science-based area.

Labour mobility is more efficiently used (i.e. shows a greater elasticity) in those regions that are more knowledge- and innovation-intensive, such as those in the European science-based area and in the Applied science area (column 1 in Table 9.7). On the one hand, the first group is composed of regions that are the most knowledge- and innovation-intensive, and endowed with those preconditions frequently associated with greater endogenous capacity of knowledge

Table 9.7 Heterogeneity in the returns to mobility and networking

Dep. var.: ln(patents)$_t$‡	(1) Focal var.= Mobility Pooled OLS	(2) Focal var.= Average degree Pooled OLS	(3) Focal var.= Connectivity Pooled OLS	(4) Focal var.= Network density Pooled OLS
ln(RD)$_{t-1}$	0.56***	0.58***	0.58***	0.53***
	(0.03)	(0.03)	(0.03)	(0.03)
ln(HK)$_{t-1}$	−0.03	0.03	0.06	−0.04
	(0.06)	(0.06)	(0.06)	(0.06)
ln(POP)$_{t-1}$	0.11**	0.03	−0.00	0.14***
	(0.06)	(0.06)	(0.06)	(0.05)
Imitative innovation area *(Focal var.)$_{t-1}$	0.00	0.34***	0.01***	−0.40***
	(0.00)	(0.03)	(0.00)	(0.05)
Smart and creative diversification area*(Focal var.)$_{t-1}$	0.03***	0.32***	0.02***	−0.56***
	(0.00)	(0.03)	(0.00)	(0.05)
Smart technological application area*(Focal var.)$_{t-1}$	0.05***	0.58***	0.02***	−0.64***
	(0.01)	(0.05)	(0.00)	(0.05)
Applied science area*(Focal var.)$_{t-1}$	0.08***	0.83***	0.03***	−0.71***
	(0.01)	(0.05)	(0.00)	(0.05)
European science–based area*(Focal var.)$_{t-1}$	0.09***	0.02***	0.04***	−0.76***
	(0.01)	(0.00)	(0.00)	(0.05)
(Mobility)$_{t-1}$		0.92***	0.02***	0.02***
		(0.07)	(0.00)	(0.00)
ln(Average degree)$_{t-1}$‡	0.34***		0.36***	0.34***
	(0.02)		(0.02)	(0.02)
(Connectivity degree)$_{t-1}$	0.02***	0.02***		0.02***
	(0.00)	(0.00)		(0.00)
ln(Network density)$_{t-1}$‡	−0.51***	−0.51***	−0.51***	
	(0.05)	(0.05)	(0.05)	
Controls	yes	yes	yes	yes
Constant	−1.07	−0.19	0.34	−1.71***
	(0.68)	(0.68)	(0.68)	(0.66)
Observations	1,722	1,722	1,722	1,722
Number of regions	287	287	287	287
Adjusted R2	0.535	0.879	0.875	0.888

Notes: *** p<0.01, ** p<0.05, * p<0.1. Standard errors in parentheses. Control variables include: ln(SpecIn)$_{t-1}$; ln(ConIn)$_{t-1}$ (% Chemistry)$_{t-1}$; (% Biotechnology)$_{t-1}$; (% Pharmaceuticals)$_{t-1}$. ‡ We added 0.01 to these variables before the logarithmic transformation. For the definition of the five groups of regions, see Chapter 7.

creation (highly educated population and presence of scientific human capital). The second group includes regions that maintain a rather strong knowledge and innovation intensity, but differently from the former ones, they are more technologically diversified. In both cases, the results would suggest that the regions in these two areas are able to translate internal and external knowledge into new specific commercial applications more efficiently than in the rest, and that part of the external knowledge could come from workers coming from other enterprises. On the contrary, regions characterised by low levels of R&D spending as well as a rather narrow innovation profile (Imitative innovation area) do not benefit from the mobility of skilled workers, their elasticity of knowledge to labour mobility being non-significant in this case.

Similarly, the average effect of the research networks on knowledge creation hides a great variety of behaviour across regions, both considering the average degree centrality and the connectivity degree indices. In fact, having an important share of inventors participating in research networks is more efficiently used (i.e. shows a greater elasticity) in regions that outperform the others in terms of their propensity to networking, such as those in the European science-based area and in the Applied science area. It must be signalled, though, that the elasticity in the case of the regions of the Smart technological application area, the Smart and creative diversification area and the Imitative innovation area is also positive and significant, although of lower magnitude. This can be explained by their rather narrow knowledge and innovation profile. Finally, the same although with a negative sign occurs for the return to network density, with regions in the European science-based area and Applied science area being hampered more deeply from the existence of dense networks. Some of these results can be observed in Maps 9.1 and 9.2.

9.5.4. Results on the existence of cross-regional linkages

In order to obtain empirical evidence concerning the relevance of cross-regional knowledge for the generation of knowledge we present the estimation that includes cross-regional collaborations in patenting as well as inter-regional mobility (Table 9.8). The results corroborate the importance of the inflow of skilled workers for a regional economy, since only the variable considering inward migration rates of such workers presents positive and significant parameters. That is, the greater the number of inventors moving into a region, the greater the patenting activity of such region. This geographical mobility of knowledge workers can be considered, thus, a source of knowledge diffusion, allowing for a recombination of previously unconnected pieces of knowledge. However, the other three variables proxying for geographical mobility of knowledge workers (net migration rate, outward migration rate and gross migration rate) offer a non-significant parameter. This would point to the fact that once the workers have moved to other regions, the contacts they maintain with their former colleagues do not seem to play a significant role in the patenting activity of a region. Outward migration of skilled individuals cannot be considered, therefore, as an alternative source

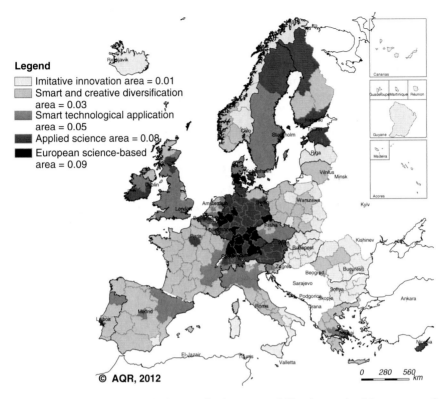

Map 9.1 Elasticity of knowledge production to mobility by territorial patterns of innovation

of knowledge flows and interactions back to the home location of the skilled employee who has left.

Again, the average results for the whole of the European regions mask substantial regional variations in the elasticities of knowledge with respect to cross-regional mobility and networking. With the inclusion of a cross-effect of the corresponding focal variable with a dummy for each region, we are able to compute a specific elasticity for each regional economy in Europe. Maps 9.3 and 9.4 show the extent of these variations.

As in the within-the-region case, we turn now to the variation in the return to geographical mobility and networking according to the territorial patterns of innovation (Maps 9.3 and 9.4).[7] The return obtained from cross-regional mobility and networks is greater in those regions that are more knowledge- and innovation-intensive, such as those in the European science-based area and in the Applied science area (Table 9.9). This is not strange since the regions in these two groups are the most knowledge- and innovation-intensive, and endowed with those preconditions frequently associated with greater endogenous capacity of knowledge

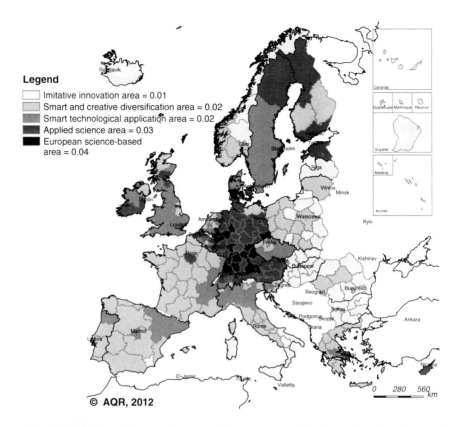

Map 9.2 Elasticity of knowledge production to connectivity by territorial patterns of innovation

creation (highly educated population and presence of scientific human capital). On the contrary, regions in the Imitative innovation area and Smart and creative diversification area, characterised by knowledge and innovation variables that show smaller values than the EU average, do not benefit from this cross-regional diffusion of knowledge.

9.6 Conclusions, implications and limitations

The research conducted here sought to assess the importance of specific knowledge flow and knowledge creation mechanisms, namely networks of co-invention and labour mobility, on regional knowledge, as opposed to the impact from R&D efforts or other mechanisms of knowledge creation and diffusion. Within a KPF framework, several hypotheses have been suggested and, although we are unable to confirm them all, a number of interesting conclusions can be identified.

Table 9.8 External links and innovation: cross-regional mobility and co-patents

Dep. var.:	(1)	(2)	(3)	(4)
ln(patents)$_t$‡	FE	FE	FE	FE
ln(RD)$_{t-1}$	0.15**	0.15**	0.14**	0.15**
	(0.07)	(0.07)	(0.07)	(0.07)
ln(HK)$_{t-1}$	0.63***	0.69***	0.71***	0.70***
	(0.10)	(0.10)	(0.10)	(0.10)
ln(POP)$_{t-1}$	1.12	0.51	0.57	0.49
	(0.81)	(0.81)	(0.82)	(0.82)
(Net migration rate)$_{t-1}$	0.55			
	(0.35)			
(Inward migration rate)$_{t-1}$		0.40*		
		(0.21)		
(Outward migration rate)$_{t-1}$			0.17	
			(0.11)	
(Gross migration rate)$_{t-1}$				0.21
				(0.22)
ln(Cross-regional patents)$_{t-1}$	0.05**	0.05**	0.05**	0.05**
	(0.02)	(0.02)	(0.02)	(0.02)
ln(SpecIn)$_{t-1}$‡	0.02	0.03	0.04	0.04
	(0.12)	(0.11)	(0.11)	(0.11)
ln(ConIn)$_{t-1}$‡	−0.03	−0.02	−0.03	−0.03
	(0.03)	(0.03)	(0.03)	(0.03)
(% Chemistry)$_{t-1}$	−0.00	−0.00	−0.00	−0.00
	(0.00)	(0.00)	(0.00)	(0.00)
(% Biotechnology)$_{t-1}$	−0.01***	−0.01***	−0.01***	−0.01***
	(0.00)	(0.00)	(0.00)	(0.00)
(% Pharmaceuticals)$_{t-1}$	0.00	0.00	0.00	0.00
	(0.00)	(0.00)	(0.00)	(0.00)
Constant	−16.03	−10.52	−10.59	−11.68
	(11.13)	(11.25)	(11.35)	(11.41)
Observations	1,722	1,722	1,722	1,722
Number of regions	287	287	287	287
R2 within	0.0996	0.1008	0.0984	0.0997
R2 between	0.4439	0.5091	0.4909	0.5071
R2 overall	0.4351	0.4984	0.4807	0.4965

Notes: *** p<0.01, ** p<0.05, * p<0.1. Standard errors in parentheses. ‡ We added 0.01 to these variables before the logarithmic transformation. Since the net migration rate ranges [−1,1], we avoid the logarithmic transformation of all the cross-regional mobility variables. In consequence, their sign and significance can be fairly informative, but any interpretation of their magnitude should be treated with caution.

Strong support for the positive relationship between regional labour market mobility and regional knowledge intensity is found. The influence of networks is also fairly important, but the strength of these ties (measured as the network density) was found to have a negative influence on knowledge. In line with studies

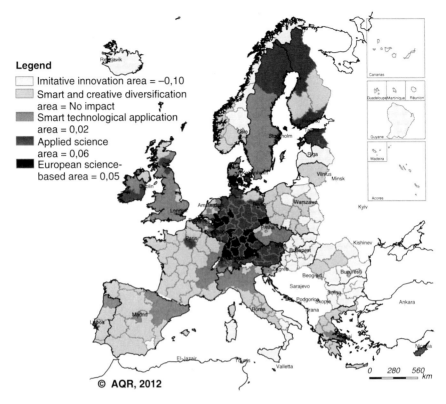

Map 9.3 Elasticity of knowledge production to cross-regional mobility by territorial patterns of innovation

elsewhere, we rely on the explanations provided by Grannovetter (1985) concerning the importance of weak ties for knowledge.

As labour mobility and research networks have been obtained to be a fundamental factor in the creation of knowledge, the unequal distribution of such features in the territory could explain regional differences in innovation performance and economic development. In this sense, policies aimed at encouraging the mobility of highly skilled workers or enhancing participation in research networks (as promoted by the European Commission through Marie Curie programmes or the Framework Programme Projects), especially in less knowledge-intensive regions, may play a critical role in the creation of knowledge, and subsequent economic growth. Clearly, though, the effectiveness of such policies, as shown by the results of this chapter, crucially depends on each region's capacity to give returns to such labour mobility and participation in research networks. In this respect, we have provided evidence that those regions that are more knowledge-intensive obtain higher returns since they are able to translate internal and external knowledge

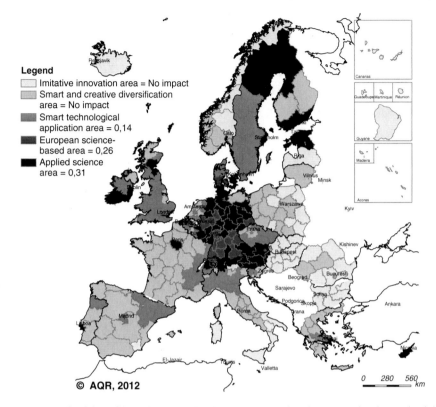

Map 9.4 Elasticity of knowledge production to cross-regional co-patenting by territorial patterns of innovation

into new specific commercial applications more efficiently than the less innovative regions. Therefore, the idea that R&D spending and knowledge production in general spill over to neighbouring regions is not so evident in the absence of a certain level of receptivity to the exploitation of external knowledge. However, certain threshold effects seem to arise as evidenced by the negative influence of the networks' strength and the null impact of mobility in certain high-performance regions.

Finally, from a policy perspective, the present chapter fleshes out empirically pivotal pillars of the smart specialization strategy put recently to the fore by the European Commission. Thus, the concepts of local *embeddedness* of the local networks and labour market, as well as the degree of *connectedness* to external sources of knowledge, constitute core ideas of the strategy. To some extent, both concepts are crucially related to the regional and cross-regional meaningful features which have been scrutinized in this chapter.

Table 9.9 Heterogeneity in the returns to cross-regional mobility and co-patents

Dep. var.: ln(patents)$_t^‡$	(1) Focal var. = IMR	(2) Focal var. = Cross regional pat
	Pooled OLS	Pooled OLS
ln(RD)$_{t-1}$	0.83***	0.83***
	(0.02)	(0.02)
ln(HK)$_{t-1}$	0.16**	0.17***
	(0.06)	(0.07)
ln(POP)$_{t-1}$	−0.12**	−0.06
	(0.06)	(0.06)
Imitative innovation area *(Focal var.)$_{t-1}$	−1.78***	−0.01
	(0.37)	(0.03)
Smart and creative diversification area*(Focal var.)$_{t-1}$	−0.58	−0.00
	(0.43)	(0.03)
Smart technological application area*(Focal var.)$_{t-1}$	2.33***	0.14***
	(0.82)	(0.04)
Applied science area* (Focal var.)$_{t-1}$	5.82***	0.31***
	(0.89)	(0.04)
European science-based area* (Focal var.)$_{t-1}$	7.27***	0.26***
	(1.63)	(0.05)
(Inward migration rate)$_{t-1}$	−0.32	
	(0.29)	
ln(Cross-regional patents)$_{t-1}^‡$	0.27***	
	(0.02)	
Controls	yes	yes
Constant	3.57***	3.18***
	(0.70)	(0.74)
Observations	1,722	1,722
Number of regions	287	287
Adjusted R2	0.859	0.848

Notes: *** $p<0.01$, ** $p<0.05$, * $p<0.1$. Standard errors in parentheses. Control variables include: ln(SpecIn)$_{t-1}$; ln(ConIn)$_{t-1}$; (% Chemistry)$_{t-1}$; (% Biotechnology)$_{t-1}$; (% Pharmaceuticals)$_{t-1}$. ‡ We added 0.01 to these variables before the logarithmic transformation. Since the net migration rate ranges [−1,1], we avoid the logarithmic transformation of all the cross-regional mobility variables. In consequence, their sign and significance can be fairly informative, but any interpretation of their magnitude should be treated with caution. For the definition of the five groups of regions, see Chapter 7.

Notes

1 Recent special issues on the subject include: 'Spatial knowledge diffusion through collaborative networks'. Guest editors: Corinne Autant-Bernard, Jacques Mairesse and Nadine Massard, *Papers in Regional Science* 2007, 86(3): 341–525; and, more specifically on the subject of networks of co-inventors, the special issue, 'Embedding network analysis in spatial studies of innovation. Guest editor: Edward M. Bergman, *The Annals of Regional Science*, 2009, 43(3): 559–833.

2 Note that, as stressed in Boschma and Iammarino (2009, p.295), 'extra-regional knowledge that is complementary, but not similar, to existing competences in the region will particularly enhance interactive learning (. . .). If the external knowledge

Annex 9.1 Variables, data construction, and data source

Variable	Proxy	Source
Patents	Patents, fractional count, 3-year moving average	REGPAT January 2010 edition
R&D	R&D expenditures (in euros), 3-year moving average	Eurostat
Human capital	Total population with tertiary education	Eurostat
Mobility	Share of multi-patent inventors with more than one applicant	REGPAT January 2010 edition
Average degree centrality	Average number of personal links in the form of co-patents per inventor	REGPAT January 2010 edition
Connectivity	Share of multi-patent inventors with at least 1 co-inventor	REGPAT January 2010 edition
Network density	$DENS_{it} = \dfrac{T_{it}}{Q_{it}(Q_{it}-1)/2}$	REGPAT January 2010 edition
Net migration rate	Inflows minus outflows of inventors to the local number of inventors	REGPAT January 2010 edition
Inward migration rate	Inflows of inventors to the local number of inventors	REGPAT January 2010 edition
Gross migration rate	Inflows plus outflows of inventors to the local number of inventors	REGPAT January 2010 edition
Outward migration rate	Outflows of inventors to the local number of inventors	REGPAT January 2010 edition
Cross-regional networks	Number of patents, fractional count, co-authored with outside inventors, to the local number of inventors	REGPAT January 2010 edition
Specialisation index	$SpIn_{it} = \dfrac{1}{2}\sum_{j}\left\vert\dfrac{PAT_{ijt}}{PAT_{it}} - \dfrac{PAT_{Cjt}}{PAT_{Ct}}\right\vert$	REGPAT January 2010 edition
Concentration index	$ConIn_{it} = \sum_{jt}\left(PAT_{ijt}/PAT_{jt}\right)^{2}$	REGPAT January 2010 edition
% Organic chemistry	Share of patents in IPC chemistry	REGPAT January 2010 edition
% Pharmaceuticals	Share of patents in IPC pharmaceuticals	REGPAT January 2010 edition
% Biotechnology	Share of patents in IPC biotechnology	REGPAT January 2010 edition

is unrelated, the industrial base of the region cannot absorb it and is unlikely to benefit from it. When the external knowledge is the same (. . .), it can be absorbed locally, but the new knowledge will not add much to the existing local knowledge base'. As we will show later on, our empirical application does not consider this distinction, which is left for future extensions.

3 SNA has been widely applied to collaboration in research and innovation studies, although a review of detailed methodological contributions falls outside the scope of this chapter. In fact, in recent years many contributions have been made to economics and economic geography using SNA tools, most notably Balconi et al. (2004), Breschi

and Catalini (2009), and Ter Wal and Boschma (2009). For a more complete theoretical discussion of the methods and applications of SNA, see Wasserman and Faust (1994).

4 International Patent Classification.

5 Although overall employment in these sectors would be a better proxy, these data are not available.

6 We added a small value, 0.01, to all the explanatory variables presenting zero values in at least one observation to allow for a logarithmic transformation.

7 We have tested the equality of the coefficients for the different groups of regions through the use of Wald tests. In all the cases, we reject the null of equality of coefficients, allowing us to conclude that the elasticities differ across categories. The results of the tests can be provided upon request.

10 Knowledge, innovation and economic efficiency across territorial patterns of innovation

Roberta Capello and Camilla Lenzi

10.1. Introduction

The large heterogeneity in innovation modes in Europe detected in Chapter 7 has called for a variety of empirical analyses aimed at measuring the efficiency of each pattern of innovation on economic performance. The previous chapters have focused on the efficiency of each territorial pattern of innovation in producing new knowledge from both internal and external knowledge inputs (Chapters 8 and 9, respectively) and in generating economic growth from knowledge inputs as suggested by the Lisbon and Europe 2020 Agendas (Chapter 8).

The key messages stemming from the previous impact analyses indicate that the way regions exploit internal knowledge (in particular R&D) and human capital to generate new local knowledge differs among innovation patterns. In particular, R&D is less effective in the regions with the lowest knowledge endowments, testifying that a certain degree of knowledge is required to generate new knowledge. This is true up to a certain threshold where increasing returns turn into decreasing returns. Similarly, the capacity of regions to exploit external knowledge to produce new knowledge differs markedly among European regions: a certain amount of absorptive capacity (in the form of internal knowledge) is necessary in order to benefit from external formal knowledge.

Moreover, knowledge requires a certain critical mass to impact on GDP. In fact, R&D is more efficiently used in those regions that already invest considerably in R&D, whereas regions characterized by lower levels of R&D experience little increase in their economic performances due to further investments in R&D. Importantly, human capital has a higher impact on GDP than R&D, especially in regions where human capital is low, which highlights the importance of human capital for growth in weak regions with respect to R&D investments. On the other hand, human capital exhibits strong decreasing returns, and its effects on growth are limited in regions highly endowed with skilled people (ESPON KIT, 2012). However, the crucial ingredient for regional performance is not high endowment with each single knowledge input but rather an efficient mix of the two. Nevertheless, achieving an efficient combination and use of knowledge inputs is a very difficult task, one much more complex than achievement of an efficient combination and use of traditional production factors, labour and capital.

To date, no evidence has been provided on the impact of innovation on the static and dynamic efficiency of economic systems. In our opinion however, each territorial pattern may represent a different way of innovating, and none of them is expected to be by definition superior to, or necessarily more efficient than, another. Rather, each pattern may provide an efficient use of local innovation activities to generate both higher productivity levels and higher growth rates.

This chapter fills this gap by assessing the capacity of the five territorial patterns of innovation in exploiting knowledge and innovation to achieve higher static and dynamic efficiency gains, the former measured in terms of productivity levels, the latter in terms of economic growth rates.

This chapter first measures the efficiency levels – in terms of total factor productivity (TFP) – across the five patterns of innovation. The results confirm the general belief that higher efficiency gains are displayed by those innovation patterns that have a high internal knowledge endowment. Contrary to general expectations, however, are the results related to the two types of creative patterns based on external knowledge: the evidence shows that the pattern based on informal knowledge (Pattern 4) records higher efficiency with respect to the pattern based on formal knowledge (Pattern 3).

This evidence raises the question of whether this unexpected result is confirmed when using a dynamic approach. While the literature largely concurs on the crucial role played by knowledge and innovation in explaining regional growth, little is known about the spatial heterogeneity of this relationship. This chapter will therefore investigate whether knowledge and innovation play a similar role in all territorial patterns of innovation or, by contrast, whether threshold effects operate in achieving higher growth rates. This will also enable understanding of whether the different patterns of innovation similarly benefit from knowledge and innovation to grow, and whether, in order to grow, single patterns rely more on innovation than on knowledge.

Efficiency in taking advantage of innovation is expected not to link with the strength of the local formal knowledge base alone; rather, different territorial patterns of innovation characterized by different levels of knowledge intensity can be similarly efficient in grasping and exploiting innovation returns and, therefore, in growing.

The rest of the chapter is organized as follows. The next section describes the empirical strategy to estimate TFP and its main results. Next, Section 10.3 briefly reviews the literature on TFP determinants and identifies the main drivers of TFP, while Section 10.4 is devoted to the econometric analysis of TFP across territorial patterns of innovation. Section 10.5 presents the empirical framework in which to study the impact of knowledge and innovation on regional growth, while Section 10.6 discusses the econometric results of the growth equation estimates. The last section makes some final remarks and concludes by considering the policy implications of all the analyses presented in the book.

10.2. TFP estimation

The paramount importance of productivity (level and growth rate) indicators in economics as well as in policymaking is generally not matched by single and uncontroversial measures and interpretations for the existing and most common statistics (Schreyer and Pilat, 2001). Often, data availability constraints (especially in international comparisons studies) and the specific purpose of productivity measurement determine the actual indicators chosen.

Put briefly, productivity describes the relationship between output and the inputs used to generate output. Two broad groups of measures can be identified: single-factor productivity measures (i.e. the output is related to a single measure of input) and multi-factor productivity measures (i.e. the output relates to a set of inputs), also called total factor productivity (TFP). The most common measure in this second group is the capital–labour multi-factor productivity measure (OECD, 2001). TFP, therefore, can be considered as a comprehensive measure of productivity and technology efficiency in the use of factor endowments.

Estimation of TFP has been a long-debated and highly controversial topic in economics. Three main approaches can be identified in the literature and, to date, no definitive consensus on a single method has been reached, since all approaches have shortcomings and are subject to criticisms (for a survey see Carlaw and Lipsey, 2003).

Initially, the most common method of calculating TFP was growth accounting (or residual method) based on Solow's 1956 and 1957 seminal papers. In this approach, TFP is 'a measure of our ignorance', and therefore obtained as the residuals of output regressed on inputs. This methodological approach has been heavily criticized in the literature, in terms of both concepts (e.g. the aggregation of the production function) and measurement (e.g. measurement of inputs and output) (see for example Griliches 1987 and 1995), although it is still well maintained (OECD, 2001; Dettori et al., 2011; Marrocu et al., 2012a; Quatraro, 2010).

A different approach is the index number approach, in which TFP is computed as the ratio between output and an index aggregating all production factors (Diewert, 1987). This approach overcomes the conceptual ambiguity of the aggregate production function inherent to the growth accounting approach, at the cost, however, of identifying the appropriate index adding up all inputs into a single scalar, again a highly debated issue.

Lastly, the distance function approach is based on the measurement of the distance from the actual production of an economy to the production efficiency frontier. For example, the data envelopment analysis (DEA) approach, first developed by Farrell (1957), belongs to this group (see Chapter 8 for an application of DEA). This is a non-parametric method aimed at identifying the best performing units whose objective is to convert multiple inputs into multiple outputs. DEA does not require specification of the functional form for the relation linking inputs to outputs, and it is able to handle multiple inputs and outputs. The best performance is characterized in terms of efficiency, so that the most performing units define the efficient frontier, which 'envelopes' all the other units. Nevertheless, this approach critically relies on the assumption that all units share the same aggregate production function linking inputs and outputs.

It is therefore evident that no method is free from limitations. In the analysis reported in this chapter, the standard method was adopted, i.e. a traditional growth accounting approach to capital–labour multi-factor productivity (OECD, 2001). Regional TFP level was estimated as the residual of the log-linearized version of the traditional Cobb-Douglas production function model, taking the following form:

$$GDP_r = \alpha + \beta K_r + \gamma L_r + \varepsilon_r \qquad (10.1)$$

where GDP_r is the regional gross domestic product, K_r is the regional capital stock, L_r is the regional employment level and ε_r represents the regional idiosyncratic error. GDP, capital stock and labour were averaged over the years 2005–2007 to smooth possible effects related to specific years of estimation. The capital stock series at the regional level is not available from public databases and official sources. The capital stock series was elaborated by CRENoS and was constructed by applying the perpetual inventory method on investment series in the years 1985–2007.[1] Specifically, $K_{r,t}$, the capital stock of region r at time t, is obtained as the sum of the flows of gross investments in the previous periods with a constant (across regions and over time) 10% depreciation rate (d), as follows:

$$K_{r,t} = (1-d) K_{r,\,t-1} + I_{r,\,t-1} \qquad (10.2)$$

The capital stock value for the initial year (i.e. 1985) was computed as the sum of investment flows, $I_{r,\,t}$, in the ten preceding years (i.e. 1975–1984).

Tables 10.1 and 10.2 report respectively the input and output variables description and summary statistics.

TFP estimates were obtained by 2SLS due to possible endogeneity problems, as it is frequently the case in spatial analyses (Fingleton and LeGallo, 2008); in fact, the Durbin-Wu-Hausman test supports the use of 2SLS over OLS.[2] Instruments are represented by one period lagged regressors as in Marrocu et al. (2012a). Factor endowments' coefficient estimates are reported in Table 10.3.

Table 10.1 TFP estimation: Data description

Indicators	Measures	Computation	Year	Source
GDP	Economic wealth	Euro (thousands)	Average value 2005–2007	Eurostat
Capital	Capital stock (factor endowment)	Euro (thousands)	Average value 2005–2007	CRENoS database
Labour	Employment (factor endowment)	Unit of labour (thousands)	Average value 2005–2007	Eurostat

Table 10.2 TFP estimation: Summary statistics

Variable	Obs.	Mean	Std. Dev.	Min.	Max.
GDP	262	43682.15	50926.75	1070.608	500369.8
Labour	262	822.10	655.33	14	5122.23
Capital	262	9009.29	11437.51	92	110349.7

Table 10.3 TFP estimation: Estimated coefficients

Dependent variable: Real GDP (Average value 2005–2007)	2SLS
Capital (Average value 2005–2007)	0.606**
	(0.412)
Labour (Average value 2005–2007)	0.329***
	(0.058)
Constant	2.658***
	(0.268)
R^2	0.75
Observations	262
Test of endogeneity: H0 (regressor is exogenous)	
Durbin–Wu–Hausman test of endogeneity	10.54***

Notes: * $p<0.10$, ** $p<0.05$, *** $p<0.01$. 2SLS robust standard errors. Instruments are one year-lagged explanatory variables. Source: rearranged from Capello and Lenzi, 2012b.

10.3. The determinants of TFP

The increasing importance of the endowment and accumulation of 'soft' factors of production vis-à-vis 'physical' and relatively 'traditional' resource endowments is widely accepted in the scientific domain and is increasingly considered as a 'stylized fact', or empirical regularity, in the empirical literature on growth (Easterly and Levine, 2001).

These 'soft' production factors, frequently also (and somewhat broadly) defined as intangible assets, have been proved to be crucial determinants of productivity increases, although specific results tend to vary with the level of analysis, the indicators used and the geographical and time coverage (IAREG, 2010).

Different streams of literature have, in turn, emphasized the importance of different assets, such as human capital (see the seminal papers by Becker, 1964 and Romer, 1989, as well as Lopez-Baso and Moreno Serrano, 2010, and Capello et al., 2010, for more recent contributions), entrepreneurship (see Audretsch and Keilbach, 2006 for a review), social capital (Putnam, 2000; Guiso et al., 2008; Tabellini, 2008), the relative role of specialization and diversification externalities (see Beaudry and Schiffauerova, 2009, for a review), knowledge and innovation (see among the many others, Cooke et al., 2011).

In particular in this chapter, we focus on the role of knowledge and innovation on TFP level as captured by the notion of territorial patterns of innovation. When measuring TFP level across the five territorial patterns of innovation, however, we also controlled for other 'soft elements' that recent studies have shown to be relevant in the process of knowledge creation and diffusion, and that are therefore important determinants of TFP level and growth in the current years, namely specialization externalities, which operate mainly within a specific industry, diversity externalities which work across sectors, and social capital, which operates across individuals (Beaudry and Schiffauerova, 2009; Dettori et al., 2011; Marrocu et al., 2012a; Marrocu and Paci, 2012), as described in Table 10.4.

Table 10.4 TFP and its determinants: Variables description

Indicators	Measures	Computation	Year	Source
TFP	Economic productivity	Residuals	Average value 2005–2007	Authors' estimation on Eurostat data
Specialization in manufacturing	Location quotient in manufacturing sectors computed on employment data	Location quotient on employment in manufacturing sectors	2002	Eurostat
EU12	Bulgaria, Cyprus, Czech Republic, Hungary, Estonia, Latvia, Lithuania, Malta, Poland, Romania, Slovakia, Slovenia	Dummy variable equal to 1 if the regions is located in a EU12 country	2004	Eurostat
Social capital	Trust	Share of people trusting each other	2000	European Value Survey
Agglomeration economies (Megas)	FUAs with the highest scores on a combined indicator of transport, population, manufacturing, knowledge, decision-making in the private sectors	Dummy variable equal to 1 if the region is classified as mega	2000	ESPON

The most common way to measure regional industrial specialization is by means of a location quotient on employment in manufacturing sectors. The long-standing debate on the relative importance of specialization vs diversification externalities (Beaudry and Schiffauerova, 2009) indicates that empirical evidence is not robust in this regard and that results are overall ambiguous. Some studies report positive effects of specialization (e.g. Cingano and Schivardi, 2004; Henderson et al., 2001) whereas others report negative effects of specialization (Frenken et al., 2007; Paci and Usai, 2008). Although, at conceptual level, the expected impact of specialization is rather unpredictable, in that it depends on the level of analysis, unit of measurement and data used (Beaudry and Schiffauerova, 2009), the development of the service sector affecting most Western European countries and the prominent localization of manufacturing activities in New EU12 countries suggest that this variable has a negative effect on TFP level (Marrocu et al., 2012a).

To capture diversity externalities, i.e. all synergies, complementarities, collective learning effects and local knowledge spillovers arising in dense agglomerations of different economic activities, which are at the basis of knowledge and innovation creation, and possible productivity gains, a dummy variable was used to capture the structure of the urban system in the region (labelled 'Megas'). This variable takes in fact value 1 in regions hosting one of the 70 functional urban areas (FUAs) with the highest scores on a combined indicator of transport, population, manufacturing, knowledge, and decision-making in the private sectors. The empirical literature has consistently shown the importance of diversified externalities for productivity increases and more generally for economic performance (Beaudry and Schiffauerova, 2009). Therefore, we expect this variable to have a positive effect on TFP level.

If knowledge spillovers at sectoral level are important determinants of TFP, also the degree of cooperative attitude and collective actions within a region is a condition for local knowledge spillovers. Higher cooperative attitudes should promote knowledge and innovation circulation and socialization, thus enhancing productivity. Similarly, trust – and therefore openness to diversity – characterizes settings that are more innovation-prone and thus more rapid in adopting innovation and profiting from the productivity gains that it yields. Trust, in fact, has been proved to facilitate cooperation (Guiso et al., 2008), to reduce transaction costs and opportunistic behavior, thereby promoting knowledge and innovation diffusion and an overall improvement in economic environment and performance. This variable is therefore expected to have a positive effect on TFP level. In this case, the regional share of people trusting each other was the indicator used to measure social capital.

Furthermore, the empirical model includes a control for the distinction between EU12 and EU15 as TFP level and dynamics have been shown to differ quite sharply according to the development stage of economies; in particular, productivity levels tend to be higher in more developed areas, despite the rapid catch-up registered in EU12 (Marrocu et al., 2012a). Country dummies were also added to control for national variations that may affect the nature and institutional setting of regional innovation processes, the general economic dynamism and the nature and pattern of development, and possible economic interdependencies across regions in the same country.

Finally, and more importantly, a set of dummy variables each aimed at capturing the five different territorial patterns of innovation was included in order to capture the role of knowledge and innovation and the variety of innovation modes characterizing European regions.

Accordingly, we estimated the following model:

$$TFP_r = F(Specialisation\ in\ manufacturing_r,\ Trust_r,\ EU12_r,\ Mega_r,$$
$$IIA_r,\ SCDA_r,\ STAA_r,\ ASA_r,\ ESBA_r) + \varepsilon_r \qquad (10.3)$$

where IIA_r, $SCDA_r$, $STAA_r$, ASA_r, $ESBA_r$ are the five dummies each capturing the different territorial patterns of innovation and ε_r the regional idiosyncratic error.

Table 10.5 reports the summary statistics of the variables.

Table 10.5 TFP and its determinants: Summary statistics

Variable	Obs.	Mean	Std. Dev.	Min.	Max.
TFP	262	1.14	0.67	0.22	5.30
Specialization in manufacturing	262	0.99	0.34	0.24	1.93
Trust	262	30.97	15.77	0	82

10.4. Productivity levels in territorial patterns of innovation

Table 10.6 reports the estimates of TFP determinants as specified in equation (10.3). The control variables are significant and with the expected sign. In fact, TFP is higher in old European countries (EU15); it benefits from agglomeration economies and a higher level of trust, whereas it is negatively affected by specialization in manufacturing.

More interestingly, the five dummies capturing the different territorial patterns of innovation are all significant with a positive sign, suggesting that all groups of regions have a positive and significant impact on TFP level. Although the five groups of regions are characterised by different (and increasing) levels of knowledge and innovation, each innovation mode can lead to productivity increases.

However, the magnitude of their impacts on TFP may differ, as displayed in Map 10.1. As expected, the *European science-based area* reports the highest efficiency level. However, the efficiency ranking does not strictly reflect the knowledge intensity ranking in the form of R&D expenditures. In fact, despite relatively limited R&D efforts and patent intensity, the *Smart and creative diversification area* comes third in the efficiency ranking of European regions, followed by the *Smart technological application area* (which shows comparable efficiency levels) and the *Imitative innovation area*.

Table 10.6 Determinants of TFP

Dependent variable: TPF (average value 2005–2007)	OLS
EU12	−0.544***
	(0.130)
Agglomeration economies – Mega	0.144***
	(0.043)
Specialization in manufacturing	−0.651***
	(0.076)
Trust	0.481**
	(0.227)
European science-based area (ESBA)	1.142***
	(0.178)
Applied science area (ASA)	0.967***
	(0.115)
Smart technological application area (STAA)	0.821***
	(0.102)
Smart and creative diversification area (SCDA)	0.864***
	(0.100)
Imitative innovation area (IIA) – Constant	0.658***
	(0.110)
Country dummies	Yes
R2	0.79
Lagrange multiplier (Spatial lag)	0.001
Lagrange multiplier (Spatial error)	0.154
N observations	262

Notes: * $p < 0.10$, ** $p < 0.05$, *** $p < 0.01$. Robust standard errors in parentheses.

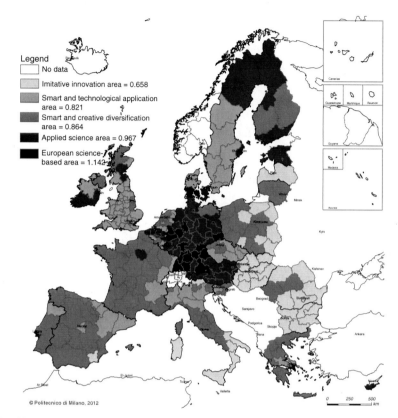

Map 10.1 Impact on TFP level by territorial patterns of innovation

To assess whether these impacts are statistically different, Table 10.7 reports the output of pair-wise tests on the coefficients of the five territorial patterns dummies obtained from estimation of equation 10.3 (reported in Table 10.6 and displayed in Map 10.1).

Three key messages stem from Table 10.7. Firstly, there is a clear divide between regions in the *Imitative innovation area* and the others. In fact in the

Table 10.7 Pair-wise comparison of impact on TFP level across territorial patterns of innovation

	ESBA	*ASA*	*STAA*	*SCDA*	*IIA*
European science-based area (ESBA)	—				
Applied science area (ASA)	n.s.	—			
Smart technological application area (STAA)	<**	<**	—		
Smart and creative diversification area (SCDA)	<**	n.s.	n.s.	—	
Imitative innovation area (IIA)	<***	<***	<*	<***	—

Notes: * $p < 0.10$, ** $p < 0.05$, *** $p < 0.01$. n.s. = not statistically significant.

former group, the impact on TFP is significantly lower than in all the others. Possibly, some sort of threshold effects in the creation and use of knowledge and innovation are at work because they require a certain critical mass to express their full potential. Regions in the *Imitative innovation area* may not yet have reached a critical mass of knowledge and innovation such that they are able to turn their benefits into higher productivity levels as much as can regions belonging to the other innovation patterns.

Secondly, the *Smart and creative diversification area* and the *Smart technological application area* do not differ in their impacts on TFP. Similarly, nor do the *Applied science area* and the *European-science based area* differ in their impacts on TFP. This seems to suggest that more formal, general and basic knowledge does not necessarily lead to higher productivity levels. Rather, also, more applied if not tacit knowledge can yield similar productivity gains.

Thirdly, the difference between the *Smart and creative diversification area* and the *Applied science area* is not significant, suggesting that this group has the potential to catch up quite rapidly with the frontier groups in terms of productivity.

Interestingly, this evidence suggests that the productivity level of European regions is not linked to the strength of the local formal knowledge base alone. In fact, by benchmarking the knowledge and innovation endowments and the impact on TFP level in the *Imitative innovation area*, in the *Smart and creative diversification area*, in the *Smart technological application area* and in the *Applied science area* with those of the *European science-based area* (i.e. the most knowledge- and innovation-intensive pattern) the results indicate that the four innovation patterns are not much less efficient than the European science-based one (Table 10.8). In particular, regions in the *European science-based* area show a productivity level barely double that of regions in the bottom group even though its R&D and innovation endowments are, respectively, six and three times greater than the R&D and innovation endowments of the *Imitative innovation area*. This confirms that it is not the pure knowledge and innovation endowment that explains the productivity level that a region is able to achieve, but rather how these endowments mix with specific territorial characteristics (Table 10.8).

Moreover, whereas the *European science-based area* shows knowledge and innovation rates more than double those of the *Smart and creative diversification area*, its impact on TFP is not particularly different from that of the *Smart and*

Table 10.8 Values of R&D, of innovation, and of the impact on TFP in the European science-based area (ESBA) with respect to the other territorial patterns of innovation

Values of ESBA with respect to:	Relative R&D on GDP	Relative share of innovative firms	Relative impact on TFP level
Applied science area (ASA)	1.39	1.35	1.18
Smart technological application area (STAA)	1.49	1.64	1.39
Smart and creative diversification area (SCDA)	2.65	2.28	1.32
Imitative innovation area (IIA)	6.19	3.48	1.73

creative diversification area. Lastly, whereas the *European science-based area* records knowledge and innovation rates respectively 1.39 and 1.35 greater than those of the *Applied science area*, their impact on TFP is not statistically different (see Table 10.7 above).

This means that the relationship between knowledge and innovation endowment, on the one hand, and productivity level on the other, is not always linear in qualitative terms: efficiency may be, in relative terms, greater than the simple endowment of knowledge and innovation, as also pointed out in Chapter 8. As a consequence, the efficiency in mixing and using knowledge and innovation does not always match the strength of the local formal knowledge base, suggesting that different territorial patterns of innovation characterized by different levels of knowledge intensity can be similarly efficient in grasping and exploiting innovation returns for growing. This is the topic of the next section.

10.5. Knowledge, innovation and regional performance: a regional growth model

The literature widely agrees on the crucial role played by knowledge and innovation in explaining regional growth (see Cooke et al., 2011 for a recent overview). However, as mentioned in the introduction to this chapter, little is known about the spatial heterogeneity of this relationship. Most previous studies have in fact focused on the 'average knowledge and innovation effect for the average region', and only very recently have some scholars tried to understand their possible differentiated impact across regions (see for example Sterlacchini, 2008; Charlot et al., 2012; Marrocu et al., 2012a). Nevertheless, spatial heterogeneity has been captured through rather basic distinctions either politically defined, e.g. advanced vs disadvantaged regions, the latter being defined as Objective 1 regions[3] (Sterlacchini, 2008 and Charlot et al., 2012), or on the basis of different socioeconomic development stages, e.g. EU15 vs EU12 (Marrocu et al., 2012a).

However, these institutional and socioeconomic distinctions do not allow one to capture important heterogeneity sources across regions in the types of knowledge needed for innovating, nor in attitudes towards innovation, which mostly depend upon specific and systemic context conditions and tend to be highly cumulative and persistent over time (Iammarino, 2005). By relying on the territorial patterns classification, built on the territorial socioeconomic conditions enabling knowledge and innovation to develop, the analysis described in the present chapter overcame this limitation. In particular, it addressed three related research questions:[4]

1) whether knowledge and innovation play a significant role in all territorial patterns of innovation or, by contrast, whether threshold effects operate and a critical mass of knowledge and innovation is needed to achieve higher growth rates (i.e. testing whether the impact of knowledge and innovation is statistically significant in all territorial patterns of innovation);

2) whether the different patterns of innovation similarly benefit from knowledge and innovation to grow (i.e. testing the differences in the elasticity of

GDP growth to knowledge and to innovation across territorial patterns of innovation);

3) whether each pattern relies more on innovation than on knowledge to grow (i.e. testing the differences in the ratio between the elasticity of GDP growth to innovation and the elasticity of GDP growth to knowledge across territorial patterns of innovation).

As said in the introduction to this chapter, our expectation was that efficiency in taking advantage of innovation does not link with the strength of the local formal knowledge base alone; rather, different territorial patterns of innovation characterized by different levels of knowledge intensity can be similarly efficient in grasping and exploiting innovation returns and, therefore, in growing.

The different strands of literature presented in Chapter 6 rely on three main groups of factors to explain regional growth: (local or external) knowledge inputs, territorially embedded elements that facilitate the creation of innovation, and the economic dynamism of the area.

Therefore, to explore the research questions advanced above, we estimated a regional growth model that combined knowledge inputs – such as R&D investments and knowledge embedded in human capital – with socioeconomic local factors that enable knowledge and innovation to take place, while controlling for the region's economic dynamics as well as for the nature and pattern of development. As a novelty of our approach, we also introduced innovation as a variable separate from R&D investments, expecting the innovation variable to have additional explanatory power with respect to pure knowledge. Possible multi-collinearity problems between the knowledge and the innovation variables were controlled for when the estimations were run, as explained in Section 10.6.

The data set presented in Chapter 7, therefore, was expanded to meet the strong requirements in terms of data availability entailed by the empirical testing of the three research questions. As regards knowledge inputs, we considered three variables capturing the intensity of:

• formal, basic knowledge, measured through R&D expenditures on GDP;
• informal knowledge embedded into professional capabilities, measured through a composite indicator on the degree of specialized workers in the region, in particular managers and technicians (see Table 10.9 for details on the indicator's construction);
• innovation, in order to account directly for the impact of new products and/or processes introduced in the market.

As regards socioeconomic local enablers of knowledge and innovation, we considered the effects of:

• trust, as a measure of social capital, cooperation capabilities and collective actions within a region. Higher cooperative attitudes should promote knowledge and innovation circulation and socialization, thus enhancing local growth potentials;

Table 10.9 GDP growth and its determinants: variables description

Indicators	Measures	Computation	Year	Source
GDP growth rate	Economic growth	Annual rate of growth	2005–2007	Eurostat
Employment growth rate in manufacturing	Employment dynamics	Annual rate of growth	2002–2004	Eurostat
Accessibility (infrastructure endowment)	Rail and road network length by usable land	Km of rail and road network on usable land	2000	ESPON
FDI	Foreign direct investments	Number of FDIs on total population	Average value 2001–2003	FDI-Regio, Bocconi-ISLA
Structural funds expenditures	Millions (euros) of expenditure on population	Natural logarithm	1994–1999	ESPON
Functional specialization	% blue-collar occupations	Share of craft and related trades workers, plant and machine operators, and assemblers in total employment (ISCO codes 7 and 8)	Average value 2002–2004	European Labour Force Survey
Capabilities	Share of managers and technicians	Factor analysis on the share of production and specialized service managers and technicians (ISCO codes 13 and 31); factor score min-max normalized	Average value 1997–2001	European Labour Force Survey
R&D	R&D expenditure	Share of R&D expenditure on GDP	Average value 2000–2002	CRENoS database
Innovation (product and/or process)	Firms introducing a new product and/or a new process into the market	Share of firms introducing product and/or process innovations	One value for the period 2002–2004	Authors' estimation on CIS (Eurostat) data

- infrastructural endowment, as a measure of accessibility to the region. The higher the accessibility of a region, the greater the probability that the region will acquire new knowledge, new ideas, new information, and therefore the greater the probability of higher growth rates;
- functional specialization of a region, as a measure of the presence/lack of innovation-prone activities. High-level functions are more likely to stimulate knowledge and innovation than are low-level functions, and therefore to increase growth rates;
- agglomeration economies meant to capture the synergies, complementarities, collective learning effects and local knowledge spillovers arising in the dense agglomerations of economic activities which are at the basis of knowledge and innovation creation, and enhanced local growth.

Lastly, as regards a region's economic dynamism as well as the nature and pattern of development, our data set included the following measures:

- employment growth rate in manufacturing, in order to account directly for the dynamics of the regional labour market ($\Delta Empl_r$);
- foreign direct investments penetration rate (FDI) as a measure of regional economic attractiveness, which is expected positively to affect GDP growth rate, and is supposed to generate a push effect on the local economy;
- a dummy variable for regions in new member countries (EU12), in order to control for the distinctive growth patterns characterizing Eastern and Western European regions;
- structural funds, in order to control for the likely positive impact of public expenditures aimed at stimulating growth in developing regions.

Accordingly, the baseline model estimated was as follows:

$$\Delta GDP_r = \alpha_0 + \beta_1 \Delta Empl_r + \beta_2 EU12_r + \beta_3 Social\ Capital_r +$$
$$\beta_4 Accessibility_r + \beta_5 FDI_r + \beta_6 Structural\ Funds_r +$$
$$\beta_7 Functional\ Specialization_r + \beta_8 Agglomeration\ Economies_r +$$
$$\beta_9 Capabilities_r + \beta_{10} R\&D_r + \beta_{11} Innovation_r + \varepsilon_r \qquad (10.4)$$

where ΔGDP is the regional annual GDP growth rate.

To unravel the large heterogeneity of innovation modes, we next interacted the R&D and innovation variables with the five dummies each aimed at capturing the different territorial patterns of innovation as defined in Chapter 7. The enlarged models to be estimated therefore became as follows:

$$\Delta GDP_r = \alpha_0 + \beta_1 \Delta Empl_r + \beta_2 EU12_r + \beta_3 Social\ Capital_r +$$
$$\beta_4 Accessibility_r + \beta_5 FDI_r + \beta_6 Structural\ Funds_r +$$
$$\beta_7 Functional\ Specialization_r + \beta_8 Agglomeration\ Economies_r +$$
$$\beta_9 Capabilities_r + \beta_{10} \sum_{r=1}^{5} D_r * R\&D_r + \varepsilon_r \qquad (10.5)$$

$$\Delta GDP_r = \alpha_0 + \beta_1 \Delta Empl_r + \beta_2 EU12_r + \beta_3 Social\ Capital_r + \\ \beta_4 Accessibility_r + \beta_5 FDI_r + \beta_6 Structural\ Funds_r + \\ \beta_7 Functional\ Specialization_r + \beta_8 Agglomeration\ Economies_r + \\ \beta_9 Capabilities_r + \beta_{10} R\&D_r + \beta_{11} \sum_{r=1}^{5} D_r * Innovation_r + \varepsilon_r \qquad (10.6)$$

where D_r represents the dummy variable for regional membership in the different territorial patterns of innovation.

Lastly, as we were aware that economic growth in one region may affect the growth of neighbouring regions, we controlled for spatial dependency with appropriate econometric techniques (namely spatial lag and spatial error models, indicated as SAR and SEM respectively) when statistically relevant. Following Anselin (1988), we used Lagrange multiplier tests to decide on the model specification i.e. SAR vs. SEM.[5] Table 10.10 reports the summary statistics of the variables.

10.6. Knowledge, innovation and regional performance across different territorial patterns of innovation

Table 10.11 reports the estimates of the regional growth model (eqs 10.4 to 10.6). The results for the variables capturing knowledge and innovation territorial enabling factors and the variables capturing regions economic dynamism, as well as those for the nature and pattern of development are overall statistically significant and with the expected sign. In particular, as regards a region's economic dynamism, GDP growth positively reacts to increases in employment, to FDIs penetration, and relatively more weakly to structural funds expenditures, and is higher in Eastern Europe regions.

As regards socioeconomic local enablers of knowledge and innovation, GDP growth is positively influenced by the synergic effects deriving from agglomeration economies, by trust and social capital, by informal knowledge embedded in technical and managerial competences. On the other hand, GDP growth is

Table 10.10 GDP growth and its determinants: summary statistics

Variable	Obs.	Mean	Std. Dev.	Min.	Max.
GDP growth rate (2005–2007)	262	3.64	2.05	−1.33	12.41
Employment growth rate in manufacturing (2002–2004)	262	−2.01	3.41	−21.32	13.41
Accessibility (infrastructure endowment)	262	27.03	39.48	0	453.51
FDI	262	0.19	0.40	0.00	4.29
Structural funds expenditures	262	33454030	56140880	0	434866600
% of blue-collar occupations	262	33.3	7.1	16.33	58.73
Capabilities	262	0.40	0.16	0	1
R&D	262	1.37	1.21	0.10	6.60
Innovation	262	35.54	13.27	7.97	87.10

Table 10.11 Determinants of regional GDP growth rate (2005–2007)

Dependent variable:	(1)	(2)	(3)	(4)
GDP growth rate 2005–2007	OLS	SEM	OLS	SEM
Employment growth rate in manufacturing (2002–2004)	0.075** (0.033)	0.072** (0.032)	0.059* (0.034)	0.071** (0.033)
EU12	0.043*** (0.015)	0.051*** (0.019)	0.049*** (0.016)	0.047** (0.020)
Trust	0.017** (0.007)	0.009 (0.009)	0.018*** (0.007)	0.008 (0.009)
Accessibility (infrastructure endowment)	−0.005** (0.002)	−0.006** (0.003)	−0.006** (0.002)	−0.006* (0.003)
FDI	0.005*** (0.002)	0.007*** (0.003)	0.005*** (0.002)	0.007*** (0.003)
Structural funds expenditures	0.001 (0.001)	0.002 (0.001)	0.001 (0.001)	0.001 (0.001)
% of blue collars occupations	−0.022 (0.017)	−0.003 (0.020)	−0.023 (0.017)	−0.001 (0.020)
Capabilities	0.031*** (0.007)	0.040*** (0.010)	0.031*** (0.008)	0.041*** (0.010)
Agglomeration economies	0.005** (0.002)	0.006** (0.002)	0.005* (0.002)	0.006** (0.002)
R&D	0.318*** (0.099)	0.310*** (0.101)		
R&D*ESBA			0.424*** (0.126)	0.304* (0.163)
R&D*ASA			0.351*** (0.127)	0.290** (0.131)
R&D*STAA			0.205* (0.107)	0.298** (0.127)
R&D*SCDA			0.363* (0.193)	0.414** (0.168)
RD*IIA			−0.173 (1.183)	0.777 (0.686)
Innovation				
Innovation*ESBA				
Innovation*ASA				
Innovation*STAA				
Innovation*SCDA				
Innovation*IIA				
Constant	0.006 (0.011)	−0.013 (0.018)	0.002 (0.011)	−0.012 (0.018)
Lagrange multiplier (spatial error)	13.612***		7.760***	
Robust Lagrange multiplier (spatial error)	4.325***		1.632	

(5)	(6)	(7)	(8)	(9)	(10)	(11)
SAR	*OLS*	*SAR*	*OLS*	*SAR*	*OLS*	*SAR*
0.056*	0.064**	0.058*	0.068**	0.061**	0.051	0.050
(0.003)	(0.032)	(0.031)	(0.033)	(0.031)	(0.034)	(0.032)
0.032*	0.063***	0.051***	0.066***	0.053***	0.067***	0.055***
(0.019)	(0.016)	(0.019)	(0.016)	(0.018)	(0.016)	(0.019)
0.013*	0.018**	0.015**	0.017**	0.014*	0.018**	0.015*
(0.008)	(0.007)	(0.007)	(0.007)	(0.007)	(0.007)	(0.007)
−0.005	−0.007***	−0.006**	−0.007***	−0.006**	−0.006***	−0.005*
(0.002)	(0.002)	(0.003)	(0.002)	(0.003)	(0.002)	(0.003)
0.005*	0.005***	0.005**	0.005***	0.005*	0.005***	0.005*
(0.001)	(0.002)	(0.003)	(0.002)	(0.003)	(0.002)	(0.003)
0.001	0.002*	0.001	0.002**	0.002	0.002*	0.001
(0.001)	(0.001)	(0.001)	(0.001)	(0.001)	(0.001)	(0.001)
−0.015	−0.039**	−0.033*	−0.032*	−0.025	−0.029*	−0.023
(0.018)	(0.017)	(0.017)	(0.017)	(0.018)	(0.017)	(0.017)
0.031***	0.031***	0.031***	0.033***	0.033***	0.031***	0.030***
(0.008)	(0.006)	(0.008)	(0.007)	(0.008)	(0.008)	(0.008)
	0.005**	0.005**	0.005**	0.005**	0.004	0.004*
	(0.002)	(0.002)	(0.002)	(0.002)	(0.002)	(0.002)
			0.191*	0.198*	0.192*	0.196*
			(0.115)	(0.105)	(0.115)	(0.104)
0.342**						
(0.159)						
0.304**						
(0.131)						
0.244*						
(0.128)						
0.390**						
(0.168)						
0.034						
0.643						
	0.044***	0.039***	0.039***	0.033***		
	(0.009)	(0.010)	(0.010)	(0.010)		
					0.037*	0.032**
					(0.022)	(0.013)
					0.045	0.040**
					(0.029)	(0.016)
					0.039	0.037*
					(0.035)	(0.019)
					0.055	0.050**
					(0.048)	(0.026)
					0.016	0.012
					(0.079)	(0.039)
−0.005	−0.015	−0.018	−0.020	−0.023	−0.021	−0.024
(0.015)	(0.012)	(0.015)	(0.012)	(0.015)	(0.017)	(0.016)
7.760***	1.934		2.608		0.842	
1.632	0.039		1.078		0.120	

Continued

Lagrange multiplier (spatial lag)	10.284***		7.531***	
Robust Lagrange multiplier (spatial lag)	0.997		1.403	
R2 (OLS) – Squared correlation (SEM and SAR)	0.38	0.36	0.39	0.35
Lambda(SEM) / Rho (SAR)		0.701***		0.728***
		(0.132)		(0.130)
Observations	262	262	262	262

Notes: * p < 0.10, ** p < 0.05, *** p < 0.01. Robust standard errors in parentheses. SEM and SAR estimates are based on a row-standardised continuous distance matrix. Source: adapted from Capello and Lenzi (2013b).

moderately hampered by a regional functional specialization in blue-collar occupations, and more significantly by the accessibility level, suggesting that density and congestion effects prevail.[6]

More interestingly, the results concerning our key variables indicate that both knowledge and innovation play a crucial role in explaining growth patterns in European regions (Models 1 and 6, Table 10.11), thus supporting the efforts to enlarge and strengthen the European knowledge base proposed in the Lisbon Agenda and Europe 2020 strategy.

The first important message from these results is that increasing average R&D spending at the EU level is certainly conducive to achieving superior GDP growth rates, also after controlling for spatial interdependencies across regions (Table 10.11, Models 1 and 2). On computing GDP growth rate elasticity to R&D, on average a one percentage point increase in R&D spending yields a 0.12% increase in GDP growth rate (Table 10.12).[7] This is largely consistent with previous findings in the literature and supports the idea that knowledge is a crucial ingredient for faster regional growth.

To gain better understanding of the spatial heterogeneity in GDP growth rate response to R&D spending, we replaced the R&D variable by interacting it with the five dummies, each intended to capture the different territorial patterns of innovation (Table 10.11, Models 3, 4 and 5). Interestingly, the results suggest that knowledge is affected by threshold effects: in fact, growth in the *Imitative innovation area* regions seems not to respond to increases in the local knowledge basis. The ranking of the elasticity of GDP growth to R&D strictly reflects the local knowledge intensity ranking (Table 10.12). Not surprisingly, regions in the *European science-based area* are better positioned to reap the growth benefits stemming from extra investments in R&D because their GDP growth rate elasticity to R&D is greater than the average value. Regions in the *Smart technological application area* and in the *Applied science area* still show above-average elasticity values although they are about 1/3 lower than in the *European science-based*

7.531***	3.761**		4.108**		3.415*	
1.403	1.867		1.678		2.693*	
0.41	0.41	0.42	0.42	0.43	0.43	0.44
0.401***		0.286*		0.297**		0.280*
(0.146)		(0.148)		(0.147)		(0.150)
262	262	262	262	262	262	262

area. Lastly, the *Smart and creative diversification area* exhibits a positive effect of R&D on GDP growth, despite being below the average.

On looking at the statistical differences among the elasticities of the five patterns (Table 10.13), the performance of the *Smart technological application area* stands out. In fact, its elasticity of GDP growth to R&D does not statistically differ from those of the most knowledge-endowed regions in the *Applied science area* and *European science-based area.* On the other hand, the *Smart and creative diversification area* shows a statistically lower elasticity of GDP growth to R&D with respect to the other groups; this suggests that additional investments in knowledge creation in this area seem less conducive to faster growth than in the other groups of regions. Therefore, these results support the idea that further investments in new formal knowledge creation should be concentrated in those regions with greater R&D spending and which are probably able to take the greatest advantages from it and seem to be the most efficient in using knowledge for growing.

Likewise, increasing innovation at the EU level has a positive effect on GDP growth rates, also after controlling for spatial interdependencies across regions (Table 10.11, Models 6 to 9). Because the R&D variable includes both private and public expenditures, we cannot exclude the possibility that the innovation variable captures the R&D efforts of innovative firms. Therefore multi-collinearity with the innovation variable may exist, as also underlined by the high and significant correlation (0.534) between the knowledge and innovation variables. When introduced together, knowledge and innovation maintain considerable effects on their own without substituting each other. Even if the inclusion of the innovation variable reduces the impact of R&D on GDP growth (see Models 1 and 8 in Table 10.11), the introduction of the latter still adds explanatory power to the regional growth model, testifying that multi-collinearity problems between the two variables do not interfere in the analysis.

This result is also robust to alternative estimation strategies. In fact, by adopting a structural equation modelling framework, we jointly estimated both the impact

Table 10.12 Elasticity of GDP growth to knowledge and innovation by territorial patterns of innovation

	GDP growth (2005–2007)	R&D on GDP	Share of innovative firms	Elasticity of GDP growth to R&D ($E_{GDP\_gr\_R\&D}$)	Elasticity of GDP growth to innovation ($E_{GDP\_gr\_Innovation}$)	$E_{GDP\_gr\_Innovation} / E_{GDP\_gr\_R\&D}$
EU average	3.64	1.37	35.54	0.12	0.32	2.67
European science-based area (ESBA)	3.29	2.56	63.16	0.24	0.63	2.63
Applied science area (ASA)	3.65	1.84	46.92	0.16	0.42	2.71
Smart technological application area (STAA)	3.17	1.71	38.43	0.17	0.40	2.39
Smart and creative diversification area (SCDA)	3.85	0.97	27.69	0.08	0.24	3.05
Imitative innovation area (IIA)	4.2	0.41	18.14	Not significant	Not significant	Not significant

Notes: elasticity values to knowledge and innovation were computed according to the estimated coefficients reported in Table 10.11. Elasticity values of GDP growth to knowledge were computed according to the estimated R&D coefficient in model 2 (EU average value), because tests implemented on the significant coefficients of the interaction variables (estimated in models 4 and 5) indicated that these coefficients were not statistically different, suggesting that the impact of R&D on GDP growth is similar in the four groups of regions. Elasticity values of GDP growth to innovation were computed according to the estimated innovation coefficient in model 9 (EU average value), because tests implemented on the significant coefficients of the interaction variables (estimated in model 11) indicated that these coefficients were not statistically different, suggesting that the impact of innovation on GDP growth is similar in the four groups of regions. Source: Capello and Lenzi (2013b).

Table 10.13 Pair-wise t-tests on the difference between the elasticity values of GDP growth to R&D across the different territorial patterns of innovation

	ESBA	ASA	STAA	SCDA
European science-based area (ESBA)	—			
Applied science area (ASA)	n.s.	—		
Smart technological application area (STAA)	n.s.	n.s.	—	
Smart and creative diversification area (SCDA)	<***	<***	<***	—

Source: Capello and Lenzi (2013b)

Notes: * p < 0.10, ** p < 0.05, *** p < 0.01. n.s. = not statistically significant. Values for the Imitative innovation area are not included as the impact of R&D on GDP growth is not statistically significant.

of R&D on innovation on the one hand, and the impact of both R&D and innovation on GDP growth on the other (while controlling for the other determinants of GDP growth described in Section 10.5). Importantly, the significance level and the magnitude of the R&D and innovation coefficients were not affected.

On computing GDP growth rate elasticity to innovation, on average a one percentage point increase in innovation yields a 0.33% increase in GDP growth rate, almost three times greater elasticity than that of R&D.[8]

Similarly to the case of R&D, to gain better understanding of the spatial heterogeneity in GDP growth rate reaction to innovation, we replaced the innovation variable by interacting it with the five dummies, each of them intended to capture the different territorial patterns of innovation. The results indicate that innovation, too, appears to have some sort of threshold advantage and to require a certain critical mass to express its full potential. In fact, economic growth in *Imitative innovation area* regions do not seem to respond to innovation (nor to knowledge). It seems likely that they have not yet reached a critical mass of knowledge and innovation so that they can turn their benefits into higher growth rate.

On computing the elasticity values of GDP growth to innovation for the different groups, the ranking is quite similar to that of the GDP growth rate elasticity to R&D (Table 10.12 and Map 10.2). Importantly, however, the effects of innovation on the GDP growth rate seem to be of larger magnitude with respect to the effect of knowledge, not only at the EU level and but also in the different groups of regions.

Similarly to R&D, pair-wise t-tests on the difference between the elasticity values of GDP growth to innovation in the different clusters indicated that *Smart technological application area* regions, *Applied science area* regions and *European science-based area* regions exhibit statistically similar values for the elasticity of GDP growth to innovation. Somewhat unexpectedly, *European science-based area* regions do not show a pronounced capacity to exploit innovation (nor knowledge) compared with *Smart technological application area* regions and *Applied science area* regions (Tables 10.12 to 10.14), suggesting that the regions with the largest endowments of knowledge and innovation do not always enjoy the greatest returns from knowledge and innovation. In other words, efficiency in translating innovation into higher growth rates does not always match the strength of the local knowledge base.

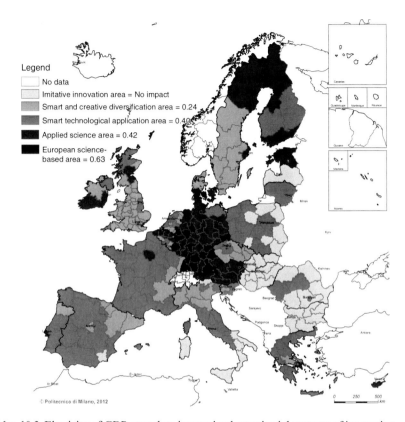

Map 10.2 Elasticity of GDP growth to innovation by territorial patterns of innovation

Table 10.14 Pair-wise t-tests on the difference between the elasticity values of GDP growth to innovation across the different territorial patterns of innovation

	ESBA	ASA	STAA	SCDA
European science-based area (ESBA)	—			
Applied science area (ASA)	<***	—		
Smart technological application area (STAA)	n.s.	n.s.	—	
Smart and creative diversification area (SCDA)	<***	< ***	<***	—

Source: Capello and Lenzi (2013b)

Notes: * p < 0.10, ** p < 0.05, *** p < 0.01. n.s. = not statistically significant. Values for the Imitative innovation area are not included as the impact of innovation on GDP growth is not statistically significant.

Lastly, although the *Smart and creative diversification area* regions have a statistically lower elasticity of GDP growth to both innovation and R&D compared with the other groups of regions (Tables 10.13 and 10.14), the relative ratio between the elasticity of GDP growth to innovation and the elasticity of GDP

Table 10.15 Pair-wise t-tests on the ratio between the elasticity values of GDP growth to innovation to the elasticity values of GDP growth to R&D across the different territorial patterns of innovation

	ESBA	ASA	STAA	SCDA
European science-based area (ESBA)	—			
Applied science area (ASA)	n.s.	—		
Smart technological application area (STAA)	n.s.	n.s.	—	
Smart and creative diversification area (SCDA)	>**	>**	>*	—

Source: Capello and Lenzi (2013b)

Notes: * $p < 0.10$, ** $p < 0.05$, *** $p < 0.01$. n.s. = not statistically significant. Values for the Imitative innovation area are not included as the impact of R&D and innovation on GDP growth are not statistically significant.

growth to R&D is statistically greater than in the other groups of regions (Tables 10.12 and 10.15). This suggests that these regions are, in relative terms, more efficient than the others in exploiting innovation rather than knowledge for growing. Accordingly, growth in these regions is more reactive to innovation than to R&D and, in relative terms, this group obtains the highest growth benefits from innovation.

We may conclude from this evidence that the growth benefits accruing from innovation do not necessarily match the intensity of the formal local knowledge base (Table 10.14), and that regions lacking a strong local knowledge base can be as successful as more knowledge-intensive regions in turning innovation into higher growth rate (Table 10.15).

These results therefore have strong policy implications in terms of the strategies to be implemented to make Europe and its regions become a knowledge-based economy and achieve smart growth, as discussed in the last chapter.

10.7. Conclusions

The results of this chapter point to several interesting findings that somewhat challenge the conventional wisdom on knowledge and innovation as generic policy tools to achieve smart growth as proposed by the most recent European strategic policy documents (namely, the Europe 2020 strategy).

Firstly, different groups of regions (in terms of knowledge and innovation intensity) may be similarly efficient in exploiting their knowledge and innovation endowments. More importantly, the productivity gains are not strictly linked to the intensity of the local formal knowledge base; nor is formal knowledge the only and chief driver leading to higher productivity.

Secondly, both knowledge and innovation play a crucial albeit different role in explaining growth patterns in European regions, thus supporting the efforts to enlarge and strengthen the European knowledge base proposed in the Lisbon Agenda and Europe 2020 strategy. However, whilst our results do not deny the importance of R&D as a strategic policy tool, they do question the general belief that additional investment in R&D may be beneficial for all types of regions. Rather, our findings indicate that only some regions are able to benefit from additional investments in knowledge creation; accordingly, R&D policy targets should be adapted to specific regional conditions.

Thirdly, the dynamic efficiency gains stemming from innovation, in the form of enhanced GDP growth, may be different from that of R&D and, importantly, are more pervasive (i.e. the impact of innovation on GDP growth is, at the European average, almost three times greater than that of R&D). Moreover, different groups of regions make exhibit different efficiency in exploiting knowledge vs innovation for growing. This suggests that R&D policies should not be considered a straightforward substitute for innovation policies, and different innovation policies and targets should be conceived and addressed to different types of regions in order to make them fully contribute to the achievement of the Europe 2020 goals.

Before moving to the last part of the book, the next chapter compares the geographical patterns of knowledge activities in Europe with crucial competitors in both advanced and emerging economies, namely the US, China and India. Moreover, in the next chapter a comparison in the elasticities of new knowledge to R&D is conducted among Europe, US, India and China, and the role of local enabling factors of innovation is highlighted. The results obtained for the other countries may provide important lessons for Europe, and together with the vast body of empirical evidence developed so far, may be useful for developing the regional innovation policies presented in Chapter 12.

Notes

1   The authors are grateful to CRENoS – University of Cagliari (Italy) for granting access to, and use of, their capital series data.
2   Using OLS instead of 2SLS does not alter the results.
3   Objective 1 regions are regions with a per capita GDP lower than 75% of the EU average.
4   A similar analysis is presented in Capello and Lenzi (2013b).
5   As a robustness check, we also controlled for endogeneity in the baseline model by running 2SLS instrumental variable regressions that could boost our confidence in causality. Variables were instrumented with lagged predictors as is customary in the growth literature in the absence of adequate instruments correlated to the explanatory variables but indirectly correlated to the dependent variable (Temple, 1999). Importantly, the Durbin–Wu–Hausman test did not allow us to reject the null hypothesis that the regressors were exogenous, suggesting that OLS estimates are preferable to 2SLS estimates.
6   To check for robustness we introduced additional variables like entrepreneurship and human capital, which, however, turned out to be non-significant. Results are available from the authors upon request.
7   The regional elasticity of GDP growth rate to R&D ($E_{GDP\_gr,\ R\&D}$) was obtained by multiplying the R&D estimated coefficient $\beta_{R\&D,EU}$ times the ratio between the EU average R&D level and the EU average GDP growth rate, as the formula below summarizes: $E_{GDP\_gr,R\&D} = \beta_{R\&D,EU} * (R\&D_{EU}/GDP\_gr_{EU})$.
8   The regional elasticity of GDP growth rate to innovation ($E_{GDP\_gr,Innovation}$) was obtained by multiplying the innovation estimated coefficient ($\beta_{Innovation,EU}$) times the ratio between the EU average innovation level and the EU average GDP growth rate, as the following formula summarizes: $E_{GDP\_gr,Innovation} = \beta_{Innovation,EU} * (Innovation_{EU}/GDP\_gr_{EU})$.

11 Regional knowledge creation in China, India and the US

Lessons for European regions

Riccardo Crescenzi and Andrés Rodríguez-Pose

11.1. Introduction

After an in-depth analysis of the processes underlying the translation of knowledge and innovation into economic performance in the European regions, this chapter aims to explore the geography of knowledge generation in other developed and emerging countries and uncover the spatial processes that explain the differential capability of regions to build upon existing knowledge. Based on a unique database on local socioeconomic conditions, R&D and patenting activity for China, India and US, this chapter develops an empirical analysis highly complementary to that adopted for the analysis of the EU regions in Chapter 8, as well as in existing comparative analyses between Europe and the US (Rodríguez-Pose and Crescenzi, 2008; Crescenzi and Rodríguez-Pose, 2009, 2011, 2013; Crescenzi et al., 2007) as also between China and India (Crescenzi et al., 2012), drawing relevant policy lessons for the European Union.

Direct benchmarking between the EU and the US on the one hand, and China and India on the other, has become particularly stringent since the year 2000, when the European Union launched the Lisbon Agenda, which aimed to make the European Union the 'most competitive and dynamic knowledge-based economy in the world' by 2010. Since then, the technological gap with the US has not only not waned, but appears to have widened – whether this is measured by scientific publications, article citations or patent intensity (Crescenzi et al., 2007). The past decade has also witnessed the dramatic rise to prominence of the 'BRICs' countries, especially India and China: Goldman Sachs suggests that by 2030, the largest three world economies will be the US, China and India (Wilson and Purushothaman, 2003). It is critical for European policymakers to understand the dynamics of this shifting, multipolar environment.

There is now a large body of evidence suggesting that innovation, competitiveness and growth are influenced by spatial factors as well as national conditions. In particular, not only is innovative activity spatially concentrated, but local/regional conditions play important mediating functions on regional (and national) innovation 'outcomes'. EU policymakers have launched research and policy initiatives into nation state competition, and in the territorial dimensions of knowledge generation (Chapter 8). This chapter thus explores a key aspect of the EU's future economic development – namely the geography of innovation of India, China and the US, making comparisons to and drawing lessons from that of the European Union.

The past two decades have seen the globalisation of production *and* the globalisation of R&D (Fu and Soete; 2010, Yeung, 2009). The US, China and India have been at the forefront of these shifts (Parayil and D'Costa, 2009; Leadbeater and Wilsdon, 2007; Popkin and Iyengar, 2007). During the 1970s and 1980s Indian and Chinese firms acted as 'production platforms' for Western firms, largely from the US, or pursued indigenous innovation strategies with varying degrees of success (Yeung, 2009). Since the 1990s, businesses in both countries have been moving up the value chain, engaging in R&D-led innovation and international partnerships (Kuchiki and Tsuji, 2010; Bruche, 2009). The result has been a number of high-tech urban hubs across South East Asia, with a complex nexus of relationships between US multinationals, local institutions and domestic firms (Yeung, 2009; Saxenian and Sabel, 2008).

In most countries innovative activity tends to be spatially clustered, reflecting the 'matching', 'sharing' and 'learning' economies of large urban areas (Duranton and Puga, 2003). The resulting 'territorialisation' of innovation is well observed in mature economies like the US and EU (Storper, 1997). Notably, similar spatial clustering is also present in 'emerging' economies. This means that it is critical to understand the *territorial* aspects of innovation systems in India and China, as well as the US, and to compare these to the EU.

Our analysis is one of the first to present a systematic, cross-country quantitative analysis of territorial innovation systems. We deploy new panel data sets to explore both the geographical patterns of knowledge generation, and the range of forces and factors shaping these outcomes. In this way we are able both to explore country-specific factors in detail, and to explore commonalities and differences across the EU, China, India and the US.

Our approach adds value for EU policymakers in three ways. First, it enables us to isolate factors shaping knowledge generation and development in different contexts. In turn, this helps the EU site its own leading and lagging regions. Second, we 'capture' both the emergence of new actors in technological competition as well as existing leaders – helping EU regions identify external competitors and opportunities. Third, our analysis supports policy transfer from the EU to non-EU partners.

The text is organised into sections, as follows. In Section 11.2 an in-depth analysis of the spatial distribution of patenting activity, by country, region and key technology fields (information and communication technologies (ICT), biotech and nanotech) is pursued. Section 11.3 reprises our conceptual framework, which informs the quantitative analysis that follows, and sets out our model and data sources. Section 11.4 gives results of the quantitative analysis, both for China, India and the US and an integrated analysis across these three countries and the EU. Section 11.5 provides brief conclusions and policy lessons. Details of variables and diagnostics are given in Annexes 11.1 and 11.2.

11.2. EU knowledge generation performance in context: Key trends in China, India and the US

11.2.1 Country-level comparative perspective

We begin with an overview of the comparative 'innovation performance' of the four territories, using the most recently available data across a range of key knowledge inputs and outputs.

Crescenzi et al (2007) and Rodríguez-Pose and Crescenzi (2008) provide systematic analysis of the EU25 innovation system. They find that the EU lags the US – the acknowledged world leader – on a range of innovation inputs such as R&D spending (especially that carried out by private firms), numbers of R&D researchers, numbers of star researchers, shares of 20-year-olds in higher education and expenditure per student. The same lag is also observed in key knowledge outputs – patent intensity, scientific publications and article citations. For example, since the start of the 1990s the US has increased its national patenting activity more or less continuously, with counts rising from around 15,000 patents to 55,000.

How do India and China compare? Figure 11.1 gives comparative patent intensity info for the EU, US, China and India. All four of these territories increased overall patenting and patent intensity during the 1990s. From 2000 onwards India patenting rates rose substantially. However, India's impressive improvements have been dwarfed by the huge jump patenting in China post-2001, shifts which significantly reflect increasing Chinese investments in innovation 'inputs' (see below). Overall patent counts rose from 1,000 to nearly 6,000, with patent intensity (per capita patenting) rising over four-fold.

During the 1990s both India and China invested heavily in innovation 'inputs', particularly China, increasing literacy rates and Higher Education (HE) enrolment, raising production of engineering graduates and increasing spend on R&D. Both countries also began to 'globalise' their economies, increasing Foreign Direct

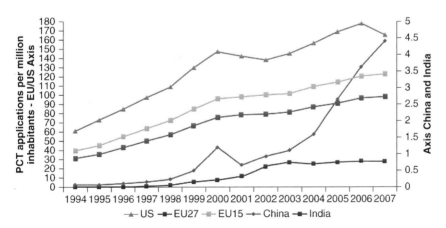

Figure 11.1 Patent intensity, PCT applications/capita, China, India, EU, US 1994–2007

Note: PCT = Patent Cooperation Treaty

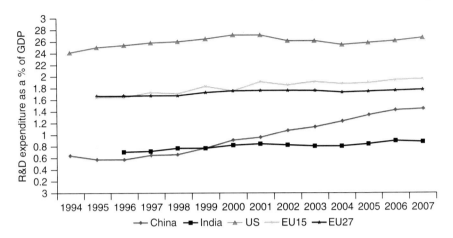

Figure 11.2 R&D expenditure as a share of GDP, 1994–2007.

Investments (FDIs) flows, licensing of foreign technology and moving students abroad (Dahlman, 2010). Figure 11.2 shows R&D as a share of GDP in China, India, EU and the US.

As a share of GDP, R&D spending in the US has moved slightly upward during this period, but still vastly outstrips the other two countries. China's R&D spending has been on an upwards trend since the late 1990s, with significant climbs since the 2000s. India's R&D share has been more or less in 'steady state'.

Another key innovation input is human capital. As outlined above, in the past two decades both China and India have significantly increased investment in human capital, especially at degree level. Figure 11.3, below, shows country-level population shares with tertiary education or above.

The US still produces vastly more graduates than Europe, India or China. However, in technology-specific fields these countries are catching up with the US.

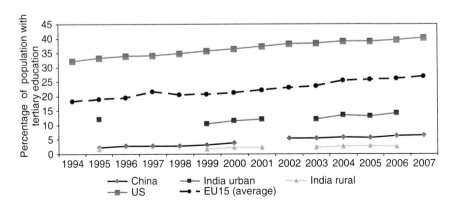

Figure 11.3 Population shares with tertiary education, 1994–2007

During the 1990s Indian universities significantly increased their production of engineering graduates – from 44,000 per year in 1992 to 184,000 in 2000. This compares with 352,000 per year in China – and just 76,000 per year in the US (Mitra, 2007). China has also exploited global knowledge by moving students abroad to study in larger numbers than India – although Indian returnees have had significant impacts on the country's ICT sector (Saxenian, 2006). Raising human capital stocks helps to build the scientific workforce. With 926 R&D researchers per million people, China now has the second-highest number of researchers worldwide (Schaaper, 2009). By contrast, India's R&D worker intensity has actually fallen since the mid-1990s.

Looking deeper into histories and policy choices helps to explain some of these differences. The US is an established technology leader which comfortably outperforms the EU, as well as India and China, in R&D, R&D workforce, research quality and university-educated workforce population shares (Crescenzi et al., 2007). The origins of the US 'national innovation system' date back to the 1945–50 Cold War rearmament period (Mowery, 1992). The US system has been built up over time via a series of large-scale projects, as well as supportive anti-trust and Intellectual Property (IP) regimes that allow easy commercialisation of ideas. The large venture capital community in the US has also helped bring new ideas to market (Reed, 2010). India and China manifest a number of similarities, but also some important differences compared to both the US and each other. Historically, both India and China used innovation and technology-led development to pursue national prestige/international positioning, for example via space flight and atomic weapons programmes (Leadbeater and Wilsdon, 2007). India and China have also moved from heavily statist models of public policy, towards market-led reforms (Fleischer et al., 2010; Fan, 2008; Jian et al., 1996).

China moved to 'globalise' its economy and innovation system earlier than India, and more comprehensively. China's trade as a share of GDP has been significantly higher than India's since the 1980s; FDI flows and licensing of foreign technology are also higher (Dahlman, 2010). China has moved through waves of planned development, with a first phase of market-orientated reforms in 1978. Special Enterprise Zones were introduced in the 1980s to concentrate FDI flows and encourage technology transfer, and in the 1990s the country joined the World Trade Organisation (WTO) (Dahlman, 2010; Liu and Buck; 2007; Jian et al., 1996). A second wave of reforms began in the mid-1990s, with encouragement of private businesses (Fleischer et al., 2010).

By contrast, until the 1991 currency crisis forced an acceleration of economic liberalization, India's development strategy had been largely autarkic, based on import substitution (Dahlman, 2010). Since then the country has shifted from 'highly regulated, autarkic' development to more market-led models, with a further acceleration in the early 2000s (Fleischer et al., 2010; Gajwani et al., 2006). More than China, India has since been able to make a virtue of cultural and historical specificities in developing innovative capacity – most obviously the English language and democratic political institutions (Bruche, 2009; Bound, 2007).

The two countries have developed different overall strengths, partly through conscious policy choices. China has become 'the manufacturing workshop of the world' (Dahlman, 2010), although its firms are now climbing up the value chain (Bruche, 2009). India has been developing a comparative advantage in pharma-ceutical and ICT sectors – a process significantly shaped by partnerships with Multinational Enterprises (MNEs) and the role of diaspora communities, and by India's English language and human capital bases (Bruche, 2009; Mani, 2004).

These historical trajectories are shaping current policy priorities. Both countries are developing their domestic innovation capacities, particularly China (Lundin and Schwaag Serger, 2007). In 2006 the country announced their 'Medium- to Long-Term Science and Technology Development Programme'. The Programme sets out a 15-year strategy to raise R&D spending from 1.3% of GDP (in 2006) to 2.5% (in 2020): this requires raising annual R&D spending by 10–15% per year. India's model focuses on developing skilled human capital, clustering activity in science parks, and providing financial instruments such as tax incentives, research grants, concessional loans and venture capital (Mani, 2004).

As China has switched to investing in domestic capacity, since the 2000s India has taken a more aggressive approach to adopting foreign technology, especially in ICT (Dahlman, 2010). A key focus of policy in the 1990s has been to promote co-location of high-tech activity, especially via a network of regional science parks (Mitra, 2007). In 2005, Chinese-style Special Economic Zones were also introduced – offering lower tax and less labour regulation in an attempt to attract and grow export-orientated firms.

11.2.2 The spatial dynamics of innovative output in US, China and India: EU regions in context

We now move on to consider the *territorial* aspects of the four territories' inno-vation systems. Looking at the spatial distribution of knowledge generation activity helps us to understand differences between and within the EU, China, India and the US. As explained in the introduction, we know that knowledge-generation activity tends to be spatially uneven and reflects agglomeration (see also Section 11.3). Second, mature and 'emerging' economic systems will have different territorial dynamics: as noted in the introduction, rapid urbanisation is an important aspect of development in India and China. This suggests different spatial configurations between the three countries – an intuition borne out in the descriptive analysis.

Figure 11.4 illustrates the cumulative distribution of patenting across space in the EU, India, China and the US from 1994 to 2007, focusing on the 20 regions with the highest patent counts. The graph should be read from right to left. The slope of the curve shows the degree of spatial clustering: the steeper the line, the more clustered. Spatial 'shares' can then be read off points on the line. For example, the figure shows that the five EU regions with the highest shares of patent applications together represent 35% of all EU patenting; for the US the corresponding figure is about 50%. By contrast, the five most innovative Indian

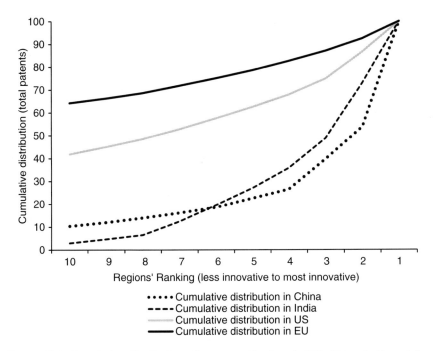

Figure 11.4 Cumulative distribution of patent applications in EU, China, India and the
US: Top 10 most innovative regions

regions cover 75% of Indian patents; in China, the five highest-patenting regions
have just fewer than 80% of all patent applications.

Two points stand out from the graph. First, there seems to be a clear difference
in the spatial features of 'mature' and 'emerging' innovation systems, with patenting in India and China far more spatially agglomerated than in the United States or
the EU, where the distribution of patenting activity is more smoothly distributed
across space. It is also notable that the EU system is substantially less clustered
in space than the US system. Second, different levels of investment in innovation
inputs also appear to influence where knowledge-generation activities take place.
For example, the six highest-patenting regions in China account for a bigger share
of knowledge production activity than those in India, although the pattern reverses
after that with a long tail of Indian regions.

Maps 11.1–11.3 take a more focused look at the US, India and China, giving
population-weighted patent counts by region. We can see that the US (Map 11.1)
has a smoother spatial distribution of patents by applicant than either China or
India. The three leading regions are San Jose–San Francisco–Oakland (Northern California), San Diego–Carlsbad–San Marcos (Southern California) and
Appleton–Oshkosh–Neenah (Wisconsin). These three account for only 32% of
all patenting by applicant, compared to 73% and 64% shares for, respectively,
the leading Chinese and Indian regions. Generally, the more innovative regions

in the US are located on the Western and Eastern seaboards, or the Great Lakes region (Michigan, Wisconsin). Less innovative areas are located in the Midwest or South, with a couple of exceptions – Houston–Baytown–Huntsville (Texas) and Denver–Aurora–Boulder (Colorado).

In China (Map 11.2), the leading regions for knowledge production tend to be in coastal areas. Outside these regions, the next group of provinces, accounting for

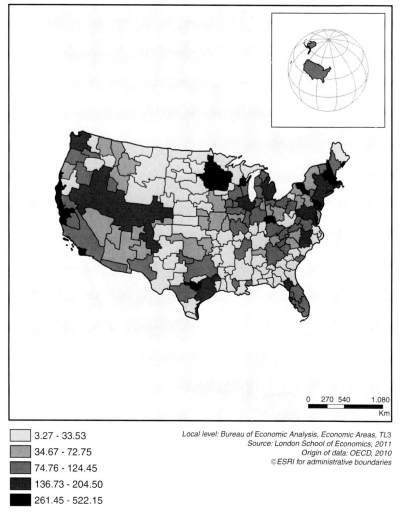

▢ 3.27 - 33.53	*Local level: Bureau of Economic Analysis, Economic Areas, TL3*
▢ 34.67 - 72.75	*Source: London School of Economics, 2011*
▨ 74.76 - 124.45	*Origin of data: OECD, 2010*
■ 136.73 - 204.50	*©ESRI for administrative boundaries*
■ 261.45 - 522.15	

Map 11.1 US: Average patents per million inhabitants, 1994–2007

Source: OECD Regional Database.

Note: Population-weighted patent counts by applicant from OECD REGPAT Database, Patents filed under the Patent Co-operation Treaty (PCT)

1–3% of total patenting on average are also situated along the coast – only Sichuan (south-west) and Hunan (central China) are not coastal provinces. The centre and west of China are less innovative. Tibet, Qinghai and Ningxia, in the far south-west or in the north-west of the country hardly generate any patents.

In India (Map 11.3), leading regions tend to be in/around Delhi and the south. Delhi and Mumbai are the main centres, and the top three provinces – Karnataka

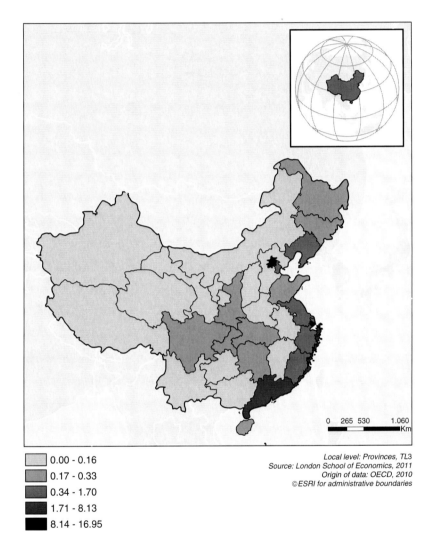

0.00 - 0.16	
0.17 - 0.33	
0.34 - 1.70	
1.71 - 8.13	
8.14 - 16.95	

Local level: Provinces, TL3
Source: London School of Economics, 2011
Origin of data: OECD, 2010
©ESRI for administrative boundaries

Map 11.2 China: Average patents per million inhabitants, 1994–2007

Source: OECD Regional Database.

Note: Population-weighted patent counts by applicant from OECD REGPAT Database, Patents filed under the Patent Co-operation Treaty (PCT)

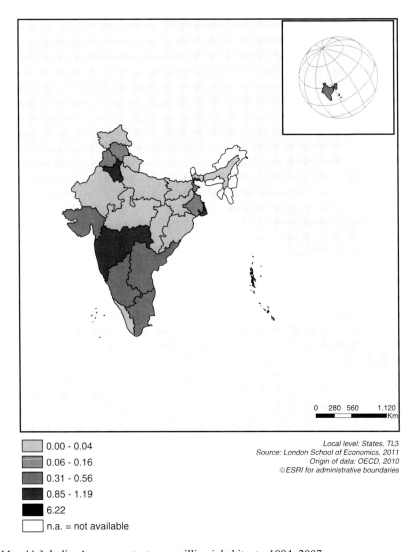

0.00 - 0.04
0.06 - 0.16
0.31 - 0.56
0.85 - 1.19
6.22
n.a. = not available

Local level: States, TL3
Source: London School of Economics, 2011
Origin of data: OECD, 2010
©ESRI for administrative boundaries

Map 11.3 India: Average patents per million inhabitants, 1994–2007

Source: OECD Regional Database.

Note: Population-weighted patent counts by applicant from OECD REGPAT Database, Patents filed under the Patent Co-operation Treaty (PCT)

(8.7%, capital Mumbai), Haryana (7%, next to Delhi) and Tamil Nadu (7%, South) – produce almost 25% of the country's patent applications. States in north-east India, or border states, are much less innovative. Some of them did not have any patents applicants until 2007 (for example Assam, despite its more than 30 million inhabitants, on the north-east border with Bhutan and Bangladesh).

Sun (2003) finds evidence of increasing spatial agglomeration of innovative activity in China during the 1990s, as measured by patents. Our results confirm this: in 1994 innovative activity in India is far more concentrated than in China. By the late 1990s the pattern is beginning to change: by 2007 patenting is more clustered in Chinese provinces than in Indian states. Indian patenting remains more concentrated in 2000, so agglomeration of patenting activity in China took place in parallel with the country's overall rise in patenting activity.

We next explore patenting trends in further detail by breaking down overall counts into key technology fields. To do this we organise patent data by 'technology field' rather than industry; OECD data follows standard International Patent Classifications (IPC), from which we explore counts for biotechnology, ICT and nanotechnology.

Breakdowns across time suggest relatively little change at specific points between 1994 and 2007. For instance, biotechnology patenting is somewhat more spatially agglomerated in China and India than overall patenting; in China, the top three 'biotech regions' account for over 80% of overall patenting in the field. As with overall counts, however, both countries have more concentrated biotech patenting activity than the US – where the top three regions account for just over 30% of all biotech patents. Similar patterns exist in the distribution of ICT patents. Technological activity is even more agglomerated in China than in India, with both countries having long tails of trailing regions. Again, both countries' ICT patenting is much more spatially clustered than in the US. In the nanotechnology patenting field, India has a more agglomerated sectoral innovation system than China, with the top three Indian regions accounting for over 80% of nanotech patenting, against an approximate 60% share for the leading Chinese regions. The US is rather less agglomerated.

11.3. Conceptual framework and empirical model for comparative territorial analysis

The descriptive analysis suggests a very complex story for each country, and makes initial comparisons between them less than straightforward. In turn, this suggests the need for a clear conceptual framework to delineate conditions and experiences. The framework should be able to explain the *dynamics* of each country's innovation system, including its *territorial components*, and help illuminate the *interactions* between component parts.

We explore the factors behind these geographies of knowledge generation by using a modified regional knowledge production function. This approach extends the 'traditional' framework à la Griliches (Griliches, 1979; Griliches, 1986) and Jaffe (1986) in order to account for the role of territorial characteristics and spatial processes discussed in the previous section (Audretsch and Feldman, 1996; Crescenzi et al., 2007; O hUallachain and Leslie, 2007; Ponds et al., 2010). In this way, we are able to take into consideration both systems of innovation conditions and other internal and external factors.

We fit the following empirical model:

$$y_{i,t} = \alpha_i + \tau_t + \beta R\&D_{i,t} + \gamma WR\&D_{i,t} + \delta SF_{i,t} + \zeta WSF_{i,t} + x_{i,t} + \varepsilon_{i,t} \qquad (11.1)$$

where:

y	represents regional patent intensity;
$R\&D$	is the share of R&D/S&T expenditure in regional GDP;
SF	is the social filter index;
$WR\&D$ and WSF	are spatial lags of R&D/S&T and SF respectively with appropriate spatial weights;
x	is a set of structural features/determinants of knowledge generation of region i;
E_{it}	is an idiosyncratic error;

and where i represents the region and t time.

We assemble panel data sets for Chinese provinces, Indian states and US BEA Economic Areas (see Annex 11.1 for details). Data for China covers 30 provinces between 1995 and 2007 inclusive. Data for India covers 19 states between 1995 and 2004. Data for the US covers 179 BEA Economic Areas, 1994–2007. The choice of empirical variables included in the model is discussed in what follows.

11.3.1 Patent intensity

Regional patent applications per capita is the dependent variable and is used as a proxy for the knowledge output of the local economy. Using patent counts to establish geographical knowledge patterns should be done with care, especially in developing country contexts. Our data is from OECD patent cooperation treaty (PCT) – so avoids problems that might arise using domestic Chinese or Indian data (Li and Pai, 2010; Wadhwa, 2010). Other innovation metrics for India and China – such as the location of multinational firms – also tend to follow similar spatial patterns to our findings (Bruche, 2009) so we can be fairly confident we have identified real trends. There are two important caveats. First, patents measure *invention* and tend to be biased towards particular sectors of the economy where inventions are primarily protected via patenting (OECD, 2009). Second, patent *applications* in India and China partly reflect patenting activity by MNEs. MNE patents may be filed in any office around the world, regardless of where the invention actually took place (Li and Pai, 2010).

11.3.2 Internal conditions

We fit a number of independent variables covering internal conditions affecting regional performance in terms of knowledge generation. These are set out below.

R&D expenditure

Endogenous growth theories highlight the importance of human capital and knowledge in advancing the technological frontier. Subsequent productivity gains drive long-term growth rates (Romer, 1990). In practice, national governments have tended to operationalise endogenous growth ideas by seeking to raise overall levels of human capital and ideas production.

Commonly used in the US and EU, 'national innovation system' models describe key actors such as businesses, central government, universities and public research institutes (Liu and White, 2001) – closely resembling the 'national science systems' explored by David Mowery and others (Mowery, 1992; Mowery and Oxley, 1995). Analyses focus on countries' performance on key inputs – R&D spending, human capital stock, university investment – and their links to key outputs such as patenting rates and 'gazelle' firms, which approximate ideas generation and diffusion respectively.

These linear, national-level perspectives of innovation systems are relevant to China and India because of both countries' current and historic emphasis on technology-led national growth (Leadbeater and Wilsdon, 2007). Both China and India are now investing heavily in 'innovation inputs', such as R&D and HE, which both feed into and feed from rapid macroeconomic growth (Kuijs and Wang, 2006). The main drawback of linear models of knowledge generation is that they pay minimal attention to space – and so do not explain why innovative activity is often spatially concentrated.

The percentage of regional GDP devoted to S&T (China) or R&D (India, US) is the main measure of economic input used to generate knowledge in each region and is also frequently used in the literature as a proxy for the local capability to 'absorb' knowledge and innovation produced elsewhere (Cohen and Levinthal, 1990; Maurseth and Verspagen, 2002). In our framework R&D expenditure is a proxy for 'the allocation of resources to research and other information-generating activities in response to perceived profit opportunities' (Grossman and Helpman, 1991b, p. 6) in order to capture the existence of a localised system of incentives (in the public and the private sector) towards intentional innovative activities.

Social filter
Originally defined by Freeman (1987) as 'the network of institutions in the public and private sectors whose activities and interactions initiate, import, modify and diffuse new technologies', innovation systems are now viewed broadly as including social institutions, education and communications infrastructures and the norms and rules that regulate economic and social interaction (Lundvall et al., 2009). Such frameworks allow incorporation of country-specific factors that new economic geography models may not include.

Regional innovation systems localise and spatialise these frameworks to specific regions and clusters (Asheim and Gertler, 2005; Cooke, 2002b; Cooke et al., 1997; Storper, 1997; Saxenian, 1994; Piore and Sabel, 1984). The central insight – shared with geographical approaches – is proximity facilitates innovation, or as Asheim and Gertler (2005) suggest, 'the geographic configuration of economic agents … is fundamentally important in shaping the innovative capabilities of firms and industries'. Regional innovation system analysis is centred on firms' capabilities, and the relationships between these and other institutions. Specifically, business performance is influenced by a number of regional-level factors at the regional level. These include other actors (e.g. universities, public agencies) networks (e.g. public–private partnerships) and institutions (rules, customs and norms). These meso-level factors are also influenced by national-level institutions (such as legal and IP frameworks, or public spending programmes), and by sectoral factors (industry-specific conditions or technological trends/shocks). Within these systems, critical dynamics are the 'triple helix' of private-university–public-sector interactions (Cooke, 2002b), and the 'untraded interdependencies' that regulate agents' behaviour (Storper, 1997).

Synthesising the debate, Storper famously sees regional outcomes as being governed by three spaces – territory, organizations and technologies. This suggests regional innovation system perspectives usefully complement national and sectoral systems approaches, as well as the endogenous growth and new economic geography perspectives explored earlier. Recent evolutionary studies also suggest the importance of deep history path-dependence in explaining regional and national innovation trajectories (Simmie et al., 2008; Storper, 1997; Martin and Sunley, 2006). Sectoral perspectives help illuminate the intersections between regional, national and industry factors, and the co-evolution of innovation systems through the interactions of their component parts (Malerba and Mani, 2009).

A growing number of researchers are attempting to recalibrate regional innovation system frameworks for developing country perspectives (Lundvall et al., 2009; Padilla-Perez et al., 2009; Scott and Garofoli, 2007, provide useful overviews). It is important to make these adaptations. First, in both China and India development in the formal economy partly depends on the performance of the broader, informal innovation system – social capital and networks, institutions and governance capacity (Lundvall et al., 2009). Second, China and India's 'innovation experiences' need to be understood as part of the globalisation of both production and R&D that has been occurring since the 1970s (Bruche, 2009; Mitra, 2007). As Yeung (2009) points out, the task is to explain innovation *under globalization*. Third, local, spatial patterns of innovation are linked to these global flows. As Saxenian and Sabel (2008) argue, research needs to explain the specific 'puzzle' of rapid development of high-tech hubs in countries without the consistent quality of institutions generally thought necessary for growth.

Unlike innovation systems in developed countries, formal institutions may be weak in developing countries, especially at regional level, with intellectual property regimes providing only partial coverage and public agencies that may not always be welfare-maximising (Altenburg, 2009; Joseph, 2009). Capital and finance may be limited, and university–industry collaborations are likely to be limited, with universities being mainly providers of human capital (of varying quality) (Padilla-Perez et al., 2009).

All of these factors place constraints on firms' ability to develop new products and services – and limits managers' incentives to collaborate with other firms (Altenburg 2009). In this context, MNEs may become important providers of both capital flows (via FDI) and new technologies (via alliances/collaborations and spillovers) (Cantwell, 2005). More than half of global R&D is currently done within MNEs; in 2007 Toyota ($8.4bn) and General Motors ($8.1bn) each spent more on R&D than India (Dahlman, 2010). Similarly, export markets become an important source of growth alongside home markets; and the national state (and national policy frameworks) may become more important than regional actors in supporting firms and mediating economic activity (Padilla-Perez et al., 2009). 'Discretionary public policies' in national development strategies are critical (Cimoli et al., 2009).

These predictions echo the themes of other literatures on the globalization of innovation (Mowery, 2001) and its impact on regional economies in developing countries. Archibugi and Iammarino (2002), studying the globalisation of innovation, identify three key processes: international exploitation of locally-generated ideas; 'global generation' of innovations by MNEs; and global 'techno-scientific collaborations'. Another stream of work focuses on MNE location strategies (Cantwell, 2005; Dunning, 1998; Dunning, 1996), and the behaviour of 'lead firms' (Yeung, 2009) which engage in different types of spatially specific 'strategic coupling' with local firms, influencing cluster formation and producing heterogeneous patterns of spatial development.

From a different perspective, Saxenian and Sabel (2008) and Saxenian (2006) emphasise the role of migrants and transnational communities in facilitating innovation, by spreading ideas, developing globalised production systems and influencing institutional reform in 'home' countries. Finally, both Leadbeater and Wilsdon (2007) and Yeung (2009) compare institutional and policy factors in shaping innovation outcomes in South/East Asian countries. They note the importance of more open markets, and public investments in human capital and other 'innovation-enabling' infrastructure.

We use the social filter to capture the unique combination 'of innovative and conservative . . . elements that favour or deter the development of successful regional innovation systems' in every space (Rodríguez-Pose, 1999, p. 82). The social filter covers three domains: educational attainment, structure of productive resources and population age structure.

11.3.3 Spillovers

Geographical approaches show how agglomeration supports innovative activity, via localised knowledge spillovers (e.g. Carlino et al. (2007); Acs et al. (2002); Audretsch and Feldman (1996); Malmberg et al. (1996); Jaffe et al., (1993)). As neither agglomeration nor innovation can be measured directly, density and patenting are typically used as proxies. Alternatively, various kinds of distance weights can be used to model local agglomerations and spillovers to other areas. A number of studies suggest that proximity–spillover–innovation links also operate in developing country contexts, with strong evidence that urbanisation boosts productive efficiency (Xu, 2009; Duranton, 2008; Scott and Garofoli, 2007). However, these effects may be constrained by the pace of urbanisation and/or institutional capacity. Specifically, rapid or chaotic urbanisation can outstrip governments' ability to provide adequate infrastructure and public services (Cohen,

2006; Venables, 2005). As such, agglomerations are also strongly correlated with poverty and informal development.

In addition to the variables related to the 'internal' characteristics of each territory, the model also includes variables representing the potential spatial effects from neighbouring regions that may affect regional knowledge generation performance in the region of interest. The innovative success of an area depends both on its internal conditions and on those of neighbouring interconnected regions. The spatially lagged R&D variable captures the 'aggregate' impact of knowledge generation activities pursued in the neighbourhood that exert a positive impact on local performance, via inter-regional knowledge exchange channels and complementarities that make localised knowledge flows possible. Conversely, centripetal forces driving the location of knowledge-enhancing activities in pre-designated 'hotspots' may lead to the generation of negative externalities: proximity to dynamic areas may 'absorb' resources from the local economy and limited complementarities/synergies might prevent any market-driven compensation for such distortion. We use a combination of first-order contiguity weights and inverse-distance weights to capture localised and far-ranging knowledge flows respectively. Weighted measures of both R&D/S&T intensity (WR&D) and the social filter (WSF) are generated. For details, see Annex 11.2.

11.3.4 Wider structural factors

The role of the key drivers for the process of knowledge creation and of their spatial organisation is assessed after controlling for the geography of other key economic variables influencing regional performance (x). These measures include:

Degree of Specialisation (Krugman Index): Following Midelfart-Knarvik et al. (2002) we call the index K the Krugman specialisation index, used to measure the specialisation of local employment by calculating:

a)   for each region, the share of industry k in that region's total employment: $v_i^k(t)$;
b)   the share of the same industry in the employment of all other regions: $v_i^{-k}(t)$; and
c)   the absolute values of the difference between these shares, added over all industries:

$$K_i(t) = \sum_k abs(v_i^k(t) - v_i^{-k}(t)) \text{ with } v_i^k(t) = \sum_{j \neq i} x_i^k(t) / \sum_k \sum_{j \neq i} x_i^k(t) \quad (11.2)$$

The index takes the value zero if region *i* has an industrial structure identical to the rest of the country, and takes the maximum value of two if it has no industries in common with the rest of the country.

Level of GDP per capita: As customary in the literature on the determinants of regional growth performance, the initial level of GDP per capita is introduced in the model in order to account for the region's initial wealth as proxy for the distance from the technological frontier as customary also in technological catch-up literature (Fagerberg, 1994). The significance and magnitude of the coefficient associated to this variable will allow us to test the existence of a process of technological catch-up.

Existing stock of transport infrastructure endowment: Transport infrastructure may affect innovative performance through a variety of mechanisms also associated with its influence on the spatial organisation of innovative activities. In order to capture the direct impact of transport infrastructure on regional growth, the model includes a specific proxy for the stock of transport infrastructure proxied by total motorways or railways in region, in kilometres, standardised by regional population (Canning and Pedroni, 2004). See Annex 11.1 for further detail.

Agglomeration: Different territorial configurations of the local economy may give rise to different degrees of agglomeration economies and spillovers. The geographical concentration of economic activity has an impact on innovation (Duranton and Puga, 2003; Charlot and Duranton, 2004), which needs to be controlled for in order to single out the differential impact of other 'knowledge' assets such us R&D intensity and Social Filter conditions. From this perspective, population is a useful – though very rudimentary – proxy for these factors.

Migration: The degree of internal labour mobility is reflected by the regional rate of migration. A positive rate of migration (i.e. net inflow of people from other regions) is a proxy for the capacity of the region to benefit from external human capital and knowledge by attracting new workers, increasing the size of its labour pool and its 'diversity' in terms of skills and cultural background (Ottaviano and Peri, 2005).

11.4. Results of quantitative comparative analysis

We fit the panel data with the model specified in equation (11.1), which we run as a two-way fixed effects regression.[1] We minimise potential spatial autocorrelation by explicitly controlling for national growth rates. Furthermore, by introducing the 'spatially lagged' variables WR&D and WSF, we take into consideration the interactions between neighbouring regions, minimising any effect on the residuals. Results also use robust standard errors clustered on state (India), province (China) or economic area (US). We deal with potential endogeneity of the right-hand side variables by fitting these as one-period lags.

Finally, because of different accounting units we express all explanatory variables as a percentage of the respective GDP or population. This is exploratory analysis – so in what follows we focus mainly on the sign and significance of coefficients, rather than the size of specific point estimates.

Results are reported for China, India and the US in the following subsections.

In each case, models (1) through (3) explore 'linear' components of the innovation system, regressing patenting rates on R&D/S&T expenditure and various spatial lags of science spending. Models (4) through (8) introduce the spatial filter and spatially weighted variants. Models (9) to (11) bring in the wider structural factors.

The model generally performs better for Chinese and American data, as we have a longer time period and more observations (because of smaller spatial units). Results for India are more volatile, as we only have state-level 92 observations over 10 years.

11.4.1 China

The main results for China are given in Table 11.1. Overall, the results suggest a traditional agglomeration story: richer regions with agglomeration activities, good infrastructure endowments and industrial specialisation have higher patenting rates. After controlling for these structural factors in the regional economy, net migration also becomes a force for innovation (although point estimates are much smaller than for structural conditions). Once agglomeration effects are included in our model, spillovers become negative significant, suggesting higher-patenting regions are drawing in resources from neighbouring areas.

Models (1) to (3) explore 'linear' elements of the innovation system. We find that regional R&D spending is not significant on patenting rates, and that spatially weighted science and technology spending is negative insignificant. This echoes other findings for the European Union, where R&D spending tends to be centralised at nation state level (Crescenzi et al., 2007). The spillovers result may also reflect effects of a centrally planned economy, in which capital and labour are shifted via policy decisions; or as suggested above, the concentration of knowledge generation in a few urban cores.

Models (4) through (8) introduce the social filter. As expected, we find the social filter is positive significant (at 5% level). However, introducing traditional agglomeration measures removes social filter significance. Spatial lags of the social filter (using first-order contiguity weights) are negative, becoming negative significant when wider structural factors are controlled for. Models (9) to (11) include wider structural factors of regional economies. As noted above, we find traditional agglomeration measures dominate the analysis. The Krugman Index and population density are both positive significant on innovation at 1%. Railway density has a large point estimate but is only marginally significant in full models, perhaps because China has focused on building roads. Net migration is positive significant at 1%, but point estimates are much smaller than for agglomeration measures. To further explore agglomeration processes, we interact science and technology spending with population density. The interaction term is negative significant at the 5% level suggesting that, although high-density areas favour knowledge generation, increases in science and technology expenditure beyond certain thresholds may yield marginal decreasing returns, underlining the potential presence of knowledge efficiency thresholds in Chinese large-scale agglomerations.

11.4.2 India

In the case of India, our results suggest a rather different and more dispersed configuration of territorial innovation from China and the US. Here, regional R&D and the social filter explain a significant amount of variation in knowledge output (Table 11.2). As with China, the interaction of R&D and population density is highly significant – but unlike China, the coefficient is positive and renders simple R&D spending insignificant. Spillover variables are also positive and significant, until net migration is introduced in the analysis. Taken together, the results suggest the importance of a number of several highly dense urban spaces driving knowledge production, plus wider social and institutional conditions – a finding that tallies with wider evidence reviewed above.

As before, models (1) to (3) explore conventional innovation 'inputs'. Unlike China, we find that regional R&D spending is important for regional knowledge generation. Point estimates are very large, although only significant at 10%. R&D spending maintains its importance as social conditions and structural factors are introduced into the analysis. In contrast with China, spillovers of R&D are positive significant at 5% (although these drop out once net migration are brought in).

Models (4) to (8), exploring social conditions and the social filter, also present different results. Unlike China, the social filter is positive significant at 5% in most specifications.

Models (9) through (11) introduce wider structural conditions in the regional economy. Compared with China, agglomeration measures generally play a much less important role in innovative activity. The Krugman Index is insignificant, but road density and net migration are both significant at 5%, the latter most salient. As noted above, interacting R&D with population density produces an important result, although in the opposite direction to the Chinese case: suggesting marginal returns to concentrating R&D that are not present in China.

11.4.3 US

Table 11.3 gives the main results for the US. As it is the only 'mature' urban and innovation system in our country set, we expect the results to be different from those for India and China. Overall, the US results indicate a stable geography of knowledge generation organised around large, specialised spatial clusters.

As before, models (1) to (3) explore linear components of the US innovation system. The results suggest a consistently strong connection between regional R&D expenditure and patenting activity – a relationship that holds throughout the specifications (except for model (11), of which more below). Unlike China and India, we find no significant effects of R&D spillovers in any specification. This reflects wider analysis that knowledge spillovers within US regions exhibit considerable distance decay, tending to die out within the economic area in which ideas are generated (Acs et al., 2002).

As with China and India, social and institutional factors exhibit a robust positive influence on innovation. Models (4) through (7) indicate that the social filter is significant on patenting at 1%, a relationship that persists in further specifications.

Table 11.1 China: social filter index, 1995–2007

VARIABLES	(1)	(2)	(3)	(4)	(5)
Regional R&D/ S&T expenditure	0.0410 (0.131)	0.0696 (0.131)	0.0349 (0.133)	0.0274 (0.123)	0.00673 (0.123)
Spatially weighted S&T (inverse dist)		−4.13e−09 (3.64e−09)		−4.64e−09 (3.36e−09)	
Spatially weighted S&T (first-order contiguity)			2.37e−10 (1.13e−09)		−4.81e−10 (1.06e−09)
Social filter				0.00316** (0.00123)	0.00322*** (0.00124)
Spatially weighted social filter (inverse dist)					
Spatially weighted social filter (first-order contiguity)					
Krugman index					
Railway density					
Population density					
Net migration					
GDP per capita					
Interaction S&T expenditure* pop. density					
Constant	−0.000546 (0.00245)	1.50e−05 (0.00246)	−0.000495 (0.00245)	0.00215 (0.00241)	0.00145 (0.00235)
Year dummies	X	X	X	X	X
Observations	390	390	390	390	390
R-squared	0.092	0.099	0.092	0.144	0.136
Number of provinces	30	30	30	30	30

Notes: Robust standard errors in parentheses. *** $p < 0.01$, ** $p < 0.05$, * $p < 0.1$

(6)	(7)	(8)	(9)	(10)	(11)
0.0249	0.0269	−0.00805	−0.0533	−0.0963	0.492*
(0.123)	(0.124)	(0.0898)	(0.0601)	(0.0701)	(0.267)
−4.08e−09	−4.91e−09	−7.93e−10	−1.63e−08***	−7.98e−09***	−7.45e−09***
(3.44e−09)	(3.42e−09)	(3.01e−09)	(3.85e−09)	(2.56e−09)	(2.28e−09)
0.00315**	0.00310**	0.00104	2.76e−06	−0.000552	−0.000377
(0.00124)	(0.00123)	(0.000878)	(0.000520)	(0.000564)	(0.000506)
−0.00374					
(0.00366)					
	0.000738	−0.00197**	−0.00141*	−0.00210***	−0.00110
	(0.00100)	(0.000985)	(0.000761)	(0.000742)	(0.00100)
		0.0300***		0.0204***	0.0213***
		(0.00566)		(0.00408)	(0.00427)
		0.183**		0.134**	0.141***
		(0.0725)		(0.0604)	(0.0496)
			0.000148***	0.000176***	0.000294***
			(5.52e−05)	(4.91e−05)	(5.86e−05)
			−1.81e−05	2.83e−05***	4.57e−05***
			(2.24e−05)	(1.04e−05)	(1.06e−05)
			8.27e−07***		
			(2.63e−07)		
					−0.00111**
					(0.000536)
0.000353	0.00267	−0.0332***	−0.0493***	−0.0798***	−0.121***
(0.00288)	(0.00272)	(0.00590)	(0.0185)	(0.0167)	(0.0215)
X	X	X	X	X	X
390	390	390	390	390	390
0.146	0.145	0.312	0.400	0.400	0.570
30	30	30	30	30	30

Table 11.2 India: social filter index, 1995–2004

Variables	(1)	(2)	(3)	(4)	(5)
Regional S&T expenditure	1.734* *(0.968)*	1.832* *(1.064)*	1.787* *(0.952)*	1.638 *(1.067)*	1.657* *(0.963)*
Spatially weighted R&D (inverse dist)		2.14e-09 *(4.41e-09)*		1.43e-09 *(4.36e-09)*	
Spatially weighted R&D (first-order contiguity)			2.37e-09** *(1.03e-09)*		2.20e-09** *(1.05e-09)*
Social filter				0.000189** *(8.87e-05)*	0.000148 *(8.90e-05)*
Spatially weighted social filter (Inverse dist)					
Spatially weighted social filter (first-order contiguity)					
Krugman index					
Road density					
Population Density					
GDP per capita					
Gross migration (inter-state)					
Interaction R&D expenditure* pop.density					
Constant	−0.00204* *(0.00110)*	−0.00385 *(0.00432)*	−0.00443** *(0.00190)*	−0.00313 *(0.00428)*	−0.00417** *(0.00194)*
Year dummies	X	X	X	X	X
Delhi trend	X	X	X	X	X
Observations	92	92	92	92	92
R-squared	0.903	0.904	0.911	0.906	0.912
Number of states	19	19	19	19	19

Notes: Robust standard errors in parentheses. *** $p < 0.01$, ** $p < 0.05$, * $p < 0.1$

(6)	(7)	(8)	(9)	(10)	(11)
1.641*	1.505*	1.456	1.314*	1.545*	0.194
(0.875)	(0.806)	(0.885)	(0.774)	(0.810)	(0.321)
2.04e-09**	1.71e-09*	1.75e-09*	1.04e-09	1.24e-09	1.06e-09
(9.16e-10)	(8.81e-10)	(9.07e-10)	(8.96e-10)	(9.54e-10)	(8.19e-10)
0.000246**	0.000261**	0.000255**	0.000253**	0.000210*	0.000194**
(0.000106)	(0.000113)	(0.000115)	(0.000108)	(0.000110)	(9.07e-05)
0.00231					
(0.00158)					
	0.00113*	0.00111*	0.000848	0.000694	0.000357
	(0.000580)	(0.000605)	(0.000517)	(0.000472)	(0.000304)
		−0.000574		−8.15e-05	−0.000985
		(0.00153)		(0.00133)	(0.000951)
		−3.94e-06		−4.53e-05**	−3.69e-05**
		(8.34e-06)		(2.12e-05)	(1.75e-05)
			−3.56e-06	1.41e-06	−7.68e-08
			(2.87e-06)	(1.26e-06)	(1.07e-06)
			−6.04e-08		
			(3.80e-08)		
			1.75e-05***	1.74e-05**	1.30e-05**
			(6.53e-06)	(7.55e-06)	(6.07e-06)
					0.000999***
					(0.000276)
−0.00441**	−0.00354**	−0.00311	0.000568	−0.00622*	−0.00288
(0.00192)	(0.00156)	(0.00211)	(0.00438)	(0.00348)	(0.00211)
X	X	X	X	X	X
X	X	X	X	X	X
92	92	92	92	92	92
0.919	0.923	0.923	0.935	0.938	0.964
19	19	19	19	19	19

Table 11.3 US, BEA: social filter index, 1995–2007

Variables	(1)	(2)	(3)	(4)	(5)
Regional R&D expenditure	2769***	2792***	2757***	2782***	2745***
	(668.4)	(672.0)	(666.3)	(671.5)	(665.9)
Spatially weighted R&D (inverse dist)		−1846		−2065	
		(1580)		(1584)	
Spatially weighted R&D (first–order contiguity)			489.0		454.2
			(454.8)		(449.1)
Social filter				0.00582***	0.00566***
				(0.00129)	(0.00130)
Spatially weighted social filter (inverse dist)					
Spatially weighted social filter (first-order contiguity)					
Krugman index					
Road density					
Population density					
Net domestic migration					
GDP per capita					
Interaction R&D expenditure* pop.density					
Constant	0.0217***	0.0267***	0.0189***	0.0260***	0.0179***
	(0.00495)	(0.00592)	(0.00578)	(0.00591)	(0.00577)
Year dummies	X	X	X	X	X
Observations	2327	2327	2327	2327	2327
R-squared	0.252	0.253	0.253	0.256	0.256
Number of regions	179	179	179	179	179

Notes: Robust standard errors in parentheses. *** $p < 0.01$, ** $p < 0.05$, * $p < 0.1$

(6)	(7)	(8)	(9)	(10)	(11)
2737***	2787***	2586***	2441***	2334***	739.0
(661.4)	(665.6)	(580.0)	(574.3)	(527.2)	(906.9)
−570.9	−1882	−1362	428.6	458.3	1137
(1603)	(1588)	(1551)	(1538)	(1525)	(1608)
0.00624***	0.00822***	0.00627***	0.00738***	0.00642***	0.00668***
(0.00131)	(0.00150)	(0.00148)	(0.00143)	(0.00144)	(0.00147)
0.0384***					
(0.00923)					
	−0.0119***	−0.00891***	−0.00587*	−0.00433	−0.00513
	(0.00358)	(0.00341)	(0.00322)	(0.00313)	(0.00323)
		−0.0868***		−0.0253	−0.0373*
		(0.0239)		(0.0225)	(0.0224)
		4.31e−05***		3.29e−05**	3.20e−05**
		(1.58e−05)		(1.42e−05)	(1.36e−05)
			0.000589***	0.000466***	0.000359***
			(0.000157)	(0.000162)	(0.000130)
		−1.50e−07**	−8.07e−08	−2.40e−08	
			(6.37e−08)	(5.75e−08)	(5.94e−08)
			5.77e−06***	5.30e−06***	4.95e−06***
			(9.60e−07)	(9.24e−07)	(8.11e−07)
					7.904*
					(4.509)
0.0165**	0.0266***	0.00743	−0.159***	−0.189***	−0.161***
(0.00673)	(0.00591)	(0.0452)	(0.0321)	(0.0469)	(0.0404)
X	X	X	X	X	X
2327	2327	2327	2327	2327	2327
0.261	0.260	0.296	0.312	0.330	0.340
179	179	179	179	179	179

Social Filter spillovers exhibit a mixed effect: inverse distance weights are positive significant, while first-order contiguity weights are negative significant, and become progressively less important as wider structural factors are introduced.

Models (9) through (11) bring in wider structural factors. These confirm what is already apparent from models (1) to (3): that traditional agglomeration factors play important roles. Population density and GDP per capita are both strongly positive on patenting. Interacting R&D spending with population density (model (11) helps explore the relative role of linear and structural factors: the interaction term and population density are both significant, while R&D spending becomes insignificant. This suggests the joint effect of agglomeration is driven by structural factors.

As in India (but not China), the Krugman Index is weakly significant or insignificant. Net inter-BEA migration is rather less important in the US than in China or India, reflecting the relative stability of the country's knowledge generation geography.

11.4.4 Comparisons of spatial dynamics: the EU vs China, India and the US

Finally, we integrate our analysis with that pursued in Chapter 8 to compare key features of all four territories. Table 11.4 presents the main results. The regional knowledge production function links patenting activity to R&D expenditures, human capital and, to control for each region's size, resident population.

Table 11.4 Knowledge production function, indicative comparison across continents

Dependent variable: patents

	Europe	US	China	India
Model	SAR	FE	FE	FE
Estimation method	ML	OLS	OLS	OLS
R&D	0.430***	0.041**	1.303***	0.995***
	(8.011)	(2.050)	(4.059)	(3.713)
Human capital	0.629***	0.627	0.022	0.631
	(3.985)	(0.739)	(0.135)	(0.798)
Included control variables				
Population	Yes	Yes	Yes	Yes
Country dummies	Yes			
Year dummies		Yes	Yes	Yes
Delhi trend				Yes
R-squared	0.847	0.365	0.731	0.776
Number of territorial units	287	179	30	19

Source: Europe, Chapter 8 (Table 8.3, reg. 5); other countries, elaboration of the authors

Notes: Total R&D for Europe and India, S&T Expenditure for China, Private R&D for the US
Panel estimation period: 2000–2007 for Europe; 1995–2007 for the other countries
All variables are log-transformed and include a constant
Robust t-statistics in parenthesis; significance: ***1%; **5%; *10%

The most striking result is that R&D expenditure turns out to be positive and significant in all macro areas considered, although it displays huge differences in the elasticity levels which follow a clear decreasing returns pattern. Indeed, the lowest elasticity of knowledge production to R&D expenditure is shown by US, the area where the R&D investment is at the highest level. The European average elasticity is equal to 0.43, while a much higher return is found for China (1.3) and India (0.99), which are two large economies in an initial stage of investing specific resources in formal innovation activities.

The second important result is that human capital exerts a relevant role on knowledge production only in Europe, whereas it appears not significant in the other three countries. However, it has to be considered that when human capital is not included alone in the regression but is incorporated as one of the components of the 'social filter' (Crescenzi and Rodríguez-Pose, 2009, 2011) then it plays a relevant role for the case of US, China and India (Crescenzi et al., 2012) as well. This means that in the European regional innovation model the availability at the local level of an adequate endowment of highly educated labour forces plays a key role per se in influencing the process of knowledge creation. On the other hand, in other territorial contexts it is the combination of elements that compose the social filter which positively enhances the creation of knowledge.

Third, the analysis confirms substantive differences between the EU's main 'innovation competitors'. Results for China suggest that the country's regional innovation systems are driven by the density–R&D nexus, and more broadly by traditional agglomeration factors. Patenting activity is concentrated in richer regions with big urban cores and good infrastructure networks. This may be because of China's sharper density gradient, plus the role of the state-directed economy – which appears to limit spillovers between regions. In our detailed country-level analysis, for instance, the social filter is positively linked to knowledge output, but the relationship has no statistical significance.

By contrast, India presents a more straightforward 'R&D plus spillovers' story, especially in a number of dense urban cores. Agglomeration measures play a less important role than in China; conversely, spillover variables are positive and (mostly) statistically significant as a driver of patenting. The country-level results for India also highlight the importance of migration: there appears to be a very dynamic spatial matching of talent across regions, perhaps reflecting freer movement of labour. Also unlike China, the Social Filter is positive and significantly linked to knowledge output.

Overall, the US system shares some superficial similarities with both China (a traditional agglomeration story) and India (a number of knowledge 'hotspots'). The generation of knowledge occurs largely in self-contained zones relying on their own R&D inputs, favourable local socioeconomic environments and on large pools of skilled individuals. However, we know from the previous territorial analysis that knowledge generation activity in both China and India is far more spatially clustered than in the US. Knowledge spillovers in the US are largely localised: but the large number of knowledge generation 'sites' helps raise the country's overall innovation performance.

11.5. Conclusions and policy lessons

Our analysis has explored the dynamics and drivers of knowledge generation activity in the US, China and India in comparison with the EU. The US is widely considered as the world's technological leader. Both China and India have experienced significant jumps in national innovation outputs in recent years; more broadly, both countries are now key locations in increasingly globalised sectoral innovation systems. Many of these sectoral networks have been led by MNEs originating in the US, via complex outsourcing and collaborative ventures. We are interested in how these national and pan-national forces are shaping the evolution of knowledge activities across space, and their interaction with country-specific social, institutional and historical factors.

Our analysis has a number of useful features for EU policymakers. We deliver rich, detailed descriptive analysis on key innovation inputs and outputs across the three countries. We site these results within an analytical framework which allows us to identify individual components of innovation systems and their interaction. We then apply this framework in regression modelling, in order to explore key relationships in more detail.

How does this type of comparative analysis add value to EU policymakers, especially at regional level? First, it enables us to isolate the factors that shape the genesis of knowledge and economic dynamism at the territorial level at different stages of the process of technological development. In turn, this helps develop a better understanding of these processes for EU leading and lagging regions at the same time.

Second, the territorial approach allows us to 'capture' the emergence of new actors in the international technological competition arena as well as to situate existing leading regions. This is important for EU regions to understand their 'competitors' as well as for EU-based firms and institutions (e.g. universities) to identify new opportunities in 'distant' markets. In this respect our analysis should be read alongside other territorial studies such as the World Bank World Development Report 2009.

Third, it supports 'policy transfer' where the EU aims to provide support to non-EU partners wishing to learn from the EU experience: comparative analysis provides a systematic framework for policy development work, for example the European Commission's 2010 China Regional Policy report.

With this in mind, what does our comparative analysis tell us? Overall, that there is no single 'best practice' or 'optimal model' for EU innovation, as territorial specificities are of crucial importance for regional/local economic development/innovation policies. Factors behind successful outcomes in China, India and the US cannot be easily replicated in different contexts. For example, Americanising EU innovation systems is not helpful. Policies need to be tailored to local conditions.

The country-specific findings throw out a number of important lessons for policymakers. First, in the US tighter functional integration (when compared to Europe) is fostering concentration and specialisation by means of factor mobility.

The EU should carefully consider how integration policies – and mobility in particular – impact on knowledge output and its geography. A narrow focus on innovation inputs may cover up crucial framework conditions. This is particularly important for leading regions but also for emerging territories as shown for China and, even more so, for India.

Second, at this relatively initial stage of technological development only a very few 'hotspots' have so far emerged in China and India, but new 'localities' are now developing, creating both new opportunities and challenges for EU innovation in the global stage. The geography of global knowledge generation and innovation is changing at increasing speed and the emergence of new and rapidly growing hubs in the developing world is raising the stakes for EU firms, institutions and policy-makers involved in these fields. This chapter has sought to provide European actors with an analytical/critical picture of their external competitors, suggesting that the EU nowadays faces competition both from 'below' (China and India) and from 'above' (US). But the picture is more complex when analysed at the sub-national level: there are also new opportunities for EU firms and investors, but they are highly localised and constantly evolving over time with ever-changing driving forces. However, the level of internal disparities in emerging countries remains very high (even when compared with the US). This might produce social and/or political tensions in the future, possibly threatening further evolution of these economies if appropriate development policies are not implemented. This risk should be carefully taken into account by EU firms for its impact on investments and trade relations.

Annex 11.1. Geographical coverage and description of the variables

A11.1.1 China: Geographical coverage

For China data are available for the Provincial-level administrative subdivisions: 22 Provinces, four Autonomous Regions, four Municipalities. Two Special Administrative Regions (Hong Kong and Macau) and One Autonomous Region (Tibet) have been excluded from the analysis due to the lack of data for the selected variables (Table A11.1).

A11.1.2 India: Geographical coverage

For India data are available for 18 States and 3 Union Territories that are covered in the analysis. Bihar and Rajasthan are included in descriptive statistics but not in the regression analysis due to limited number of observations available over time (Table A11.2).

A11.1.3 US: Geographical coverage. BEA Economic Areas (EAs)

'BEA's economic areas define the relevant regional markets surrounding metropolitan or micropolitan statistical areas. They consist of one or more economic

Table A11.1 Geographical coverage for China

Provincial subdivisions	Available data
Anhui	YES
Beijing	YES
Chongqing	YES
Fujian	YES
Gansu	YES
Guangdong	YES
Guangxi	YES
Guizhou	YES
Hainan	YES
Hebei	YES
Heilongjiang	YES
Henan	YES
Hubei	YES
Hunan	YES
Inner Mongolia	YES
Jiangsu	YES
Jiangxi	YES
Jilin	YES
Liaoning	YES
Ningxia	YES
Qinghai	YES
Shaanxi	YES
Shandong	YES
Shanghai	YES
Shanxi	YES
Sichuan	YES
Tianjin	YES
Xinjiang	YES
Yunnan	YES
Zhejiang	YES
Hong Kong (SAR)	NO
Macau (SAR)	NO
Tibet (AR)	NO

nodes – metropolitan or micropolitan statistical areas that serve as regional centres of economic activity – and the surrounding counties that are economically related to the nodes. The economic areas were redefined on November 17, 2004, and are based on commuting data from the 2000 decennial population census, on redefined statistical areas from OMB (February 2004), and on newspaper circulation data from the Audit Bureau of Circulations for 2001.'
http://www.bea.gov/regional/docs/econlist.cfm
Regional definitions from BEA:
http://www.bea.gov/regional/definitions/#P
Definitions of GDP vs personal income and their availability:
http://www.bea.gov/regional/about.cfm

Table A11.2 Geographical coverage for India

States of India	Available data
Andhra Pradesh	YES
Arunachal Pradesh	
Assam	
Bihar	Limited availability / excluded from regression analysis
Chhattisgarh	
Goa	YES
Gujarat	YES
Haryana	YES
Himachal Pradesh	YES
Jammu and Kashmir	YES
Jharkhand	YES
Karnataka	YES
Kerala	YES
Madhya Pradesh	YES
Maharashtra	YES
Manipur	
Meghalaya	
Mizoram	
Nagaland	
Orissa	YES
Punjab	YES
Rajasthan	Limited availability / excluded from regression analysis
Sikkim	
Tamil Nadu	YES
Tripura	
Uttar Pradesh	YES
Uttarakhand	
West Bengal	YES
Union Territories	
Andaman and Nicobar Islands	
Chandigarh	YES
Dadra and Nagar Haveli	
Daman and Diu	
Lakshadweep	
National Capital Territory of Delhi	YES
Puducherry	YES

The Bureau prepares GDP by metropolitan area estimates only, beginning with 2001. Conversely Local area personal income is the only detailed, broadly inclusive economic time series for local areas that is available annually beginning with 1969 (BEA Website 2011. http://www.bea.gov/regional/about.cfm). Only the latter is also available for the 179 BEA Economic Areas (EA).

A11.1.4 Definitions of variables

Table A11.3 Definitions of variables for China

Variable	Definition	Source(s)
Patenting indicator (Dependent variable)		
PCT applications per capita (per 1000 persons)	Number of provincial PCT applications (count) / total regional population	OECD.Stat
Innovation efforts		
Regional S&T expenditure	Intramural expenditure on Science and Technology (S&T) as a share of total regional GDP.	China statistical yearbook on science and technology, 1991–2008
Social filter		
Agricultural employment	Agricultural employment as a share of total provincial employment	China statistical yearbook, 1991–2008
Unemployment rate	Unemployment rate at the provincial level (in urban areas only)	China statistical yearbook, 1991–2008
Young population (15–24)	People aged 15–24 as share of total population in the province	China population census data
Human capital accumulation (Tertiary education)	People with college-level or higher degrees as a share of total provincial population (aged 6 and above)	China statistical yearbook, 1991–2008
Structure of the local economy		
GDP per capita	Total regional GDP/ total provincial population (units)	China statistical yearbook, 1991–2008
Population density	Calculated as average population (units) in year t /surface of the province (Sq kms)	China statistical yearbook, 1991–2008
Krugman index	Provincial-level Krugman index calculated on the basis provincial employment in 15 major sectors defined by the 1990 official statistical classification of industrial sectors.	China statistical yearbook, 1991–2008
Railway density	Length of railways in operation (Kms) in the province / total surface of the province (Sq km)	
Net migration	Net inter-provincial migration per 1000 persons, calculated as the difference between total migratory inflows minus total migratory outflows	China population census data

Table A11.4 Definitions of variables for India

Variable	Definition	Sources
Patenting indicator (Dependent variable)		
PCT applications per capita (per 1000 persons)	Number of State PCT applications (Count) / total regional population	OECD.Stat
Innovation efforts		
Regional R&D expenditure	Combines central government extramural and state total expenditure in R&D as a share of regional GDP	Research and development statistics 2004–05 and 2007–08; Research and Development in Industry 2000–01, Ministry of Science and Technology, Govt. of India; Planning Commission, India
Social filter		
Unemployment rate	Rate of unemployment at the state level (urban areas)	Planning Commission, Govt. of India.
Agricultural employment	Agricultural employment as a share of total employment at the state level	Census of India 1991, 2001
Human capital accumulation (tertiary education)	People with college, diploma or higher degrees (in urban areas) as a share of total state population (aged 7 and above)	National sample survey
Young people	People aged 15–24 as a share of total state population	Census of India 1991, 2001
Structure of the local economy		
Population density	Calculated as average population (units) in year t /surface of the state (Sq-kms)	Central statistics office
GDP per capita	Calculated as regional gross domestic product/regional population (units)	Central statistics office
Krugman index	Statel-level Krugman index calculated on the basis state GDP in 13 major sectors	Central statistics office
Gross migration	Inter-state migratory in-flows per 1000 persons	Census of India 1991, 2001
Religious fractionalization index (R_index)	The index is calculated on the basis of 7 major religious groups $$1 - \sum_{k=1}^{K} p_k^2, K \geq 2$$ K is different religious group, and pk indicates the share of group k in the total state population	Census of India 1991, 2001
Road density	Calculated as the length of state roads (Kms) /surface of the state (Sq kms)	Basic road transport statistics of India, Ministry of Transport and Highways

Table A11.5 Definitions of variables for US, BEA economic areas

Variable	Definition	Sources
Patenting indicator (Dependent variable)		
PCT applications per capita (per 1000 persons)	Number of state PCT applications (Count) / total regional population	OECD.Stat
Innovation efforts		
Regional R&D expenditure	Regional private R&D expenditure as a percentage of regional total personal income	Compustat from Standard & Poor's – Wharton research data services (WRDS), available in LSE library
Social filter		
Unemployment rate	Rate of unemployment at the BEA-EA level	US Bureau of Labour Statistics, local area unemployment statistics
Agricultural employment	Agricultural employment as a share of total employment at the BEA-EA level.	US Census Bureau counties data files
Human capital accumulation (tertiary education)	People with bachelor's degree and higher as a share of total BEA-EA population (aged 25 and above)	US Census Bureau counties data files
Young people	People aged 15–24 as a share of total BEA-EA population	US Census Bureau counties data files
Structure of the local economy		
Population density	Calculated as average population (units) in year t /surface of the BEA-EA (Sq-kms)	US Census Bureau, US counties data files/Bureau of Economic Analysis
Personal income per capita	This is used as a proxy for GDP per capita (see note) as is calculated as total personal income on the BEA EA /regional population (units)	US Census Bureau, US counties data files/Bureau of Economic Analysis
Krugman index	EA-level Krugman index calculated on the basis BEA-EA employment in 10 major sectors	US Census Bureau, US counties data files/Bureau of Economic Analysis
Net migration	Domestic inter-EA net migratory in-flows per 1000 persons	US Census Bureau, US counties data files/Bureau of Economic Analysis
Road density	Calculated as the length of highways (Kms) /surface of the Economic Area (Sq kms)	US Bureau of Transport Statistics, National Transportation Atlas Database.

Annex 11.2. Principal component analysis results

Table A11.6 Principal component analysis: eigenanalysis of the correlation matrix

	China			
Component	*Eigenvalue*	*Difference*	*Proportion*	*Cumulative*
Comp1	1.78367	0.607117	0.4459	0.4459
Comp2	1.17655	0.390576	0.2941	0.7401
Comp3	0.785977	0.532178	0.1965	0.9366
Comp4	0.2538	—	0.0634	1

	India			
Component	*Eigenvalue*	*Difference*	*Proportion*	*Cumulative*
Comp1	1.42679	0.397231	0.3567	0.3567
Comp2	1.02956	0.140551	0.2574	0.6141
Comp3	0.889012	0.234381	0.2223	0.8363
Comp4	0.654631	—	0.1637	1

	US, BEA			
Component	*Eigenvalue*	*Difference*	*Proportion*	*Cumulative*
Comp1	1.4628	0.380224	0.3657	0.3657
Comp2	1.08258	0.107053	0.2706	0.6363
Comp3	0.975522	0.49642	0.2439	0.8802
Comp4	0.479102	—	0.1198	1

Table A11.7 Principal component analysis: principal components' coefficients

	China				
Variable	*Comp1*	*Comp2*	*Comp3*	*Comp4*	*Unexplained*
Young population (15–24)	−0.0159	−0.7543	0.6441	0.1262	0
Population with tertiary educ.	−0.6743	0.2201	0.1046	0.6971	0
Unemployment rate (urban)	0.2586	0.6176	0.7407	−0.0559	0
Agricultural employment	0.6915	−0.0337	−0.1602	0.7036	0

	India				
Variable	*Comp1*	*Comp2*	*Comp3*	*Comp4*	*Unexplained*
Young population (15–24)	0.5725	−0.2819	0.5164	−0.571	0
Population with tertiary educ.	0.6567	0.1375	0.15	0.7262	0
Agricultural employment	−0.4901	−0.1991	0.786	0.3184	0
Unemployment rate (urban)	−0.0285	0.9284	0.3033	−0.2127	0

Table A11.7 Continued

	US, BEA				
Variable	*Comp1*	*Comp2*	*Comp3*	*Comp4*	*Unexplained*
Young population (15–24)	−0.1487	0.4121	0.8939	−0.095	0
Population with tertiary educ.	−0.727	−0.0067	−0.045	0.6852	0
Unemployment rate	0.4163	−0.6588	0.4222	0.4631	0
Agricultural employment	0.5254	0.6294	−0.1439	0.5542	0

Note: For the calculation of the social filter index the score for Comp1 in China, US BEA-Economic Areas has been pre-multiplied by −1 to match the interpretation of the index computed for India (proxy for 'innovation proneness')

Note

1 Breusch-Pagan tests suggest fixed effects estimation is preferred due to the high significance of the individual effects.

Part III

Innovation policy implications

12 Towards a conclusion

Smart innovation policies

Roberto Camagni and Roberta Capello

12.1. Introduction

This chapter examines the policy implications that stem from the analyses presented in the previous chapters, and it considers how sectoral policies, like innovation policies, can be appropriately translated into a regional setting. Regional policy suggestions are derived both from the theoretical framework developed, built on the concept of 'territorial patterns of innovation', and from interpretation of the results of the empirical analysis on the impact of knowledge and innovation on regional growth. Territorial patterns of innovation are understood – as explained in Chapter 6 – as being differentiated spatial variants of the linear knowledge → invention → innovation → development logical path, implying varied inter-regional cooperation processes in knowledge development and acquisition, and varied innovation and development outcomes.

Much can be learnt from the results obtained, since most of the territorial evidence described in the previous chapters runs counter to some general beliefs behind traditional normative choices. These counter-intuitive results may provide the basis for reorienting regional policy strategies in the field of innovation towards more efficient visions and styles.

The policy suggestions presented in this chapter are closely embedded in the present EU regional policy debate animated in particular by official documents like the Commission's report titled *Regional Policy Contributing to Smart Growth in Europe* (EC, 2010b), where a first attempt to translate innovation policies into a regional context is made. In fact, this report calls for identification in each region of sectors and technological domains to which regional policies should be tailored in order to promote local innovation processes. The document fully subscribes to the 'regional innovation smart specialization' strategy (RIS3) suggested by the 'Knowledge for Growth' expert group advising the former European Commissioner for Research, Janez Potocnik (Foray, 2009; Foray et al., 2009). It convincingly advocates a consistent match between investments in knowledge and human capital and the present industrial and technological 'vocations' and competences of territories. 'Strategies have to consider the heterogeneity of research and technology specialization patterns' (Giannitsis, 2009, p. 1).

The results of our work make it possible to take a step forward with respect to the suggestions made by the smart specialization approach. A first important achievement is that the regional taxonomy advocated by the smart specialization strategy on which to target different innovation policies – distinguishing an advanced 'research area' (the core) and a 'co-application area' of general purpose technologies (GPTs) (the periphery) – is not appropriate in a widely diversified regional context. The empirical evidence presented in this book suggests that the geography of innovation is much more complex than a simple core–periphery dichotomy: the capacity to move from knowledge to innovation and from innovation to regional growth differs among regions according to the varied presence of innovation preconditions and crucial elements of territorial capital; therefore, the identification of specific 'innovation patterns' is essential for building targeted normative strategies.

But this is only one of the unconventional results contained in this book. This chapter highlights the unexpected evidence (Section 12.2) that, together with theoretical reflections on the limitations of the smart specialization strategy (Section 12.3) and on how to overcome them (Section 12.4), helps in advocating targeted innovation policies at regional level. These policies – labelled 'smart innovation policies' (Section 12.5) – may be defined as policies able to increase the innovation capability of an area by boosting the effectiveness of accumulated knowledge and fostering territorial applications and diversification, doing so on the basis of local specificities and the characteristics of already-established innovation patterns. New policy tools and styles are suggested in order to attain the European goals of *smart growth* and *Innovation Union* (Section 12.6).

12.2. Knowledge, innovation and territorial evidence: unexpected policy warnings

12.2.1. General beliefs and unconventional empirical evidence

The general aim of increasing European competitiveness through knowledge and innovation is a strategic and correctly formulated goal of the Europe 2020 Agenda (EC, 2010a), which presents the general context in which Europe will act in the next decade. The first Report proposes a strategy based on three pillars – namely, smart, sustainable and inclusive growth. In particular, smart growth may become the occasion for relaunching a knowledge-intensive growth model for Europe on a regional basis, supplying operational responses to the requirement of one of its 'Flagship Initiatives', namely 'Innovation Union'.

The general orientation towards smart growth rests on a number of general beliefs. The first is the well-known idea that knowledge is the most strategic asset on which the competitive advantage of nations, regions and firms depends, because the present knowledge economy paradigm is bound to become pervasive in all advanced economies. Given the wide R&D gap between Europe and some key trading partners, the Europe 2020 Agenda has called for the achievement of a 3% share of R&D in GDP, a target already expressed in a previous official document, the Lisbon Agenda (EC, 2000).

The second general belief is that a strong linkage exists between knowledge production and innovation capacity. This is shared by the promoters of the flagship initiative 'Innovation Union', for whom the presence of knowledge and human capital guarantees more innovative performance in Europe and across Europe.

These statements recall a number of common beliefs fully acceptable when a European level of analysis is adopted. But the empirical evidence presented in the previous chapters shows that much more caution is required when a regional perspective is adopted, with regard to:

a)   the pervasiveness of the knowledge economy;
b)   the smart specialization strategy (behind the Flagship Initiative 'Innovation Union');
c)   R&D investments as innovation policy tools (the Europe 2020 Agenda);
d)   the linkage between R&D investments and innovation;
e)   the linkage between knowledge, innovation and smart growth.

a)   The pervasiveness of the knowledge economy
As mentioned several times in this book, there is no unique definition of the knowledge economy because it can manifest itself in different forms, which are expected to complement each other but sometimes substitute for each other. The knowledge economy can be measured at regional level through either the presence of high-tech manufacturing and service sectors (technologically advanced regions), or the presence of scientific activities (human capital and research activities: scientific regions), or the capacity of regions to cooperate – intentionally or unintentionally – with other regions (knowledge networking regions). The regional types empirically identified and mapped on this basis testify that the knowledge economy in Europe is rather fragmented, with a substantial number of regions engaged only in external cooperation networks (mainly in central Europe), and only three technologically advanced regions hosting scientific functions at the same time, while most of the technologically advanced areas are also networking regions (see Chapter 5).

The territorial evidence testifies that, when a regional perspective is adopted, the picture is rather impressive (or depressive): in most European regions the knowledge economy is still in its infancy.

b)   The smart specialization strategy behind the Flagship Initiative 'Innovation Union'
The official document *Elements for a Common Strategic Framework* (EC, 2012b) recalls that the Flagship Initiative *Innovation Union* states 'that the funds should be fully exploited to develop research and innovation capacities across Europe, based on smart specialization strategies' (p. 2), the latter advocating differentiated policies for 'core' and 'periphery' regions. Regions hosting high-tech sectors and top R&D activities are considered to be 'core' regions leading new knowledge creation and the transformation of the economy, and acting as Europe's drivers in the international technological competition. All other regions are assigned the role of adopters/adapters of technological frontier inventions within their 'knowledge domains', on the basis of their production specificities (Foray, 2009; Foray et al., 2009; Giannitsis, 2009; Pontikakis et al., 2009).

But the ways in which knowledge may be created, acquired, utilized and transformed into innovation are far more complex in a regional context; and the preconditions for knowledge creation, for turning knowledge into innovation, and for turning innovation into growth are unevenly distributed and differently linked to the territorial culture of each region. This means that each region follows its own path in undertaking the different abstract phases of the innovation process, depending on the context conditions: its own 'pattern of innovation', in the terminology of this research work. If a taxonomy is drawn up on the basis of our conceptual expectations, i.e. on the complex interplay between phases of the innovation process and the territorial context, *the territorial evidence shows that there is a variety of possible innovation patterns larger than the simple core/periphery dichotomy* (Chapter 7).

c) The Europe 2020 Agenda and R&D investments as an innovation policy tool
The overall policy recommendation of the Europe 2020 Agenda is that a policy target of 3% of R&D over GDP should be achieved. This policy aim has a strong meaning when an aggregate EU perspective is adopted, but it proves fragile when it is translated into a regional setting.

The empirical evidence shows that, in recent years, R&D spending over GDP has been characterized by a strong regional variation ranging from values lower than 0.5% to ones of more than 6%, while a very small number of regions in Europe have reached 3% of R&D expenditure on GDP. Even more striking is that a large number of regions are still below the 0.5% level, testifying that achievement of the 3% goal is still an ambitious aim (Chapter 5).

Our territorial evidence adds something even more impressive to these descriptive results. Inference analysis shows that a substantial impact of R&D over GDP is achieved only in those regions where a critical mass of R&D activities is present. The estimated elasticity of GDP to R&D by patterns of innovation is in fact higher for those patterns that have higher stocks of R&D over GDP (Figure 12.1) (Chapter 8). Furthermore, econometric results show that R&D investment is characterized by decreasing returns: in fact, the elasticity of new knowledge (measured in terms of patenting activity) to R&D for the different patterns of innovation takes an inverted U-shaped form when patterns are ordered by increasing intensity of R&D/GDP (Figure 12.2) (Chapter 8).

The lessons to be learned from these results are that, contrary to general beliefs, the linkage between knowledge production and its exploitation for growth is not a direct one; moreover, R&D investments in knowledge-intense production areas should be reoriented towards new technological domains in order to avoid the decreasing returns that accompany R&D activities.

As a last important result, the elasticity of GDP to R&D proves to be much lower than that of GDP to human capital. Especially in the areas where a limited R&D activity is present, the elasticity of GDP to human capital is more than double that to R&D (Table 12.1). In normative terms, this suggests that investments in human capital in knowledge-devoid areas play an important role in boosting growth. This statement is reinforced by the results of the data envelope analysis

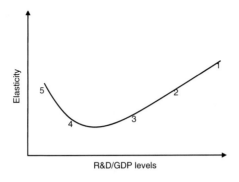

1 = European science-based area   4 = Smart and creative diversification
2 = Applied science area   area
3 = Smart technological application   5 = Imitative innovation area
     area

Figure 12.1 Elasticy of GDP to R&D for different levels of R&D / GDP intensity

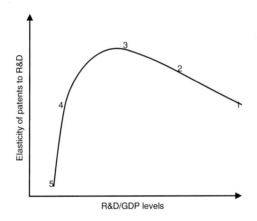

1 = European science-based area   4 = Smart and creative diversification
2 = Applied science area   area
                                              5 = Imitative innovation area
3 = Smart technological application
     area

Figure 12.2 Elasticity of knowledge to R&D by patterns of innovation

(DEA): a tentative comparison between regional efficiency in knowledge production – through knowledge inputs such as human capital and R&D – and efficiency
in the use of production inputs shows a much higher level of heterogeneity in the
former than in the latter. This result suggests that an efficient combination and use
of knowledge inputs is much more difficult to achieve than an efficient combination and use of production factors. Innovation policies should, inter alia, also be
oriented towards the reinforcement and the efficient combination of all factors that
generate knowledge production, rather than the reinforcement of single separate
factors (Chapter 8).

Table 12.1 GDP elasticity to R&D and human capital

Elasticities *Territorial patterns of innovation*	*Elasticity of GDP to R&D*[a]	*Elasticity of GDP to human capital*[b]
European science-based area	0.148	0.168
Applied science area	0.126	0.255
Smart technological application area	0.111	0.309
Smart and creative diversification area	0.115	0.303
Imitative innovation area	0.120	0.310

Source: a) Chapter 8 in this book; b) ESPON KIT (2012).

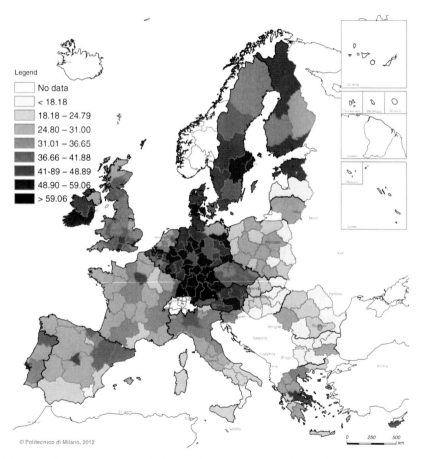

Legend
- No data
- < 18.18
- 18.18 – 24.79
- 24.80 – 31.00
- 31.01 – 36.65
- 36.66 – 41.88
- 41-89 – 48.89
- 48.90 – 59.06
- > 59.06

© Politecnico di Milano. 2012

0   250   500 km

Map 12.1 Shares of firms introducing product and/or process innovation

d) The linkage between innovation and R&D investments

The policy recommendations of the Agenda 2020 make explicit the general belief that knowledge produced through R&D investments leads to innovation and to efficiency gains. Whilst this is true at an aggregated geographical level, at regional

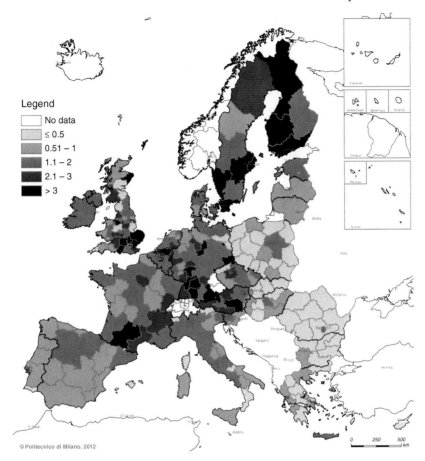

Map 12.2 R&D expenditures on GDP (2006–2007)

level the invention–innovation short circuit is not valid. The evidence for this statement is forthcoming from different parts of the empirical analysis contained in this book. Brief comparison between the map of the spatial distribution of R&D investments/GDP (Map 12.1) and that of the share of product and/or process innovation shows that the former indicator is much more concentrated than the latter (Map 12.2).

Moreover, if one inspects the innovative performances of different types of knowledge-based region, a similarity emerges between scientific regions, defined as those with an above-average endowment of knowledge production factors, and other types of regions, like networking regions (Table 12.2 and Chapter 5). External knowledge therefore plays an important role in the innovative activity of firms, compensating for their limited capacity to produce internal knowledge and counterbalancing the diseconomies of scale linked to internal knowledge production. In line with most conceptual approaches on innovation and regional growth, external knowledge makes it possible to overcome the 'entropy death' to which areas with no cross-regional scientific cooperation are subject (Figure 12.3 and Chapter 9). However, in this case, too, our empirical findings warn against the overly hasty generalization that external knowledge may automatically substitute for a lack of internal knowledge production. The empirical evidence suggests that

Table 12.2 Share of innovative firms by type of regions

Type of regions	Share of innovative firms	Share of firms developing product innovation	Share of firms developing process innovation	Share of firms developing product and/or process innovation	Share of firms developing marketing and/or organizational innovation
Technologically advanced regions only	14.05		11.49	35.03	24.68
Scientific regions only	13.55		11.85	37.26	23.88
Knowledge networking regions only	12.35		11.32	39.59	29.73
Technologically advanced regions and scientific regions	14.45		10.89	44.79	27.28
Non-knowledge intensive regions	6.68		10.62	29.35	21.55

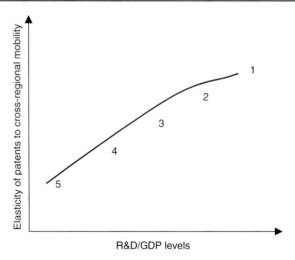

1 = European science-based area
2 = Applied science area
3 = Smart technological application area
4 = Smart and creative diversification area
5 = Imitative innovation area

Figure 12.3 Elasticity of patents to cross-regional mobility of inventors by patterns of innovation

a form of 'absorptive capacity' à la Cohen and Levintal (Cohen and Levintal, 1990) is required for it to be possible to exploit external knowledge (Chapter 9).

Contrary to general belief, local knowledge intensity does not necessarily guarantee higher innovation performance. The latter is also associated with the exploitation of external knowledge.

e) The linkage between knowledge, innovation and smart growth

The ultimate goal of the Agenda 2020 is to achieve a smart growth which boosts regional economic performances through innovation. However, similarly to R&D, innovation appears to have scale advantages of some sort and to require a certain critical mass to express its full potential. The analysis of the elasticity of GDP to innovation produces interesting results. Economic growth in *Imitative innovation* regions does not seem to respond to innovation (nor to knowledge); it seems likely that these regions have not yet reached a critical mass of knowledge and innovation so that they can turn their benefits into a higher growth rate. An interesting result is that the *Applied science* regions show an elasticity to innovation similar to that of *European science-based* regions, even though the average R&D and innovation intensities of this latter cluster are almost 40% greater than those of the former (Table 12.3 and Chapter 10).

If total factor productivity is analysed as a proxy for economic performance, Figure 12.4 contains some important results. The spatial distribution of total factor productivity (TFP) values across territorial patterns of innovation is similar to the distribution of innovative firms, and instead differs substantially from the spatial distribution of R&D over GDP. R&D-intensive patterns of innovation do not register relatively higher TFP values with respect to R&D-devoid patterns.

All these results suggest that the growth benefits deriving from innovation do not necessarily match the strength of the formal local knowledge base, and that regions innovating in the absence of a strong local knowledge base can be as successful as more knowledge-intensive regions in turning innovation into a higher growth rate.

Table 12.3 Indicators of R&D and innovation intensity, elasticity of GDP to knowledge and innovation in the European science-based area with reference to the other patterns of innovation

Values of the European science-based area with respect to:	Relative R&D on GDP	Relative share of innovative firms	Relative elasticity of GDP growth to R&D	Relative elasticity of GDP growth to innovation
Imitative innovation area	6.19	3.48	Not significant	Not significant
Smart and creative diversification area	2.65	2.28	3	2.63
Smart technological application area	1.49	1.64	1	1
Applied science area	1.39	1.35	1	1

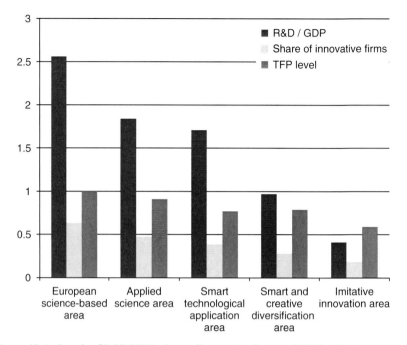

Figure 12.4   Levels of R&D/GDP, share of innovative firms and TFP levels by patterns of
innovation

12.2.2. Unconventional policy warnings

The empirical evidence presented in the previous subsection highlights the need
to supersede some general beliefs concerning the logics and economics of innovation if sound policy recommendations are to be devised. From this evidence
ensue some unconventional policy warnings in regard to excessive expectations
concerning the role of knowledge and innovation as drivers of growth. When a
regional approach is adopted, the following policy messages emerge:

- a knowledge economy is not everywhere a driver of growth opportunities;
- R&D expenditure is not everywhere the most effective policy tool for the
  development of new knowledge;
- formal knowledge is not the main and most strategic knowledge asset on
  which a knowledge economy relies in all regions;
- external knowledge is not a substitute for the lack of internal knowledge;
  rather it is relevant everywhere;
- innovation is not necessarily linked to internal formal knowledge production.

The variety of innovation patterns demonstrates that European innovation policies must move away from a thematically/regionally neutral and generic strategy
and instead look for selective and regionally appropriate strategies. If innovation

policies are to support modernization in *all* European regions, they must comply with the specificities and potentials of individual regions, avoiding the opposite risks of a dispersion of public resources in undifferentiated ways, on the one hand, and of a concentration of all resources in a few regions where traditional R&D policy is apparently bound to yield the highest returns, leaving other regions unsupported, on the other.

However, the suggestion of the most recent proposal of the smart specialization strategy to develop specific innovation policies for each region (EC, 2012) does not look fully consistent: specificities of single regions are fundamental for the implementation of projects, but the definition of strategies calls for the identification of common approaches for similar types of regions defining innovation pathways with the highest success probability and preventing unlikely local policies. For this reason, a sound territorial taxonomy, as the one proposed in this book, could allow to design achievable regional innovation paths and to pursue a rational use of public resources.

12.3. The smart specialization debate: Embeddedness and connectedness

The smart specialization strategy (RIS3) was developed in order to find an explanation – and a consequent rational strategy – for the wide R&D gap between Europe and some key trading partners. The most straightforward reason for the knowledge gap was posited as the smaller share of the European economy consisting of high-tech, R&D intensive sectors. A second reason cited for the gap was the spatial dispersion of the limited R&D efforts: this generated insufficient critical mass and investment duplications, inefficient resource allocation, and consequent weak learning processes (Pontikakis et al., 2009).

On the basis of this diagnosis, a rational and concrete proposal was put forward by the 'Knowledge for Growth' expert group. It advocates differentiated policies for 'core' and 'periphery' regions, the former able to host laboratories and research activities on general purpose technologies (GPTs), the latter oriented towards the identification of their 'knowledge domain' in which to specialize and towards cooperation with external R&D providers ('co-application of innovation') (Foray et al., 2009; Foray, 2009; Giannitsis, 2009).

The advantages of such a strategy are strongly underlined in the smart specialization debate, namely:

- the possibility to achieve at the same time a 'polarization' and a 'distribution' of research activities in space. GPT research activities would achieve the critical mass of financial and human resources necessary to their efficient development, reinforcing the idea of a European Research Area (ERA) (EC, 2000); peripheral areas would not be penalized, taking advantage of financial resources to support the application of technological advances to their specific specialization fields;
- the achievement of a more productive use of the potentials of each region – defined in terms of traditional competence and skills, tacit knowledge and

specific innovation processes – that would be reinforced by investments in human capital and research able to match each region's innovation profile;
- the development of cumulative learning in advanced R&D activities and the consequent exploitation of increases in R&D productivity;
- the creation of synergic effects between GPT and co-applications, thus increasing the size of GPT markets and the returns on R&D investment, enlarging at the same time the potential for technological adoption, adaptation and diffusion.

An important caveat is stressed concerning the achievements of the above-mentioned advantages: the RIS3 approach makes the strong assumption that an area is able to discover new specialization fields inside its 'knowledge domain', i.e. well-defined innovation niches on the basis of its present competences and human capital endowment, in which it can hope to excel in the future also thanks to synergetic policy support (Pontikakis et al., 2009). Some members of the group are explicit in this sense: 'the concept of smart specialization (. . .) assumes that there are criteria to judge which specializations, and consequently which policy targets, are smart' (Giannitsis, 2009, p.4). In other words, a consistent matching between investments in knowledge and human capital and the present territorial 'vocations' represents a difficult and crucial challenge, impinging on a creative and by no means mechanistic decision process.

On this particular aspect, the RIS3 argument is very clear: the search and discovery process around the traditional specialization has to be a bottom-up process, in which local entrepreneurs are identified as the leading actors, being the main knowledge and creativity keepers, interested in efficiently exploiting existing cognitive resources and driving their reorientation towards new innovative but related fields. For the same reasons, the smart specialization expert group warns against the use of a top-down approach for the identification of specialization, which could be disruptive for an otherwise efficient policy strategy.

Besides specialization and embeddedness in the local knowledge domain, the RIS3 calls for particular attention to the connectedness among different geographical areas and knowledge domains; cooperation linkages represent the main potential for learning, either through the integration of different knowledge bases, a general purpose and an applied one, or through best practice of innovation application.

The main policy message of the smart specialization argument is the inappropriateness of the 'one-size-fits-all' policy which could be derived from a fast and superficial reading of the Lisbon 2000 and Europe 2020 agendas. When a regional perspective is adopted, in fact, an aggregate policy goal of 3% of the EU GDP to be invested in R&D/innovation shows its fragility in supporting the increase of the innovation capacity of each region; on the other hand, different evolutionary specializations based on specific local competences and vocations call for differentiated and region-specific innovation policy targets (Pontikakis et al., 2009).

What is acceptable and what is not in the smart specialization argument from a regional science and regional policy perspective? In answering to this question, one has to keep in mind that the RIS3 discourse was born in a sectoral, national and industrial policy context, nurtured mainly by industrial economics specialists, and that only very recently their argument was assumed into a regional policy context.

The main ideas behind the strategy – namely specialization, embeddedness and connectedness – are for sure fully acceptable and welcome. As the main literature in the field of regional innovation suggests – from the *milieu innovateur* theory to the regional innovation system approach and the learning region (Camagni, 1991; Lundvall and Johnson, 1994; Tödtling and Trippl, 2005) – the way in which regions evolve and innovate is deeply rooted into slow localized learning processes, fed with information, interaction, long-term production trajectories, appropriate investments in research and education. Like all learning processes, they are inherently localized and cumulative, as they embed in human capital, interpersonal networks, specialized and skilled labour markets, local governance systems; therefore they are highly selective in spatial terms and require ad hoc local policy interventions to be adequately supported (Camagni, 2001; Quévit and Van Doren, 1997; Camagni and Maillat, 1995). Thanks to the smart specialization approach, the inadequacy of a 'one-size-fits-all' policy for innovation at regional level is decisively transferred from the scientific literature into the institutional debate.

The need for connectedness is also stringent in modern times and widely acknowledged: since knowledge has an ever more complex nature, cooperation and networking with selected external competence sources is necessary for the attainment of complementary pieces of knowledge, avoiding lock-in with respect to local historical specializations (Camagni, 1991).

Also the RIS3 proposition concerning the nature of the search and discovery process about the appropriate differentiation and upgrading strategy of local specialization fields looks particularly interesting, as it touches two relevant theoretical points:

- the collective nature of the learning processes inside those special places, characterized by intense local synergies and interpersonal interactions that are the industrial districts/milieus and the cities, where the learning process embeds into the dense fabric of SMEs and into the local labour market (Camagni, 1991; Capello, 1999; Keeble and Wilkinson, 1999; Camagni and Capello, 2002);
- the similar role played by the local milieu – fostering co-operation, collective action, incremental innovative solutions to technological and market problems, fast diffusion of innovation inside the local territory – with respect to the role of von Hayek's market as 'social spontaneous order' and 'discovery process' (von Hayek, 1978): local knowledge and strategic capability is inherently dispersed in a host of local actors whose decisions and entrepreneurial creativity have to be coordinated in a self-organized way and eventually supported by pro-active and smart policies.

The remarks made by the RIS3 literature about the necessity of achieving a critical mass for R&D spending are more than convincing. Polarization of research activity in space is not only necessary to provide sufficient support in restricted budget conditions, but it is requested if investment in research has to be efficient, since not all regional contexts are able to take advantage from R&D or human capital investments. Areas in which a very limited amount of knowledge and endogenous innovative activities are present do not receive any advantage from additional, but limited, R&D spending (Chapter 8). On the other side, dispersion of knowledge also in remote places following the principle of providing 'inclusive and smart growth' to all Europe is a political necessity, as well as a forward-looking economic strategy.

For all these reasons, the smart specialization approach looks highly valuable, appropriate and a good starting point for further reflections. However, as rightly pointed out (McCann and Ortega-Argilés, 2011), the translation of a sector policy, like innovation policy, to a regional setting is not a simple task, and this is where additional efforts can be made.

12.4. The need for a territorial approach to innovation policies

While the general philosophy behind the smart specialization argument is widely acceptable, its direct application in regional development policies is questionable. Its pure sectoral logic; its concentration on R&D as the only source of knowledge and innovation; and its dichotomous perception of regional innovation processes and patterns are all aspects that have to be overcome or improved in a theoretical, empirical and normative sense.

When utilized in a regional context, the sectoral logic presents two main limits. The first refers to the idea that formal knowledge is the only source of innovation. Instead, different sources of knowledge exist in local economies, with similar importance, appropriateness and positive effects. They mainly concern informal knowledge creation and development, such as creativity, craft capability, practical skills – often embedded in long-standing competence and production tradition in a host of niche specializations – which have recently been labelled as synthetic and symbolic knowledge (Asheim et al., 2011). The second limit is that, starting from formal knowledge in order to identify the degree and capability of each region to innovate, the sectoral logic ignores the variability of regional paths towards innovation itself, on which innovation policies should carefully focus.

Regional innovation paths strongly depend on territorial elements, rooted in the local society, its history, its culture, its typical learning processes. In fact:

A)   knowledge creation is the result of the presence of a combination of material and non-material elements, formal and informal sources. The material elements, like presence of universities and research centres, are for sure important assets, but what makes the difference in knowledge creation are, increasingly, intangible aspects linked to creativity, culture, taste, that represent for local communities a fertile ground for the development of specialized and skilled labour markets, qualified human capital, continuous learning processes, and local interpersonal cooperation networks;

B) if the distinction between factors enhancing development of new knowledge and those stimulating innovation holds at the national level, it is even more stringent at the local level where specificities in learning processes, quality of human capital, and knowledge externalities are present in different intensity. It is certainly true that basic knowledge is created in some regions where most inventions take place; however, there are also regions developing inventions and product innovations in their specialization fields, either using off-the-shelf GPTs developed elsewhere, or acquiring some crucial knowledge from out-side (patents, scientific or technological skills), or establishing inter-regional co-operation networks (as in the RIS3 model of co-invention of applications). Last but not least, there are imitative regions which have limited capability of adaptation on already existing innovations, but which are able to find their position on markets even without any kind of knowledge;

C) the existence and importance of knowledge spillovers has been widely acknowledged for some decades (Jaffe et al., 1993; Acs et al., 1994). But this reminds us about the importance of proximity and spatial conditions in the dialectic between knowledge creation and knowledge receptivity. Over time, proximity has been interpreted less in terms of geographical space and increasingly in terms of cognitive and social space, deriving from similarities/differences in stocks of social and relational capital among regions (Basile et al., 2012). The capacity of an economic system to gain advantage from knowledge created elsewhere is again dependent on its culture, creativity and openness to external stimuli; in a word, on its 'cognitive and social space' (Boschma, 2005; Capello, 2009b). Different regions develop different 'cognitive and social spaces' and this explains the degree of their virtual connection, their receptivity and, consequently, the potential knowledge spillovers they may benefit from;

D) economic growth is not necessarily linked with cognitive or technological catching-up. The strong economic performance of new member countries up to 2008 is certainly not related to growth of the knowledge economy, as these countries (and their regions) have witnessed a weak performance in scientific indicators, both of input (R&D) and of output (patenting activity) (Chapters 8 and 10). Of course, if some forms of technological or knowledge advancement had taken place, economic growth in these countries could have been more robust or continuous. But these advancements should not have taken the form of a traditional, generic investment in R&D, but rather the form of knowledge spillover generation from large multinational plants into the local fabric of small and medium enterprises, supported by public / private bargaining and agreements (the equivalent of the old-established practice of agreements on 'local content') and creatively utilized by local potential entrepreneurs;

E) what is really meant by referring to the importance of local territories is the fact that, while some important production factors like financial capital, general information, consolidated technologies and codified knowledge are today readily available virtually everywhere, the ability to organize these factors into continuously innovative production processes and products is by no means pervasive and generalized, but instead exists selectively only in some places where tacit knowledge is continuously created, exchanged and utilized, and business ideas find their way to real markets (Camagni and Capello, 2009).

For all these reasons, the translation of a sectoral policy – like innovation policy was intended to be, traditionally – into a regional spatial setting is not an easy task, and calls for a *territorial approach*, considering all the specificities of the single regions. The preconditions for knowledge creation, for turning knowledge into innovation, and for turning innovation into growth are all embedded in the territorial culture of each region. This means that each region follows its own path in performing the different abstract phases of the innovation process, depending on the context conditions: its own 'pattern of innovation', in our terminology.

On the other hand, following the RIS3 model, a dichotomous regional taxonomy emerges. In fact, the way in which the model suggests targeting regions with different innovation policies leads to a simplified partitioning of the European research territory into a core and a periphery. But the ways in which knowledge may be created, acquired, utilized and transformed into innovation are far more complex when regional conditions are taken in full consideration, as theoretically conceptualized in this book (Chapter 6).

The identification of a taxonomy able to capture the regional conditions behind regional innovation modes is not a simple exercise (Chapter 7). The more diffused taxonomies are substantially rooted in local formal knowledge as the main driver of innovation; even approaches coming from a regional science milieu do not really accept the conceptual possibility of differentiation in regional innovation patterns. The regional innovation system approach (Trippl, 2010) claims that any regional innovation system is constituted by two subsystems: a subsystem of knowledge generation and diffusion (knowledge infrastructure dimension) and a subsystem of knowledge application and exploitation (business dimension), made up of the companies located in the region. It identifies local success conditions in the intense interactions and circulation of knowledge, human capital and resources within and between these subsystems, for any type of regions. We see here a contradiction: even if regional specificities are considered, as embedded in the two subsystems, at the same time any regional innovation system is supposed to need both subsystems, despite the variability in local capabilities, knowledge sources, knowledge intensity and typology of innovation. Our claim is that in some cases a subsystem of knowledge generation may be present, in some others not, and knowledge could be acquired from outside; for regions belonging to this latter case, the suggestion of developing and reinforcing the knowledge subsystem (Tödtling and Trippl, 2005) looks somehow misplaced and it is probably not what their innovation mode requires.[1]

New thematically and/or regionally focused innovation policies require the identification of context specificities in the knowledge-to-innovation process, much as a 'place-based' approach is postulated for a renewed EU regional development policy (Barca, 2009). To achieve such a goal, a theoretically and empirically sound regional innovation taxonomy is required, to be tested on the European space.

12.5. Towards 'smart innovation policies'

The five – conceptually differentiated – innovation patterns detected in this book may pave the way towards a renewed, spatially sound inclusion of the smart specialization strategy in R&D policies into an appropriate regional innovation policy framework, along similar lines of the Reform of the EU Regional Development Funds, explicitly intended as a 'key means of turning the priorities of the Innovation Union Flagship Initiative into practical action on the ground' (EC, 2010b, p. 2). The logical pathway towards 'smart innovation' policies is drawn in Figure 12.5.

'Smart innovation' policies may be defined as those policies able to increase the innovation capability of an area by boosting effectiveness of accumulated knowledge, fostering new applications and diversification, enlarging and deepening the local knowledge base, starting from local specificities and the established innovation patterns in each region.

The two key concepts of 'embeddedness' and 'connectedness' – put forward in the recent smart specialization debate – are a useful starting point. However, smart innovation policies adapt the two concepts to the specificities of each pattern of innovation, and look for ad hoc interventions, appropriate for each single territorial innovation pattern, with the aim to reinforce the virtuous aspects that characterize each pattern, and increase each pattern's efficiency (Table 12.4).

This general policy strategy should not be open to doubts or criticisms concerning the possible risk of locking regions into their traditional specialization, jeopardizing their specific resilience in a fast-changing economic environment.[2] In fact, the smart innovation strategy assumes, in its application to each regional innovation pattern, an evolutionary attitude, targeting, suggesting and supporting local learning processes towards the detection of new needs, new creative applications and diversification of established technologies, new forms of blending knowledge advancements and local specialization, the discovery, and possibly the orientation, of future technological trends. Even 'jumps' over a different innovation pattern might be foreseen in some regional cases, even if, given the responsibility in the management of public money, policy makers should better stick

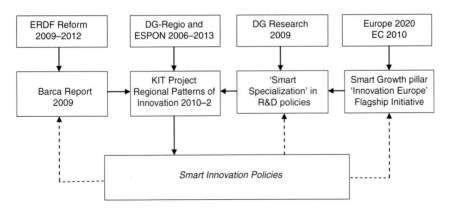

Figure 12.5 Logical pathway and contributions to Smart Innovation Policies

Table 12.4 Smart innovation policies by territorial innovation patterns

Policy aspects	Territorial patterns of innovation				
	European science-based area (Pattern 1)	Applied science area (Pattern 2)	Smart technological application area (Pattern 3)	Smart and creative diversification area (Pattern 4)	Imitative innovation area (Pattern 5)
Policy goals	Maximum return to R&D investments		Maximum return to applications and co-operation in applications		Maximum return to imitation
Policy actions for local knowledge generation	Support to R&D in:		Support to creative application, shifting capacity from old to new uses, improving productivity in existing uses, through:		Fast diffusion of existing innovation
(Embeddedness)					Enhancing receptivity of existing innovation
	new basic fields	specialized technological fields	incentives to technological development and upgrading	identification of international best practices	Support to local firms for complementary projects with MNCs
	general purpose technologies	variety in applications	variety creation	support to search in product/market diversification	Support to local firms for specialized subcontracting
				support to entrepreneurial creativity	
Policy actions for exploitation of knowledge spillovers	Incentives to inventors attraction and mobility		Incentives for creative applications through:		Incentives for MNCs attraction
	Support of research cooperation in:				
(Connectedness)	GPT and trans-territorial projects (ERA)	specific technologies and trans-territorial projects (ERA), in related sectors/domains	co-operative research activities among related sectors	participation of local actors to specialized international fairs	bargaining on innovative 'local content' procurement by MNCs

Policy style				
encouraging of labour mobility among related sectors/domains	Reach a critical mass in R&D activities through concentration of public support; Priority to triangular projects by Universities-Research Centres-Enterprises; Peer assessment of R&D programmes; Support to knowledge and technological transfer mechanisms to related sectors; Thematical/regional orientation of R&D funding: in GPTs; in specific fields of research and technological specialization of the area	co-operative search for new technological solutions; attraction of "star" researchers even for short periods; work experience in best practice knowledge creation firms of the same domains	Ex-ante careful assessment of innovation and differentiation strategies and projects; Continuity in public support, subject to in-itinere and ex-post assessment of outcomes; Support to bottom-up identification of industrial vocations, by raising awareness on local capabilities and potentials ('strategic industrial planning'); Thematical/regional orientation of innovation funding, in order to: strengthen present formal and tacit knowledge through co-operation with strong external partners in the specialization sectors; enhance local technological receptivity, creativity and product differentiation capability in specializ. sectors	Favour local spill-overs of managerial and technological knowledge from MNCs; Support to co-operation projects between MNCs and local firms; Support to technological transfer and diffusion
Beneficiaries				
Local firms	University, research centers, large local firms	Local firms	Local entrepreneurs	Local firms

Source: Camagni and Capello, 2013

to strengthening the upgrading and diversification processes inside each single innovation pattern – the least risky process, and the most likely successful one.

Regional innovation policies for each pattern should differ first of all in terms of policy goals.

A) The maximum return to R&D investments is the right policy goal for regions belonging to the European science-based and the Applied science patterns, characterized by a sufficient critical mass of R&D endowment already present in the area. Regions belonging to these two innovation patterns can in fact exploit the indivisibilities associated with research activity and take advantage from additional R&D funding coming from joint and integrated efforts of regional, national and EU bodies. Given their different research specialization, the two patterns can reinforce their efficiency when innovation policies take into full consideration the regional research specificities: in the European science-based area the maximum return on R&D spending is obtained through policy actions devoted to R&D spending in GPTs, and a strong specialization is fundamental to achieving a critical mass of research. On the other hand, applied scientific fields of research should absorb much of the R&D funds in the Applied science area, diversifying efforts in related sectors of specialization, i.e. in diversified sectors within the same knowledge domain in which the region excels.

B) Support to basic research is not the most natural policy goal for the Smart technological application and the Smart and creative diversification patterns. In these areas the relatively low R&D endowment does not guarantee the presence of a critical mass of R&D in order to exploit economies of scale in knowledge production: returns to R&D of such kinds of policy are modest, as shown in some empirical analyses (Chapter 8). Innovation policy aims in these patterns can be found in the maximum return to new applications and to inter-regional cooperation in applications, deeply linked to the ability of regions to change rapidly in response to external stimuli (such as the emergence of a new technology) and to realize creative search processes concerning product and market diversification. To achieve such a goal, support to creative application, shifting capacity from old to new uses, and improving productivity in existing uses are the right policy tools for maximizing the return to co-inventing application. In a word: support to 'D', and to cooperative 'D' rather than to 'R'. In the first case (Pattern 3) policy actions for the achievement of such goals can take into account incentives to technological projects that foresee new and creative use of existing scientific knowledge; in the second case (Pattern 4), support and incentives to search in products/markets diversification and to entrepreneurial creativity look more appropriate.

C) Finally, in the Imitative innovation area attention has to be devoted to the achievement of the maximum return to imitation, through fast diffusion of already existing innovation, strengthening of local receptivity to innovation (or reducing social/psychological or institutional barriers to change) and supporting favourable negotiations between local firms and multinational corporations (MNCs) on complementary projects and innovative, specialized subcontracting.

Beyond the previous policy recommendations aiming at fostering the creation of local knowledge, policy interventions should also aim at knowledge acquisition from outside the region, what has been called 'connectedness'. As for the case of embeddedness, also in this case implementation varies according to the specificities of the different patterns of innovation.

A) In the first two patterns, the appropriate policy tools to attract external knowledge are incentives to inventors' attraction and mobility, and support to research cooperation: in GPT and trans-territorial projects in the European science-based area, and in related sectors belonging to specific fields of technological specialization in the Applied science area. This suggestion is in line with the creation of the ERA put forward by the European Commission, an area composed of all research and development activities, programmes and policies in Europe which involve a transnational perspective. The Applied science area could also be favoured by the encouragement of regional and inter-regional labour mobility between related sectors, which makes skills and experience move around and blend with each other across sectors and regions.

B) Policy tools for knowledge acquisition in the third and fourth patterns are incentives for creative applications. For such a purpose, cooperative research activities in related sectors in those regions where a little applied science base exists are an efficient policy tool for the Smart technological application area. On the one hand, participation of local actors in specialized international fairs, the attraction of 'star' researchers even for short periods of time, or support for work experiences in best-practice knowledge-creation firms in related sectors are the right incentives to stimulate innovation in the Smart and creative diversification area whose innovation capacity lies in the brightness of local entrepreneurs to find outside their area the right applied science in which to innovate and move towards a specialized diversification in related sectors.

C) The traditional incentives to attract MNCs remain the most efficient tool to attract new knowledge in areas with very limited – formal or informal, scientific or technical – knowledge. Traditional bargaining on 'local content' in MNCs' procurement could also be used, with enhanced attention to cooperation in specialized subcontracting.

The policies suggested require renewed styles in their design-to-delivery phases in order to enhance efficiency and effectiveness (Camagni, 2008; Camagni and Capello, 2011). As in more general regional development policies, strong attention should be devoted to the following elements:

•   transparency, which means clear justification of the spatial allocation of funds in the different measures, from spatial concentration in some cases (reaching a critical mass in R&D, particularly in Patterns 1 and 2) to spatial pervasiveness in others (tapping local creativity, diversification and adoption capabilities: Patterns 3 to 5);

- control on local strategies followed, in order to avoid rent-seeking attitudes by local élites (in politics, in the economy, but also in the higher education and research fields). This means favouring active cooperation among the main local actors: universities, research centres and firms. The internal strategies of the single actors in the research and innovation fields, though perfectly possible, may not be the best ones for the entire regional community, or the most appropriate in terms of risk assumption by the public sphere; therefore, programmes and projects presented jointly by all three main actors should be solicited and given high priority (especially in Patterns 1 and 2);
- peer ex-ante assessment of main R&D and innovation projects presented to public support;
- knowledge transfer, knowledge diffusion through inter-sectoral and inter-regional co-operation and general knowledge dissemination should be favoured, in order to boost productivity of the publicly supported R&D;
- favour continuity over time in public support decisions – a crucial precondition for local learning processes – at the condition of fair and effective intermediate and ex-post assessment of outcomes;
- build a formalized, but flexible, organizational model for supporting the identification of regional specializations, in R&D and production, and for strengthening the search process of new thematic application fields and diversification areas, inside and outside the present technological and production domains: a local, participatory model that could be labelled as 'strategic industrial planning';
- favour creativity and entrepreneurial spirit in all regional conditions. This means, on the one hand, detecting and supporting present local skills, traditions, social values, positive attitudes towards the environment and local culture and cultural diversity (especially in Patterns 3 and 4); on the other hand, to create an innovation-friendly business environment, reduce barriers or resistance to change, enhance receptivity to external stimuli and opportunities, and discover new local potentials through the engagement of insufficiently utilized local resources (in Patterns 3 and 4 and especially 5);
- favour the strengthening of local spillovers from large firms and MNCs present in the different regional contexts, in the field not just of technical knowledge and research potential but also in the field of production organization and managerial styles and practices, mainly through local subcontracting and cooperation with local firms.

New keywords, complementing embeddedness and connectedness, should be: *justification* of the spatial allocation of funds, *tripartite cooperation* (universities, research centres, firms), *peer assessment* of R&D programmes and projects, *continuity* in public support subject to in-itinere control, tapping *creativity and entrepreneurial spirit*, informal but also lightly structured *local search* processes.

The 'patterns of innovation' taxonomy previously identified supplies precise rationale and potential operationality to the above-mentioned policy goals, actions and styles, assigning differentiated priorities to each regional condition in the knowledge-to-innovation process.

Beneficiaries of these policy recommendations differ among patterns. University, research centres and large R&D laboratories of private firms are the natural beneficiaries in Patterns 1 and 2 – the European science-based area and of the Applied science area. Local firms are the natural recipients in Pattern 3, namely the Smart technological application area; entrepreneurs and small firms are the natural recipients of policies in the Smart and creative diversification area (Pattern 4) and the Imitative innovation area.

The previous policy suggestions are meant to increase the efficiency and effectiveness of innovation processes inside each single pattern. However, within each pattern, regions exist that are more advanced than others, and that could potentially move to a different pattern. For these regions, 'evolutionary policies' can be foreseen, devoted to the achievement of an upgrading of innovation processes.

Figure 12.6 shows the relative position of each pattern in terms of the elasticity of GDP to R&D, as measured in Chapter 8. First of all, it shows how R&D activities require a certain critical mass in order to become effective; and this evidence supports the general suggestion concerning the necessary spatial concentration of R&D support, in the direction of an already endowed area. Secondly, Figure 12.6 represents the potential dynamic trajectories that the most efficient regions belonging to each pattern could follow in order to achieve superior efficiency rates – and the associated policies supporting these trajectories.

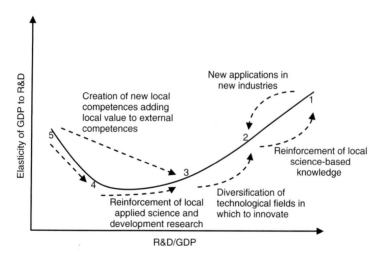

1 = European science-based area   4 = Smart and creative diversification area
2 = Applied science area   5 = Imitative innovation area
3 = Smart technological application area

Figure 12.6 Evolutionary trajectories and policies by patterns of innovation

The most efficient regions in the Imitative innovation area (Pattern 5) could jump either into a Smart and creative diversification area (Pattern 4) or a Smart technological application area (Pattern 3) through the creation of new local competence and entrepreneurial spirit, adding local value to external knowledge. The case study on the automotive industry in Bratislava, developed inside the empirical analysis (ESPON KIT, 2012) is a telling example in this respect: following the creation of local suppliers with specific competences, the main local innovation processes moved away from an imitative pattern, building on the knowledge that local subsidiaries and subcontractors had accumulated through strong interaction with the parent company. The innovation pattern in this area is increasingly approaching a Smart technological application pattern (Pattern 3).

The most efficient regions in Pattern 4 could be supported in order to move towards Pattern 3 (Smart technological application) through the reinforcement of local applied science and development research.

The European science-based area (Pattern 1) could be stimulated to avoid some evidence on decreasing returns of R&D activities in terms of knowledge creation[3], by diversifying research into new application fields in new industries, merging aspects of the Applied science area (Pattern 2). On the other hand, some regions belonging to the latter area could strengthen their science base in GPT fields, if already present with some critical mass, moving towards the first Pattern, namely European science-based.

Finally, efficient regions belonging to the Smart technological application area (Pattern 3) could overcome the low returns of R&D activities, limited to some tiny specialization sectors, by diversifying the technological fields in which to invest and innovate, acquiring some characteristics of Pattern 2.

Engagement in these kinds of 'evolutionary' strategies and policies should be carefully assessed and controlled, in order to avoid misallocation of public resources, backing impossible local dreams. In fact, this possible engagement requires: a) the identification of the most efficient regions within each pattern; b) the presence of some context precondition typical of the targeted pattern, and in particular of a sufficient critical mass in existing activities (R&D, technological knowledge, production know-how, managerial competences); c) the presence of reliable (new) local actors, capable of managing new crucial functions; and d) the presentation of credible and well-assessed research and innovation projects. Only in these conditions would evolutionary policies find a fertile ground on which to produce virtuous effects.

If it is true that in some – textbook – cases innovation is the result of unforeseeable events, of totally unexpected creative 'jumps' and the breaking up of existing technological trajectories, it is also important to remember the systemic, complex and incremental character of the bulk of innovation processes, based on necessary slow, smooth and 'localized' learning processes. Therefore, it is rational to claim that regional innovation policies, managing public funds, should mainly stick to clearly defined innovation trajectories, based on existing context conditions and capabilities, presenting reasonable risks and the highest expected returns for the entire regional economy.

12.6. Conclusions

The results of the empirical work carried out in this book, together with the present debate on regional policy design to fit the Europe 2020 Agenda, call for additional reflections on the way sectoral policies can be translated appropriately into a regional setting. In particular, policies addressed to the achievement of the smart growth goal have the evident problem of matching the sectoral dimension – knowledge excellence, R&D support, technological innovation – to the regional scale.

This book has presented the rationale for a regionalized conception, design and delivery of innovation policies. If these policies have to support modernization and innovation processes in *all* European regions, they have to diversify their approach in order, first, to comply with the specificities and potentials of the single regions, and secondly to avoid the opposite risks of dispersion of public resources in undifferentiated ways, or conversely to concentrate all resources in a few regions where the traditional policy action, namely R&D support, is due to grant the highest returns.

In order to build 'smart innovation policies', the present regional patterns of innovation have to be identified, resulting from the different modes of performing the different phases of the innovation process – knowledge production/acquisition, invention, innovation, growth – according to territorial specificities. In some cases, a policy of support to R&D can turn to be extremely useful, namely when a critical mass of research activities is already present, while it could produce no effect in regions where the path to innovation is not based on the development of an internal, formal knowledge base.

This book puts forward some new ideas on how to conceptualize regions in terms of their innovative capacity. All empirical evidence stresses the importance of a sound taxonomy of regional innovative capacity, and five patterns of innovation are conceptually and empirically defined in the case of European regions, going from cases in which the full 'linear' model of innovation – from R&D to innovation – is present, to cases in which external knowledge is applied with differentiated local creative contributions to innovation, to cases in which innovation is mainly the effect of imitative processes.

The general concepts of embeddedness and connectedness, put forward in the recent debate on smart specialization, are right policy principles also for 'smart innovation policies'. However, these latter policies call for the adaptation of the two principles to the specificities of each pattern of innovation, and call for ad hoc interventions with the aim of supporting, strengthening and diversifying the virtuous aspects of each regional innovation process.

Beyond the necessity to fully embed policy strategies into regional specificities through a bottom-up search process involving knowledge and project design capability of local actors, and to strengthen inter-regional cooperation in knowledge creation and transfer, new policy styles are requested by the new policy model. They refer to justification of the spatial allocation of funds and of differentiation of policy tools, tripartite cooperation between universities, research centres and firms in main R&D projects, peer assessment of R&D programmes and projects, continuity in public support subject to intermediate and ex-post assessment of outcomes, tapping creativity and entrepreneurial spirit, and definition of informal but also lightly structured local processes of 'strategic industrial planning'.

Innovation policies should mainly operate inside each innovation pattern, intended as the natural and more promising way of supporting regional innovation processes. But in some special cases, some regions could 'jump' over different and more advanced innovation patterns; 'evolutionary' policies could support these paths, with extreme attention and careful assessments, provided that context conditions and reliability of actors and strategies/projects could reduce risks of failure.

'Smart innovation policies', designed according to these principles and guidelines, could supply a conceptually and operationally sound answer to the need of renewed policy tools fit to attain the goals of smart growth and Innovation Union, consistent with the smart specialization strategy proposed by DG Research and the necessary place-based reform of the EU regional policy advocated by the Barca Report and the recent documents of DG Regio.

Notes

1 If we do not agree with the idea of developing R&D facilities with the same intensity everywhere, for the same reasons we do not agree that knowledge subsystems and the business subsystem have to be present everywhere with the same intensity.
2 A similar criticism was in fact addressed to the RIS3 strategy. See: Cooke, 2009.
3 There is significant econometric evidence of decreasing returns of knowledge creation (patenting) to investments in R&D in European regions: see ESPON KIT, 2012.

References

Abreu M., Grinevich V., Kitson M., Savona M. (2008), 'Absorptive capacity and regional patterns of innovation', *DIUS RR-08-11*

Acosta M., Coronado D., Leòn M. D., Martìnez M. A. (2009), 'Production of university technological knowledge in European regions: evidence from patent data', *Regional Studies* 43(9): 1167–1181

Acs Z. J., Anselin L., Varga A. (2002), 'Patents and innovation counts as measures of regional production of new knowledge', *Research Policy* 31(7): 1069–1085

Acs Z. J., Audretsch D. B., Braunerhjelm P., Carlsson B. (2004), 'The missing link: the knowledge filter and entrepreneurship in endogenous growth', CEPR Discussion Paper 4783

Acs Z. J., Audretsch D. B., Feldman M. P. (1994), 'R&D spillovers and recipient firm size', *Review of Economics and Statistics* 76(2): 363–367

Afifi A., Clarck V., May S. (2004), *Computer-aided multivariate analysis*, Chapman and Hall, Boca Raton, FL

Agrawal A., Cockburn I., McHale J. (2006), 'Gone but not forgotten: labour flows, knowledge spillovers, and enduring social capital', *Journal of Economic Geography* 6(5): 571–591

Agrawal A., Kapur D., McHale J. (2008), 'How do spatial and social proximity influence knowledge flows? Evidence from patent data', *Journal of Urban Economics* 64(2): 258–269

Agrawal A., Kapur D., McHale J., Oettl A. (2011), 'Brain drain or brain bank? The impact of skilled emigration on poor-country innovation', *Journal of Urban Economics* 69(1): 43–55

Allen T. J. (1977), *Managing the flow of technology: technology transfer and the dissemination of technological information within the R&D organization*, Cambridge, Massachusetts: MIT Press

Almeida P. and Kogut B. (1997), 'The exploration of technological diversity and the geographic localization of innovation, *Small Business Economics* 9(1): 21–31

Almeida P. and Kogut B. (1999) 'Localisation of knowledge and the mobility of engineers in regional networks', *Management Science* 45(7): 905–917

Altenburg T. (2009), 'Building inclusive innovation systems in developing countries: challenges for IS research', in Lundvall B. A., Vang J., Joseph K. J., Chaminade C. (Eds) *Handbook of innovation systems in developing countries*, Cheltenham: Edward Elgar, 35–56

Anselin L. (1988), *Spatial econometrics: methods and models*, London: Kluwer

Anselin L., Acs Z. J., Varga A. (1997), 'Local geographic spillovers between university research and high technology innovations', *Journal of Urban Economics* 42(3): 422–48

Anselin L., Varga A., Acs Z. (2000), 'Geographic and sectoral characteristics of academic knowledge externalities', *Papers in Regional Science* 79(4): 435–443

Antonelli C. (1989), 'A failure inducement model of research and development expenditure: Italian evidence from the early 1980s', *Journal of Economic Behaviour and Organization* 12(2): 159–180

Antonelli C. (2008), *Localised technological change. Towards the economics of complexity*, London and New York: Routledge

Archibugi D. and Iammarino S. (2002), 'The globalization of technological innovation: definition and evidence', *Review of International Political Economy* 9(1): 98–122

Arrow K. J. (1962a), 'Economic welfare and the allocation of resources for invention', in Nelson R. R. (Ed.), *The rate and direction of inventive activity: economic and social factors*, Princeton, NJ: Princeton University Press for NBER, 609–625

Arrow K. J. (1962b), 'The economic implications of learning by doing', *Review of Economic Studies* 29(3): 155–173

Arthur W. B. (1989), 'Competing technologies, increasing returns, and lock-in by historical events', *Economic Journal* 99(394): 116–131

Arthur W. B. (1994), *Increasing returns and path dependence in the economy*, Ann Arbor: University of Michigan Press

Arundel A., Patel P., Sirilli G., Smith K. (1997), *The future of innovation measurement in Europe: concepts, problems and practical directions*, IDEA Paper N. 3, STEP Group Oslo

Asheim B. and Coenen L. (2005), 'Knowledge bases and regional innovation systems: comparing Nordic clusters', *Research Policy* 34(8): 1173–1190

Asheim B. and Gertler M. (Eds) (2005), *The geography of innovation: regional innovation systems*, Oxford: Oxford University Press

Asheim B. T. and Isaksen, A. (1997), 'Location, agglomeration and innovation: towards regional innovation systems in Norway?', *European Planning Studies* 5(3): 299–330

Asheim B., Boschma R., Cooke P. (2011), 'Constructing regional advantage: platform policies based on related variety and differentiated knowledge base', *Regional Studies*, 45(7): 893–904

Audretsch D. B. and Feldman M. P. (1996), 'R&D spillovers and the geography of innovation and production', *American Economic Review* 86 (3): 630–640

Audretsch D. B. and Feldman M. P. (2004), 'Knowledge spillovers and the geography of innovation', in Henderson V. and Thisse J. (Eds), *Handbook of urban and regional economics*, Amsterdam: Elsevier, 4: 2713–2739

Audretsch D. B. and Keilbach M. (2010), 'Entrepreneurship and growth', in Malerba F. (Ed.), *Knowledge-intensive entrepreneurship and innovation systems: evidence from Europe*, London: Routledge, 286–296

Audretsch D. B. and Lehmann E. E. (2005), 'Does the knowledge spillover theory of entrepreneurship hold for regions?', *Research Policy* 34(8): 1191–1202

Autant-Bernard C. and LeSage J. P. (2011), 'Quantifying knowledge spillovers using spatial econometric models', *Journal of Regional Science* 51(3): 471–496

Autant-Bernard C., Mairesse J., Massard N. (2009), 'Spatial knowledge diffusion through collaborative networks. Introduction', *Papers in Regional Science* 86(3), 341–50

Autant-Bernard C. and Massard N. (2009), 'Underlying mechanisms of knowledge diffusion', IAREG Working Paper 4.7

Aydalot P. (Ed) (1986), *Milieux innovateurs en Europe*, GREMI, Paris

Bahlmann M. D., Huysman M. H., Elfring T., Groenewegen P. (2008), 'Global pipelines or global buzz? A micro-level approach towards the knowledge-based view of clusters', VU University Amsterdam, Serie Research Memoranda 0002

Balconi M., Breschi S., Lissoni F. (2004), 'Networks of inventors and the role of academia: an exploration of Italian patent data', *Research Policy* 33(1), 127–45

Balconi M., Brusoni S., Orsenigo L. (2010), 'In defense of a linear model', *Research Policy* 39(1): 1–13

Banker P. C., Charnes A., Cooper W. W. (1984), 'Some models for estimating technical and scale inefficiencies in data envelopment analysis', *Management Science* 30(9): 1078–1092

Baptista R. and Swann P. (1998), 'Do firms in clusters innovate more?', *Research Policy* 27(5): 525–540

Barca F. (2009), *An agenda for the reformed cohesion policy*, Report to the Commissioner for Regional Policy, Brussels, April

Basile R., Capello R., Caragliu A. (2012), 'Technological interdependence and regional growth in Europe: proximity and synergy in knowledge spillovers', *Papers in Regional Science* 91(4): 697–722

Bathelt H., Malberg A., Maskell P. (2004), 'Clusters and knowledge: local buzz, global pipelines and the process of knowledge creation', *Progress in Human Geography* 28(1): 31–56

Beaudry C. and Schiffraeuova A. (2009), 'Who's right, Marshall or Jacobs? The localization vs urbanization debate', *Research Policy* 38(2): 318–337

Becattini G. (1979), 'Dal 'settore' industriale al 'distretto' industriale. Alcune considerazioni sull'unità d'indagine dell'economia industriale', *Rivista di Economia e Politica Industriale* 5(1): 7–21

Becattini G. (Ed.) (2004), *Industrial districts: a new approach to industrial change*, Cheltenham: Edward Elgar

Becker G. S. (1964), *Human capital*, Chicago: University of Chicago Press

Bellet M., Colletis G., Lung Y. (1993), 'Introduction au numéro spécial sur économie et proximité', *Revue d'Economie Régionale et Urbaine* 3: 357–361

Bengs C. and Schmidt-Thomé K. (Eds) (2005), 'Urban-rural relations in Europe: ESPON 1.1.2 Final Report', Helsinki (FI): Centre for Urban and Regional Studies, Helsinki University of Technology

Benhabib J. and Spiegel M. (1994), 'The role of human capital in economic development: evidence from aggregate cross-country data', *Journal of Monetary Economics* 34(2): 143–174

Bergman E. M. (2009), 'Embedding network analysis in spatial studies of innovation', *The Annals of Regional Science* 43(3): 559–65

Bergman E. M. and Maier G. (2009), 'Network central: regional positioning for innovative advantage', *The Annals of Regional Science* 43(3): 615–644

Bernstein J. I. and Nadiri M. I. (1988), 'R&D spillovers, the rates of return and production in high-tech industries', *American Economic Review* 78(2): 429–434

Bernstein J. I. and Nadiri M. I. (1989), 'Research and development and intraindustry spillovers: an empirical application of dynamic duality', *Review of Economic Studies* 56(2): 249–267

Bettencourt L., Lobo J., Helbing D., Kühnert C., West G. (2007a), 'Growth, innovation, scaling, and the pace of life in cities', *Proceedings of the National Academy of Sciences* 104(17): 7301–7306

Bettencourt L., Lobo J., Strumsky D. (2007b), 'Invention in the city: increasing returns to patenting as a scaling function of metropolitan', *Research Policy* 36(1), 107–120

Beugelsdijk S. and van Schaik T. (2005), 'Social capital and growth in European regions: an empirical test', *European Journal of Political Economy* 39(2): 301–324

Bode E. (2004), 'The spatial pattern of localized R&D spillovers: an empirical investigation for Germany', *Journal of Economic Geography* 4(1): 43–64

Bogliacino F. and Pianta M. (2010), 'Innovation and employment: a reinvestigation using revised Pavit classes', *Research Policy* 39(6): 799–809

Boschma R. (2005), 'Proximity and innovation: a critical assessment', *Regional Studies* 39(1): 61–74

Boschma R. and Frenken K. (2010), 'The spatial evolution of innovation networks. A proximity perspective', in Boschma R. and Martin R. (Eds), *The handbook of evolutionary economic geography*, Cheltenham: Edward Elgar, 120–135

Boschma R. and Iammarino S. (2009), 'Related variety, trade linkages and regional growth', *Economic Geography* 85(3): 289–311

Boschma R., Eriksson R., Lindgren U. (2009), 'How does labour mobility affect the performance of plants? The importance of relatedness and geographical proximity', *Journal of Economic Geography* 9(2): 169–190

Bottazzi L. and Peri G. (2003), 'Innovation and spillovers in regions: evidence from European patent data', *European Economic Review* 47(4): 687–710

Bound K. (2007), *India: the uneven innovator*, London: Demos

Braczyk H., Cooke. P., Heidenreich. M. (1998), *Regional innovation systems*, London: UCL Press

Breschi S. (2000), 'The geography of innovation: a cross-sector analysis', *Regional Studies*, 34(2): 213–229

Breschi S. and Catalini C. (2009), 'Tracing the linkages between science and technology: an exploratory analysis of the research networks among scientists and inventors', *Research Policy* 39(1): 14–26

Breschi S. and Lenzi C. (2011), 'Net-city. How co-invention networks shape the inventive productivity of US cities', paper presented at the 51st ERSA Conference, Barcelona

Breschi S. and Lissoni, F. (2001a), 'Knowledge spillovers and local innovation systems: a critical survey', *Industrial and Corporate Change* 10(4): 975–1005

Breschi S. and Lissoni, F. (2001b), 'Localised knowledge spillovers vs. innovative millieux: knowledge 'tacitness' reconsidered', *Papers in Regional Science* 80(3): 255–273

Breschi S. and Lissoni F. (2004), 'Knowledge networks from patent data: methodological issues and research targets', in Moed H., Glänzel W., Schmoch U. (Eds) *Handbook of quantitative science and technology research: the use of publication and patent statistics in studies of S&T systems*, Berlin: Springer Verlag, 613–643

Breschi S. and Lissoni F. (2006), 'Cross-firm inventors and social networks: localised knowledge spillovers revisted', *Annales d'Economie et de Statistique* 79–80: 189–209

Breschi S. and Lissoni F. (2009), 'Mobility of skilled workers and co-invention networks: an anatomy of localized knowledge flows', *Journal of Economic Geography* 9(4): 439–468

Breschi S., Lenzi C., Lissoni F., Vezzulli A. (2010), 'The geography of knowledge spillovers: the role of inventors' mobility across firms and in space', in Boschma R. and Martin R. (Eds) *The handbook of evolutionary economic geography*, Cheltenham: Edward Elgar, 353–369

Bronzini R. and Piselli P. (2009), 'Determinants of long-run regional productivity with geographical spillovers: the role of R&D, human capital and public infrastructure', *Regional Science and Urban Economics* 39(2): 187–199

Bruche G. (2009*), A new geography of innovation – China and India rising Columbia FDI perspectives*, New York: Vale Columbia Center, Columbia University

Calleja Crespo D. and Groebner V. (Eds) (2012), 'European competitiveness report: reaping the benefits of globalization', Brussels: European Commission

Camagni R. (1985), 'Spatial diffusion of pervasive process innovation', *Papers of the Regional Science Association* 58(1): 83–95

Camagni R. (1991), 'Technological change, uncertainty and innovation networks: towards dynamic theory of economic space', in Camagni R. (Ed.) *Innovation networks: spatial perspectives, London: Belhaven-Pinter*, 121–144

Camagni R. (1993), *Principi di economia urbana e territoriale*, Rome: Carocci

Camagni R. (1999),'The city as a milieu: applying the Gremi approach to urban development', *Revue d'Economie Régionale et Urbaine* 3: 591–606

Camagni R. (2001), 'Policies for spatial development', in OECD (Ed.) *Territorial outlook*, Paris, 147–169

Camagni R. (2004), 'Uncertainty, social capital and community governance: the city as a milieu', in Capello R., Nijkamp P. (Eds), *Urban dynamics and growth: advances in urban economics*, Amsterdam: Elsevier, 121–152

Camagni R. (2008), 'Towards a conclusion: regional and territorial policy recommendations', in Capello R., Camagni R., Fratesi U., Chizzolini B. (Eds) *Modelling regional scenarios for the enlarged Europe*, Berlin: Springer Verlag, 283–306

Camagni R. (2011), 'Local knowledge, national vision: challenges and prospect for the EU regional policy', Post-Seminar Publication, Polish Ministry of Regional Development, Ostróda, 18–19 July

Camagni R. and Capello R. (2002), 'Milieux innovateurs and collective learning: from concepts to measurement', in Acs Z. J., de Groot H. L. F., Nijkamp P. (Eds) *The emergence of the knowledge economy*, Berlin: Springer Verlag, 15–46

Camagni R. and Capello R. (2009), 'Knowledge-based economy and knowledge creation: the role of space', in Fratesi U. and Senn L. (Eds) *Growth and innovation of competitive regions: the role of internal and external connections*, Berlin: Springer-Verlag, 145–166

Camagni R. and Capello R. (2011), 'Macroeconomic and territorial policies for regional development: theory and empirical evidence from the EU', in Stimson B., Stough R. and Nijkamp P. (Eds) *Endogenous regional development: perspective, measurement and empirical investigations*, Cheltenham: Edward Elgar, 204–236

Camagni R. and Capello R. (2013), 'Regional innovation strategies and the EU regional policy reform: Towards smart innovation policies', *Growth and Change*, 44(2): 355–389

Camagni R. and Maillat D. (Eds) (1995), *Milieux innovateurs. Théories et politiques*, Paris: Economica

Canaleta C. G., Arzoz P. P., Garate M. R. (2003), 'Productivity, public capital and convergence: a study of the Spanish regions', *Tijdschrift voor Economische en Sociale Geografie* 94(5): 537–553

Canning D. and Pedroni P. (2004), *The effect of infrastructure on long-run economic growth*, Boston, Mass.: Harvard University

Cantwell J. (2009), 'Location and Multinational Enterprise', *Journal of International Business Studies* 40(1): 35–41

Cantwell J. (2005), 'MNCs, local clustering and science-technology relationships', in

Santangelo G. (Ed.), *Technological change and economic catch-up: the role of science and multinationals*, Cheltenham: Edward Elgar, 75–94

Cantwell J. and Iammarino S. (2003), *Multinational corporations and European regional systems of innovation*, London: Routledge

Capello R. (1988), 'La diffusione spaziale dell'innovazione: il caso del servizio telefonico', *Economia e Politica Industriale* 58: 141–175

Capello R. (1999), 'Spatial transfer of knowledge in high-technology milieux: learning vs. collective learning processes', *Regional Studies* 33(4): 353–365

Capello R. (2007), *Regional economics*, Abingdon: Routledge

Capello R. (2009a), 'Indivisibilities, synergy and proximity: the need for an integrated approach to agglomeration economies', *Tijdschrift voor Economische en Sociale Geografie* 100 (2): 145–159

Capello R. (2009b), 'Spatial spillovers and regional growth: a cognitive approach', *European Planning Studies* 17(5): 639–658

Capello R. (2012), 'Territorial patterns of innovation', in Cappellin R., Ferlaino F., Rizzi P. (Eds), *La città nell'economia della conoscenza*, Milan: FrancoAngeli, 51–80

Capello R. and Caragliu A. (2012), 'Proximities and the intensity of scientific relations: synergies and non-linearities', paper presented at the Tinbergen Institute Seminar, Amsterdam, 7–8 May

Capello R. and Faggian A. (2005), 'Collective learning and relational capital in local innovation processes', *Regional Studies* 39(1): 75–87

Capello R. and Lenzi C. (2012a), 'Territorial patterns of innovation: a taxonomy of innovative regions in Europe', *Annals of Regional Science*, DOI 10.1007/s00168-012-0539-8

Capello R. and Lenzi C. (2012b), 'Knowledge, innovation and productivity across regional patterns of innovation', mimeo available from the authors

Capello R. and Lenzi C. (2013a), 'Knowledge, innovation and economic growth nexus: spatial heterogeneity in Europe', *Journal of Regional Science* forthcoming

Capello R. and Lenzi C. (2013b), 'Territorial patterns of innovation and economic growth in European regions', *Growth and Change*, 44(2): 195–227

Capello R., Caragliu A., Nijkamp P. (2010), 'Territorial capital and regional growth: increasing returns in knowledge use', *Tijdschrift voor Economische en Sociale Geografie* 102(4): 385–405

Capello R., Caragliu A., Lenzi C. (2012), 'Is innovation in cities a matter of knowledge-intensive services? An empirical investigation', *Innovation: The European Journal of Social Science Research* 25(2): 151–174

Cappellin R. (2003a), 'Territorial knowledge management: towards a metrics of the cognitive dimension of agglomeration economies', *International Journal of Technology Management* 26(2–4): 303–325

Cappellin R. (2003b), 'Networks and technological change in regional clusters', in Bröcker J., Dohse D., Soltwedel R. (Eds), *Innovation clusters in interregional competition*, Berlin: Springer Verlag, 53–78

Cappellin R. and Nijkamp P. (Eds) (1990), *The spatial context of technological development*, Aldershot: Avebury

Carlaw K. I. and Lipsey R. G. (2003), 'Productivity, technology and economic growth: what is the relationship?', *Journal of Economic Surveys* 17(3): 457–495

Carlino G. A., Chatterjee S., Hunt R. M. (2007) 'Urban density and the rate of innovation', *Journal of Urban Economics* 61(3): 389–419

Castellani D. and Zanfei A. (2006), *Multinational firms, innovation and productivity*, Cheltenham: Edward Elgar

Charlot S. and Duranton G. (2004), 'Communication externalities in cities', *Journal of Urban Economics* 56(3): 581–613

Charlot S., Crescenzi R., Musolesi A. (2012), 'An 'extended' knowledge production function approach to the genesis of innovation in the European regions', Working Paper GAEL 2012–06

Charnes A., Cooper W. W., Rhodes E. (1978), 'Measuring the efficiency of decision making units', *European Journal of Operational Research* 2(4): 429–444

Ciciotti E. (1982), 'Differenze regionali nella capacità innovativa', *Politica ed Economia* 3: 42–48

Ciciotti, E. and Wettman, R. (1981), *The mobilization of the indigenous potential*, Commission of the European Communities. Internal documentation on Regional Policy n.10, Bruxelles

Cimoli M., Dosi G., Nelson R., Stiglitz J. (2009), 'Institutions and policies in developing economies', in Lundvall B. A., Chaminade C., Joseph K. J., Vang, J. (Eds) *Handbook of innovation systems and developing countries: building domestic capabilities in a global context*, Cheltenham: Edward Elgar, 337–359

Cingano F. and Schivardi F. (2004), 'Identifying the sources of local productivity growth', *Journal of the European Economic Association* 2(4): 720–742

Clark N. G. (1971), 'Science, technology and regional economic development', *Research Policy* 1(1): 296–319

Coe N. M. and Bunnell T. (2003), 'Spatializing' knowledge communities: towards a conceptualisation of transnational innovation networks', *Global Networks* 3(4): 437–456

Coe D. T. and Helpman E. (1995), 'International R&D spillovers', *European Economic Review* 39(5): 859–887

Coelli T. J. (1996), 'A Guide to DEAP Version 2.1: a data envelopment analysis computer program', CEPA Working Paper 8/96, The University of New England

Cohen B. (2006), 'Urbanization in developing countries: current trends, future projections, and key challenges for sustainability', *Technology in Society* 28(1–2): 63–80

Cohen W. and Levinthal D. (1990), 'Absorptive capacity: a new perspective on learning and innovation', *Administrative Science Quarterly* 35(1): 128–152

Combes P. P., Duranton G., Gobillon L. (2008), 'Spatial wage disparities: sorting matters!', *Journal of Urban Economics* 63(2): 723–742

Cook W. D. and Seiford L. M. (2009), 'Data envelopment analysis (DEA) – thirty years on', *European Journal of Operational Research* 192(1): 1–17

Cooke P. (2002a), *Knowledge economies. Clusters, learning and cooperative advantage*, London: Routledge

Cooke P. (2002b), 'Regional innovation systems: general findings and some new evidence from biotechnology clusters', *Journal of Technology Transfer* 27(1): 133–145

Cooke P. (2005), 'Regionally asymmetric knowledge capabilities and open innovation. Exploring 'Globalization 2' – A new model for industry organization', *Research Policy* 34(8): 1128–1149

Cooke P. (2009), *The knowledge economy, spillovers, proximity and specialization*, JRC, European Commission, Directoral General for Research, Brussels, 29–39

Cooke P., Asheim B., Boschma R., Martin R., Schwartz D., Tötdling F. (Eds) (2011), *Handbook of regional innovation and growth*, Cheltenham:Edward Elgar

Cooke P., Uranga M., Extebarria G. (1997), 'Regional innovation systems: institutional and organizational dimensions', *Research Policy* 26(4–5): 475–491

Cooper W. W., Seiford L.M., Tone K. (2007), *Data envelopment analysis*, Berlin: Springer-Verlag, 2nd edition

Corredoira R. A. and Rosenkopf L. (2006), 'Learning from those who left: the reverse transfer of knowledge through mobility ties', Management Department Working Paper

Courlet C. and Pecqueur B. (1992), 'Les systems industriels localizes en France: un nouveau modèle de développement', in Benko G. and Lipietz A. (Eds) *Les régions qui gagnent*, Paris: PUF, 81–102

Cowan R. and Jonard N. (2004), 'Network structure and the diffusion of knowledge', *Journal of Economic Dynamics and Control* 28(8): 1557–1575

Crescenzi R. and Rodríguez-Pose A. (2009), 'Systems of innovation and regional growth in the EU: endogenous vs. external innovative efforts and socio-economic conditions', in Fratesi U. and Senn L. (Eds) *Growth and innovation of competitive regions: the role of internal and external connections*, Berlin: Springer-Verlag, 167–192

Crescenzi R. and Rodríguez-Pose A. (2011), *Innovation and regional growth in the European Union*, Berlin: Springer-Verlag

Crescenzi R. and Rodríguez-Pose A. (2013), 'R&D, socio-economic conditions, and regional innovation in the U.S.', *Growth and Change* 44(2): 287–320

Crescenzi R., Rodriguez-Pose A., Storper M. (2007), 'The territorial dynamics of innovation: a Europe–United States comparative analysis', *Journal of Economic Geography* 7(6): 673–709

Crescenzi R., Rodriguez-Pose A., Storper M. (2012), 'The territorial dynamics of innovation in China and India', *Journal of Economic Geography* 12(5): 1055–1085

Crespi G., Geuna A., Nesta L. (2007), 'The mobility of university inventors in Europe', *Journal of Technology Transfer* 32(3): 195–215

Cullinane K., Song D. W., Wang T. F. (2004), 'An application of DEA windows analysis to container port production efficiency', *Review of Network Economy* 3(2): 184–206

Dahlman C. (2010), 'Innovation strategies of three of the BRICS: Brazil, India and China. What can we learn from three different approaches', in Fu X. and Soete L. (Eds) *The rise of technological power in the South*, Basingtoke: Palgrave MacMillan, 15–48

Dasgupta P. and Stiglitz J. (1980), 'Uncertainty, industrial structure and the speed of R&D', *Bell Journal of Economics* 11(1): 1–28

David P. A. (1985), 'Clio and the economics of QWERTY', *American Economic Review* 75(2): 332–337

David P. A. (1993), 'Knowledge property and the system dynamics of technological change', in Summers L. and Shah. S. (Eds) *Proceedings of the World Bank Annual Conference on Development Economics, Washington DC: The World Bank*, 215–248

David P. A. and Foray D. (1995), 'Accessing and expanding the science and technology knowledge base', *STI Review* 16: 16–38

Decoster E. and Tabaries M. (1986), ''L'innovation dans un pôle scientifique: le cas de la cité scientifique Île de France Sud', in Aydalot P. (Ed.) *Milieux innovateurs en Europe*, Paris: GREMI, 79–100

Del Gatto M., Di Liberto A., Petraglia C. (2011), 'Measuring productivity', *Journal of Economic Surveys* 25(5), 952–1008

Department of Trade and Industry (2006), 'Innovation in the UK: indicators and insights', Occasional Paper No. 6, available at http://www.bis.gov.uk/files/file31569.pdf

D'Este P. and Iammarino, S. (2010), 'The spatial profile of university-business research partnerships', *Papers in Regional Science* 89(2): 335–350

Dettori B., Marrocu E., Paci R. (2011), 'Total factor productivity. Intangible assets and spatial dependence in the European regions', *Regional Studies* DOI: 10.1080/00343404.2010.529288

Diewert E. (1987), 'Index numbers', in Eatwell J., Milgate M., Newman P. (Eds) *The new Palgrave, a dictionary of economics*, London: MacMillan, 767–780

Döring T. and Schnellenbach J. (2006), 'What do we know about geographical knowledge spillovers and regional growth? A survey of the literature', *Regional Studies* 40(3): 375–395

Dosi G. (1982), 'Technological paradigms and technological trajectories: a suggested interpretation of the determinants and directions of technical change', *Research Policy* 11(3): 147–162

Dosi G. (1988), 'Sources, procedures and microeconomic effects of innovation', *Journal of Economic Literature* 26(3): 1120–1171

Drucker P. (1969), *The age of discontinuity: guidelines to our changing society*, New York: Harper and Row

Dunning J. (1996), 'The geographical sources of competitiveness in firms: Some results of a new survey', *Transnational Corporations* 5(3): 1–21

Dunning J. (1998), 'Location and the multinational enterprise: a neglected factor?', *Journal of International Business Studies* 29(1): 45–66

Dunning J. (2001), 'The eclectic (OLI) paradigm of international production: Past, present and future', *International Journal of the Economics of Business*, 8(2): 173–190

Dunning J. (2009), 'Location and the multinational enterprise: John Dunning's thoughts on receiving the *Journal of International Business Studies* 2008 decade award', *Journal of International Business Studies*, 40(1): 20–34

Duranton G. (2008), 'Viewpoint: From cities to productivity and growth in developing countries', *Canadian Journal of Economics/Revue Canadienne d'Économique* 41(3): 689–736

Duranton G. and Puga D. (2001), 'Nursery cities: urban diversity, process innovation and the life-cycle of product', *American Economic Review* 91(5): 1454–1477

Duranton G. and Puga D. (2003), 'Micro-foundations of urban agglomeration economies', NBER Working Paper 9931

Duranton G. and Puga. D. (2004). 'Micro-foundations of urban agglomeration economies', in. Henderson J.V. and Thisse J.F. (Eds) *Handbook of regional and urban economics, cities and geography*, Amsterdam: Elsevier, 4: 2063–2117

Easterly W. and Levine R. (2001), 'It's not factor accumulation: stylized facts and growth models', *World Bank Economic Review* 15(2): 177–219

EC – Commission of the European Communities (2000), *Towards a European Research Area*, Communication from the Commission, COM(2000) 6, European Commission, Brussels

EC – Commission of the European Communities (2008), *Green Paper on territorial cohesion: turning territorial diversity into strength*, COM(2008), European Commission, Brussels

EC – Commission of the European Communities (2010a), *Europe 2020. A strategy for smart, suitable and inclusive growth*, Communication from the Commission, COM(2010), European Commission, Brussels

EC – Commission of the European Communities (2010b), *Regional policy contributing to smart growth in Europe*, COM(2010)553, Brussels

EC – Commission of the European Communities (2011a), *Regional innovation monitor: innovation patterns and innovation policy in European regions – trends, challenges and perspectives*. Project No. 0932. Enterprise and Industry Directorate-General

EC – Commission of the European Communities (2011b), *Report from the Commission to the European Parliament, the Council, the European Economic and Social Committee and the Committee of the Regions*, State of the Innovation Union 2011

EC – Commission of the European Communities (2012a), *Guide to research and innovation strategies for smart specialisations (RIS3)*, Smart Specialization Platform, May, http:// s3platform.jrc.ec.europa.eu/c/document_library/get_file?uuid=a39fd20b-9fbc-402b-be8c-b51d03450946&groupId=10157

EC – Commission of the European Communities (2012b), *Elements for a common strategic framework 2014 to 2020*, Brussels, 14.3.2012 SWD(2012) 61 final

Edgerton D. (2005), 'The linear model did not exist. Reflections on the history and historiography of science and research in industry in the twentieth century', in Grandin K., Worms N. and Widmalm S. (Eds). *The science industry nexus*. Science history publications, Sagamore Beach, 31–57

Edwards B. K. and. Starr R. (1987), 'A note on indivisibilities, specialization, and economies of scale', *The American Economic Review* 77(1): 192–194

Elhorst J. P. (2010), 'Applied spatial econometrics: raising the bar', *Spatial Economic Analysis* 5(1): 10–28

Enflo K. and Hjertstrand P. (2009), 'Relative sources of European regional productivity convergence: a bootstrap frontier approach', *Regional Studies* 43(5): 643–659

ESPON KIT (2012), *Knowledge, innovation, territory (KIT)*, final report available at http://www.espon.eu/main/Menu_Projects/Menu_AppliedResearch/kit.html

Etzkowitz H. and Leydesdorff L. (1997), *Universities in the global economy: a triple helix of university–industry–government relations*, London: Cassell

Etzkowitz H. and Leydesdorff L. (2000), 'The dynamics of innovation: from national systems and 'mode 2' to a triple helix of university– industry–government relations', *Research Policy* 29(2): 109–123

European Council (2000), Presidency Conclusions Lisbon European Council, 23–24 March 2000 (No. 100/1/00): European Council

Evangelista R., Iammarino S., Mastrostefano V., Silvani A. (2001), 'Measuring the regional dimension of innovation. Lessons from the Italian innovation survey', *Technovation* 21(11): 733–745

Ewers H.-J. and Allesch J. (Eds) (1990), *Innovation and regional development*, Berlin: De Gruyter

Fagerberg J. (1994), 'Technology and international differences in growth rates', *Journal of Economic Literature* 32(3): 1147–1175

Fagerberg J., Mowery D. C., Nightingale P. (2012), 'Introduction: The heterogeneity of innovation—evidence from the Community Innovation Surveys', *Industrial and Corporate Change* 21(5): 1175–1180

Fan P. (2008), 'Innovation capacity and economic development in China and India', UNU-WIDER Research Paper No. 2008/31. Helsinki: UNU World Institute for Development Economics Research

Farrell M. J. (1957), 'The measurement of productive efficiency', *Journal of the Royal Statistical Society*, Series A, General 120: 253–281

Feldman M. P. (1994), 'Knowledge complementarity and innovation', *Small Business Economics* 6(5): 363–372

Feldman M. P. (1999), 'The new economics of innovation, spillovers and agglomeration: a review of empirical studies', *Economics of Innovation and New Technology* 8(1–2): 5–25

Feldman M. P. and Audretsch D. B. (1999), 'Innovation in cities: science-based diversity, specialization and localized competition', *European Economic Review* 43(2): 409–429

Filippetti A. and Peyrache A. (2012), 'Labour productivity and technology gap in European regions: a non-paramatric approach, CEPA Working Paper WP0x/2008

Fingleton B. and LeGallo J. (2008), 'Estimating spatial models with endogenous variables, a spatial lag and spatial dependent disturbances, *Papers in Regional Science* 87(3): 319–339

Fischer M. and Varga A. (2003), 'Spatial knowledge spillovers and university research', *Annals of Regional Science*, 37(2): 303–322

Fleisher B., Li H., Zhao M. Q. (2010), 'Human capital, economic growth, and regional inequality in China', *Journal of Development Economics* 92(2): 215–231

Fleming L., King C., and Juda A. (2007), 'Small worlds and innovation', *Organization Science* 14(5): 375–93

Foddi M. and Usai S. (2013), Regional knowledge performance in Europe, *Growth and Change* 44(2): 258–286

Foray D. (2000), *L'économie de la connaissance*, Paris: La Découverte

Foray D. (2009), 'Understanding smart specialisation', in Pontikakis D., Kyriakou D., van Bavel R. (Eds) *The question of R&D specialisation*, JRC, European Commission, Directoral General for Research, Brussels, 19–28

Foray D. and Lundvall B. A. (Eds) (1996), *Employment and growth in the knowledge-based economy*, Paris: OECD

Foray D., David P., Hall B. (2009), 'Smart specialisation – the concept', *Knowledge Economists Policy Brief* n. 9: 1–5

Fratesi U. and Senn L. (2009), 'Regional growth, connections and economic modelling: an introduction', in Fratesi U. and Senn L. (Eds) *Growth and innovation of competitive regions: the role of internal and external connections*, Berlin: Springer-Verlag, 3–28

Freeman C. (1987), *Technology policy and economic policy: lessons from Japan*, London: Pinter

Frenkel A. (2001), 'Why high-technology firms choose to locate in or near metropolitan areas', *Urban Studies* 38(7): 1083–1101

Frenken K., van Oort F. G., Verburg T. (2007), 'Related variety, unrelated variety and regional economic growth', *Regional Studies* 41(5): 685–697

Fu X. and Soete L. (Eds) (2010), *The rise of technological power in the South*, Basingstoke: Palgrave MacMillan

Gajwani K., Kanbur R., Zhang X. (2006), 'Comparing the evolution of spatial inequality in China and India: a fifty-year perspective', International Food Policy Research Institute (IFPRI), DSGD Discussion paper, Nr. 44. Washington DC IFPRI

Garofoli G. (1981), 'Lo sviluppo delle aree periferiche nell'economia italiana degli anni Settanta', *L'industria* 2(3): 391–404

Gertler M. S. (1997), 'The invention of regional culture', in Lee R. and Wills J. (Eds) *Geographies of economies*, London: Arnold, 47–58

Gertler M. S. (1995), ''Being there': proximity, organization, and culture in the development and adoption of advanced manufacturing technologies', *Economic Geography* 71(1): 1–26

Gertler M. S. and Levite Y. M. (2005), 'Local nodes in *Global Networks*: the geography of knowledge flows in biotechnology innovation', *Industry and Innovation* 12(4): 487–507

Giannitsis T. (2009), 'Technology and specialization : strategies, options, risks', *Knowledge Economists Policy Brief* n. 8: 1–7

Gittelman M. (2007), 'Does geography matter for science-based firms? Epistemic communities and the geography of research and patenting in biotechnology', *Organization Science* 18(4): 724–741

Glaeser E. (1998), 'Are cities dying?', *Journal of Economic Perspectives* 12(2): 139–160

Glaeser E. (2010), 'Introduction', in Glaeser E. (Ed.), *Agglomeration economics*, National Bureau of Economic research, Chicago: University of Chicago Press, 1–14

Glaeser E., Kallal H., Scheinkman J., Schleifer. A. (1992), 'Growth in cities', *Journal of Political Economy* 100(6): 1126–1152

Glaeser E., Laibson D., Sacerdote B. (2002), 'An economic approach to social capital', *Economic Journal* 112(483): 437–458

Goddard J. B. and Thwaites A. T. (1986), 'New technology and regional development policy', in Nijkamp P. (Ed.) *Technological change: employment and spatial dynamics*, Berlin: Springer Verlag, 91–114

Gomes-Casseres B., Hagedoorn J., Jaffe A.B. (2006), 'Do alliances promote knowledge flows?', *Journal of Financial Economics* 80(1): 5–33

Gordon I. (2001), 'Unemployment and spatial labour markets: strong adjustment and persistent concentration', in Martin R. and Morrison P. (Eds) *Geographies of labour market inequality*, London: Routledge, p. 55–82

Grabher G. (1993), 'The weakness of strong ties: the lock-in of regional development in the Ruhr area', in Grabher G. (Ed.) *The embedded firm*, London: Routledge, 255–277

Granovetter M.S. (1985), 'The strength of weak ties', *American Journal of Sociology* 78(6): 1360–1380

Greunz L. (2003), 'Geographically and technologically mediated knowledge spillovers between European regions', *The Annals of Regional Science* 37(4): 657–680

Griliches Z. (1957), 'Hybrid corn: an exploration in the economics of technological change', *Econometrica* 25(4): 501–525

Griliches Z. (1979), 'Issues in assessing the contribution of research and development to productivity growth', *The Bell Journal of Economics* 10(1): 92–116

Griliches Z. (1986), 'Productivity, R&D, and basic research at the firm level in the 1970s', *American Economic Review* 76 (1): 141–54

Griliches Z. (1987), 'Productivity: measurement problems', in Eatwell J., Milgate M., Newman P. (Eds) *The new Palgrave, a dictionary of economics*, London: MacMillan

Griliches Z. (1990), 'Patent statistics as economic indicators: a survey', *Journal of Economic Literature* 28(8): 1661–1707

Griliches Z. (1991), 'Patent statistics as economic indicators: a survey', NBER Working Paper 3301

Griliches Z. (1992), 'The search for R&D spillovers', *Scandinavian Journal of Economics* 94(0): 29–47

Griliches Z. (1995), 'The discovery of the residual', NBER Working Paper 5348

Groot de H., Nijkamp P. and Stough R. (Eds) (2004), *Entrepreneurship and regional economic development: a spatial perspective*, Cheltenham: Edward Elgar

Groot H. L. F. de, Poot J., Smit M. (2009), 'Agglomeration externalities, innovation and regional growth: theoretical reflections and meta-analysis', in Capello R. and Nijkamp P. (Eds) *Handbook of regional growth and development theories*, Cheltenham: Edward Elgar, 256–281

Grossman G. M. and Helpman E. (1991a), *Innovation and growth in the global economy*, Cambridge, Massachusetts: MIT Press

Grossman G. M. and Helpman E. (1991b), 'Quality ladders in the theory of growth', *The Review of Economic Studies* 58(1): 43–61

Guiso L., Sapienza P., Zingales L. (2008), 'Social capital as good culture. Alfred Marshall Lecture', *Journal of European Economic Association*, 6(2–3): 295–320

Hägerstrand T. (1952), 'The propagation of innovation waves', *Lund Studies in Geography, Human Geography series* B 4: 3–19

Hägerstrand T. (1967), 'Aspects of the spatial structure of social communication and the diffusion of innovation', *Papers of the Regional Science Association* 16(1): 27–42

Haken H. (1993), 'Synergetics as a theory of creativity and its planning', in Andersson A., Batten D., Kobayashi K., Yoshikawa K. (Eds) *The cosmo-creative society. Logistical networks in a dynamic economy*, Berlin: Springer-Verlag, 45–52

Hall B. H., Jaffe A, Trajtenberg M. (2001), 'The NBER patent citations data file: lessons, insights and methodological tools', NBER Working Paper 8498

Hausman J. A. (1978), 'Specification test in econometrics', *Econometrica* 46(6): 1251–1271

Hausman J. A., Hall B. H., Griliches Z. (1984), 'Econometric models for count data with an application to the patent-R&D relationship', *Econometrica* 51(4): 909–938

Hayek von F. A. (1978), 'Competition as a discovery procedure', in Hayek F., *New studies in philosophy, politics, economics and the history of ideas*, University of Chicago Press, 179–190

Henderson V., Kuncoro A., and Turner M. (1995), 'Industrial development in cities', *Journal of Political Economy* 103(5): 1067–1090

Henderson V., Lee T., Lee Y. (2001), 'Scale externalities in Korea', *Journal of Urban Economics* 49(3): 479–504

Hodgson G. M. (1988), *Economics and institutions. A manifesto for a modern institutional economics*, Cambridge: Polity

Hodgson G. M. (1998), 'The approach of institutional economics', *Journal of Economic Literature* 36(1): 166–192

Hoekman J., Frenken K., van Oort F. (2009), 'The geography of collaborative knowledge production in Europe', *The Annals of Regional Science* 43(3): 721–38

Hoisl K. (2007), 'Tracing mobile inventors: the causality between inventor mobility and inventor productivity', *Research Policy* 36(5): 615–36

Hoisl K. (2009), 'Does mobility increase the productivity of inventors?', *Journal of Technology Transfer* 34(2): 212–25

Hollanders H., Tarantola S., Loschky A. (2009a), 'Regional innovation scoreboard (RIS) 2009', Pro Inno Europe Paper n. 14, Entreprise and Industry Magazine, Brussels available at http://www.proinno-europe.eu/page/regional-innovation-scoreboard

Hollanders H., Tarantola S., Loschky A. (2009b), 'Regional innovation scoreboard (RIS) 2009 – Methodology report', available at http://www.proinno-europe.eu/page/regional-innovation-scoreboard

Hong S., Oxley L., McCann P. (2012), 'A survey of innovation surveys', *Journal of Economic Surveys* 26(3): 420–444

Hoover E. M. Jr (1936), 'The measurement of industrial localization', *Review of Economics and Statistics* 18 (4): 162–171

Hübner D. (2009), 'Towards third generation of regional innovation policy', paper presented at the Conference on 'Innovation, research and development in the framework of the European regional policy, held in Athens, 26 February

Iammarino S. (2005), 'An evolutionary integrated view of regional systems of innovation: concepts, measures and historical perspectives', *European Planning Studies* 13(4): 497–519

IAREG (2010), Intangible assets and regional economic growth, Scientific executive summary, available at http://www.iareg.org/

INSEAD (2011), *Global innovation index 2011*, INSEAD

Jacobs J. (1969), *The economy of cities*, New York: Random House

Jacobs J. (1984), *Cities and the wealth of nations*, New York: Random House

Jaffe A. B. (1986), 'Technological opportunity and spillovers of R&D: Evidence from firms' patents, profits, and market value', *American Economic Review* 76(5): 984–1001

Jaffe A. B. (1989), 'Real effects of academic research', *American Economic Review* 79(5): 957–970

Jaffe A. B., Trajtenberg M., Henderson R. (1993), 'Geographic localisation of knowledge spillovers as evidenced by patent citations', *Quarterly Journal of Economics* 108(3): 577–598

Jian T., Sachs J., Warner A. (1996), 'Trends in regional inequality in China', *China Economic Review* 7(1): 1–21

Johannisson B. and Spilling O. (1983), *Strategies for local and regional self-development*, Oslo: NordRefo

Johansson B. and Karlsson C. (2009), 'Knowledge and regional development', in Capello R. and Nijkamp P. (Eds) *Handbook of regional growth and development theories*, Cheltenham: Edward Elgar, 239–255

Joly P. B. (1997), 'Chercheurs et laboratoires dans la nouvelle économie de la science', *Revue d'Economie Industrielle* 79(1): 77–94

Joseph K. J. (2009), 'Sectoral innovation systems in developing countries: the case of India's ICT industry', in Lundvall B. A., Vang J., Joseph K. J., Chaminade C. (Eds) *Handbook of innovation systems in developing countries: building domestic capabilities in a global setting*, Cheltenham: Edward Elgar, 183–213

Keeble D. (1990), 'Small firms, innovation and regional development in Britain in the 1990s', *Regional Studies* 31(3): 281–293

Keeble D. and Wilkinson F. (1999), 'Collective learning and knowledge development in the evolution of regional clusters of high-technology SMEs in Europe', *Regional Studies* 33(4): 295–303

Keeble D. and Wilkinson F. (2000), *High technology clusters, networking and collective learning in Europe*, Aldershot, Ashgate

Kerr W. R. (2008), 'Ethnic scientific communities and international technology diffusion', *The Review of Economics and Statistics* 90(3): 518–537

Kim J., Lee S. J., Marschke G. (2006), 'International knowledge flows: evidence from an inventor-firm matched data set', NBER Working Paper 12692

Kroll H. (2009), 'Spillovers and proximity in perspective: a network approach to improving the operationalisation of proximity', Fraunhofer ISI Working Papers Firms and Regions No. R2/2009

Krugman P. (1991a), *Geography and Trade*, Cambridge, Massachusetts: MIT Press

Krugman P. (1991b), 'Increasing returns and economic geography', *Journal of Political Economy* 99(3): 483–499

Kuchiki A. and Tsuji M. (Eds) (2010), *From agglomeration to innovation: upgrading industrial clusters in emerging economies*, Basingstoke: Palgrave Macmillan

Kujis L. and Wang T. (2006), 'China's pattern of growth: moving to sustainability and reducing inequality', *China & World Economy* 14(1): 1–14

Lambooy J.G. and Boschma R.A. (2001), 'Evolutionary economics and regional policy', *Annals of Regional Science* 35(1) 113–133

Laudel G. (2003), 'Studying the brain drain: can bibliometric methods help?', *Scientometrics* 57(2): 215–237

Leadbeater C.and Wildson J. (2007), *The atlas of ideas: how Asian innovation can benefit us all*, London: Demos

Lenzi C. (2009), 'Patterns and determinants of skilled workers' mobility: evidence from a survey of Italian inventors', *Economics of Innovation and New Technology* 18(2): 161–179

Lenzi C. (2010), 'Technology mobility and job mobility: On the use of patent data for inventors' career analysis', manuscript available from the author

Leone R. and Struyk R. (1976), 'The incubator hypothesis: evidence from five Sma's', *Urban Studies* 13(3): 325–332

LeSage J. P. and Pace R. K. (2009), *Introduction to spatial econometrics*, Boca Raton: CRC

Li X. and Pai Y. (2010), 'The changing geography of innovation activities: what do patent indicators imply?', in Fu X. and Soete L. (Eds), *The rise of technological power in the South*, Basingstoke: Palgrave MacMillan, 69–88

Licht G. (2009), 'How to better diffuse technologies in Europe', *Knowledge Economics Policy Brief* 7:1–5

Lissoni F (2001), 'Knowledge codification and the geography of innovation: the case of Brescia mechanical cluster', *Research Policy* 30(9): 1479–1500

Liu X. and Buck T. (2007), 'Innovation performance and channels for international technology spillovers: evidence from Chinese high-tech industries', *Research Policy* 36(3): 355–366

Liu X. and White S. (2001), 'Comparing innovation systems: a framework and application to China's transitional context', *Research Policy* 30(7): 1091–1114

Lobo J. and Strumsky D. (2008), 'Metropolitan patenting, inventor agglomeration and social networks: a tale of two effects', *Journal of Urban Economics* 63(3): 871–84

Lopez-Bazo E. and Moreno Serrano R. (2010), 'Regional variability in the impact of human capital on regional growth', IAREG WP2/3

Lorenz E. (1996), 'Collective learning processes and the regional labour market', unpublished research note, European network on networks, collective learning and RTD in regionally-clustered high-technology SMEs

Lucas R. (1988), 'On the mechanics of economic development', *Journal of Monetary Economics* 22(1): 3–24

Lundin N. and Schwaag Serger S. (2007), 'Globalization of R&D and China – empirical observations and policy iimplications', Research Institute of Industrial Economics, Working Paper, 710, Stockholm: Research Institute of Industrial Economics.

Lundvall B. A. (Ed.) (1992), *National systems of innovation. Towards a theory of innovation and interactive learning*, London: Pinter

Lundvall B. A. and Johnson B. (1994), 'The learning economy', *Journal of Industry Studies* 1(2): 23–42

Lundvall B. A., Vang J., Joseph K. J., Chaminade C. (Eds) (2009), *Handbook of innovation systems in developing countries*, Cheltenham: Edward Elgar

MacDonald S. (1987), 'British science parks: reflections on the politics of high technology', *R&D Management* 17(1): 25–37

Machlup F. (1962), *The production and distribution of knowledge in the United States*, New York: Princeton University Press

Maffezzoli, M. (2006), 'Convergence across Italian regions and the role of technological catch-up', *The B.E. Journal of Macroeconomics* 1(1): 1–15

Maggioni M. (2002), *Clustering dynamics and the location of high-tech firms*, Berlin: Physica-Verlag

Maggioni M. A. and Uberti, T. E. (2011), 'Networks and geography in the economics of knowledge flows', *Quality and Quantity* 45(5): 1031–1051

Maggioni M. A., Nosvelli M., Uberti, T. E. (2007), 'Space versus networks in the geography of innovation: a European analysis', *Papers in Regional Science* 86(3): 471–493

Maggioni M. A. and Uberti T. E. (2008), 'Knowledge networks across Europe: which distance matters?', *The Annals of Regional Science* 43(3): 691–720

Mahmood I. and Singh J. (2003), 'Technological dynamism in Asia', *Research Policy* 32(6): 1031–1054

Maier G. and Sedlacek S. (Eds) (2005), *Spillovers and innovations: space, environment and the economy*, Vienna: Springer Verlag

Malecki E. J. (1980), 'Corporate organisation of R&D and the location of technological activities', *Regional Studies* 14(3): 219–234

Malecki E. J. (1997), *Technology and economic development: the dynamics of local, regional and national competitiveness*, Cambridge: Addison-Wesley, Longman

Malecki E. J. and Varaiya P. (1987), 'Innovation and changes in regional structure', in P. Nijkamp (Ed.), *Handbook of regional and urban economics*, Amsterdam: North Holland, 629–645

Malerba F. (Ed.) (2004), *Sectoral systems of innovation*, Cambridge: Cambridge University Press

Malerba F. and Mani S. (Eds) (2009), *Sectoral systems of innovation and production in developing countries: actors, structure and evolution*, Cheltenham: Edward Elgar

Malmberg, A. and Maskell P. (2002), 'The elusive concept of localization economies: towards a knowledge-based theory of spatial clustering', *Environment and Planning* A 34(3): 429–449

Malmberg, A., Solvell O., Zander I. (1996), 'Spatial clustering, local accumulation of knowledge and firm competitiveness', *Geografiska Annaler Series B: Human Geography* 78(2): 85–97

Mani S. (2004), 'Institutional support for investment in domestic technologies: an analysis of the role of government in India', *Technological Forecasting and Social Change* 71(8): 855–863

Mankiw N. G., Romer D., D. Weil (1992), 'A contribution to the empirics of economic growth', *Quarterly Journal of Economics* 107(2): 407–437

Mansen J. (2008), 'Economic growth, TFP convergence, and the world export of ideas: a century of evidence', *Scandinavian Journal of Economics* 110(1): 145–167

Mansfield E. (1961), 'Technological change and the rate of imitation', *Econometrica* 29(4): 741–766

March J. G. (1991), 'Organizational consultants and organizational research', *Journal of Applied Communication Research* 19(1–2): 20–31

Marrocu E. and Paci R. (2012), 'Education or creativity: what matters most for economic performance?', *Economic Geography* 88(4): 369–401

Marrocu E., Paci R., Usai S. (2011), 'The complementary effects of proximity dimensions on knowledge spillovers', Working Paper CRENoS 2011/21

Marrocu E., Paci R., Usai S. (2012a), 'Productivity growth in the old and new Europe: the role of agglomeration externalities', *Journal of Regional Science* DOI: 10.1111/jors.12000

Marrocu E., Paci R., Usai S. (2012b), 'Proximity, networking and knowledge production in Europe: what lessons for innovation policy?' forthcoming in *Technological Forecasting and Social Change*

Marsan G. A. and Maguire K. (2011), 'Categorisation of OECD regions using innovation-related variables', Organisation for Economic Co-operation and Development (OECD) Regional development Working Paper 2011/03

Marshall A. (1920), *Principles of economics*, London: Macmillan republished in 2009, New York: Cosimo Books

Martin P. and Ottaviano G. (1999), 'Growing locations: industry location in a model of endogenous growth', *European Economic Review* 43(2): 281–302

Martin R. and Sunley, P. (2006), 'Path dependence and regional economic evolution', *Journal of Economic Geography* 6(4): 395–437

Martìnez-Fernàndez M.Â., Capò-Vicedo J., Vallet-Bellmunt, T. (2012), 'The present state of research into industrial clusters and districts. Content analysis of material published in 1997–2006', *European Planning Studies* 20(2): 281–304

Marx M., Strumsky S., Fleming L. (2007), 'Noncompetes and inventor mobility: specialists, stars, and the Michigan experiment, Harvard Business School WP 07-042

Maskell P., Bathelt H., Malmberg, A. (2006), 'Building global knowledge pipelines: the role of temporary clusters', *European Planning Studies* 14(8): 997–1013

Massard N. and Riou S. (2002), 'L'impact des structures locales sur l'innovation en France: specialisation ou diversite?', *Region et Developpement* 16(22): 111–136

Massey D., Quintas P., Wield D. (1992), *High tech fantasies: science parks in society, science and space*, London: Routledge

Maurseth P. B. and Verspagen B. (2002), 'Knowledge-spillovers in Europe: a patent citation analysis', *Scandinavian Journal of Economics* 104(4): 531–545

McCann P. (2004), 'Urban scale economies: statics and dynamics', in Capello R. and Nijkamp P. (Eds), *Urban dynamics and growth: advances in urban economics*, Amsterdam: Elsevier, 31–56

McCann P. and Ortega-Argilés R. (2011), 'Smart specialisation, regional growth and applications to EU cohesion policy', Document de treball de l'IEB 2011/14, Institut d'Economia de Barcelona

Melo P. C., Graham D.J., Noland R. B. (2009), 'A meta-analysis of estimates of urban agglomeration economies', *Regional Science and Urban Economics* 39(3): 332–342

Metcalfe J. S. (1981), 'Impulse and diffusion in the study of technological change', *Futures* 13(5): 347–359

Midelfart-Knarvik K. H., Overman H., Redding S., Venables A. (2002), 'The location of European industry' European Economy – Economic Papers 142, Directorate General Economic and Monetary Affairs, European Commission Brussels: European Commission

Miguélez E. and Gómez-Miguélez I.G. (2011), 'Singling out individual inventors from patent data', IREA Working Paper 2011/05

Mitra R. (2007), 'India's emergence as a global R&D center – an overview of the Indian R&D system and potential' Working Paper R2007:012. Ostersund: Swedish Institute for growth Policy Studies

Monk C. S. P., Porter R. B., Quintas P., Storey D., Wynarczyk P. (1988), *Science parks and the growth of high technology firms*, London: Croom Helm

Moreno R., Paci R., Usai S. (2005a), 'Geographical and sectoral clusters of innovation in Europe', *The Annals of Regional Science*, 39(4): 715–739

Moreno R., Paci R., Usai S. (2005b), 'Spatial spillovers and innovation activity in European regions', *Environment and Planning A* 37(10): 1793–1812

Moreno R., Paci R., Usai S. (2006), 'Innovation clusters in the European regions', *European Planning Studies* 14(9): 1209–1234

Moretti E. (2004), 'Human capital externalities in cities', in Henderson V. and Thisse J. (Eds), *Handbook of urban and regional economics*, Amsterdam: Elsevier, 4: 2243–2291

Morrison A., Rabellotti R., Zirulia L. (2011), 'When do global pipelines enhance knowledge diffusion in clusters?', Papers in Evolutionary Economic Geography (PEEG) 1105, Utrecht University

Mowery D. C. (1992), 'The US national innovation system: origins and prospects for change', *Research Policy* 21(2): 125–144

Mowery D. C. (2001), 'Technological innovation in a multipolar system: analysis and implications for U.S. policy, *Technological Forecasting and Social Change* 67(2): 143–157

Mowery D. C. and Oxley J. E. (1995), 'Inward technology transfer and competitiveness: the role of national innovation systems', *Cambridge Journal of Economics* 19(1): 67–93

Mowery D. C. and Rosenberg N. (1998), *Path of innovation: technological change in 20th century in America*, Cambridge, Mass: Cambridge University Press

Muller E. and C. Nauwelaers (2005), *Enlarging the ERA: identifying priorities for regional policy focusing on research and technological development in the New Member States and Candidate Countries*, Final report COP6-CT.2004.00001

Navarro M., Gibaja J. J., Aguado R., Bilbao-Osorio B. (2008), 'Pattern of innovation in the EU-25 regions: a typology and policy recommendations', Orkestra Working Paper Series in Territorial Competitiveness, Number 2008-04, Deusto Foundation, Donostia/San Sebastian

Navarro M., Gibaja J. J., Bilbao-Osorio B., Aguado R. (2009), 'Patterns of innovation in EU-25 regions: a typology and policy recommendations', *Environment and Planning C: Government and Policy* 27(5): 815–840

Nelson R. R. (1959), 'The simple economics of basic scientific research', *Journal of Political Economy* 67(3): 297–306

Nelson R. R. (1993), *National innovation systems: a comparative analysis*, Oxford: OUP

Nelson R. R. and Winter S. G. (1977), 'In search of a useful theory of innovation', *Research Policy* 6(1): 36–76

Nelson R. R. and Winter S. G. (1982), *An evolutionary theory of economic change*, Cambridge. MA: Harvard University Press

O Huallachain B. and Leslie T. F. (2007), 'Rethinking the regional knowledge production function', *Journal of Economic Geography* 7(6): 737–752

Oakey R. P., Thwaites A. T., Nash P. A. (1980), 'The regional distribution of innovative manufacturing establishments in Britain', *Regional Studies* 14(3): 235–253

OECD (1996), 'Special theme: the knowledge-based economy', in *OECD, Science, Technology and Industry Outlook 1996*, Paris, 229–256

OECD (2001), *OECD productivity manual*, available at http://www.sourceoecd.org/

OECD (2004), *Global knowledge flows and economic development*, Paris

OECD (2005), *Science, technology and industry scoreboard*, Paris

OECD (2009), *OECD regions at a glance 2009*, Paris

OECD (2010), *Typology of regional innovation systems*, 20th session of the working party on Territorial Indicators

OECD (2011), *Territorial outlook*, Paris

Oettl A. and Agrawal A. (2008), 'International labor mobility and knowledge flow externalities', *Journal of International Business Studies* 39(8): 1242–1260

Okubo Y. (1997), 'Bibliometric indicators and analysis of research systems: methods and examples', STI Working Paper 1/97, OECD, Paris

Ottaviano G. and Peri, G. (2005), 'Cities and cultures', *Journal of Urban Economics* 58(2): 304–337

Owen-Smith J. and Powell W. W. (2004), 'Knowledge networks as channels and conduits:

the effects of spillovers in the Boston biotechnology community', *Organization Science* 15(1): 5–21

Paci R. and Marrocu E. (2013), 'Knowledge assets and regional performance', *Growth and Change*, 44(2): 228–257

Paci R. and Usai S. (1999), 'Externalities, knowledge spillovers and the spatial distribution of innovation', *GeoJournal* 49(4): 381–390

Paci R. and Usai S. (2000), 'Technological enclaves and industrial districts: an analysis of the regional distribution of innovative activity in Europe', *Regional Studies* 34(2): 97–114

Paci R. and Usai S. (2008), 'Agglomeration economies, spatial dependence and local industry growth', *Revue d'Economie Industrielle* 123(3): 87–109

Paci R. and Usai S. (2009), 'Knowledge flows across European regions', *The Annals of Regional Science* 43 (3): 669–690

Padilla-Perez R., Vang J. and Chaminade C. (2009), 'Regional innovation systems in developing countries: integrating micro and meso-level capabilities', in Lundvall B. A., Vang J., Joseph K. J., Chaminade C. (Eds) *Handbook of innovation systems in developing countries: building domestic capabilities in a global setting*, Cheltenham: Edward Elgar, 140–182

Padmore T. and Gibson H. (1998), 'Modeling systems of innovation, part II: a framework for industrial cluster analysis in regions', *Research Policy* 26(6): 625–641

Parayil G. and D'Costa A. (2009), *The new Asian innovation dynamics: China and India in perspective*, Basingstoke: Palgrave Macmillan

Pavitt K. (1984), 'Sectoral patterns of technical change: towards a taxonomy and a theory', *Research Policy* 13(4): 343–373

Peri G. (2005), 'Determinants of knowledge flows and their effect on innovation', The *Review of Economics and Statistics* 87(2): 308–322

Perrin J. C. (1995), 'Apprentissage collectif, territoire et milieu innovateur: un nouveau paradigme pour le développement', in Ferrão J. (Ed.), *Políticas deiInovação ed desenvolvimento regional et local*, Lisboa: Edição do Instituto de Ciencias Sociais de Universidade de Lisboa, republished in Camagni R. and Maillat D. (Eds) (2006), *Milieux innovateurs*, Paris: Economica-Anthropos, 99–128

Pianta M. (2001), 'Innovation, demand and employment', in Petit P. and Soete L. (Eds), *Technology and the future of European employment*, Cheltenham, Edward Elgar, 142–165

Piore M. J. and Sabel C. (1984), *The second industrial divide: possibilities for prosperity*, New York: Basic Books

Ponds R., Van Oort F. G., Frenken K, (2007), 'The geographical and institutional proximity of research collaboration', *Papers in Regional Science* 86(3): 423–443

Ponds R., Van Oort F. G., Frenken K, (2010), 'Innovation, spillovers and university-industry collaboration: an extended knowledge production function approach', *Journal of Economic Geography* 10(2): 231–255

Pontikakis D., Chorafakis G., Kyriakou D. (2009), 'R&D Specialization in Europe: from stylized observations to evidence-based policy', in Pontikakis D., Kyriakou D., van Bavel R. (Eds), *The question of R&D specialisation*, JRC, European Commission, Directoral General for Research, Brussels, 71–84

Popkin J. M. and Iyengar P. (2007), *IT and the East: how China and India are altering the future of technology and innovation*, Boston, Mass.: Harvard Business School Press

Porter M. E. (1990), *The competitive advantage of nations*, London: Macmillan

Puga, D. (2010), 'The magnitude and causes of agglomeration economies', *Journal of Regional Science* 50(1): 203–219

Putman R. D. (2000), *Bowling alone: the collapse and revival of American community*, New York: Simon and Schuster

Quatraro F. (2010), 'Knowledge coherence, variety and economic growth. Manufacturing evidence from Italian regions', *Research Policy* 39(10):1289–1302

Quévit M. and van Doren P. (1997), 'The problem of innovative milieux and territorial structural adjustment policies', in Ratti R., Bramanti A., Gordon R. (Eds), *The dynamics of innovative regions – the GREMI approach*, Aldershot: Ashgate, 343–365

Quigley J. M. (1998), 'Urban diversity and economic growth', *Journal of Economic Perspectives* 12(2): 127–138

Rallet A. and Torre A. (Eds) (1995), *Économie industrielle et économie spatiale*, Paris: Economica

Rauch J. (1993), 'Productivity gains from geographic concentration of human capital: evidence from the cities', *Journal of Urban Economics* 34(3): 380–400

Redding S. J. (2010), 'The empirics of new economic geography', *Journal of Regional Science* 50(1): 297–311

Reed H. (2010), *Reinventing venture capital: towards a new economic settlement*, London: Demos

Rodríguez-Pose A. (1999), 'Innovation prone and innovation averse societies: economic performance in Europe', *Growth and Change* 30(1): 75–105

Rodriguez-Pose A. and Crescenzi R. (2008), 'R&D, spillovers, innovation systems and the genesis of regional growth in Europe', *Regional Studies* 42(1): 51–67

Roelandt T. J. A. and den Hertog P. (Eds) (1998), 'Cluster analyses & cluster-based policy in OECD-countries', The Hague/Utrecht: OECD-TIP Group

Roman M. (2010), 'Regional efficiency of knowledge economy in the new EU countries: The Romanian and Bulgarian case', MPRA Paper 23083, University Library of Munich, Germany

Romer P. M. (1986), 'Increasing returns and long-run growth', *Journal of Political Economy* 94(5): 1002–1037

Romer P. M. (1989), 'Human capital and growth: theory and evidence', NBER Working Paper 3173

Romer P. M. (1990), 'Endogenous technological change', *Journal of Political Economy* 98(5): 71–102

Rosenkopf L. and Almeida P. (2003), 'Overcoming local search through alliances and mobility', *Management Science* 49(6): 751–766

Rousseau S. and Rousseau R. (1998), 'The scientific wealth of European nations: taking effectiveness into account', *Scientometrics* 42(1), 75–87

Sassen S. (1994), *Cities in a world economy*, Thousands Oaks: Pine Forge Press

Saxenian A. L. (1994), *Regional advantage: culture and competition in Silicon Valley and Route 128*, Boston, Mass.: Harvard University Press

Saxenian A. L. (2006), *The new argonauts: regional advantage in a global economy*, Boston, Mass.: Harvard University Press

Saxenian A. L. and Sabel C. (2008), 'Venture capital in the "periphery": the new argonauts, global search and local institution-building', *Economic Geography* 84(4), 379–394

Schaaper M. (2009), 'Measuring China's innovation system: national specificities and international comparisions', STI Working Paper 2009/1, Paris: OECD

Schilling M. A. and Phelps C. C. (2007), 'Interfirm collaboration networks: the impact of large-scale network structure on firm innovation', *Management Science* 53(7): 1113–1126

Schreyer P. and Pilat D. (2001), 'Measuring productivity', *OECD Economic Studies*, 33: 127–170

Schumpeter J. A. (1934), *The theory of economic development*, Cambridge, Mass.: Harvard University Press

Schumpeter J. A. (1942), *Capitalism, socialism and democracy*, New York: Harper and Row

Scott A.J. (Ed.) (2001), *Global city-regions: trends, theory, policy*, Oxford University Press, Oxford

Scott A. J. and Angel D. P. (1987), 'The US semiconductor industry: a locational analysis', *Environment and Planning* A 19(7): 875–912

Scott A. and Garofoli G. (Eds) (2007), *Development on the ground: clusters, networks and regions in emerging economies*, Oxford: Routledge

Shalem R. and Trajtenberg M. (2008), 'Software patents, inventors and mobility', unpublished manuscript

Sharma S. and Thomas V. J. (2008), 'Inter-country R&D efficiency analysis: an application of data envelopment analysis', *Scientometrics* 76(3): 483–501

Shearmur R. (2012), 'The geography of intrametropolitan KIBS innovation: distinguishing agglomeration economies from innovation dynamics', *Urban Studies* 49(11): 2331–2356

Simmie J., Carpenter J., Chadwick A., Martin R. (2008), *History matters: path dependence and innovation in British city-regions*, London: NESTA

Simonen J. and McCann P. (2008), 'Firm innovation: the influence of R&D cooperation and the geography of human capital inputs', *Journal of Urban Economics* 64(1): 146–154

Singh J. (2005), 'Collaborative networks as determinants of knowledge diffusion patterns', *Management Science* 51(5): 756–770

Singh J. and Agrawal A. K. (2011), 'Recruiting for ideas: how firms exploit the prior inventions of new hires', *Management Science* 57(1): 129–150

Smith K. (2005), 'Measuring innovation', in Fagerberg J., Mowery D. C., Nelson R. R. (Eds) (2005), *The Oxford handbook of innovation*, Oxford: Oxford University press, 148–177

Solow R. M. (1957), 'Technical change and the aggregate production function', *Review of Economics and Statistics*, 39(3): 312–320

Song J., Almeida P., Wu G. (2003), 'Learning-by-hiring: when is mobility more to facilitate interfirm knowledge transfer?', *Management Science* 49(4): 351–65

Starrett D. A. (1978), 'Market allocations of location choice in a model with free mobility', *Journal of Economic Theory* 17 (1): 21–37

Steinmueller W. E. (2000), 'Will new information and communication technologies improve the 'codification' of knowledge?' *Industrial and Corporate Change* 9(2): 361–376

Sterlacchini A. (2008), 'R&D, higher education and regional growth: uneven linkages among European regions', *Research Policy* 37(6–7): 1096–1107

Sternberg R. (1996), 'Reasons for the genesis of high-tech regions. theoretical explanation and empirical evidence', *Geoforum* 27(2): 205–223

Stöhr W. and Tödling F. (1977), 'Spatial equity: some anti-theses to current regional development doctrine', *Papers of the Regional Science Association* 38(1): 33–53

Storey D. J. and Tether B. S. (1998), 'Public policy measures to support new technology-based firms in the European Union', *Research Policy* 26(9): 1037–1057

Storper M. (1997), *The regional world: territorial development in a global economy*, New York: Guilford

Storper M. and Scott A. J. (1995), 'The wealth of regions: market forces and policy imperatives in local and global context', *Futures* 27(5): 505–526

Sun Y. (2003), 'Geographic patterns of industrial innovation in China during the 1990s', *Tijdschrift voor Economische en Sociale Geographie* 94(3): 376–389

Tabellini G. (2008), 'Institutions and culture: presidential address', *Journal of the European Economic Association* 6(2–3): 255–294

Tappeiner G., Hauser C., Walde J. (2008), 'Regional knowledge spillovers: fact or artifact?', *Research Policy* 37(5): 861–874

Temple J. (1999), 'The new growth evidence', *Journal of Economic Literature* 37(1): 112–156

Ter Wal A. L. J. and Boschma R. (2009), 'Applying social network analysis in Economic Geography: framing some key analytic issues', *The Annals of Regional Science* 43(3): 739–756

Thurieaux B., Arnold E., Couchot C. (Eds) (2000), *Innovation and enterprise creation: Statistics and indicators*, Luxembourg: European Commission (EUR17038)

Tödtling F. and Trippl M. (2005), 'One size fits all? Towards a differentiated regional innovation policy approach', *Research Policy* 34(8): 1203–1219

Torre A. and Rallet A. (2005), 'Proximity and localization', *Regional Studies* 39(1): 47–59

Trippl M. (2010), 'Developing cross-border regional innovation systems: key factors and challenges', *Tijdschrift voor Economische en Sociale Geographie* 101(2): 150–160

Trippl M. and Maier G. (2007), 'Knowledge spillover agents and regional development', SRE-Discussion 2007/01

Trippl M. and Maier G. (2010), 'Knowledge spillover agents and regional development', *Papers in Regional Science* 89(2): 229–233

Tseng C. (2009), 'Technological innovation and knowledge network in Asia: evidence from comparison of information and communication technologies among six countries', *Technological Forecasting and Social Change* 76(5): 654–663

UNU-Merit (2010), 'The regional impact of technological change in 2020', Synthesis report of Framework service contract 150083-2005-02-BE, DG-Regio

Usai S. (2011), 'The geography of inventive activity in OECD regions', *Regional Studies* 45(6): 711–731

Uzzi B. (1996), 'The sources and consequences of embeddedness for the economic performance of organizations', *American Sociological Review* 61(4): 674–698

Van Oort F. and Raspe O. (2006), 'Economic growth and the urban knowledge economy', Utrecht University Papers in Evolutionary Economic Geography (PEEG) n. 06/07

Varga A. (2000), 'Local academic knowledge transfers and the concentration of economic activity', *Journal of Regional Science* 40(2): 289–309

Varga A., Anselin L., Acs Z. (2005), 'Regional innovation in the US over space and time', in Maier G. and Sedlacek S. (Eds), *Spillovers and innovation: space, environment and the economy*, Vienna: Springer-Verlag, 93–104

Veltz P. (1993), 'D'une géographie des coûts à une géographie de l'organisation: quelques thèses sur l'évolution des rapports entreprises/territoires', *Révue Economique* 44(4): 671–686

Venables A. J. (2005), 'Spatial disparities in developing countries: cities, regions, and international trade', *Journal of Economic Geography* 5(1): 3–21

Verspagen B. (2010), 'The spatial hierarchy of technological change and economic development in Europe', *The Annals of Regional Science* 45(1): 109–132

Verspagen B. and Schoenmakers W. (2004), 'The spatial dimension of patenting by multinational firms in Europe', *Journal of Economic Geography* 4(1): 23–42

Von Tunzelmann N. and Acha V. (2005), 'Innovation in 'low-tech' industries', in Fagerberg J., Mowery D.C., Nelson R. R. (Eds*), The Oxford handbook of innovation*, Oxford: Oxford University Press, 407–432

Wadhwa, V. (2010), Chinese and Indian entrepreneurs are eating America's lunch. *Foreign Policy*, 28/12/2010, available at http://www.foreignpolicy.com/articles/2010/12/28/chinese_and_indian_entrepreneurs_are_eating_americas_lunch

Wang E.C. (2007), 'R&D efficiency and economic performance: a cross-country analysis using the stochastic frontier approach', *Journal of Policy Modelling* 29(2), 345–360

Wang E. C. and Huang W. (2007), 'Relative efficiency of R&D activities: a cross-country study accounting for environmental factors in the DEA approach', *Research Policy* 36(2): 260–273

Wasserman S. and Faust K. (1994), *Social network analysis: methods and applications*, Cambridge: Cambridge University Press

Watts D. J. and Strogatz S. H. (1998), 'Collective dynamics of 'small-world' networks', *Nature* 393(6684): 440–442

Whitley R. (1992), *Business systems in east Asia: firms, markets and societies*, London: Sage

Whitley R. (2003), 'Developing innovative competences: the role of institutional frameworks', *Industrial and Corporate Change* 11(3): 497–528

Wilson D. and Purushothaman R. (2003), 'Dreaming with BRICS: the path to 2050', Global Economics Paper 99, Goldman Sachs

Wintjes R. and Hollanders H. (2010), *The regional impact of technological change in 2020*, Report to the European Commission, Directorate General for Regional Policy, on behalf of the network for European Techno-Economic Policy Support (ETEPS AISBL) http://ec.europa.eu/regional_policy/sources/docgener/studies/pdf/2010_technological_change.pdf

World Bank (2009), *World development report 2009: reshaping economic geography*, Washington

Xu Z. (2009), 'Productivity and agglomeration economies in Chinese cities', *Comparative Economic Studies* 51(3): 284–301

Yeung H. (2009), 'Regional development and the competitive dynamics of global production networks: an East Asian perspective', *Regional Studies* 43(3): 325–351

Zabala-Iturriagagoitia J.M., Voigt P., Gutierrez-Gracia A., Jimenez-Saez F., (2007), 'Regional innovation systems: how to assess performance', *Regional Studies* 41(5): 661–672

Zheng X. P. (2007), 'Economies of network, urban agglomeration, and regional development: a theoretical model and empirical evidence', *Regional Studies* 41(5): 559–569

Zucker L. G., Darby M. R., Armstrong J. (1998), 'Geographically localized knowledge: spillovers or markets?', *Economic Inquiry* 36(1): 65–86

Index